WORLD WAR II 365 DAYS

For Chaplain Albert B. Wagner, Second Lieutenant Mary Catherine McGarr (Angelos), and all the other men and women who served and sacrificed for the Allied cause.

Preface

In spring 1939, as the Sino-Japanese conflict raged in Asia and Hitler plotted the invasion of Poland, the World's Fair opened in Flushing Meadows, New York. With the singular exception of Germany, all the nations that would soon be embroiled in the most devastating war this planet has yet known were represented at the fair, where they mounted exhibitions that both looked toward the future and celebrated past accomplishments. The British displayed one of the milestones in the development of democracy, the Lincoln Cathedral copy of the Magna Carta, that seminal charter of liberties to which English barons forced King John to give his consent in 1215. Unwilling to risk this precious document's destruction after the war in Europe started in September, the British transported it to Washington and placed it in the safekeeping of the Library of Congress. Here it joined more than three thousand treasures from the national library of China that our Library was also safeguarding, "refugee" materials from other combatant countries, and the more than six million items then comprising the Library of Congress collections—including the Declaration of Independence and the Constitution of the United States.

Shortly thereafter, Librarian of Congress Archibald MacLeish faced a huge task that had not been anticipated in the Fiscal Year 1941 budget request: sorting through the collections to determine which items should be evacuated from Washington and which should remain but be shifted to safer quarters within the Library buildings should the United States be swept into war. Since there was no money to pay for new help or staff overtime, he asked for volunteers. The response was overwhelming. Some seven hundred staff members contributed more than ten thousand hours of their time to help complete this important work, preparing the Library for one of the most remarkable events in its history. On December 26, 1941, less than three weeks after the Japanese attack on Pearl Harbor, Library staff and military guards removed the Declaration of Independence, the Constitution, the Magna Carta, Lincoln's Gettysburg Address, the Gutenberg Bible, and other special treasures to the reinforced bullion vaults of For

Knox, Kentucky. Over 4,700 cases of other rare, valuable, and essential materials—the equivalent of eight *miles* of shelved materials—were removed to different locations outside the District of Columbia. At the same time the Library entered a wartime period of quietly frenetic activity, serving members of Congress and government departments on a twenty-four-hour-a-day schedule and remaining a hub of information and inspiration to the entire nation throughout the war.

Today, with collections now in excess of 135 million items, the Library of Congress continues to serve Congress, the nation, and the international community. Our three buildings on Capitol Hill welcome more than a million visitors a year. Millions more visit this great institution, and examine its growing digitized collections, via our Website, www.loc.gov. Still others discover the Library's rich store of information through books such as *World War II 365 Days*.

This unique compendium, drawn from the Library's vast collections, presents the story of a tumultuous era in which the very survival of democracy—and the free flow of knowledge on which democracy depends—was at issue. In these pages you will find photographs, maps, political cartoons, drawings, posters, and paintings created by people of many nations. You will read the words of wartime political leaders, Axis propa-gandists, anti-fascist resistance leaders, nurses, and soldiers. You will encounter singular revelations of the war's unparalleled devastation and appalling crimes. And you will discover moving testaments to the sacrifices and stubborn resistance of people struggling to preserve the light of freedom in a darkening world. In this new century, faced with new challenges, the Library of Congress honors their struggle with the publication of this book—and with our continuing dedication to keeping the torch of knowledge alight.

James H. Billington
The Librarian of Congress

Introduction

"A word is not a crystal, transparent and unchanged, it is the skin of a living thought, and may vary greatly in color and content according to the circumstances and the time in which it is used," Supreme Court Justice Oliver Wendell Holmes, Jr., once observed.[1]

"War," by whatever name—*"bellum," "krieg," "guerre," "sensou," "voina"*—has been the descriptive skin that has enveloped countless armed clashes since time out of mind. But like every unhappy family, every war makes for unhappiness—and sometimes, for glory—in its own way. Some wars, indeed, generate such colossal carnage and consequence that they beggar the effort of conventional language to define them—and few more so than World War II. "War" seems hardly an adequate term to capture the enormity and the effects of the epic catastrophe that wreathed the planet in incalculable woe and destruction in the middle years of the twentieth century.

World War II was in many ways the mother and father of all wars, as well as the undisputed progenitor of the modern era. It dwarfed all previous conflicts in its global dimensions.

It spawned more fiendish innovations than any previous armed struggle, marking it as a uniquely gruesome event in human history. It was the first war in which more noncombatants than armed warriors died; the first war waged largely from the air, often against civilian targets; the first war to see the use of atomic weapons; and the first war to encompass industrial-scale genocide, a term officially added to the world's vocabulary of shame in the war's immediate aftermath. World War II was also the last war ever likely to be fought between massed armies, navies, and air fleets in gigantic combat formations dependent on prodigious quantities of supplies pouring from their homeland fields and factories for years on end. And it was one of the rare wars in which history judges the victors to have fought for a just cause, and to have achieved an outcome of unarguable moral clarity.

When the fighting was finished, some 60 million people lay dead. Fascism in Italy, Nazism in Germany, and militarism in Japan were all extinguished. So thorough was their defeat that Germans would call the moment of their surrender on

May 8, 1945, *Stunde Null*, or zero hour, when time itself was sundered and history's clock had to be set anew. Adolf Hitler had committed suicide just days earlier. At almost the same time, Italy's Benito Mussolini, the swaggering *Duce* who had led his people only to humiliation and misery, was summarily executed by anti-fascist Italian partisans, his mutilated body hung by the heels in Milan's Piazzale Loreto. Japan's war-time leader, General Hideki Tojo, botched his own suicide attempt in September 1945 and was hanged in 1948, after being tried and convicted for war crimes.

Yet the war wounded the victors, too. France had been humiliated, genuflecting before the invading Germans in 1940 with little more than a flourish of the matador's cape, and lying supinely impotent under the Nazi heel for years thereafter. The war severely impoverished Britain and led ultimately to the extinction of the once mighty British Empire. It annihilated some 26 million Soviet citizens, and turned much of the Soviet Union into a wasteland—a loss once described by President John F. Kennedy as "equivalent to the destruction of this country east of Chicago."[2] It slaughtered nearly 10 million Chinese and paved the way for the triumph of Mao Tse-tung's Communist Party. It left a bitter residue of barely suppressed hatreds and vengeance-lust in the Balkans, which erupted into bloody "ethnic cleansing" some two generations later.

Among all the belligerents, Axis and Allies alike, only the United States emerged from the war invigorated and robust—more stable, more secure, more prosperous, more powerful, and more self-confident. To be sure, more than 400,000 American soldiers, sailors, marines, and airmen had given the last full measure of devotion to secure the Allied victory. But proportionate to losses in other nations' fighting forces, that toll was fortunately modest. Meanwhile, the war claimed but a handful of American civilian lives, and the continental United States was mercifully spared from the fighting and bombardment that scarred the soil of so many other nations.

In many ways, America's World War II was unlike everybody else's. Here it ended a century and a half of American isolationism, banished the Great Depression that had plagued the nation for more than a decade, and somewhat improbably deposited the United States, as Winston Churchill remarked at war's end in 1945, "at the summit of the world," a position from which it has yet to be dislodged, more than half a century later.

World War II set the stage for the Cold War that pitted the erstwhile Allies, the Soviets and the Americans, against one another for more than four decades, turning Eastern and Central Europe into a tense zone of hair-trigger military confrontation and ideological competition, even while engendering the pacification and prosperity of Western Europe and setting the

European continent as a whole on the path toward a degree of political unity not seen since the time of Charlemagne.

The war also catalyzed the end of colonialism in Asia, not to mention Africa. It might even be said that Japan accomplished its cardinal war objective of expelling the Western imperial powers from Asia, an historic achievement that was only temporarily reversed at war's end. The United States withdrew from the Philippines in 1946; Britain from India in 1947, from Ceylon (Sri Lanka) and Burma (Myanmar) in 1948, and from Malaya in 1957; the French departed from Vietnam in 1954, and the Netherlands from the Dutch East Indies (Indonesia) in 1949. With the British handover of Hong Kong in 1997 and Macao in 1999 to the People's Republic of China, the age of Western imperialism in Asia definitively ended—writing *finis* to a centuries-old drama in which World War II was the effective dénouement.

Given World War II's panoramic sweep and the infinitude of individual tales it bred, words alone can give but a partial account of its teeming reality. The narrative that follows in these pages is admirable for its comprehensiveness and concision, as well as for its color and clarity. In vivid and often lyrical language, it artfully breathes life into the totality of the war as few accounts have succeeded in doing. It is creatively complemented by a running time line that highlights the war's most notable events, and further enhanced by generous excerpts from diaries and memoirs of participants. And if one accepts the old maxim about the worth of a picture relative to words, then the abundance of images in this book can be said to amplify its value a thousand fold.

Drawn from the vast collections of the Library of Congress, an archive that boasts materials from all countries and continents caught up in the war, the illustrations in this volume—many of them rarely if ever previously published—provide uncommonly evocative documentation of the conflict's complexity and cruelty as well as its frequent humanity. Images from the several home fronts—including posters and political cartoons as well as on-the-scene sketches and hand-drawn maps—date from before the outbreak of the shooting through the war's conclusion in 1945. And thanks to notable advances in photographic techniques and technologies in the early decades of the twentieth century, the photographic record of the fighting war is especially rich.

Most American as well as other countries' armed forces had official photographic units. Many of them employed legendary figures like Margaret Bourke-White, the first woman correspondent accredited to the U.S. Army, and Edward Steichen, the dean of American photographers, former head of the Army's photo section in World War I, who became chief of the Navy's photographic unit. The war made new legends out of others, notably Joe Rosenthal, the Associated Press photographer who on February 23, 1945, snapped the shot of six Marines raising the American flag on Mt. Suribachi, on the island of Iwo Jima—probably the war's most famously iconic image, and the inspiration for the official Marine Corps monument near Arlington National cemetery.

Photos served to document combat operations for training purposes and for later analysis by the military. No less important, they also served to convey the reality of the fighting front to the civilian populations whose continued support for the war effort was indispensable. To that end, Steichen instructed his photographers "above all" to "concentrate on the men. The ships and planes will become obsolete, but the men will always be there."[3]

And yet contemporary Americans on the home front were long denied the kind of direct, unmediated visual record of the war that television would make commonplace for the later generations that sent troops to Vietnam and the Persian Gulf. Photos of the wreckage at Pearl Harbor on December 7, 1941, for example, showed burning and blasted ships, but nothing of the bloated and mangled bodies that littered much of the harbor. War Department rules forbade publishing photos of dead G.I.s until September 20, 1943, when *Life* magazine was permitted to print George Strock's striking image of three soldiers dead on the invasion beach of Buna, in New Guinea, none of whose faces could be seen.

The combination of words and images in the pages that follow makes *World War II 365 Days* an extraordinary historical account. It does not merely recreate the war as contemporaries experienced it. It also offers perspectives and images that were denied to the generation that fought the war, but are now, thanks to the Library of Congress's researchers, available to us. Together the text and illustrations that constitute this book weave a memorable literary as well as visual tapestry of history's most fearsome conflict.

David M. Kennedy

David M. Kennedy, is the Donald J. MacLachlan Professor of History at Stanford University. His book *Freedom From Fear: The American People in Depression and War, 1929–1945* was awarded the Pulitzer Prize in 2000.

[1] Oliver Wendell Holmes, Jr., *Towne v. Eisner*, 245 U.S. 418, 425 (1918)

[2] John F. Kennedy, American University Address, June 10, 1963. www.americanrhetoric.com/speeches/jfkamericanuniversityaddress.html

[3] Steichen quoted in Susan D. Moeller, *Shooting War: Photography and the American Experience of Combat (New York: Basic Books, 1989), 192.*

About this Book

Books in the 365 Days series do not have page numbers; each text page bears a date, from January 1 through December 31. Readers will note that in *World War II 365 Days*, the main text and images do not pertain to the particular date on which they appear. Rather, each month is devoted to a theme or period in the complex story of the Second World War. In order of presentation, these are: January—Prelude (the buildup to and causes of the war); February—Wars East and West, 1937–1939; March—Blitzkrieg! 1940; April—A Global Conflict, 1941; May—Interlude, Allies versus the Axis; June—Axis Ascendant, 1942; July—Interlude, Total War; August—The Tide Begins to Turn, 1943; September—The Allies Close In, 1944; October—Interlude, The Most Terrible Conflict; November—Unconditional Surrenders, 1945; and December—Aftermath.

The daily events that run at the bottom of each lefthand page throughout the book—like the words in a crawler or news-ticker at the bottom of a television screen—are generally not connected to the text and images on the same two-page spread; instead, these entries constitute a separate running diary of noteworthy World War II–related events.

Prelude

At 11 A.M. on November 11, 1918, the Great War that had shaken the world for more than four years ended when a cease-fire went into effect between the defeated Central Powers (primarily Germany and the Austro-Hungarian and Ottoman empires) and the victorious Allied nations. With the exception of the United States (which had joined the Allied war effort in 1917 as an "associated power"), all the major combatants in what is now called World War I were exhausted by this unprecedented bloodletting, in which death had been abetted by new and terrible weapons: air forces, organized submarine warfare, tanks, flame throwers, and poison gas.

Along the four-hundred-mile western front that stretched from Switzerland to the English Channel, the conflict had quickly devolved into the corrosive anguish of static trench warfare. Until 1918, attempts to break this stalemate comprised massive charges across the shell-hole-pocked muck of "no-man's-land" through storms of artillery and machine gun fire—the surviving attackers often trapped and slaughtered on the barbed-wire defenses fronting the enemy's trenches. The toll of those killed and wounded from just two of the myriad western front battles—Verdun (February–December 1916) and the Somme (July–November 1916)—was an estimated two million men. By the end of the war, an estimated nine to thirteen million men had been killed, including 116,516 Americans.

Western Europe may have been the worst charnel house;

JANUARY 1

1933 As Japan consolidates its occupation of Manchuria (which the Japanese rename Manchukuo), Chinese and Japanese forces clash at Shanhaikuan, on the border between Manchuria and northern China.

but major combat raged from Africa through the Middle East and into the Balkans. In Eastern Europe, where the czar's unprepared forces suffered a costly defeat by Germany at the 1914 Battle of Tannenberg, the war did much to spark the revolution of 1917 that transformed imperial Russia into the world's first Communist state—an event that sent shock waves around the globe.

Throughout a radically changed postwar world—as the territories of defeated empires were redistributed, borders altered, and new countries formed—the very idea of another such conflict seemed so untenable that the Great War of 1914–18 was called "the war to end war." "Shame on military glory," French writer and Great War combat veteran Henri Barbusse wrote in his classic novel *La Feu* ("Under Fire," 1916), "shame on armies, shame on the soldier's calling that changes men by turns into stupid victims and ignoble brutes."

Yet for many people on both sides, the thirst for peace was matched by a hunger for vengeance. As Allied delegates to the Paris Peace Conference of 1919 framed a treaty filled with the seeds of future conflict, a megalomaniac Austrian ex-corporal named Adolf Hitler began dreaming of leading Germany down a fiery path that would erase the humiliation of defeat. At the same time, a complex of factors launched the former Allied nations of Italy and Japan on quests for empire that would lead them to ally with Hitler's Germany. From the beginning, that alliance was characterized chiefly by mistrust and the dictates of self-interest, but its leaders did share one conviction that would lead the world to disaster:

"War alone . . . puts the stamp of nobility upon the peoples who have the courage to meet it," Benito Mussolini asserted.

"War is the father of creation and the mother of culture," a 1930s Japanese Imperial Army pamphlet declared, "both in individuals and competing nations."

"Any alliance whose purpose is not the intention to wage war," Hitler wrote in 1925, "is senseless and useless."

Artwork for a British World War I poster. Color lithograph by Gerald Spencer Pryse, c. 1915.

Returning home at the end of the Great War, the surviving professional military officers of the Central Powers and Allied armed forces faced some similar postwar challenges: Military budgets were slashed, manpower was reduced precipitously, and distrust of the presumably barbaric *psychologie du militaire professional* (psychology of the military professional) prevailed. German warriors such as the daring and much-decorated Luftwaffe (air force) officer Hermann Göring were also plunged into the social and economic chaos of a defeated nation and the ugly recriminations of a people unused to military defeat. "Officers were being insulted in the streets by the men," his wartime aide Karl Bodenschatz later reported, "the medals they had risked their lives to earn torn from their breasts." As Göring spoke of "a great crusade to raise the Fatherland back to the heights from which it had fallen," Captain George C. Marshall, who had been among the first members of the American Expeditionary Force to reach Europe in 1917, was determined to help rectify the many flaws in the U.S. Army that its wartime experience had revealed. Marshall exerted increasing influence and slowly advanced in rank as he sought to prepare the small core of professional American ground-force officers for organizing and training the citizen armies that would have to fight through the "cloud of uncertainties" that would characterize a future, presumably much more technological and mobile war.

ABOVE: *Psychologie du militaire professional.* Socialist antiwar poster. Color lithograph by Maximilien Luce, Paris, c. 1930.

LEFT: Oblt. Hermann Göring, German Luftwaffe, c. 1914–18.

RIGHT: Capt. George C. Marshall, United States Army, c. 1914–18.

JANUARY 2

1942 The Japanese occupy Manila, the capital of the Philippines.

1945 Danish underground forces destroy a factory in Copenhagen producing parts for German V-2 rockets.

igh hopes surrounded the delegates who gathered for the Paris Peace Conference in January 1919—and particularly centered on U.S. president Woodrow Wilson. A year earlier, Wilson had proposed Fourteen Points that seemed a promising basis for a lasting peace. Yet the ideals expressed in Wilson's program quickly drowned in treacherous currents of vengeance and national self-interest. Point I—"Open covenants of peace, openly arrived at"—was the first to succumb, as preparatory deliberations by the Allies' Council of Ten (two delegates each from the United States, Britain, France, Italy, and Japan) proved so frustrating that the leaders of the Big Three (the United States, Britain, and France) eventually retreated into private quarters to haggle among themselves. The Treaty of Versailles that emerged after months of convoluted negotiations disappointed the Italians (who expected greater territorial rewards for their costly participation in the war); offended the Japanese (who were rebuffed when they proposed including a racial equality provision in the Covenant of the League of Nations); and included a roster of bitterly punitive terms toward Germany. These were adopted despite a prophetic warning from British prime minister David Lloyd George: "You may strip Germany of her colonies, reduce her armaments to a mere police force and her navy to that of a fifth-rate power; all the same, in the end if she feels that she has been unjustly treated . . . she will find means of exacting retribution from her conquerors."

At the Trianon Palace Hotel, German delegates listen to a speech by French premier George Clemenceau on the terms of the Treaty of Versailles, May 27, 1919.

JANUARY 3

1935 As it struggles to deal with an invasion by the more technologically advanced forces of Italy, the government of Ethiopia appeals to the League of Nations to take actions that will "safeguard peace."

solationism ran deep among the American people after World War I, fed by resentment among some in the military over what they saw as British manipulation of Americans during the conflict; distaste at the haggling during the Paris Peace Conference; and a growing conviction that fat-cat war profiteers were chiefly responsible for unnecessary American involvement. Having emerged from the conflict comparatively unscathed—in fact, the United States replaced Britain as the leading financial power in the postwar world—most Americans were content to rely on the country's two flanking oceans to protect its security as they hungered for a "return to normalcy." That slogan helped elect Warren G. Harding in 1920, a year after a conservative Republican Congress refused to ratify the Versailles Treaty—thus rejecting U.S. membership in the newly formed League of Nations. This decision bitterly disappointed a dedicated minority who fervently believed that without full American participation, the League would not succeed in maintaining a lasting peace. As Mrs. Frank Day Tuttle, chairman of the Women's Pro-League Council, wrote in July 1923: "America holds the balance of power . . . . So we are told that, as America goes, so goes the world. America is to choose, then . . . . [S]he must either cooperate with the nations of the world and build up a new world founded upon law and order, or she must compete in the old mad way in building up armaments which leads to universal disaster."

A prayer for the spiritual union of mankind. Issued by the Women's Pro-League [of Nations] Council, New York, 1924.

JANUARY 4

1932 In the "jewel" of the British Empire, the Indian National Congress votes to resume civil disobedience in its quest for national sovereignty. Mahatma Gandhi is arrested; boycotts, picketing, and "days of strike and mourning" (*hartals*) begin again.

1934 President Roosevelt addresses Congress, telling members that national economic recovery program costs will grow to $10.5 billion by June.

✶ A PRAYER ✶

For the Spiritual Union of Mankind.

WAR HAS FAILED
TO END WAR.

DIPLOMACY HAS FAILED
TO END WAR.

ONLY TIES OF THE SPIRIT INFALLIBLY UNITE.

Therefore We Pray For

The Divine Alliance of Nations.

Eternal God, Father of All Souls,

Grant unto us such clear vision of the Sin of War
That we may earnestly seek that Co-operation between Nations
Which Alone can make War Impossible.

As man by his inventions has made the whole world
Into One Neighborhood,
Grant that he may, by his co-operations, make the Whole World
Into One Brotherhood.

Help us to break down all race prejudice:
Stay the greed of those who profit by war, and
The ambitions of those who seek an imperialistic conquest
Drenched in Blood.

Guide all Statesmen to seek a Just Basis
For International Action in the Interests of Peace.
Arouse in the Whole Body of the People an
Adventurous Willingness,
As they Sacrificed Greatly for War,
So, also, for International Good-Will,
To Dare bravely, Think wisely, Decide resolutely,
And to Achieve Triumphantly. Amen.

Feel As You Pray That Endless Others Are Aspiring With You.

"More Things Are Wrought By Prayer Than This World Dreams Of."

Apply to Women's Pro-League Council
303 Fifth Avenue, Room 2010,
For More Cards Like This.

Please Keep This Card In Plain Sight.
Try to Give One Away Every Day.

By 1917, more than 1.3 million Russian soldiers had been killed in battle and some six million more had been either wounded or captured. Behind the battle lines, prices had skyrocketed and food was so scarce that workers struck and people marched through city streets shouting antiwar slogans and demanding to be fed. On February 26, the Duma (legislature) refused the czar's order to close down and instead called for the formation of a provisional government in which the people could have more confidence. Four days later, after additional encouragement from his military leaders, the czar abdicated. As various factions struggled within the country, the German government, seeing an opportunity to end the war in Eastern Europe, made it possible for exiled Marxist revolutionary Vladimir Lenin and twenty-seven associates to return to Russia by train. Thus began the revolution that would take Russia out of the war and result in the creation of the Union of Soviet Socialist Republics (USSR) within the next five years. The governing ideology of this, the world's first Communist nation, rejected religion and called for worldwide revolution by workers and the abolition of private enterprise. This was a terrifying prospect to governments and people in the Western democracies. In the East, where imperial Russia and Japan had long vied for territory and influence, the Japanese, too, viewed the Communists' ascension with alarm. But they also viewed Russia's political turmoil as a possible opportunity.

LEFT: *May 1, 1920—through the wreckage of capitalism to the world brotherhood of workers!* Reproduction, c. 1965–80, of a poster originally produced in 1920.

RIGHT: *V. I. Lenin Declares the Power of the Soviets.* Reproduction of a painting by Vladimir Aleksandrovich Serov (1910–68), published in Moscow, 1967.

JANUARY 5

1920 As the Russian Civil War continues, along with a bitter territorial conflict between Russians and Poles, the Bolsheviks suffer a setback when the Poles and Letts capture Dvinsk. A month later, however, the Bolsheviks will take Odessa.

In March 1918, the Russian government of Vladimir Lenin signed the Treaty of Brest-Litovsk with Germany, ending Russian participation in World War I. At about the same time, factional disputes sparked the Russian Civil War (1918–20), which pitted Lenin's Bolshevik Communist faction (Red) against an unruly alliance of moderates, liberals, dissident Communists, and right-wing czarists (White) that was supported by Imperial Russia's former Western Allies. As British, French, and American forces occupied Murmansk and Archangel in the north, the U.S. government invited the Japanese to participate in a joint expedition to Siberia to rescue a Czechoslovakian force that had been cut off when the Allied eastern front collapsed. The invitation was well timed to further a plan within the Imperial Japanese Army to occupy the Russian Far East and turn it into a politically and economically useful buffer state. Many more Japanese troops poured into Siberia than the Allies had requested, and they stayed well after the Czechs had been rescued and the British and American troops had withdrawn. As Japanese civilians followed the troops to exploit economic assets, combat continued, sometimes seared by episodes of criminal brutality: In May 1920, Bolshevik soldiers tortured and massacred seven hundred Japanese men, women, and children at Nikolaevsk. By June 1922, with no end in sight and civilian support for the Siberian incursion at low ebb, the Imperial Japanese Army withdrew from Siberia.

The Japanese Army Occupied Vragaeschensk [Blagoveshchensk] [Siberia]. Color lithograph by Shobido & Co., Tokyo, 1919.

JANUARY 6

1929 King Alexander of the Kingdom of the Serbs, Croats, and Slovenes suspends the country's constitution, appoints his bodyguard prime minister, and chooses a cabinet composed mostly of Serbs. The country is renamed Yugoslavia.

1944 Maj. Gen. James H. (Jimmy) Doolittle assumes command of the U.S. Eighth Air Force, based in Britain.

Throughout its history, strategically located Poland had been subjected to conquest and partition by stronger powers—most particularly Russia and Prussia/Germany. Each of these powers mounted intensive "Russification" and "Prussification" programs in the Polish territory they controlled, yet Polish nationalists' greatest resentments were directed toward Russia. During World War I, Polish Legions fought alongside Germans against the czar's forces—then chafed at the rigid control Germany insisted on maintaining over the Polish government. Not until the Allies defeated the Central Powers in November 1918 (when Russia was violently transforming into the Soviet Union) did Poland actually regain its status as an independent nation. Almost immediately, however, the Poles faced a new Russian challenge and a new war. A territorial dispute stemming from provisions of the Versailles Treaty flared into the Russo-Polish War of 1919–20, a bitter contest in which the Poles, assisted by the French, managed to push the Russians back. Poland subsequently confirmed its claim to a border that was farther east than the Russians wished. Many Germans also deeply resented the territories Germany had been required to surrender to resurgent Poland. When Nazi leader Adolf Hitler spoke of Germany's need for greater *lebensraum* (living space), his eyes were turned eastward—toward Poland, and beyond.

Polish army volunteers (with scythes) at the time of the Russo-Polish War. Photograph by W. A. F., Warsaw, Poland, July 18, 1920.

JANUARY 7

1935 In Rome, the aspiring imperial nations of France and Fascist Italy sign a treaty that grants Italy some concessions in Africa and opens the possibility of Franco-Italian cooperation against Germany.

The world map changed radically in the aftermath of World War I, as the Allies dismembered or reduced the holdings of the major Central Powers. The shattered Austro-Hungarian Empire became Austria, Czechoslovakia, and Hungary. The Ottoman Empire (Turkey) was greatly diminished in size, a large portion of its former territory becoming the new nation of Iraq, established under British administration. The British also gained control of Palestine and Trans-Jordan, while Syria and Lebanon fell under French supervision. Yugoslavia was born—an amalgam of the former Austro-Hungarian territories of Croatia, Slovenia, and Bosnia-Herzegovina and the independent states of Serbia and Montenegro. Germany lost its colonial holdings (those in the Far East went to Japan), while Germany itself not only lost territory to Poland, but was severed from its East Prussia lands by the newly created Polish corridor (which gave reborn Poland access to the sea). At this time, German military leaders viewed Poland as a greater risk to their country's security than Communist-controlled Russia (which officially became the Union of Soviet Socialist Republics in 1922). Since both the USSR's Red Army and the German Wehrmacht needed assistance the other could provide, in late 1921 the two armed forces began a clandestine collaboration in military training and the manufacture of planes and weapons.

Europe and Asia Minor in 1914, left, and Europe and Asia Minor in 1924, right. Maps by Col. Lawrence Martin, from International Conciliation, 1924.

JANUARY 8

1940 Britain begins rationing food.

1945 A thousand U.S. bombers attack Frankfurt, Germany.

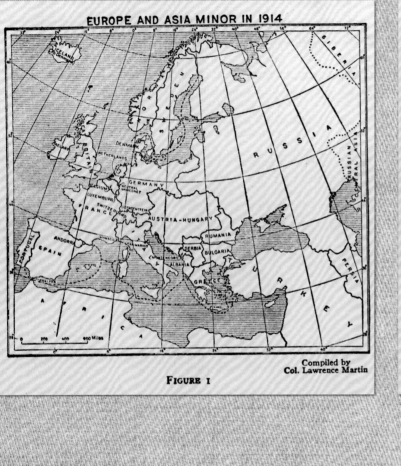

EUROPE AND ASIA MINOR IN 1914

Compiled by
Col. Lawrence Martin

FIGURE 1

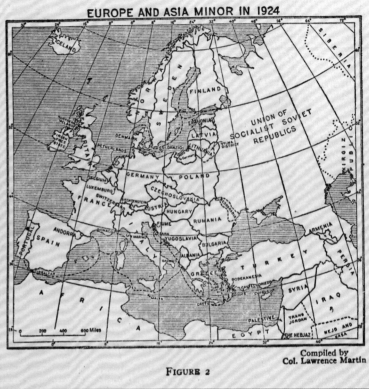

EUROPE AND ASIA MINOR IN 1924

Compiled by
Col. Lawrence Martin

FIGURE 2

At the Paris Peace Conference of 1919, Prince Faisal, leader of the Arab revolt against Turkish rule, stood before the leaders of the major Allied nations and argued passionately, but without success, for Arab independence. Faisal's Arab forces—including the ferocious Bedouin fighters of chieftain Auda Abu Tayeh—had fought alongside British troops to wrest their lands from Turkish control. With the assistance of the inventive, Arabic-speaking British liaison officer T. E. (Thomas Edward) Lawrence ("Lawrence of Arabia"), they gained some spectacular victories. (As a delegate to the peace conference, Lawrence, too, argued for Arab independence.) Yet, the Allies placed Arab lands under the colonial administration of Britain and France. Ejected from Syria by the French in 1920, a bitterly disappointed Faisal joined other Arab leaders the following year in discussions organized by Britain's new colonial minister, Winston Churchill, who had convened a conference in Cairo to decide the future of Mesopotamia. Directed to improve British-Arab relations in the area (without sacrificing British interests), Churchill brought Lawrence into the Colonial Office as an adviser, and also called on the celebrated explorer and Middle East expert Gertrude Bell (whom the Arabs had dubbed a "daughter of the desert"). Faisal emerged from these discussions as the new king of Iraq, a country in which the British would actively support their own interests long after it achieved its independence in 1932.

ABOVE: Gertrude Bell (1868–1926), 1921.

RIGHT: Bedouin and Circassian leaders, with T. E. Lawrence ("Lawrence of Arabia," third from right) and other European representatives. Photograph by the American Colony Photo Department, April 1921.

JANUARY 9

1932 A Korean nationalist attempts to assassinate Emperor Hirohito of Japan.

1945 U.S. Sixth Army forces land at Lingayen Gulf in Luzon, one hundred miles north of Manila, in the Philippine Islands.

In 1918, Field Marshal Erich Ludendorff—the powerful chief of staff to Germany's supreme World War I military commander Paul von Hindenburg—advocated a peace settlement with the Allies. Quickly reversing himself, he proceeded to spark the decidedly unfounded legend that the German army lost the war because it had been stabbed in the back. "The political leadership disarmed the unconquered army and delivered over Germany to the destructive will of the enemy," he stated in February 1919. That same year, Germany's postmonarchical leaders, their country in turmoil, signed the detested Treaty of Versailles. Barred by the Allies from negotiating better terms, they were forced to accept unprecedented financial reparations; the surrender of all Germany's colonies; the loss of iron-rich Alsace-Lorraine to France (which also gained control of vital coal mines in Germany's Saar region); and Allied occupation of the left bank of the Rhine River (the Rhineland). In 1923, as political crises proliferated and the economy worsened (by November, it took four *billion* German marks to purchase one U.S. dollar), a bitter and unstable Ludendorff marched beside Adolf Hitler and other leading Nazis during the now-famous "Beer Hall Putsch," Hitler's abortive attempt to take over the government of the German state of Bavaria. Thereafter, Ludendorff's star faded. Hitler, meanwhile, used the time he spent in prison for leading the putsch to write *Mein Kampf* ("My Struggle," 1925), his turgid—and revealing—political biography.

LEFT: *And This is No Scrap of Paper*. Pen-and-ink drawing by William Allen Rogers (1854–1931), published in the *New York Herald*, November 7, 1918.

RIGHT: German Field Mar. Erich Ludendorff. Color photomechanical print on a postcard, c. 1914–18.

JANUARY 10

1937 In Britain, the government invokes a nineteenth-century law to keep British citizens from participating in the Spanish Civil War.

1943 The U.S. Twenty-fifth Division begins the final offensive to clear Guadalcanal.

At midday on September 1, 1923, a major earthquake ripped through Japan, collapsing most buildings in Tokyo and the port city of Yokohama and destroying surrounding villages. Wind-whipped fires swept through the ruins of wood and paper buildings, roaring hotter and higher into a terrifying night as oil storage tanks and gas pipes ruptured. In all, some one hundred forty thousand people were killed and thousands more injured. The devastation caused by the quake wrought economic havoc on Japan, and loosed a frenzy of irrational retribution against immigrant Korean workers and political dissidents. Meanwhile, aid began reaching Japan from Western nations, particularly the United States. Yet Japanese gratitude was tempered by the reminder inherent in this Western largesse that their country was relatively poor in resources. The previous year, limitations on Japan's political influence and military power had been underlined by the terms of the Five-Power Naval Limitation Treaty, which restricted the Japanese navy to fewer warships than its former World War I allies, Britain and the United States. In 1924, the Japanese would receive another reminder of their unequal status when the U.S. Congress passed the Oriental Exclusion Act, effectively barring immigrants from Asia. Such treatment fed the growing sentiment for building Japan's own empire in the East—as a source of economic and political power, and a means of breaking Western influence in Asia.

The whirlwind of fire attacked Yoshiwara Street. Color lithograph from an album of fourteen posters depicting the 1923 Japanese earthquake. Gift to the people of the United States from the government of Japan, 1925.

JANUARY 11

1923 After Germany defaults on coal deliveries, French troops move in to occupy Germany's economically important Ruhr Basin. Soon inflation in Germany will soar out of control.

"**M**anchuria [northeast China] is . . . important from the point of view of Japanese capitalism," Lieutenant General Seishiro Itagaki wrote. "No fundamental solution can be found within the boundaries of naturally poor Japan that will ensure a livelihood for the people at large." A staff officer of Japan's Manchuria-based Kwangtung Army, Itagaki and his fellow officer Kanji Ishihara believed that all Manchuria could be opened for Japanese economic exploitation. The Kwangtung Army had already brought a measure of law and order to the limited area of Manchuria it had patrolled since Japan's victory in the Russo-Japanese War of 1904–05. Yet the Tokyo government resisted the army's pressure to forcefully extend its control over the whole region. So the army proceeded on its own: In 1928, it assassinated Manchuria's governing Chinese warlord, Marshal Chang Tso-lin. Then, in September 1931—after the warlord's son and successor, Chang Hsueh-liang (the "young marshal"), had declared his loyalty to the Chinese Nationalist government of Chiang Kai-shek—Kwangtung forces dynamited a section of the South Manchurian railway, blamed nearby Chinese troops for the explosion, and used the incident as an excuse for military action that by January 1932 secured all of Manchuria for Japan. This unauthorized expansion brought only the mildest of reproaches from Tokyo. The Chinese government, meanwhile, turned to the twelve-year-old League of Nations for help.

LEFT: Wu Ti (Kuan Ti), the Chinese war god, with his squire, Chou-tsang. Color woodcut, created before 1928.

RIGHT: Lt. Gen. Seishiro Itagaki, Japanese Imperial Army. Reproduction of a painting by Tadaichi Hayashi, published in *Seisen Gafu* ("A Picture Album of the Holy War"), Tokyo, 1939.

JANUARY 12

1940 The Luftwaffe conducts its first bombing raid on London.

1942 The Inter-Allied Conference (exiled leaders of nine occupied nations and China) issues a resolution that establishes the principle of postwar war crimes trials.

China was plagued by difficulties when it faced much-smaller Japan's Manchurian aggression. The Nationalist government of Chiang Kai-shek, though ostensibly democratic, was in fact a corrupt, disorganized one-party dictatorship, served by armed forces that were generally well below par. The country was riven by factions, had little industry or expertise in weapons development, and its transportation systems were unreliable. China had long been parrying the territorial ambitions of Japan and Russia. It had also been accommodating—sometimes under threat—the economic interests of several Western powers. But in 1931, these Western powers resisted entanglement in Manchuria. The risks were too great, and many felt, as British foreign secretary Lord Grey stated, "Japan had a strong case in Manchuria, where her interests were being threatened by lawlessness." Thus, the League of Nations relegated the problem to a five-man commission of inquiry (the Lytton Commission), whose deliberations were assisted by two "assessors" from the disputing nations: former Chinese prime minister Dr. Wellington Koo and Japanese diplomat Isaburo Yoshida. Months of fact-gathering (which continued through a bloody clash between Japanese and Chinese troops in Shanghai) ended in October 1932 with a report whose tepid conclusions—that China had been provocative, but Japan had been an aggressor—did nothing to change the Manchurian situation. It did, however, cause Japan to withdraw from the League.

LEFT: Isaburo Yoshida. Photograph by the National Photo Company, c. 1924

RIGHT: Dr. Vi-Kyuin Wellington Koo (1887–1985). Photograph by Underwood & Underwood, November 19, 1921.

JANUARY 13

1935 The League of Nations conducts a plebiscite in the Saar Basin. Residents vote nine to one for reuniting with Germany, rather than uniting with France or being ruled by the League. The Saar again becomes part of Germany in March.

1940 Uncertain of Hitler's intentions, Belgium orders full-scale mobilization.

After reading the long speech Hitler delivered during his trial for leading the 1923 Beer Hall Putsch (see January 10), doctor of philosophy and aspiring writer Joseph Goebbels gushed that the Nazi leader's words comprised "the catechism of a new political faith amid the despair of a collapsing, godless world." Fanatically devoted to Hitler and the Nazi Party for the next twenty years, Goebbels proved himself a master propagandist and organizer. In Berlin in the late 1920s and early 1930s, he worked to transform the motley assortment of warped idealists and down-on-their-luck thugs who constituted the Nazi *Sturmabteilung* (SA) into a disciplined, ideologically committed Nazi militia—in the process, winning the admiration of one young recruit. "There was nothing he couldn't handle," Horst Wessel wrote. "Goebbels—he was like Hitler himself." Goebbels, in turn, thought Wessel a born leader and helped move him up the Nazi ladder. After Wessel was shot in retaliation for SA attacks on Communists, Goebbels—who well understood the value of having a Nazi martyr—did not hesitate to brilliantly exploit the propaganda opportunities presented by the young Nazi's lingering death. These culminated with Wessel's funeral, a well-orchestrated and provocative event that concluded with the singing of "Raise High the Flag," an SA song Wessel had written. Renamed "The Horst Wessel Song," this wholly undistinguished air became Germany's alternate national anthem after Hitler rose to power in 1933.

LEFT: Joseph Goebbels (1897–1945) with unidentified fellow Nazis, Nuremberg, 1933.

RIGHT: Horst Wessel (1907–1930). Photoprint, c. 1930, from Hauptarchiv de NSDAP.

JANUARY 14

1942 German U-boats begin attacking ships off the east coast of the United States, torpedoing the Panamanian tanker *Norness* off Cape Hatteras, North Carolina.

On October 29, 1929, the U.S. stock market crashed, a first violent tremor in the Great Depression that was to engulf the entire world. By 1932, an estimated 20 to 25 percent of the U.S. working population was unemployed. That May, twenty-five thousand destitute World War I veterans, many accompanied by wives and children, converged on Washington, D.C. to press Congress and President Herbert Hoover for the immediate release of the $500 bonuses the government was to pay them in 1945. Although orderly, dignified, and unarmed, the people of this "Bonus Expeditionary Force" (BEF) were viewed as both threat and embarrassment by the president and Attorney General William D. Mitchell, while many newspapers labeled them Communists and urged action against them. Violence erupted on a stiflingly hot day in late July: Police attempted to clear a BEF camp on Pennsylvania Avenue, the veterans resisted, and President Hoover ordered the military to deal with this "defiance of civil authority." Personally taking command, Army Chief of Staff Douglas MacArthur declared, "We're going to break the back of the BEF," and unleashed a full-scale military assault that, by midnight, pushed the veterans out of the nation's capital as soldiers set fire to their makeshift homes. "The whole scene was pitiful," MacArthur's aide, Major Dwight D. Eisenhower, later wrote. "The veterans . . . were ragged, ill-fed, and felt themselves badly abused. To suddenly see the whole encampment going up in flames just added to the pity one had to feel for them."

Encampment built by World War I veterans of the "Bonus Expeditionary Force" in Washington, D.C. Photograph by Theodor Horydczak (1890–1971), 1932.

JANUARY 15

1944 A British cabinet committee recommends the partition of Germany after the war.
Dwight D. Eisenhower assumes command of the Allied Expeditionary Force preparing to liberate France.

"When we arrived in Washington on the night of March 2, [1933]," Raymond Moley, adviser to Franklin D. Roosevelt, wrote, "terror held the country in its grip." A renewed financial panic had forced thirty-two governors to close all the banks in their states. Frightened Americans were hoarding what little they had. Herbert Hoover had proved incapable of leading the country back to less treacherous economic ground. What would the new president do? A son of wealth and privilege, Roosevelt was a consummate politician who had served as assistant secretary of the navy and New York State senator and governor—and in the midst of his career fought a life-altering battle with polio. At the center of this national crisis, he remained buoyantly confident and generally unflappable as he listened to hosts of conflicting opinions without revealing the course he would chart for the country. After declaring, in his March 4 inaugural address, "The only thing we have to fear is fear itself," he called a special session of Congress, which passed the Emergency Banking Act on March 9. Four days later, in the first of his *Fireside Chat* radio broadcasts, he assured Americans that "it is safer to keep your money in a reopened bank than under the mattress"—and most responded by redepositing their funds. The new administration had ended one crisis, but many terrible problems remained. Meanwhile, in Germany, the Nazis were exploiting Depression-sparked troubles to at last gain control of the government.

Chief Justice Charles Evans Hughes administering the oath of office to Franklin Delano Roosevelt on the east portico of the U.S. Capitol, March 4, 1933.

JANUARY 16

1920 The Eighteenth Amendment to the U.S. Constitution—banning the manufacture, sale, and transportation of alcoholic beverages nationwide—goes into effect. Chiefly a boon to bootleggers, the amendment will be repealed with ratification of the Twenty-first Amendment on December 5, 1933.

"**I**ntrigues are everywhere afoot," Joseph Goebbels wrote in his diary on June 2, 1932. "We are playing a risky game." At stake was ultimate power, which, after a tumultuous decade culminating in the Great Depression, the Nazi Party was within reach of achieving legally. Two months earlier, Hitler had received 37 percent of the vote in the presidential election that returned Field Marshal Paul von Hindenburg to the office. Legislative elections had given the Nazi Party the largest block of seats in the Reichstag (legislature), and in August, Hermann Göring was elected Reichstag president. Still, Hindenburg refused even to consider appointing the "Bohemian corporal" chancellor of Germany—and Hitler would accept nothing less. In this roiling year of economic distress, nonstop electioneering, backroom political intrigue, and bloody clashes between Communists and rampaging Nazi storm troopers, first Fritz von Papen, then General Kurt von Schleicher headed the faction-riven German government. All the while Hitler, Göring, and Goebbels continued to wheel, deal, propagandize, and bully their way to control. Finally, after securing the support of Hindenburg's son, Oskar (possibly by means of blackmail), and the grudging alliance of Papen, the Nazis won their prize: On January 30, 1933, Hindenburg appointed Hitler chancellor of Germany. "The final decision has been made," an elated Goebbels gloated in his diary. "Germany is at a turning point in her history."

German president Paul von Hindenburg leads a procession, including Chancellor Adolf Hitler and Hermann Göring, at the Tannenberg Festival, probably in Berlin during the summer of 1933.

JANUARY 17

1945 Russian and Polish Communist forces take Warsaw.

The night Hitler became chancellor, young Melita Maschmann witnessed the celebratory parade. She later remembered "the somber pomp of the . . . flags, the flickering light of the torches . . . and the songs. . . . For hours the columns marched by. Again and again amongst them we saw groups of boys and girls scarcely older than ourselves. . . . I longed to hurl myself into this current, to be submerged and borne along by it." The Nazis longed to have her—and every "racially pure" German youth—firmly in their thrall. The Nazis saw them as the armies of tomorrow and the fertile Aryan females who would people the thousand-year Reich. In June 1933, after Hitler appointed Baldur von Schirach the Youth Leader of the entire German Reich, the Nazis began to eliminate or absorb all other youth groups into the Nazi Jungvolk (for young boys), Jungmädel (for young girls), and Hitler Youth. School curricula and textbooks were gradually altered along party lines, efforts were made to replace family ties with reliance on the party, and young people were encouraged to pray to Hitler ("Führer, my Führer given me by God, Protect and preserve my life"). In 1934, on a visit to Germany, U.S. journalist Dorothy Thompson passed a Hitler Youth camp and was shocked to see a banner "so huge that . . . every child could see it many times a day. It was white, and there was a swastika painted on it, and besides that only seven words, seven immense black words: 'YOU WERE BORN TO DIE FOR GERMANY!'"

LEFT: Letter and collage from a portfolio of eighty-nine pieces of Bavarian children's art presented to Adolf Hitler on his forty-fourth birthday in 1933.

RIGHT: An adoring group of young people surrounds Hitler in a rathskeller. Photograph between 1930 and 1936, reproduced in a Nazi souvenir album confiscated by American troops.

JANUARY 18

1919 Representatives of twenty-seven victorious Allied nations convene the Versailles Peace Conference in France. One week later they will unanimously adopt a resolution that will result in the creation of the League of Nations.

1942 Germany, Italy, and Japan sign a military convention in Berlin, laying down "guidelines for common operations against the common enemies."

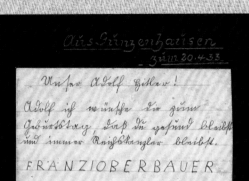

Aus Günzenhausen
zum 20.4.33

Unser Adolf Hitler!

Adolf ich wünsche dir zum
Geburtstag daß du gesund bleibst
und immer Reichskanzler bleibst.

FRANZI OBERBAUER

Günzenhausen Osiandustraße
14 b.

By 1933, Jewish communities had existed in Germany for more than one thousand six hundred years. When Hitler became chancellor, they constituted less than 1 percent of the population, some 554,000 of the country's sixty-five million people. Nearly all regarded themselves as Germans who were Jewish, rather than as Jews living in Germany. Hitler thought otherwise. In *Mein Kampf* (1925), he accused Jews of being the driving force behind Communism and stated, "No one need be surprised if among our people the personification of the devil as the symbol of all evil assumes the living shape of the Jew." Anti-Semitism was far from unknown in Germany, and Hitler and his henchmen skillfully exploited old prejudices and more recent angers born of military defeat and economic depression to make a scapegoat of Germany's Jews and promote Nazi racial policies. Immediately after coming to power, they launched an increasingly repressive anti-Semitic campaign: Jewish businesses were boycotted; books by Jewish authors were burned; Jews were dismissed from the civil service, barred from the national labor union, denied national health insurance, and forbidden to serve in the military. There were portents of far greater horrors to come. In July 1933, the Nazi newspaper *Der Stürmer* editorialized: "The Jewish people must be exterminated from the face of the earth."

Nazi authorities harassing Jewish people somewhere in Greater Germany, c. 1933–37.

JANUARY 19

1941 The Allies invade Italian-occupied Ethiopia. Since entering the war against Italy, Britain and France have been allied with the Ethiopian resistance.

Immediately after handling the banking crisis in March 1933 (see January 16), President Roosevelt launched a program that melded his own interest in conservation with a method of providing unemployment relief. By signing the Emergency Conservation Work (ECW) Act on March 31, he launched the Civilian Conservation Corps (CCC). During its nine-year existence, CCC put more than three million young men to work planting trees and generally improving public lands (at thirty dollars per month, twenty-five of which they had to send home to their families). Over the protests of General Douglas MacArthur, who feared the effects this massive undertaking would have on military readiness, the army was ordered to mobilize the CCC and run its camps—and did so in the fastest, most orderly mobilization in U.S. Army history. Within seven weeks, 310,000 men had arrived at 1,315 camps. The program did not include any military training, yet living in army-run camps did give CCC workers experience with military discipline that would prove invaluable when many later entered the wartime armed forces. Military officers involved in running the program also learned from the experience—including Colonel George C. Marshall, whose efficient administration of nineteen CCC camps brought him to President Roosevelt's attention. Marshall, who would be Roosevelt's chief military adviser throughout World War II, called his CCC experience "the most instructive service I have ever had, and the most interesting."

LEFT: *A young man's opportunity for work, play, study & health, CCC.* Silk-screen poster by Albert M. Bender, published by the Chicago, Illinois, WPA Art Project, c. 1941.

RIGHT: President Franklin D. Roosevelt having lunch at Camp Fechner, a Civilian Conservation Corps facility at Big Meadows, Virginia. Also at the table (left to right): Louis Howe, Secretary of the Interior Harold Ickes, CCC director Robert Fechner, Roosevelt, Secretary of Agriculture Henry Wallace, and Assistant Secretary of Agriculture Rexford Tugwell.

JANUARY 20

1933 President Herbert Hoover and President-elect Franklin D. Roosevelt have a second meeting to discuss the international debt situation. Hoover continues to consider his successor "a very ignorant . . . well-meaning young man."

1937 Franklin D. Roosevelt becomes the first U.S. president to be inaugurated on January 20. Previously, presidential inaugurations occurred in March.

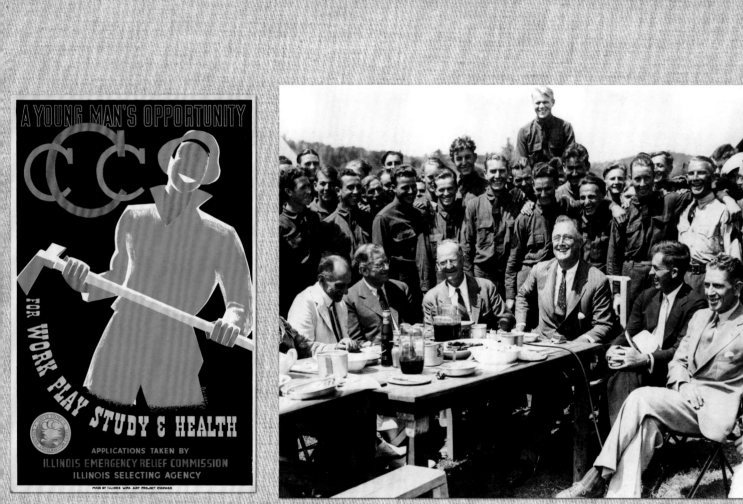

The United States grappled with the Depression as virtually the only modern industrial nation without a national system of unemployment compensation and pensions for elder citizens. This lack inspired California physician Francis E. Townsend to propose that all people over age sixty who agreed to retire be paid $200 per month, provided they pledged to spend each payment in the month they received it. Analysis quickly determined that the "Townsend Plan" was not workable; yet some twenty-five million Americans signed petitions urging its adoption. Meanwhile, President Roosevelt was asking Secretary of Labor Frances Perkins to take charge of what would prove to be the exceedingly complex task of framing legislation that would create a national "social security" program. The resulting historic legislation that the president sent to Congress on January 17, 1935—based on a model of private insurance and including contributions from workers who would later draw benefits from the program—was far less than the sweeping program Roosevelt had originally envisioned. Yet it offered at least some protection to twenty-six million American workers. "No one can guarantee this country against the dangers of future depressions," Roosevelt said in the message accompanying the bill, "but . . . we can eliminate many of the factors that cause economic depressions, and we can provide the means of mitigating their results." On August 14, 1935, the Social Security Act became law.

A monthly check to you for the rest of your life, beginning when you are 65. Color lithograph by the U.S. Social Security Board, 1935.

JANUARY 21

1942 Rommel takes his Afrika Korps on the offensive in Libya, surprising the British, who fall back to Agedabia.

In 1935, as Hitler brought Germany's heretofore clandestine rearmament into the open, German military attaché Friedrich von Boetticher reported to Berlin from Washington, D.C.: "As always, the Americans are neglecting their army in peacetime." Since 1918, the U.S. Army had shrunk from the 3.7 million men who had served during World War I to the world's seventeenth largest army, comprising some twelve thousand commissioned officers and one hundred twenty-five thousand enlisted men. Sharp budget reductions left little money for weapons development and procurement; transition from horse cavalry to mechanized units was slow and uneven; debate raged over the most effective use of armor and air power; and prevailing assumptions led to the development of contingency plans centered on hemispheric defense rather than overseas deployment. As a result of the 1931 Japanese occupation of Manchuria, U.S. military planners regarded war with Japan as a distinct possibility, but that would be primarily a naval war. Yet the navy, too, had suffered cutbacks—as had the marines —and was also operating under restrictions imposed by international naval limitations treaties. Navy and marine planners were, however, developing what would prove to be extremely sound amphibious warfare doctrine. Meanwhile, general assumptions about the character of, and the adversaries the United States would face in, a future war began to change when, in violation of the Versailles Treaty, German troops remilitarized the Rhineland in 1936 (see January 30).

On the Battlefield of Tomorrow, What Will I Wish I Had Done Today? Frame enlargement from the U.S. Signal Corps film, "The Japanese Soldier," 1942.

JANUARY 22

1936   The government of Pierre Laval falls in France.

1944   An Allied force invades the coastal area around Anzio, Italy.

During the summer of 1934, Adolf Hitler took two steps that consolidated his power in Germany. First, he gained army support by restraining what threatened to be the runaway power of his own Nazi militia, the *Sturmabteilung*, during the bloody round of thuggery and assassinations of SA leaders that became known as the "Night of the Long Knives." Then, after the death of the elderly president Paul von Hindenburg in August, he assumed the duties of president as well as chancellor, to become Germany's führer (leader). Two months earlier, the Nazi leader had traveled to Venice for his first face-to-face meeting with Italy's Fascist dictator Benito Mussolini. It was a less than successful visit: Il Duce was irritated by Hitler's near-nonstop discourses. Hitler, distressed that he had brought only civilian clothes while Mussolini was in uniform, was disgusted at the "degenerate" modern art the Fascists allowed in their galleries. Yet this lukewarm beginning was an important step toward a closer alliance—and Mussolini soon took another. After Hitler's visit, Il Duce began effecting plans for building his "new Fascist empire" in a way that would lead to chillier relations with Britain and France. On December 30, he issued a directive on Ethiopia (Abyssinia), where Italy had suffered a humiliating defeat less than forty years earlier: "The problem of Italo-Abyssinian relations has moved . . . onto a new plane. From a problem of diplomacy it has become a problem . . . which must be resolved by . . . the use of arms."

Adolf Hitler (center) with Fascist dictator Benito Mussolini (hands on hips), secretary of the National Fascist Party Achille Starace (second from left), and other Italian officials during a visit to Venice, June 14–16, 1934. Photograph by Silvio Ottolenghi.

JANUARY 23

1936 Ethiopian forces suffer eight thousand casualties versus the Italians' one thousand one hundred at the First Battle of Tembien.

At dawn on October 3, 1935, twenty-five Italian divisions well supported by aircraft swept across the Ethiopian border, repeating the Italian invasion of nearly forty years before. In the first Italo-Ethiopian war, Italy's forces had been decisively repelled at the 1896 Battle of Adowa—a defeat that initiated an era of extreme caution in the Italian high command. In 1935, however, Italy's numerical superiority and modern technology overwhelmed Emperor Haile Selassie's ill-equipped Ethiopian armed forces. In violation of the prevailing rules of war (the Hague Conventions, which the Italians had signed), the Italians used poison gas, determined that, as one Fascist commander said, "the *Duce* shall have Ethiopia with the Ethiopians or without them." The Ethiopian campaign continued despite tepid League of Nations sanctions until, on May 9, 1936, Mussolini exulted to a jubilant crowd in Rome, "Italy has at last her Empire—a Fascist Empire." The victory boosted Il Duce's support at home: "Mussolini today," philosopher Giovanni Gentile said, "has not just founded empire in Ethiopia. He has . . . created a new Italy." The new Italy was not looked upon favorably by many abroad—especially as Italian brutality continued against Ethiopians under a Mussolini directive of June 1936 to "initiate and systematically conduct [a] policy of terror and extermination against rebels and populations." Meanwhile, invigorated by success, Mussolini soon agreed to another costly military venture in Spain.

ABOVE: Haile Selassie (1892–1974), emperor of Ethiopia, 1934–74. Hand-illuminated photographic detail from a 1923 map of Ethiopia once owned by the emperor.

RIGHT: Italians guard wounded Ethiopians. Photograph from an album chronicling the 1935–36 Italian campaign in Ethiopia.

JANUARY 24

1942   U.S. destroyers sink four Japanese transports in the Battle of Makassar Strait, the first major naval engagement of World War II in the Pacific.

In 1931, before Hitler's rise to power, the International Olympic Committee (IOC) awarded the 1936 Olympics to Germany, an act that signaled general willingness to welcome the country back into the world community. By 1935, however, the character of Hitler's Nazi government, particularly its vicious treatment of "non-Aryans," had sparked calls in many nations to boycott the summer games. After sometimes-heated debates, the United States chose to participate, including among its 312-person contingent a number of Jewish athletes and eighteen black Americans. The Nazis, fully aware of the games' propagandist potential, removed anti-Semitic signs from Berlin, while propaganda minister Joseph Goebbels instructed the German press not to use "the racial point of view . . . in reporting sports results; above all . . . Negroes . . . must be treated with respect as Americans." African Americans sorely tested the Nazis' restraint, particularly track star Jesse Owens, who repeatedly bested "Aryans" as he collected four gold medals. John Woodruff, who won the gold medal for the eight-hundred-meter run, later reported his pride "for myself . . . for my race, and for my country" in helping debunk Hitler's master race theory. Woodruff's pride soon turned to bitter disappointment, however, when he was prevented from running in a track meet at the U.S. Naval Academy at Annapolis, Maryland, simply because he was black. "That let me know just what the situation was," he said later. "Things hadn't changed."

LEFT: *German—XIth Olympiad Berlin 1936.* Color lithograph by Willy Dzubas (b. 1887), attributed to Reichsbahnzentrale fur den Deutschen Reiseverkehr, 1936.

RIGHT: *Jesse Owens at the start of his record breaking 200 meter race.* Reproduction of a photograph in "Die Olympischen Spiele, 1936."

JANUARY 25

1942   Thailand declares war on the United States and Britain, and Thai forces immediately join in the Japanese invasion of Burma.

Hermann Göring, Germany's aviation minister and commander in chief of the Luftwaffe, hosted a special guest in his box at the opening ceremonies of the 1936 Summer Olympics—famed American aviator Charles A. Lindbergh, who had made the first nonstop solo flight across the Atlantic nine years before. Lindbergh was visiting Germany at the invitation of Major Truman Smith, U.S. military attaché in Berlin, who was hoping that Göring would reveal more to Lindbergh about Luftwaffe strength and capabilities than Smith had been able to learn. The air minister was delighted to escort "Lucky Lindy" on tours of aircraft factories and Luftwaffe installations. He also invited the American to inspect and fly a variety of military aircraft. Lindbergh brought away from this, and five subsequent visits he made to Germany, a deepened respect for German industry and technology —and an inflated estimate of Luftwaffe capabilities that Göring had carefully fostered. "If she wishes to do so," Lindbergh told U.S. ambassador to Britain Joseph P. Kennedy in September 1938, "Germany has now the means of destroying London, Paris, and Prague." In fact, the Luftwaffe's long-range strategic bombing capabilities were, and would remain, relatively weak. Its ability to provide tactical support for ground campaigns, and in the process wreak havoc on defenseless civilians, was becoming formidable, however— something the Germans would demonstrate in less than a year over the Spanish town of Guernica (see February 1).

Reichsminister Hermann Göring meets with Charles Lindbergh (center) and Anne Morrow Lindbergh (far left) in Germany, July 28, 1936.

JANUARY 26

1934 Germany and Poland sign a ten-year nonaggression pact proposed by Chancellor Adolf Hitler.

1942 The first contingent of U.S. forces to reach Europe arrives in Northern Ireland. U.S. forces in Britain establish headquarters in London.

On July 19, 1936, Spanish army generals who belonged to the right-wing National Front launched an attempted coup against the elected left-leaning government of the five-year-old Spanish Republic. Over the next three days, the man who would quickly emerge as the National Front leader, General Francisco Franco, asked both Mussolini and Hitler for help. As the coup devolved into vicious civil war, both dictators answered the call. Mussolini eventually dispatched some sixty thousand men and a host of aircraft—despite the prophetic warning from one of his generals that "Spain is like quicksand. If you stick in a hand, everything will follow." Hitler sent planes, tanks, technicians, and the Luftwaffe's Condor Legion—overall, a smaller investment than Italy's, but one from which Hitler was to reap greater gains. In Spain, the Germans honed the combat tactics they later used, to stunning effect, on a much greater stage—the longer the war, the greater the number of Germans who were rotated in to get combat experience. Hitler also had political reasons, as he told his generals, for not being interested in helping Franco quickly attain a "hundred percent victory. . . . Rather we are interested in a continuance of the war and in keeping up the tension in the Mediterranean." The longer Mussolini stubbornly kept his increasingly battered forces in Spain, the greater the likelihood that Italy would become permanently estranged from Britain and France, and that Il Duce would enter a permanent alliance with Germany.

ABOVE: *Francisco Franco with Two Faces*. Drawing by Miguel Covarrubias (1904–1957), c. 1925.

RIGHT: *C.N.T.—F.A.I, 19 Julio 1936*. [Confederación Nacional del Trabajo/National Confederation of Labor -Federación Anarquista Ibérica/Iberian Anarchist Federation.] Color lithograph by Toni Vidal, published in Barcelona by Ediciones Tierra y Libertad, 1937.

JANUARY 27

1936 Over President Roosevelt's veto, the U.S. Congress passes the Adjusted Compensation Act to give bonuses to World War I veterans.

1941 Joseph C. Grew, U.S. ambassador to Japan, advises Washington of reports of a possible Japanese attack on Pearl Harbor.

Three months before the Spanish Civil War began, violence erupted in Palestine, which Britain controlled under a League of Nations mandate. Since World War I, the area had been roiling with Arab-versus-Arab factional rivalries and increasing tension between Palestinian Arabs and the territory's growing Jewish population. In April 1936, an Arab attack on a Jewish bus marked the beginning of the Arab Revolt, three years of violent clashes and guerrilla warfare involving Arabs, Jews, and the British military. At the same time, Hitler was relentlessly nudging Europe toward another full-scale war. In such a conflict, the Middle East would be of vital strategic importance to Britain. The Suez Canal was an essential conduit to British territories in the East, and Britain needed the oil in Arab-controlled regions. In May 1939, as the Arab Revolt concluded, the British government issued a White Paper that ended its commitment (expressed in the Balfour Declaration of 1917) to "the establishment in Palestine of a National Home for the Jewish People." Britain proposed that a Palestinian (Arab) state be established within ten years; that Jewish immigration be restricted to seventy-five thousand over the next five years; and that all subsequent Jewish immigration be subject to Arab consent. In September, when the war in Europe began, Jewish leader David Ben-Gurion promised, "We shall fight the war against Hitler as if there were no White Paper, and we shall fight the White Paper as if there were no war."

A demonstration by Jewish residents of British Mandate Palestine against British proposals for the future of Palestine escalates into a riot, May 27, 1939.

JANUARY 28

 1944 The last Germans are eliminated from the Ardennes salient, ending the bitter and costly Battle of the Bulge.

1945 Clark Field, Philippines, is retaken by U.S. forces.

On June 27, 1936, Franklin D. Roosevelt accepted the Democratic Party's nomination for president. Over the previous four years, his administration had guided through Congress much of the legislative program that comprised the heart of the New Deal. The country had seen some economic and social improvements: Farm prices had risen, automobile production was up by 20 percent, and Civilian Conservation Corps instructors had taught thirty-five thousand illiterate young men basic skills in reading, writing, and math. Yet Americans were still in the throes of multiple crises: Eight million workers remained unemployed; hundreds of thousands of farmers in what was now known as the "Dust Bowl" had been blown off their land by billowing "black blizzards" of topsoil born of drought and bad farming methods; and political demagogues, from Louisiana governor Huey Long (assassinated in September) to Father Charles Coughlin, were propounding various revolutionary gospels to the nation's struggling poor. In this atmosphere, Roosevelt chose to fire rhetorical salvos at the relatively few American business titans he dubbed "economic royalists." The campaign alienated the titans (and distressed many FDR loyalists), but it captured the electorate. In November, voters chose Roosevelt over his chief opponent, Kansas governor Alf Landon, by an overwhelming majority and sent an equally overwhelming force of Democrats to Congress.

LEFT: Alfred M. Landon (1887–1987), 1936.

RIGHT: Cook Franklin Roosevelt stirs a pot of money in an illustration also featuring Democratic Party Chairman James Farley (the Duchess, cradling "Administration Mistakes") and Republican candidate Alf Landon (the Cheshire Cat): "'I'm glad he's not my child,' said Alice, weighing every word, 'a child like that should not be seen and also not be heard.'" Drawing in India ink over pencil with watercolor by Gregor Duncan, 1936.

JANUARY 29

1932 In the midst of Sino-Japanese political conflict over Japan's occupation of Manchuria, Japanese forces open fire on Shanghai, wreaking havoc on an eight-mile-square section of the city. In the ensuing month of fighting, thousands of Chinese troops and civilians will be killed.

1942 Britain, Russia, and Iran conclude a treaty of alliance. Ecuador severs diplomatic relations with Germany, Italy, and Japan.

The year 1936 was a pivotal one for Nazi Germany and the Hitler dictatorship. The year's big gamble was the führer's violation of the Versailles Treaty on March 7, when he sent troops to reoccupy the demilitarized German Rhineland. French and British intelligence estimated this force at thirty-five thousand. In fact, it was much smaller and could easily have been repulsed. But the French would not send in troops without the British, and Britain refused to risk war. The German move "deals a heavy blow to the principle of the sanctity of treaties," British foreign secretary Anthony Eden said on March 9. "Fortunately, we have no reason to suppose that Germany's present action threatens hostilities." Austrian chancellor Kurt von Schuschnigg was not reassured. The Nazis had assassinated his predecessor, and the Rhineland gave further warning of Hitler's audacity in pursuit of his goals—one of which was *Anschluss*, the joining of Austria and Germany. In July, Austria signed an agreement with Germany that seemed to guarantee the status quo. In secret provisions, however, Schuschnigg made concessions that would lead the country into catastrophe (see February 13). In October, Germany and Italy signed a secret protocol outlining a cooperative foreign policy; in November, Germany and Japan signed the Anti-Comintern Pact, ostensibly directed against international Communism, but with a secret provision regarding relations with the Soviet Union. The Axis was taking shape.

German troops enter Cologne during Germany's remilitarization of the Rhineland. March 17, 1936.

JANUARY 30

1933 Adolf Hitler is appointed chancellor of Germany. Just over a month later, Franklin Delano Roosevelt is inaugurated as the thirty-second president of the United States.

1941 Germany warns that ships of any nation carrying aid to Britain will be torpedoed.

O n the morning of February 26, 1936, the American ambassador to Japan, Joseph Grew, cabled the U.S. State Department from Tokyo: "The military took partial possession of the government and city early this morning and it is reported to have assassinated several prominent men." The perpetrators of what historian John Toland later called "the most ambitious coup in the history of modern Japan" were part of the "Imperial Way" faction in the Japanese army, which favored resolving Japan's severe Depression-era problems by instituting a more dictatorial government at home. They were opposed by the army's "Control" faction, which believed continued overseas expansion (see January 12) was the key to a brighter future. Over three bloody days, during which Imperial Way soldiers murdered several of the country's most influential proponents of constitutional monarchy, the Control faction emerged victorious. Breaking precedent in a country where assassination had become an accepted tool of reform, the coup's leaders were executed. But both the coup and its defeat had demonstrated the domestic power of the military—and the incident proved a turning point for Japan. By the end of the year, the army, and to a lesser extent the navy, had assured that the military would be the prevailing influence in Japanese politics. It would attempt to demonstrate its absolute loyalty to the emperor by securing a "Greater East Asian Co-Prosperity Sphere" that Japan would dominate and from which it would prosper.

Emperor Hirohito (on white horse) reviewing troops of the Imperial Japanese Army. Illustration from *Yoi kodomo kakezu, Shotōka dai 1-gakunen Zenki*, Tokyo, 1941.

JANUARY 31

1933　In Switzerland, the Geneva Disarmament Conference reconvenes.

1944　The Marshall Islands become the first of Japan's prewar territories to fall to military forces of the United States.

Wars East and West: 1937–39

The unquiet world of 1937 was an amalgam of enterprise, hope, and fear. In the United States—despite continuing economic woes (the stock market began another descent in August)—industrial production was stuttering upward, interrupted occasionally when violence breached the glowering truce between captains of industry and the burgeoning labor movement. Intriguing items were introduced to the public, including automatic transmissions for personal automobiles, grocery shopping carts, and Spam. On May 6, the first coast-to-coast radio broadcast described to listeners the crash of the German dirigible *Hindenburg* at Lakehurst, New Jersey. One week later, the coronation of King George VI of England occasioned the first worldwide radio broadcast.

The coronation was one happy event in a world festering with troubles. In the Soviet Union, Lenin's successor as Communist dictator, Joseph Stalin, embarked on a two-year orgy of purges, executing thousands of real and suspected enemies and imprisoning tens of thousands more. In Spain, vicious civil war continued. On April 26, Francisco Franco's German ally gave the world its first shocking preview of aerial blitzkrieg when planes from the Luftwaffe's Condor Legion, accompanied by a few Italian aircraft, destroyed most of Guernica, a Basque town sheltering seven thousand citizens and three thousand war refugees. British journalist George Steer was on the scene and described, in his 1938 book, *The Tree of Gernika* [sic], how Heinkel 51 fighters strafed terrified

---

FEBRUARY 1

1941   The U.S. Navy creates the Atlantic Fleet, headed by Rear Adm. Ernest J. King. Its primary purpose is to escort convoys. Nazi sympathizer Vidkun Quisling is proclaimed minister president of Norway.

people attempting to flee as bombers dropped fifty-, hundred-, and thousand-pound explosives—and smaller incendiaries: "Tubes of two pounds, long as your forearm . . . So, as the houses were broken to pieces over the people, sheathed fire descended from heaven to burn them up." The merciless raid, which killed 1,654 people and wounded 889, provoked a fierce international outcry.

In July, Japan used a small clash between Chinese and Japanese soldiers as a pretext for embarking on full-scale war. In August, a fellow army officer assassinated Iraqi strongman Bakr Sidqi. Six months earlier, an attempt to assassinate the Italian commander in occupied Ethiopia had sparked a massacre of Ethiopian partisans and civilians.

Surveying the volatile state of the world, President Roosevelt declared, in a speech in Chicago on October 5, that "the peace, the freedom and the security of 90 percent of the population of the world is being jeopardized by the remaining 10 percent" and advocated international action "to uphold laws and principles on which alone peace can rest secure." Reflecting the country's prevailing isolationism, public and political reaction was overwhelmingly negative—two congressmen even threatened to impeach the president. This response, Secretary of State Cordell Hull later wrote,

"undoubtedly emboldened the aggressor countries, and caused the democracies of Europe to wonder if we could ever be with them in more than words."

One month after the president's speech, Hitler met in a secret session with his military high command (as Colonel Friedrich Hossbach took detailed minutes). Germany, the führer said, had to acquire "greater living space than in the case of other peoples." Further, the required *lebensraum* could only be secured "by means of force . . . it was while the rest of the world was still preparing its defenses that we were obliged to take the offensive."

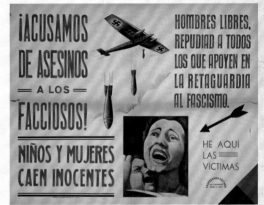

Acusamos de asesinos a los facciosos! Niños y Mujeres Caen Inocentes ("We accuse the fascists of being murderers! Innocent women and children are falling"). Color lithograph poster published by the Confederación Regional del Trabajo de Levante, between 1936 and 1939.

The governments of France, Britain, and the United States saw the Spanish Civil War in very different lights, but all were determined not to become embroiled in the conflict. American neutrality legislation forbade the sale of munitions to any belligerent nation—but this did not prevent U.S. businesses from supplying Franco's Nationalists with other useful goods. At the same time, many Americans joined volunteers from fifty-two countries in supporting the Republicans, seeing in the Spanish conflict, as British journalist Jason Gurney reported, "the great symbol of the struggle between Democracy and Fascism everywhere." In addition to the Americans who formed combat units—including the Abraham Lincoln Battalion, the George Washington Battalion, and the John Brown Battery—125 U.S. citizens served with the American Medical Bureau. African American nurse Salaria Kee's experiences as she cared for the wounded included being bombed and strafed by Nationalist planes, captured by Franco's forces, and wounded so severely she had to be furloughed home. After a long convalescence, she traveled around the country, urging African Americans to support the Republican cause: "Negro men have given up their lives [in Spain] as courageously as any heroes of any age," she said. "Surely Negro people will just as willingly give of their means to relieve the suffering of a people attacked by the enemy of all racial minorities—fascism—and its most aggressive exponents—Italy and Germany."

LEFT: *Aidez L'Espagne* ("Help Spain"). Color poster, pochoir with lithographed text, by Joan Miró (1893–1983), published by Imprimerie Moderne, Paris, 1937.

RIGHT: Cover of the fourteen-page pamphlet *A Negro nurse in Republican Spain*, featuring a photograph of American nurse and activist Salaria Kee. Published in 1938 by the Negro Committee to Aid Spain, headquartered in New York City.

FEBRUARY 2

1942   In China, U.S. Maj. Gen. Joseph ("Vinegar Joe") Stilwell is named chief of staff to Chiang Kai-shek.

A NEGRO NURSE IN REPUBLICAN SPAIN

5¢

Issued by
THE NEGRO COMMITTEE TO AID SPAIN
with the
**MEDICAL BUREAU AND NORTH AMERICAN COMMITTEE
TO AID SPANISH DEMOCRACY**

381 Fourth Avenue   Room 201   New York City

1938?

On July 7, 1937, as fighting raged on in Spain, a company of Japan's North China Army, on nighttime maneuvers near the Lukouchiao (Marco Polo) Bridge, not far from Peking (Beijing), heard gunshots. Believing they were under attack from Chinese soldiers, the Japanese returned fire. The subsequent confusion of skirmishes and negotiations eventually brought the angry Japanese to the gates of the nearby town of Wanping—which the Chinese, yelling insults from the city walls, refused them permission to search. As tensions mounted, the high command in Tokyo debated whether to seize this opportunity to begin military action that would bring them more Chinese territory or reserve their strength for action against the Soviet Union's Far Eastern forces. They opted for immediate gain from what they believed would be a short China war. "Crush the Chinese in three months and they will sue for peace," War Minister (and army general) Hajime Sugiyama asserted, as the Japanese dispatched five more divisions to China. On July 26, the Japanese ordered all Chinese troops out of Peking. They bombed Langfang and occupied Wanping. In Tungchow, Chinese militiamen massacred Japanese and Korean civilians after the Japanese garrison had left for Wanping; then Japanese soldiers returned and slaughtered all the Chinese they could find. And so it began: The Japanese pressed ruthlessly forward; the Chinese started a slow, battle-punctuated retreat into the interior of their vast country.

The Chinese Open Fire. Reproduction of a painting by Japanese combat artist Mikichi Todoriki, its title supporting the Japanese argument that the Chinese provoked war. Published in *Seisen Gafu* ("A Picture Album of the Holy War"), Tokyo, 1939.

FEBRUARY 3

1941 British Forces in Libya destroy the Italian Tenth Army at the battle of Beda Fomm.

1943 Germany begins a three-day mourning period after its eastern army's costly defeat at Stalingrad.

WARS EAST AND WEST: 1937–39

"The four Northeastern provinces have already been lost to us [occupied by the Japanese] for six years," Nationalist Chinese leader Chiang Kai-shek declared on July 19, 1937. "Now the point of conflict—Lukowchiao—has reached the very gates of Peiping. If we allow one more inch of our territory to be lost . . . then we shall be guilty of committing an unpardonable crime against our Chinese race. . . . China's sovereign rights cannot be sacrificed, even at the expense of war, and once war has begun there is no looking back." At about this time, Chiang finally agreed to form a United Front with the Chinese Communists against further Japanese aggression, a step long advocated by Chinese Communist leader Mao Tse-tung—and by Soviet dictator Joseph Stalin. But this would prove to be little more than a nominal alliance. Chiang continued to view the growing Communist movement as the principal threat to his Nationalist regime; and Mao, while as ardent a China partisan as Chiang, also viewed the Nationalists as a greater enemy than the invader. In *The Rising Sun*, historian John Toland reports a briefing Mao gave to his troops in the fall of 1937: "Our policy is to devote 70 percent of our effort to this end [increasing Communist strength], 20 percent to coping with the Government, and 10 percent to fighting the Japanese." By the time of that briefing, a German attempt to broker a peace between Japan and China had failed, and the vicious Sino-Japanese War was spreading.

LEFT: Communist Chinese leader Mao Tse-tung (right) with Chang Kuo-t'ao in the courtyard of supreme Communist headquarters, March 5, 1938.

RIGHT: Chinese Nationalist leader Chiang Kai-shek addressing cadets of the Central Military Academy, Nanking, 1935.

FEBRUARY 4

1938 Hitler assumes the role of commander in chief of the German army and names Anglophobe Joachim von Ribbentrop as Germany's new foreign minister.

In August 1937, Chiang Kai-shek opened a second fighting front, some seven hundred miles to the southeast of the Chinese defeats near Peking, by luring the Japanese into battle at the port city of Shanghai. Ordering his units to fight to the last man, Chiang removed himself to a town northwest of the embattled city. From there, he issued detailed battle orders without proper, up-to-date knowledge of the situation—something he would continue to do throughout the war. In the struggle for Shanghai, the Japanese repeatedly out-flanked Chinese forces, wreaking havoc on soldiers and civilians alike, as Swedish observer Gunnar Andersson reported in his 1939 book *China Fights for the World*: "every means of destruction this powerfully mechanized enemy had at his disposal was let loose in a rain of explosives, fire and steel." On November 8, Chiang at last ordered Chinese troops to with-draw. Refugees and soldiers clogged the roads as the army set one section of the city ablaze to cover the retreat. The fire raced out of control, eventually covering five miles as it con-tinued to burn for many days. In the nearly three months of bitter combat that preceded this fiery conclusion, it is estimated that between one hundred eighty thousand and three hundred thousand Chinese soldiers, seventy thousand Japanese, and an unknown number of civilians were lost. "What is it really worth, this wonderful machine of civilization," Andersson wrote, "if it has no inherent force to prevent a destruction like this?"

The Shanghai Conflagration. Reproduction of a painting by Tenkyo Ohta, published in *Seisen Gafu* ("A Picture Album of the Holy War"), Tokyo, 1939.

FEBRUARY 5

1940 Preparing to send troops through neutral Norway to assist the Finns in their war with Russia, the Allied Supreme War Council (Britain and France) decide to take control of the Swedish iron ore works that lay near their line of march. This would deprive Germany of essential resources. (See March 7)

1943 Mussolini assumes control of the Italian ministry of foreign affairs, ousting his son-in-law, Count Galeazzo Ciano.

On December 8, 1937, Chiang Kai-shek and his Nationalist government withdrew from the Chinese capital of Nanking, leaving behind General Tang Shengzhi in command of a 22,500-member Nanking "Defense Corps." These far-from-battle-ready troops suffered heavy casualties in the fierce hand-to-hand fighting that occurred when the Japanese stormed the city a few days later. Severely battered and widely scattered, the Chinese troops were unable to stage an orderly withdrawal when that order finally arrived from Chiang. Chaos ensued after General Tang made good on his own escape. Leaderless soldiers and panicked civilians surged through a horror of explosions and raging fires to reach the Yangtze River through the one narrow avenue of escape, the Ichang Gate. Thousands died at the gate; thousands more who managed to get through it died as overloaded boats sank or were bombed. The fall of Nanking on the night of December 12–13 marked only the beginning of what an American observer called "a hell on earth," as the Japanese embarked on a weeks-long orgy of killing, looting, and raping that has since become infamous as the Rape of Nanking. Some thousands of Chinese were saved after a group of Westerners living in the city, led by German Nazi John Rabe, established a safety zone to shelter civilians. Many more, however, could not be saved. The Japanese massacred at least ten thousand, and perhaps as many as three hundred thousand Chinese people during this hellish rampage.

Japanese Troops Entering Nanking by the Chungshan Gate. Reproduction of a painting by Eijiro Suzuki, published in *Seisen Gafu* ("A Picture Album of the Holy War"), Tokyo, 1939.

FEBRUARY 6

1941 Erwin Rommel is named commander of two German divisions to help rescue the Italians in North Africa. This force will become legendary as the Afrika Korps.

When Chiang Kai-shek withdrew from Nanking (see February 6), he was accompanied by his wife, the former May-ling Soong. Member of a prominent Chinese family and a graduate of Wellesley College, Madame Chiang had become thoroughly immersed in national politics since her 1927 marriage. In the early 1930s, she served as a member of the Legislative Yuan (one of five *yuan*, or branches of the Nationalist government), and she was secretary-general of the Chinese Aeronautical Affairs Commission when the war with Japan broke out. Tough and adept at Machiavellian stratagems, Madame Chiang employed her charm, beauty, and fluency in both written and spoken English to further Chiang's and China's cause throughout the war—particularly during a successful 1943 tour of the United States. As she withdrew from Nanking with her husband in 1937, millions of American moviegoers were becoming acquainted with the movie version of Pearl S. Buck's Pulitzer Prize–winning 1931 novel *The Good Earth*, which had been released in theaters in August. Buck had spent her early life in China, where her parents, and later Buck herself, had been missionaries. Though it had nothing to do with the Sino-Japanese conflict, *The Good Earth*'s touching portrayal of struggling Chinese peasants helped Americans put a human face on the war raging half a world away and greatly reinforced American sympathy for China.

LEFT: Madame Chiang Kai-shek (May-ling Soong) (1897–2003). Photograph, by Louis Fabian Bachrach (1881–1963), between 1939 and 1941.

RIGHT: Pearl S. Buck. Photograph, by Arnold Genthe (1869–1942), c. 1932.

FEBRUARY 7

1942 President Roosevelt approves a congressional resolution authorizing up to five hundred million dollars in financial aid to China.

E ven as American moviegoers were empathizing with the struggles of Pearl S. Buck's fictional Chinese peasants (see February 7), farmers in the United States continued to suffer. By 1937, the Midwestern drought had eased, and the worst of the dust storms were over. Yet thousands of displaced farmers continued to roam the nation's highways trying to find enough work to keep their families from starving. "They're goin' in every direction," one lucky landed farmer told photographer Dorothea Lange in August 1938, "and they don't know where they're going." The troubles of tenant farmers were exacerbated when those from whom they rented land bought new tractors that allowed the owners to work more acreage themselves. Thousands of these "tractored-out" tenants swelled the ranks of agricultural migrants, many of whom headed for California; some three hundred thousand crossed that state's borders between the middle of 1935 and May 1939. In California, however, small farms were rapidly giving way to "industrial agriculture," and many new arrivals were forced to become migrant workers in these big-business-owned fields. Some migrants picked peas for one cent a pound, others harvested lettuce or pulled carrots. "They'll sleep in the row (to hold a place in the field)," one observer told Lange, "to earn 60 cents a day." Despair was widespread—but it didn't kill optimism or a stubborn determination "to stick together to get by these hard times." (See February 9)

Migratory field-worker's home on the edge of a frozen pea field, Imperial Valley, California. Photograph by Dorothea Lange (1895–1965), March 1937.

FEBRUARY 8

1943 Legendary British major general Orde Wingate's Chindit group of British, Indian, and Ghurka fighters begin their first campaign of irregular warfare behind Japanese lines in Burma.

By 1937, with economic indicators inching upward, American workers—encouraged by such New Deal legislation as the National Recovery Act (1933) and the Wagner National Labor Relations Act (1935)—were becoming more organized and aggressive in seeking to improve their circumstances. This meant, in the words of labor leader John L. Lewis, securing "shorter hours, the prohibition of child labor . . . and a wage that will enable them to maintain themselves and their families in health and modern comfort . . . and to provide against sickness, disability, and death." Many business leaders, long devoted to maintaining low wages, objected to these goals—often employing infiltrators, stool pigeons, and private labor-busting "armies" to thwart them. Yet, despite lingering fears of Communist influence in the labor movement, public sympathy for labor was on the upswing, spurred by sympathetic novels, plays, and movies—and the investigative reports of Robert M. La Follette Jr.'s U.S. Senate committee, which was charged with examining "undue interference with the right of labor to organize and bargain collectively." Then, in 1937, labor made well-organized use of a new weapon, the sit-down strike, to achieve a stunning breakthrough. In February and March, both General Motors, then the largest U.S. automobile manufacturer, and the giant corporation U.S. Steel recognized labor organizations and made additional concessions. Other businesses, however, including Republic Steel, proved extremely reluctant to follow suit.

Tear gas breaks the picket line surrounding the Republic Steel–owned Newton Steel Plant in Monroe, Michigan, allowing nonstriking workers to enter, June 11, 1937.

FEBRUARY 9

1943   All organized Japanese resistance on
        Guadalcanal ends.

In its August 1, 1938, issue, *Time* magazine said of Kansas Republican senatorial hopeful Gerald B. Winrod: "in his weekly radiorations over two Kansas stations and in his monthly magazine, The Defender, [he] has made noises like a fascist: taken slaps at Jews and Catholics, gone hard after all Communists." Winrod was one of several American radicals who reacted to the social turmoil of the 1930s by echoing fascism. Father Charles Coughlin, radio personality and leader of the five-million-strong National Union for Social Justice, praised the "social justice" of Nazi Germany and included verbatim Nazi propaganda in many of his sermons. In 1935, William Dudley Pelley, who had founded the fascist Silver Legion of America in 1933, announced his candidacy for president, saying "the time has come for an American Hitler." In 1936, the pro-Nazi, quasi-military organization, Friends of the New Germany changed its name to the German-American Bund. Ostentatious, if relatively small (in 1939, it included about twenty thousand members), the Bund received guidance and financial support from Germany, provided military training to its members, and included a contingent of "storm troopers," modeled after the Nazi *Sturmabteilung* (see January 14). But a national fascist dictator came to life only in American fiction: Berzelius Windrip got an iron grip on the nation in Sinclair Lewis's 1935 semisatirical cautionary novel *It Can't Happen Here* and the subsequent play by Lewis and John C. Moffitt.

LEFT: Poster advertising the play *It Can't Happen Here*, by John C. Moffitt and Sinclair Lewis. Color silk screen, published by the Michigan Federal Art Project, c. 1936.

RIGHT: The German-American Bund parades along East Eighty-sixth Street in New York City, October 30, 1939.

FEBRUARY 10

1941 Britain breaks off diplomatic relations with Romania because the Romanians are allowing German troops to be based on their soil.

In late October 1938, the Nazis began expelling all Polish-born Jews living in Germany from the country. Some twenty thousand people, among them the father of seventeen-year-old Herschel Grynszpan, were forced to leave their homes, taking only what they could carry with them. From Paris, the young Grynszpan wrote to his parents: "I must protest in such a way that the world will hear me"—and proceeded, on November 7, to shoot and mortally wound the Third Secretary in the German Embassy, Ernst von Rath. Hitler exploited the young man's protest with a vengeance. On November 9, the führer approved a massive attack on the Jews of Greater Germany. During this *Kristallnacht* (Night of Broken Glass), Nazis raged through cities and towns wreaking havoc on Jewish shops, homes, and synagogues. A hundred Jews were murdered; more than twenty thousand were arrested and sent to concentration camps. Other countries reacted to this state-sponsored riot with revulsion. In America, Herbert Hoover, Al Smith, Alf Landon, and Harold Ickes were among the public figures to denounce the violence on radio. The United States recalled its ambassador to Germany; Germany reciprocated. In the meantime, to add insult to vicious injury, the German government demanded that Jews clean up the mess that the Nazi thugs had created—and charged the Jewish people of Greater Germany more than one billion Reichsmarks to cover the cost of insurance claims.

LEFT: Jewish shop owners in Berlin survey some of the damage from *Kristallnacht*, November 10, 1938.

RIGHT: *Simplified Finance*. A cartoon protesting the Nazi policy of forcing Jewish people to pay for the damage done to them and their property by Nazi thugs. Ink brush, crayon, and opaque white drawing over a blue pencil underdrawing by Herbert Block ("Herblock"), 1938.

FEBRUARY 11

1942 The Japanese issue an ultimatum for Singapore's surrender.

On December 19, 1937, American lawyer Samuel Untermeyer declared, in a speech to the Temple and Synagogue Brotherhoods in Baltimore, Maryland: "I cannot understand why Catholics, Protestants, Organized Labor, Rotarians, Masons and Americans generally have been so indolent, callous and shortsighted as to have failed long since to effect a mutual protective organization to safeguard civilization . . . when they have within easy reach the means of self-protection for themselves and their brethren in Germany—by the simple expedient of the boycott of German goods and services." In 1933, Untermeyer established the Non-Sectarian Anti-Nazi League to Champion Human Rights, which asserted in its publications that an economic boycott "would be particularly effective against a great Nation that has reverted to barbarism and would thus be cut off from commercial relations with other nations until it mends its ways. . . . Its success would depend, of course, upon the extent to which it is actively supported by world-sentiment." World sentiment proved insufficient to the task, however—even after the anti-Semitic *Kristallnacht* riots threw an international light on the dark character of the Nazi regime (see February 11). Yet Untermeyer and the league persisted, urging Americans not to let Nazism "draw strength and courage from our indifference," but to "strike back, and *now* . . . with the weapons available to the people of a democracy: legislation, propaganda, education and the boycott."

A "Boycott Nazi Germany" program draws a crowd to New York City's Madison Square Garden on March 15, 1937.

FEBRUARY 12

1941 In the first Luftwaffe action in Africa, German planes attack Benghazi, Libya.

Although Germany was barred by World War I treaties from uniting with Austria, Austrian-born Hitler worked steadily to achieve that forbidden *Anschluss*—assisted by Austrian Nazis whose terror tactics included the assassination of Austrian chancellor Engelbert Dollfuss in 1934. On February 12, 1938, Hitler summoned Dollfuss's replacement, Kurt von Schuschnigg, to his headquarters at Berchtesgaden and, at the end of a thunderous diatribe, presented the Austrian leader with a multipart ultimatum. His demands included the appointment of certain pro-Nazis—prominent among them, Dr. Artur Seyss-Inquart— to important government posts. Under threat of German invasion, Schuschnigg agreed. In a speech broadcast on February 24, however, he defied continuing Nazi pressure for *Anschluss*: "Thus far and no further . . . Red-White-Red [the Austrian national colors] until we are dead!" In response, Austrian Nazis rioted in the streets—unrestrained by police, who were by then under Interior Minister Seyss-Inquart's authority. Schuschnigg's announcement on March 9 that a plebiscite would be held to determine if a majority of Austrians favored union with Germany set off the final round of Nazi bullying and pressure tactics that resulted in the Austrian chancellor's resignation on March 11. New chancellor Seyss-Inquart asked the Germans to send troops to "help prevent bloodshed"—and by March 13, Hitler was able to declare that Austria had become the German province of "Ostmark."

LEFT: Austrian chancellor Dr. Kurt Schuschnigg in Paris. Photograph by Lucien Aigner (1901–1999), 1935.

RIGHT: The motorcade of German interior minister Dr. Wilhelm Frick arrives in Eisenstadt, Austria, three weeks after the *Anschluss* transformed the country of Austria into the German province of "Ostmark," 1938.

FEBRUARY 13

1945 British and U.S. planes begin two days of raids over Dresden, causing massive damage and an estimated thirty-five thousand deaths.

WARS EAST AND WEST: 1937–39

With achievement of the *Anschluss* (see February 13), Austria's resources became Germany's, and the Germans incorporated the Austrian military into the Wehr-macht (minus two-thirds of the officers, who were interned). Moreover, German territory now surrounded Czechoslovakia on three sides, increasing the threat to Czech sovereignty Hitler had expressed in a speech to the Reichstag on February 20, 1937, regarding the three million ethnic Germans living in Czechoslovakia's Sudetenland area: "To the interest of the German Reich belong the protection of those German peoples who are not in a position to secure along our frontiers their political and spiritual freedom by their own efforts." Before moving against Czechoslovakia, however, the Germans had to solidify their control of "Ostmark"—and, with the assistance of Artur Seyss-Inquart's puppet government, they quickly embarked on a campaign of repression and terror. Tens of thousands of Austrians, including Catholics, Social Democrats, Socialists, and Communists, were arrested and sent to concentration camps. Perhaps the greatest suffering, however, was endured by some thirty thousand Jews, who were subjected to what Austria-based American correspondent William S. Shirer termed "an orgy of sadism. . . large numbers of Jewish men and women could be seen scrubbing gutters . . . with jeering storm troopers standing over them, [as] crowds gathered to taunt them . . . . Tens of thousands more were jailed."

Gestapo officials record data on incoming prisoners at an unnamed German concentration camp as other prisoners wait, under guard. Photograph by the [American Jewish] Joint Distribution Committee, between 1939 and 1945.

FEBRUARY 14

1941   The new Japanese ambassador to the United States, Admiral Kichisaburo Nomura, presents his credentials to President Roosevelt.

Just over a month after Germany enveloped Austria (see February 13), Konrad Henlein, leader of the Sudeten German Party (SDP)—which secretly received substantial subsidies from the German government—announced eight demands on the Czechoslovakian government, including complete autonomy for Sudetenland. Czech president Eduard Benes rejected Henlein's *Karlsbad Program*—but this was only the beginning of German-SDP pressure. On September 12, after Hitler declared in a broadcast speech that the "oppression of the Sudeten Germans must end," some six thousand of Henlein's followers rioted throughout the Sudenteland, wrecking homes and killing twenty-three people. The Czech government declared martial law as the crisis continued. Nervous European powers sought to ease the situation without getting too deeply involved. "However much we may sympathize with a small nation confronted by a big and powerful neighbor," British prime minister Neville Chamberlain told the House of Commons on September 27, before leaving for a meeting with Hitler, "we cannot . . . undertake to involve the whole British Empire in war simply on her account." Two days later in Munich, Hitler, Chamberlain, French prime minister Edouard Daladier, and Italian dictator Benito Mussolini held a twelve-hour meeting (while Czech officials waited in another room) and agreed that the Sudetenland must be transferred to Germany. With no other nation willing to help them, the Czech government was forced to agree.

British prime minister Neville Chamberlain (center, with umbrella) and German foreign minister Joachim von Ribbentrop (center, holding hat and gloves) with Nazi officials at Munich airfield, September 1938.

FEBRUARY 15

1933 After giving a speech in Miami, President-elect Franklin D. Roosevelt is in his car chatting with Chicago mayor Anton J. Cermak when a deranged unemployed bricklayer fires at Roosevelt—but Cermak falls, mortally wounded.

1942 Singapore and its surviving garrison of sixty-four thousand British, Indian, and Australian defenders (nine thousand men had died in the fighting) fall to the Japanese.

"We are going blindfolded towards an abyss," France's finance minister, Paul Reynaud, said in a speech broadcast on November 12, 1938. The elation spurred by the Munich agreement of late September (see February 15) was rapidly being tempered by fears that, despite continuing (if confused) diplomatic efforts, the country was headed for another war with Germany—one for which it was ill prepared. Although the French military was strong on paper, its armory included much obsolescent equipment, and its top commanders were marked by complacency and strategic thinking that would prove to be monumentally outmoded. Moreover, the entire country had been through almost five years of political and social turmoil presided over by eight different governments. With Reynaud in the finance ministry, the current government of Prime Minister Edouard Daladier was increasing defense spending; but French industry was not organized to build new armament quickly. Much hope was placed on the Maginot Line, a three-and-a-half- to six-mile-deep complex of pillboxes, fortified houses, sunken fortresses, and blockhouses interconnected by sixty-two miles of tunnels and two hundred eighty miles of railroad and bristling with artillery and minefields. The line, however, did not extend all the way across France; and it could not prevent waves of bombers from obliterating French targets from the air—as the Luftwaffe had destroyed the Spanish town of Guernica (see February 1).

LEFT: Cross-sectional drawing of fortifications along France's defensive Maginot Line, April 14, 1938.

RIGHT: *Vulnérabilité de la France* ("The vulnerability of France"). Civil defense poster with a map showing French vulnerability to air attack. Color lithograph, 1939.

FEBRUARY 16

1940
Crew of the British destroyer *Cossack* board a German supply ship in Norwegian waters and liberate 299 British seamen whose vessel had been sunk by the German warship *Graf Spee*. The raid will contribute to Hitler's decision to invade and secure Norway.

1944
U.S. warships attack the Japanese base at Truk in the Carolines, effectively eliminating the island's threat to U.S. advances.

After Lenin died in 1924, Joseph Stalin became dictator of the Soviet Union, maintaining iron-fisted control over the political bodies that ostensibly governed the country. Capable of great charm (especially when he was seeking to impress foreign visitors), Stalin was contemptuous of the Soviet peasantry, distrustful of military officers and party functionaries who had served under Lenin, and implacably ruthless in his determination to rapidly transform his backward nation into a modern industrial state. In the early 1930s, his war on the kulaks (well-to-do peasants) forced "collectivization" of Soviet farmland and resulted in millions of deaths. People who resisted were starved and brutalized, many dying as they were deported to the inhospitable north on "death trains." Millions more starved when the government confiscated food for the industrial workers who were laboring under near-slavery conditions. All this paled in comparison to the Great Terror of 1936–38, when Stalin loosed the NKVD (secret police) against anyone even vaguely suspected of disloyalty. "Everyone was a traitor," one NKVD officer wrote, "until he proved the contrary by exposing someone else as a traitor." Tens of thousands were tortured and executed; millions were deported to a living death in Siberian labor camps. Army chief of staff Mikhail Tukhachevsky and thousands of the nation's most experienced military officers were among the victims, something that weakened Soviet forces on the eve of their epic confrontation with the German Wehrmacht.

LEFT: Mar. Mikhail Tukhachevsky (1893–1937). Until a few days before his arrest, torture, show "trial," and speedy execution, he was a hero of the Russian Revolution and the chief of staff of the Red Army, c. 1929.

RIGHT: *Träumerei an einem Moskauer kamin* ("Reverie at a Moscow Fireplace"). Ink and watercolor drawing, 1936, by German artist Josef Plank ("Seppla"), caricaturing Communist leader Joseph Stalin's harsh policies toward his enemies.

FEBRUARY 17

1943 The Allies activate the Mediterranean Air Command.

"Väterchen" in seinem Jagdzimmer

TRÄUMEREI an einem MOSKAUER KAMIN

During the last half of September 1938, the distinctive voice of CBS newscaster H. V. Kaltenborn often cut into regular U.S. radio programs with bulletins on developments in the Czechoslovakian crisis (see February 15). After Hitler was appeased, the radio schedule returned to normal—until the night of October 30, when people who tuned into the CBS *Mercury Theater* were startled by another series of bulletins. With eerie sounds and explosions in the background, increasingly hysterical "newscasters" described the Martian monsters that had just landed in New Jersey and were eradicating every force sent to stop them. Nearly two million people across the country, who had missed the opening announcement that Orson Welles and his *Mercury Theater* troupe were staging a radio version of H. G. Wells's *War of the Worlds* in honor of Halloween, took to the streets in panic, heading for churches, government offices, or just out of town. As the furor died down, Hitler cited reports of the panic as proof that his low estimate of American intelligence was justified. Meanwhile, in Britain, a possibly bemused H. G. Wells was still writing. In his 1914 book, *The World Set Free*, he had predicted the "catastrophe of the atomic bombs." On December 13, 1938, German scientists would take a giant step toward creating those terrible weapons when they achieved nuclear fission at the Kaiser Wilhelm Institute for Chemistry.

LEFT: American actor Orson Welles rehearsing a radio broadcast of *The Campbell Playhouse*, 1938.

RIGHT: *Mr. [H.G.] Wells Evolving a Cosmic Thought*. Pastel drawing by William Henry Cotton (1880–1958), c. 1935.

FEBRUARY 18

1944 London begins to endure a new wave of bombing. Severe enough to recall the most terrible days of the Battle of Britian, this assault is dubbed the Little Blitz.

W COTTON   Mr. Wells evolving a Cosmic Thought.

The vast majority of Americans were united in their desire to avoid involvement in any future European war. On many other issues, however, the nation remained divided. Early in 1939, one bitter divide was the focus of public attention after the celebrated African American contralto Marian Anderson was refused permission to give a concert at Washington, D.C.'s Constitution Hall. At first, the hall's owners, the Daughters of the American Revolution (DAR), cited scheduling difficulties. When it soon became clear that the color of Anderson's skin was the DAR's principal objection, one prominent DAR member submitted her resignation. "I belong to an organization . . . [that has] taken an action which has been widely talked of in the press," First Lady Eleanor Roosevelt wrote in her "My Day" newspaper column of February 27, 1939. "To remain as a member implies approval of that action, and therefore I am resigning." Roosevelt attended a concert at a substitute venue. On Easter Sunday, April 9, Anderson sang at the Lincoln Memorial before a live audience of seventy-five thousand that included many prominent members of the Roosevelt administration—and a radio audience of many thousands more. "My country 'tis of thee," she sang in one of the most moving portions of her program, "Sweet land of liberty, To thee we sing/ Land where my fathers died / Land of the Pilgrims' pride, From every mountainside, Let freedom ring."

ABOVE: Marian Anderson (1897–1993), 1939.

RIGHT: Accompanied on the piano by Kosti Vehanan, Marian Anderson sings at the Lincoln Memorial on April 9, 1939.

FEBRUARY 19

1942 Carrier-based Japanese aircraft attack the Australian city of Darwin, killing 240 people, injuring 150, and sinking more than a dozen ships—including a U.S. destroyer.

On March 13, 1939, less than six months after assuring the world that he had no more territorial ambitions, Hitler summoned Czechoslovakia's president, Dr. Emil Hácha, to Berlin and informed him that Prague would be reduced to "a heap of ruins" by aerial attack if the Czech government did not accede to the führer's demands—most particularly that the Czech heartland, Bohemia and Moravia, become a "Reich Protectorate." After two days of unremitting pressure, Hácha and his foreign minister, František Chvalovsky, were forced to sign a declaration that they had willingly "placed the fate of the Czech people and country in the hands of the Fuehrer of the German Reich." German troops were already moving into the Czech town of Moravská Ostrava; by March 16, all of Czechoslovakia was in German hands. Since guarantees of Czech territorial integrity made at the Munich conference the previous September (see February 15) had not actually been signed, neither France nor Britain attempted to stop this latest German conquest. Yet by now it was clear that Hitler's word could not be trusted, and the führer might have to be restrained by measures beyond negotiation. On March 31, Prime Minister Chamberlain told the House of Commons that, should Hitler threaten Poland, "His Majesty's Government would feel themselves bound at once to lend the Polish Government all support in their power . . . I may add that the French Government . . . stand in the same position in this matter."

Dr. Emil Hácha, president of Czechoslovakia, meets with Hitler, Hermann Göring, and other Nazi officials in Berlin—unaware that the German occupation of the rest of his country is already in progress, March 14, 1939.

FEBRUARY 20

1938 British foreign secretary Anthony Eden resigns in protest over Prime Minister Neville Chamberlain's appeasement policies.

1942 U.S. Navy pilot Lt. Edward "Butch" O'Hare shoots down five Japanese bombers in five minutes to become the first navy ace of World War II (O'Hare Airport, Chicago, will be named after him).

Hitler absorbed Czechoslovakia without giving prior notice to the man who was ostensibly his closest ally. Mussolini learned of the event on March 15, as it was taking place. The Italian people did not favor the German move, and Il Duce was far from amused. "Every time Hitler occupies a country he sends me a message," he pouted, after a German emissary officially informed him. Effusive communications from Hitler improved Il Duce's disposition—as did Fascist victories in Spain. But Hitler's move had fed Mussolini's own ambitions and those of his son-in-law and foreign minister, Count Galeazzo Ciano. They turned their attention to neighboring Albania, where Italy had long had political and economic influence. Within two weeks, they moved to emulate Germany by making Albania an Italian protectorate in the "new Roman empire." When conquest by legal agreement failed because of Albanian King Zog's resistance to the proffered Italian terms, Mussolini sent in his troops. Despite difficulties that foreshadowed the deep problems the Italian military would experience when total war came to the Mediterranean, by April 13 Italian king Victor Emmanuel III was able to declare the "personal union" of Italy and Albania under his crown. The Italians established an Albanian Fascist government under Shefqet Verlaci—while the worried British and French governments extended assurances of assistance to Greece and Romania in case Italy or Germany moved against them.

LEFT: *This'll Teach You a Lesson!* Mussolini tries to impress France and Britain with Fascist Italy's new conquest, Albania. Drawing by Clifford Berryman (1869–1949), April 9, 1939.

RIGHT: Ahmed Zogu, Zog I, king of the Albanians (1895–1961), between 1928 and 1939.

FEBRUARY 21

1945 U.S. P-47 "Thunderbolt" fighter-bombers attack Hitler's Berchtesgaden retreat.

In May 1939, as the Great Terror was coming to an end in the Soviet Union (see February 17), trouble erupted on the border between Outer Mongolia (where Red Army forces were stationed by dint of a mutual assistance treaty) and Japanese-occupied Manchukuo (Manchuria). A probe by Mongolian cavalry into disputed territory flared into a months' long battle that drew little notice in the West, where most were preoccupied with the ominous events in Europe. Yet the "Nomonhan Incident" was full-scale warfare, involving thirty thousand Japanese troops under Lieutenant General Michitaro Komatsubara, fifty-seven thousand Soviets and Mongolians under rising Red Army star Georgi Zhukov, and hundreds of planes and tanks. By the time it concluded in September, the encounter—characterized by vicious, often hand-to-hand fighting—had killed or wounded nearly twenty-seven thousand men. For the Japanese, it was a costly and humiliating defeat that pointed out major faults in their logistics, equipment, tactics, armor, and antitank doctrines. Growing Soviet strength in the Far East, coupled with the wholly unexpected conclusion of a German-Soviet Non-aggression Pact (see February 23) contributed to the Japanese high command's decision two years later to pursue an Eastern empire in the resource-rich south instead of moving north against the Soviets.

All Quiet at the Mongolian Frontier. Reproduction of a painting by Hakutei Ishii published in *Seisen Gafu* ("A Picture Album of the Holy War"), Tokyo, 1939.

FEBRUARY 22

1942   President Roosevelt orders Gen. Douglas MacArthur to leave the Philippines, naming him commander of Allied forces in Australia.

In August 1939, having secured Czechoslovakia (with all of its military and industrial assets), Hitler prepared to move against Poland. First, however, he sought to discourage intervention by Britain and France—and to protect Germany's rear against the threat of Russian military action—by means of a diplomatic maneuver that contradicted years of virulently anti-Communist Nazi propaganda. He directed his foreign minister, Joachim von Ribbentrop, to seek an alliance with the Soviet Union. Stalin, meanwhile, had been engaged in halfhearted negotiations regarding an alliance with the British; but the Communist dictator did not relish the prospect of getting swept into a war against Germany at the side of capitalist Britain and France. What Hitler offered was far more attractive. Thus, on August 23, 1939, the two heretofore bitterly antagonistic nations stunned the world—especially Germany's Japanese allies—by signing a ten-year mutual nonaggression pact. On the surface, a general expression of nonaggressive intent, it included a secret protocol that defined the "spheres of influence" each signatory would control "in the event of territorial and political rearrangement" in the Baltic States (which Stalin coveted), Poland (which both states coveted), and southeastern Europe. Under a credit and trade accord signed by the two governments on August 19, the USSR also agreed to supply Germany with food and raw materials—an obligation the Soviets kept to the very eve of the 1941 German invasion of their country.

LEFT: *Wonder How Long the Honeymoon Will Last?* Drawing by Clifford Berryman (1869–1949), October 9, 1939.

RIGHT: *Under Two Flags.* Drawing by Edwin Marcus (1885–1961), December 3, 1939.

FEBRUARY 23

1942 Japanese submarine I-17 fires at the Elwood oil refinery near Santa Barbara, California.

WONDER HOW LONG THE HONEYMOON WILL LAST?

AGGRESSION

Although the world was rapidly falling apart, delegations from many minor and all major powers—except Nazi Germany—came together in New York City in 1939 to celebrate their national arts and achievements. Writing for *Harper's* magazine, Sidney M. Shalett described the New York World's Fair as "the acme of all crazy vulgarity . . . the pinnacle of all inspiration." Fairgoers were wowed by the General Motors Futurama, which presented a (largely inaccurate) vision of what the United States would be like in 1960. The Soviet Union won the grand prize with a model of Moscow's elaborate Mayakovskaya subway station, part of an underground system that was built at the cost of many lives—and that would shortly save lives when it was used as an air raid shelter. The British celebrated democracy by displaying the Lincoln Cathedral copy of the Magna Carta. They also displayed their king and queen, George VI and Elizabeth, who arrived for a visit in mid-June. After inspecting the fair, the royal couple proceeded to the Roosevelt home at Hyde Park (where the king enjoyed his first "delightful hot-dog sandwich"). In Washington, they were greeted by six hundred thousand people as the Roosevelt administration emphasized U.S. friendship for the island nation that would shortly be America's principal ally in a total war.

The World's Fair, New York City.
Photograph by Rollin R. Klein,
September 15, 1939.

FEBRUARY 24

1945 Egyptian Prime Minister Ahmed Maher Pasha is assassinated just after reading a declaration of war on Germany and Japan.

With "minor exceptions German national unification has been achieved," Hitler told his senior military commanders on May 23, 1939, referring to the conquests of Austria and Czechoslovakia. "Poland . . . will try and deprive us of our victory. There is therefore no question of sparing Poland . . . There will be war." The high command's meticulous plans for a full-scale invasion were set in motion by a small-scale fraud. On the evening of August 31, 1939, eight Germans dressed as Polish soldiers staged a fake raid on a German radio station. This served as the excuse to unleash a well-prepared force of 1.5 million against Polish forces that were not fully mobilized: Both Britain and France had counseled the Polish government to avoid provoking Hitler by appearing to prepare for war. Eventually, the Poles were able to field one million men, but their army was quickly swept aside by the Wehrmacht's blitzkrieg (lightning war) tactics involving deep thrusts by armored columns and close coordination between ground and air forces. Within a week Krákow had fallen; by September 27, Warsaw was in German hands. (On September 17, meanwhile, the Soviets invaded Poland from the east, occupying territory specified under the August German-Soviet agreement.) As Poland began a long nightmare of savage occupation, Hitler visited the bomb-battered Polish capital and crowed to foreign journalists: "Take a good look around Warsaw. This is how I can deal with any European city."

Two illustrations by pacifist and artist Frans Masereel, provide some idea of the effect the German blitzkrieg of September 1939 had on the Polish people. Published in *Destins 1939–1940–1941–1942*, Zurich and New York, 1943.

FEBRUARY 25

1942 Mass evacuations of West Coast Japanese Americans begin when the U.S. Navy notifies Japanese American residents of Terminal Island near Los Angeles Harbor that they must leave their homes in 48 hours.

From the first day, exceptional viciousness marked the German advance into Poland. Three SS "Death's Head" regiments followed close behind the first-line troops with orders to "incarcerate or annihilate" every person who might pose a threat to Nazi rule. Part of the elite combat arm of Heinrich Himmler's dreaded *Schutzstaffel (SS)*, these regiments brutalized and murdered civilians, priests, municipal officials, teachers, and other intellectuals. From the beginning, too, Jews were singled out for special torment in this country that would house the largest number of concentration and death camps in Nazi-occupied lands. Yet almost as soon as the Polish government capitulated, Poles began forming resistance groups, including the ZZW (Jewish Fighting Union), the AK (Armie Krajowie), and the Communist NSZ (Narodowe Sily Zbrojne). Many people who fled the country found ways to aid these underground efforts, and the refugees were aided by British and American relief. Arthur Szyk, a Polish artist who arrived in the United States in 1940, became, in his own words, "Franklin D. Roosevelt's soldier in art"—donating his drawings to relief organizations, creating illustrations for U.S. Treasury Department bond drives, celebrating democracy in a series of stunning drawings, and skewering Axis figures with ink and paint in political cartoons and on magazine covers. He fought the Axis, Eleanor Roosevelt said, "as truly as any of us who cannot actually be on the fighting fronts."

Poland Fights Nazi Dragon, Polish War Relief. Offset lithograph by Arthur Szyk (1894–1951), in which Poland is depicted as St. George, 1943.

FEBRUARY 26

1940 The War Department creates the Air Defense Command to integrate U.S. air defenses against air attack.

O n September 3, 1939, Britain and France, both allied by treaty with Poland, declared war on Germany. That same day, German submarine U-30 torpedoed the British passenger liner *Athenia*, killing 112 passengers, including twenty-eight Americans. These were the first casualties in the years-long Battle of the Atlantic, a contest for control of the ocean lanes that were the supply lifeline of the British Isles. The *Athenia*'s sinking, although the result of an identification error (U-30 commander Fritz Julius Lemp believed the ship was an armed merchant cruiser), raised the specter of the unrestricted submarine warfare the Germans had employed during World War I (and that would soon be the case in World War II). A ship commissioned during the 1914–18 war, the carrier HMS *Courageous*, was prominent among the warships dispatched to combat this new U-boat threat. On September 17, *Courageous* was on antisubmarine patrol southwest of Ireland, where U-boats had just sunk the British merchantman *Kafristan*, when U-29, captained by Otto Schuhart, began to stalk the carrier. As *Courageous* turned into the wind to launch its aircraft, Schuhart launched his torpedoes at the imposing target—to devastating effect. Wracked by explosions, *Courageous* sank in fifteen minutes; nearly half its twelve-hundred-man crew died, including commanding officer W. T. Makeig-Jones.

ABOVE: King George VI of Great Britain, wearing the uniform of a Royal Navy admiral. Photograph, 1951.

RIGHT: The sinking of HMS *Courageous*, 1939. Reproduction of a painting by Adolf Bock (1890–1968), published in *Kamp unter der Kriegsflagge*, Berlin, 1944–45.

FEBRUARY 27

1939   The governments of France and Britain officially recognize the Spanish government of Francisco Franco.

1942   The three-day Battle of the Java Sea—fought between the Japanese and a combined force of U.S., British, and Dutch men-of-war—begins; it will end March 1 in a stunning defeat for the Allied force.

T he Red Army having easily secured the eastern third of Poland, including oil-rich Galicia, Stalin now turned his attention to Finland, which included within its borders territory he thought vital as a Soviet defensive shield. On November 28, the Soviets denounced their seven-year-old nonaggression treaty with the Finns; two days later, Soviet forces attacked Finland by land, sea, and air. More than sixty people were killed in the first air attack, the bombing of Finland's capital, Helsinki—infuriating the Finns and adding steel to the strong resistance that quickly arrested the Red Army's progress. Instead of achieving victory in a matter of weeks, the Soviets were stymied by a much smaller force that made deft use of everything from the fortified Mannerheim Line to the handy portable "Molotov Cocktail." As this "Winter War" lengthened, volunteers streamed into Finnish embassies abroad; Britain and France promised to send the Finns weapons; and former president Herbert Hoover organized a U.S. drive for Finnish relief, while Congress granted Finland ten million dollars in credits. On December 12, the League of Nations expelled the Soviet Union. Later that month, at Suomussalmi, the Finns stunned the world—and enraged Stalin—by utterly destroying two Soviet divisions. Hitler, meanwhile, viewed Soviet difficulties in Finland as proof that German armies would have little trouble defeating the USSR when he turned the Wehrmacht east.

One of the first pictures to reach the United States of the battleground at Suomussalmi, site of a resounding Finnish victory over Soviet forces in late December 1939, January 1940.

FEBRUARY 28

1942   The Japanese Sixteenth Army lands on the north coast of Java.

Blitzkrieg! 1940

The swirling currents of Fascist and Japanese aggression, Soviet military and political maneuvers, factional and anticolonial clashes, and the worried calculations of smaller, less powerful nations swept the planet's 2.3 billion people toward the abyss of world conflict in 1940. In February, President Roosevelt dispatched Undersecretary of State Sumner Welles on a "fact-finding" mission to Rome, Berlin, Paris, and London. The principal fact that the president wished to find (although he did not state it publicly) was whether it might be possible for the United States to mediate a peace settlement, which would be far preferable to a peace imposed on Hitler's terms. Welles came away from interviews with Mussolini and Hitler believing, as he later reported, "that it was only too tragically plain that all decisions had already been made. The best that could be hoped for was delay, for what little that might be worth."

Hitler erased even that small hope. A month after the Soviet Union's Winter War with Finland concluded in March, the führer abruptly ended the quiet period of "Phony War" that had prevailed in the rest of Europe since November by initiating blitzkrieg attacks—first into Scandinavia, then against the Low Countries and France. As the Wehrmacht sliced through Allied forces, a weary Neville Chamberlain was succeeded as Britain's prime minister by the eloquent, challenging Winston Churchill: "I have nothing to offer but blood, toil, tears, and sweat," he told the British people on

MARCH 1

1944 German slave labor chief Fritz Sauckel reports that there are five million foreign workers in Germany; only two hundred thousand of them are there voluntarily.

May 13. The Allied gloom deepened when Mussolini, impressed with the Wehrmacht's victories and determined to secure some of the spoils of war, brought his country into the conflict on June 10—an action that would plunge Italy into difficulties far beyond Il Duce's reckoning.

As these events unfolded, Roosevelt reminded Americans: "In modern times it is a shorter distance from Europe to San Francisco, California, than it was for the ships and legions of Julius Caesar to move from Rome to Spain. . . . I am a pacifist," he continued, "but I believe that by overwhelming majorities . . . you and I, in the long run if it be necessary, will act together to protect and defend by every means at our command our science, our culture, our American freedom and our civilization."

The Far East also seemed uncomfortably close as the Japanese Imperial Army, still deeply entangled in the war with China, moved into French Indochina. Seeking to restrain Japanese expansion, the U.S. government embargoed shipments of aviation fuel and premium scrap metals in July, and increased financial aid to the Nationalist Chinese in December. By that time, Italy, Japan, and Germany had signed the Tripartite Pact, a ten-year military and economic agreement. Adjusting military contingency

plans to reflect the growing possibility it might have to fight a two-front war, the U.S. government initiated conscription. Yet Roosevelt still strove to support Britain and other anti-Fascist states by all possible methods—short of war.

Hitler, on the other hand, was determined to broaden the conflict. On December 18, he signed a draft of "Barbarossa," the plan for invading the Soviet Union. The following day, he politely received the credentials of V. G. Dekanozov, the new Soviet ambassador to Germany.

Nazi Dove of Peace. Drawing by Lute Pease (1869–1963), October 1939.

In a rambling speech before the Reichstag on January 30, 1939, Hitler pointed to "international Jewish financiers" as the instigators of the war the führer himself would soon begin. If these "financiers" should succeed "in plunging the nations once more into a world war," he ranted, "then the result will not be the bolshevization of the earth, and thus the victory of Jewry, but the annihilation of the Jewish race in Europe." The Nazis' anti-Semitic laws and atrocities such as *Kristallnacht* had by then prompted many Jews to seek refuge outside of Greater Germany. But it was becoming increasingly difficult to secure permission to emigrate—and few countries were eager to accept Jewish refugees. Four months after Hitler's speech, the United States, Colombia, Paraguay, Argentina, and Chile all refused to admit the 927 German-Jewish refugees aboard the SS *St. Louis*, forcing the ship to return to Europe—where 254 of the passengers eventually perished. Japanese diplomats, on the other hand, had for some time been issuing transit visas to Jews for travel through Japan and China—often stretching the law to accommodate a refugee's desperate request. Despite Japanese Foreign Minister Arita Hachirō's declaration before Japan's House of Peers that Jewish people "never will be denied entry simply because of their race," very few Jews settled in the Japanese home islands during the war. Yet some twenty-one thousand did find refuge in Japanese-occupied Shanghai.

LEFT: A Soldier Standing in Front of a Barbed-Wire Fence. Drawing, c. 1939–40, by Ralph Harpuder (b. 1934), a German Jewish refugee child living in Shanghai.

RIGHT: *Der Jude* ("The Jew"). Color poster by Hans Schweitzer ("Mjölnir"), c. 1940.

MARCH 2

1943 The Battle of the Bismarck Sea begins; Allied forces thwart a Japanese attempt to reinforce positions in New Guinea.

Chaos and incompetence characterized the Red Army's initial assault on Finland in November–December 1939 (see February 28). Supplies were inadequate and much equipment was shoddy; the men were insufficiently trained and not clothed properly for winter warfare; and many units were poorly led. Stalin's Great Terror (1936–38, see February 17) had deprived the army of thousands of experienced officers and replaced many with politically correct but inexperienced men afraid to display initiative or take reasonable risks. Units were surrounded and destroyed piecemeal. Waves of soldiers armed only with rifles were hurled into the teeth of Finnish artillery. "We are going to certain death," one soldier moaned in December. "They are swatting us like flies." A revelation to the world, the Soviets' poor performance boosted Hitler's confidence that the USSR would be easily conquered—a belief he retained despite the Red Army's eventual victory over the Finns. What the Soviets lacked in quality, they made up in quantity, pouring in reinforcements. On February 10, 1940, they broke through the Mannerheim Line and began inexorably rolling the Finnish defenders back. On March 7, Finland's prime minister, Risto Ryti, flew to Moscow; five days later, he signed the treaty that ended the war. Finland remained independent but surrendered swaths of territory that increased the USSR's defensive perimeter. Stalin then turned his attention to improving his armed forces; but progress was exceedingly slow.

The frozen body of a Russian soldier lies unattended on the battlefield where the Red Army suffered the worst defeat of the Winter War. Suomussalmi, Finland, January 1940.

MARCH 3

1942 Two Japanese "Emily" flying boats attempt a night bombing attack on Pearl Harbor; cloudy conditions are among the factors that make them miss their targets by miles.

In 1940, Tokyo's Hokuseido Press published an English translation of Masaru Taniguchi's account of his experiences in Japan's "holy war" in China, *The Soldier's Log, 10,000 Miles of Battle*. "Mountain . . . pillboxes . . . kept up a constant fire on us there on the level plain," Taniguchi reported in one chapter. "Then four of our naval planes flew over and bombed them. . . . One after another, like a hawk diving after a snake, they dove, and at every dive, reinforced concrete pillboxes, trees, rocks, heavy machine guns, and the enemy were blown up and out and in every direction. . . . The spectacle of the great execution of our airplanes made us wild with joy." At the time the book was published, there was little joy in the Japanese high command, however. The trouncing the Soviets' Far Eastern Army had dealt their forces at Nomonhan (see February 22) had highlighted severe deficiencies in equipment and doctrine. Moreover, conquered Manchuria was proving to be less of an asset than they had hoped (see January 12), their German allies had signed a pact with the Soviets—and they had been mired in their "short war" with China for more than two years. In November 1939, Chiang Kai-shek committed half his Nationalist Chinese armies to a Winter Offensive, and by the end of January Japanese forces had faced more than two thousand attacks. Yet the Nationalists proved unable to maintain their momentum, and by spring, Chiang's Winter Offensive had failed.

Back from Their Bombing Adventure. Reproduction of a painting by Goro Tsuruta, published in *Seisen Gafu* ("A Picture Album of the Holy War"), Tokyo, 1939.

MARCH 4

1944 U.S. Eighth Air Force planes attack Berlin for the first time.

1944 Maj. Gen. Joseph ("Vinegar Joe") Stilwell leads the First Chinese Army and Merrill's Marauders into the Battle of Walawbum in northern Burma.

"The defeat of England is essential to final victory," Hitler wrote in his Directive Number 9, issued November 29, 1939. Beginning "Instructions for warfare against the economy of the enemy," this detailed, eight-section document presented a scheme to wound Britain's economy so severely that the English would be unable to remain in the war. Tasks assigned to the navy and air force under the directive's section 4 included "Attacks on the principal English ports by mining and blocking the sea lanes leading to them, and by the destruction of important port installations"; and "Attacks on English merchant shipping and on enemy warships protecting it." The Germans remembered how close a similar naval campaign had come to knocking Britain out of World War I. The British remembered, too: As soon as they entered the war, they instituted a convoy system to protect their shipping similar to the one they had successfully employed in 1917. Allied warships (and later aircraft) escorted merchantmen filled with essential supplies as they ran a gauntlet of Axis "wolf packs" (groups of as many as twenty submarines) and endured hit-and-run aerial attacks and the occasional pounce by "auxiliary cruisers" (Axis warships disguised as merchantmen). Convoy duty was lonely, tough, and unremittingly nerve-racking. At any time, ships could be overtaken by raging weather or storms of gunfire and torpedo blasts— often culminating, for those sailing the North Atlantic, with a deadly plunge into icy waters.

Convoy. U.S. Navy photograph, between 1940 and 1946.

MARCH 5

1944 Major General Orde C. Wingate's Special Force lands at Broadway (North Burma) in a night glider operation.

Unleashed on September 1, 1939, the German army awed the world with its stunning sweep through Poland. Led in the field by experienced and well-schooled commanders, this well-honed war machine had the formidably effective panzer divisions as its first-strike "fist"—and many supremely motivated "graduates" of the Hitler Youth in its ranks. "We all hope that we'll be transferred to the front soon," young Karl Fuchs wrote to his father on February 9, 1940. "This must be the highest and most noble goal: a man must prove himself in battle." Soldiers also cited preservation of family and the German people and the struggle to establish "a new rational world order" as reasons for their rush to the front. Most were also inspired by the aura surrounding Germany's dictator—an aura developed and perpetually burnished by the dictator himself, assisted by the well-oiled Nazi propaganda machine. "We Sudenten-German SA men want to be in the very front-line," one soldier wrote, "in order to render a fraction of our thanks for the liberation of our beautiful homeland by our magnificent Führer." On March 1, 1940, Hitler ordered Wehrmacht commanders "to prepare for the occupation of Denmark and Norway . . . It is of the utmost importance that our operations should come as a *surprise* to the Northern countries as well as to our enemies in the West." Their troops were ready: "We are merely front-soldiers," one wrote, "who will remain in this situation and never rest, till Germany is completely victorious."

A phalanx of German troops at a Nazi rally, Nuremberg, Germany. between 1935 and 1938

MARCH 6

1943 Erwin Rommel fights his last battle in Africa, directing an unsuccessful offensive against British positions at Medenine, Tunisia.

In 1940, German naval staff officers and their commander in chief, Grand Admiral Erich Raeder, were eager to secure bases in Norway that would help achieve a total blockade of Britain (and keep the Royal Navy from blockading the North Sea as it had during World War I). Hitler agreed, especially after he learned that Britain and France planned to send troops to help the Finns in their war with the Soviets. Moving through Norway, the Allied force would be able to disrupt the flow of iron ore from Sweden to Germany. To prevent that, and to secure Germany's northern flank during *Fall Gelb* (Case Yellow), the impending assault on the Low Countries and France, Hitler launched Operation *Weseruebung* (Weser Exercise). The morning of April 9, forty thousand German troops rolled into Denmark and occupied that neutral country in less than a day, thus securing the Wehrmacht's line of supply. Meanwhile, German planes bombed key Norwegian installations, paratroops landed at strategic points, and warships secured major ports and off-loaded infantry. Out-manned and out-gunned, the Norwegians still mounted a stout defense, helped by the British navy and elements of French and free Polish forces. Wind, snow, the Luftwaffe, and lack of their own air support turned the Allied defense into a painful disaster—in the midst of which (May 10) Hitler launched *Fall Gelb*. By June 9, Norway had officially capitulated. Its royal family became refugees, while the Norwegian underground dug in to continue the struggle.

LEFT: *Vor Narvik*. German photograph taken during the Wehrmacht's invasion of Norway, 1940.

RIGHT: When the law was powerless. Norwegian policemen watch a detachment of German troops marching through the streets of Oslo, Norway, May 11, 1940.

MARCH 7

1945 The U.S. Ninth Armored Division crosses the Rhine River at Remagen, fording the last natural barrier to the German heartland.

Oslo, the Norwegian capital, fell to the Germans on April 9, 1940, the first day of their northern operation (see March 7). That same evening, Vidkun Quisling, a former Norwegian minister of defense and now the head of Norway's Fascist National Union party, announced that he was head of a new government and ordered that all resistance end. (It did not.) Quisling remained "head of government" for a full six days, until the Germans unceremoniously replaced him, initially with an Administrative Council of six (well-supervised) leading Norwegian citizens—including Paal Berg, president of the Supreme Court and later head of the Norwegian resistance. Then, on April 24, Hitler appointed loyal German Nazi Josef Terboven as Reich Commissar for Norway. (Terboven remained the true, and increasingly brutal, ruler of Norway for the rest of the war. Yet the immensely unpopular and supremely ineffective Quisling also remained. In 1942 he was designated premier and remained in that post until Norway was liberated. Meanwhile, his last name, lowercase, appeared in diction-aries as a synonym for "traitor.") With Terboven in charge, Hitler turned his attention to his major gamble of 1940: the big push into Western Europe. Under the ambitious *Fall Gelb* plan, which included a bold move suggested by General Erich von Manstein, 136 divisions of the German army would have to smash through an array of fortified lines and geographic barriers and 135 French, British, Belgian, and Dutch divisions to crush the Allies.

LEFT: Vidkun Quisling (1887–1945) c. 1935.

RIGHT: *All on One Hand*. Drawing by Edwin Marcus, May 12, 1940.

MARCH 8

1942 The Burmese capital of Rangoon, the last port through which supplies could be funneled to the Burma Road for delivery to China, falls to the Japanese.

THE BIG PUSH

GERMANY'S FUTURE

On May 10, 1940, the Germans began their assault on the Low Countries and France, "favoring" the Dutch with the first large-scale airborne attack in history. By May 14 the Netherlands, lacking adequate air and armor support, was forced to surrender by the combined might of German paratroop, infantry, armor, and air assaults (including the Luftwaffe's savage bombing of Rotterdam). Meanwhile, the Germans easily flicked aside Luxembourg's tiny ceremonial military force, occupying that country as Grand Duchess Charlotte and her government escaped. Both Charlotte and Queen Wilhelmina of the Netherlands formed governments-in-exile; both made morale-boosting radio broadcasts to their captive peoples throughout the war. At the same time, King Leopold III of Belgium was witnessing a repeat of 1914, as German invaders battered his country. In a stunning move, a small force of glider-borne Wehrmacht commandos easily captured the formidable Fort Eben-Emael, opening the way to the heart of the country. A greater shock occurred when German armored columns easily penetrated the Ardennes Forest (see March 11). Finally, on May 28, with many of his soldiers among the Allied forces trapped near the port of Dunkirk, Leopold surrendered—angering many of his countrymen as well as Allied leaders, whom he had not consulted. Unlike Wilhelmina and Charlotte, the king declined to fight on from abroad, telling members of his cabinet, "The cause of the Allies is lost."

LEFT: *Surrender of Belgium*. Drawing by Willard Wetmore Combes (b. 1901), 1940.

RIGHT: Charlotte, Grand Duchess of Luxembourg (1896–1985) c. 1940.

MARCH 9

1945 American B-29s stage a devastating nighttime incendiary bombing raid on Tokyo, causing a firestorm that incinerates much of the city and kills an estimated one hundred thousand Japanese.

When the Nazis occupied her country (see March 9), Grand Duchess Charlotte of Luxembourg became a refugee with a noble purpose: to maintain a working government-in-exile and to do what she could to keep up the morale of her people at home and abroad. Some forty thousand of her countrymen fled into France with the more immediate purpose of staying alive and maintaining some measure of freedom. Poles who had managed to escape from their now divided and occupied country and Dutch people and Belgians rushing to escape the Wehrmacht's fast-moving columns were also among the thousands of people seeking refuge in France. The French government, which had already evacuated three hundred thousand civilians from the areas near the Maginot Line, struggled to accommodate the new foreign arrivals—even as more French civilians began to flee the approaching German armies. Meanwhile, British and American newspapers began printing stories about German spies and saboteurs who were helping the Wehrmacht. Although this so-called fifth column of Nazi sympathizers would prove to be largely ephemeral, the rumors caused wariness that affected international assistance to refugees. In June 1940, shortly after President Roosevelt cited the fifth column danger in a *Fireside Chat*, the U.S. Department of State ordered American consuls to deny travel visas to aliens petitioning to enter the United States if they had even the slightest doubts about the petitioner.

Refugees walk past houses destroyed during the first day of the German invasion. Mondorf, Luxembourg, May 10, 1940.

MARCH 10

1938 To counter any possible interference in his plans for *Anschluss* by Italy, long considered an Austrian protector, Hitler sends a letter to Mussolini filled with false accusations of an Austrian-Czechoslovakian plot against Germany. "Consider this step only as one of national self-defense," Hitler writes.

1943 The U.S. Fourteenth Air Force is activated under the command of Claire Chennault.

On the first day of the German campaign against the Low Countries and France, an armored force comprising three columns of tanks, each stretching back a hundred miles behind the Rhine River, entered the Ardennes Forest. This daring maneuver, which had been suggested by Staff Officer Erich von Manstein and eagerly embraced by Hitler, proved to be more successful than even most Germans had hoped. Contrary to previous assumptions, the forest proved perfectly passable by this huge armored force. The Germans swiftly outflanked the Maginot Line, smashed through the French Ninth and Second armies on May 14, and began racing toward the English Channel—their goal to trap and destroy retreating Allied troops. On May 16, Britain's new prime minister Winston Churchill flew to Paris to get a firsthand report on the growing disaster—and to ask about the deployment of Allied strategic reserves. He was stunned by the answer: With most planes knocked out of the fight and the principal lines of defense broken, there were no reserve troops to break the Germans' forward momentum. Inexorably, the Wehrmacht pushed on until hundreds of thousands of Allied troops were trapped in a small area around the port of Dunkirk. With the Germans in hot pursuit, there seemed to be no hope of evacuation. Then, on May 24, the German high command, possibly on the orders of Hitler, ordered their armored columns to stop. This allowed the British to put into motion their own daring plan (see March 12).

ABOVE: Col. Gen. Heinz Guderian (1888–1954), German expert on armored warfare and leader of the Nineteenth Panzer Corps during the campaign in France.

RIGHT: The German advance through Belgium and France toward Paris. Newspaper map, June 7, 1940.

MARCH 11

1938   Nazi Artur Seyss-Inquart replaces Kurt von Schuschnigg as Austrian chancellor.

1942   Gen. Douglas MacArthur, his wife and son, leave Corregidor for Australia.

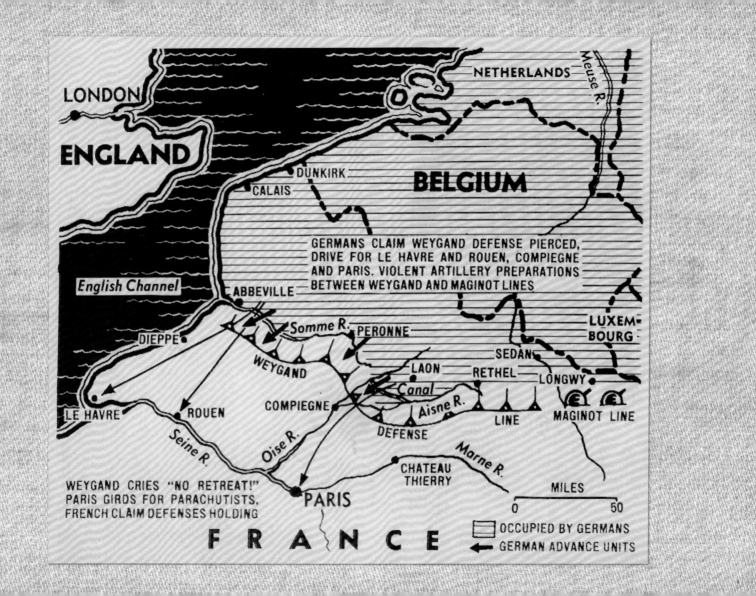

On May 19, with Allied troops trapped in a pocket on the French coast, their backs to the sea, Prime Minister Winston Churchill ordered the British Admiralty to assemble "a large number of vessels" to engage in a rescue mission. Code-named Operation Dynamo, this desperate attempt to save perhaps forty-five thousand members of the British Expeditionary Force blossomed into the "Miracle of Dunkirk" that brought 338,226 British, French, and Belgian troops to safety in Britain. Calling on civilians for help, the admiralty assembled a motley nine-hundred-vessel armada that included warships, yachts, ferryboats, fishing boats—anything capable of navigating the Channel and bringing passengers home. As the vessels brought back load after load of exhausted men, pilots of the Royal Air Force did their best to fend off Luftwaffe assaults from the sky. Meanwhile, outside Dunkirk, French and Belgian units were delaying the German ground advance in fighting around Cassel and Lille. On June 3, Operation Dynamo ended. Dunkirk itself had been ravaged by fighting, and the Allies had lost huge amounts of equipment. With help, the equipment could be replaced—and the rescued troops reinforced. On June 4, as fighting continued in France, Winston Churchill vowed, in a speech to the House of Commons, that England's people "will not flag or fail. . . . We shall defend our island, whatever the cost may be . . . until in God's good time, the new world, with all its power and might, steps forth to the rescue and the liberation of the old."

A crowded waterfront scene in England, where some of the hundreds of vessels used to achieve the "Miracle of Dunkirk" offload men transported from France. June 1940.

MARCH 12

1944 The Czech government-in-exile based in London calls for an armed civilian uprising in Czechoslovakia.

On May 21, 1940, as the British Admiralty was organizing the "Miracle of Dunkirk" (see March 12), other authorities arrested the head of the British Union of Fascists (BUF), Sir Oswald Mosley. A World War I veteran and former member of Parliament, Mosley had become disenchanted with British politics when, in 1932, he traveled to Italy and met Benito Mussolini. Impressed by Il Duce's dynamism and apparent achievements, he returned to Britain and formed the BUF. By January of 1934, Britain's *Daily Mirror* was running commentary by sympathetic Lord Rothermere chastising "timid alarmists" who had "been whimpering that the rapid growth in numbers of the British Blackshirts [BUF] is preparing the way for a system of rulership by means of steel whips and concentration camps . . . the Blackshirts will respect those principles of tolerance which are traditional in British politics." Bitterly anti-Semitic and strongly anti-Communist, Mosley married his second wife, fellow Fascist Diana Mitford, when he was visiting Germany in 1936. The ceremony took place in Joseph Goebbels's drawing room, with Hitler as a guest. Arrested four years later as persons who might "endanger the safety of the realm," both Mosleys were treated gently in prison, where they were permitted to have their own small house and a vegetable garden. They were released in November 1943, to widespread protest—including one from Mosley's sister-in-law, Jessica Mitford, who called the act "a slap in the face of anti-fascists in every country."

British Fascist Oswald Mosley (1896–1980) reviews a contingent of female Fascists, October 14, 1934.

MARCH 13

1943   Two German general officers make an unsuccessful attempt to kill Hitler with a package containing a bomb. The detonator fails.

On May 19, 1940, as Winston Churchill activated the plan to rescue Allied forces at Dunkirk (see March 12), in the United States, the Non-Partisan Committee for Peace through Revision of the Neutrality Law, which had been formed after the outbreak of the European war in 1939, was reorganized as the Committee to Defend America by Aiding the Allies. Headed by Kansas newspaperman William Allen White and Clark M. Eichelberger of the League of Nations Association, the committee quickly acquired more than six hundred branches throughout the country, in U.S. territories, and Canada—and one "Americans in Britain" chapter in England—as it worked to support many of the Roosevelt administration's efforts to assist the combatant Allies by all measures short of war. This included sending Britain substantial numbers of the warplanes that were by then coming more rapidly off U.S. assembly lines. Such measures not only vexed the Axis; they also concerned the American high command (which feared it would harm the combat readiness of U.S. forces) as well as American isolationists. On September 3, Roosevelt announced an exchange agreement whereby Britain would receive fifty "over-age" U.S. destroyers in return for allowing the United States to lease some naval and air bases in Newfoundland, on several Caribbean islands, and in British Guiana. The next day the newly formed America First Committee denounced the exchange as a move that "threatens to involve America in war abroad."

LEFT: *Defend America by aiding the Allies.* Color lithograph poster published by the Committee to Defend America by Aiding the Allies, c. 1940.

RIGHT: Axis bombs severing Roosevelt and Churchill's "hands across the sea." Pen-and-ink drawing by Josef Plank ("Seppla," b. 1900) c. 1940.

MARCH 14

1938 In the wake of the German move into Austria, Winston Churchill urges the British government, during a debate in the House of Commons, to take effective measures against Germany's increasing aggression.

1942 Mar. Philippe Pétain names Pierre Laval premier of Vichy France.

After the Allies successfully evacuated from Dunkirk (see March 12), the Germans turned south, smashed through a defensive line established by head of French forces Maxime Weygand, and pushed on toward Paris. Terror reigned on French roads as retreating soldiers and fleeing civilians were strafed by German planes. The Luftwaffe also attacked Paris until the French declared it an open city (unresistant and thus not subject to attack). By June 14, when German ground forces reached the French capital, two-thirds of the local population had fled and the government had escaped to Bordeaux. In that new, impromptu capital, French ministers spent days arguing, agonizing—and dispatching a futile plea to President Roosevelt for a declaration of war or an open declaration of support. When the majority finally decided that it was impossible to continue fighting, even from bases in France's North African colonies, President Paul Reynaud resigned. He was succeeded by the venerable World War I hero Marshal Philippe Pétain, who immediately sought an armistice. On June 21, a triumphant Hitler presented surrender terms to French representatives in a railway car set in a clearing in the woods outside Compiègne—the same place the Germans had capitulated to the Allies at the end of World War I. "The French had no warning that they would be handed the terms at the very site of the negotiations in 1918," German general Franz Halder later wrote in his diary. "They were apparently shaken by this arrangement."

One day after Hitler presented terms to the French delegation, French and German officials sign an armistice agreement in the same railroad coach in which the French had presented armistice terms to the Germans at the end of World War I, June 22, 1940.

MARCH 15

1945   U.S. bombers complete two days of destructive raids on Osaka, Japan.

By signing the armistice on June 22, the French agreed to divide their country into two zones: Two-thirds of the nation—the north and west and the entire Atlantic coast—would be occupied and governed by the Germans; the south and southeast would remain under the nominal control of the French (minus a small area that would go to the now-combatant Italians under an armistice signed on June 24). The day after the signing, Hitler made his only visit to Paris with an entourage that included architect Albert Speer. Their whirlwind, three-hour tour included the ornate Paris Opéra (with which the führer seemed particularly taken), the Champs Élysées, the Arc de Triomphe and Tomb of the Unknown Soldier, the church of Sacre Coeur on Montmartre, and the Eiffel Tower (where the French had cut the elevator cables, hoping to make Hitler walk to the top; but he only looked). That evening, after leaving the French capital behind, Hitler summoned Speer, who reported the ensuing conversation in his postwar memoir, *Inside the Third Reich*. "'Wasn't Paris beautiful?' [Hitler said]. 'But Berlin must be made far more beautiful. In the past I often considered whether we would not have to destroy Paris,' he continued with great calm, as if he were talking about the most natural thing in the world. 'But when we are finished [building and renovating] in Berlin, Paris will only be a shadow. So why should we destroy it?'"

Adolf Hitler inspects the newly conquered city of Paris, June 23, 1940.

MARCH 16

1943   A three-day battle between thirty-eight German U-boats and two Allied convoys begins along the east coast of Newfoundland; twenty-one merchant ships and one naval escort are lost.

In addition to industrial mobilization, battlefield conflict, and strategic bombing, World War II included all-out media combat. In this media war, both sides used new and improved technologies to gather, transmit, interpret, and disseminate more information—and disinformation—than in any previous war. Both Axis and Allied nations engaged in extensive propaganda campaigns, employing visual, written, and/or verbal material to persuade and influence target audiences about an idea, cause, or ideology. The totalitarian nations exercised greatest control over the media and proved singularly adept at twisting the truth to fit their own party lines and immediate objectives. ("The victor will not be asked afterwards," Hitler said, "whether he told the truth.") Democratic Britain and the United States, on the other hand, engaged in only partial control and urged that media be guided by voluntary restrictions. Each side employed armies of talented and creative people, including writers, photographers, radio commentators, and filmmakers. Caricaturists and cartoonists used their pens, pencils, and paintbrushes both to celebrate their side's (real or apocryphal) achievements and to skewer selected targets—sometimes zeroing in on the same basic theme from *very* different perspectives.

LEFT: French caricature of "octopus" Adolf Hitler, his tentacles encircling the globe. Between 1935 and 1939.

RIGHT: German caricature of "octopus" Winston Churchill, his tentacles encircling the globe. Drawing by Josef Plank ("Seppla," b. 1900), c. 1940.

MARCH 17

1942 Rear Adm. Adolphus ("Dolly") Andrews assumes command of the U.S. Eastern Sea Frontier—an area stretching from the Canadian border to Jacksonville, Florida. Waging war against German U-boats, he will develop the "Bucket Brigade," in which local boats escort shipping from port to port.

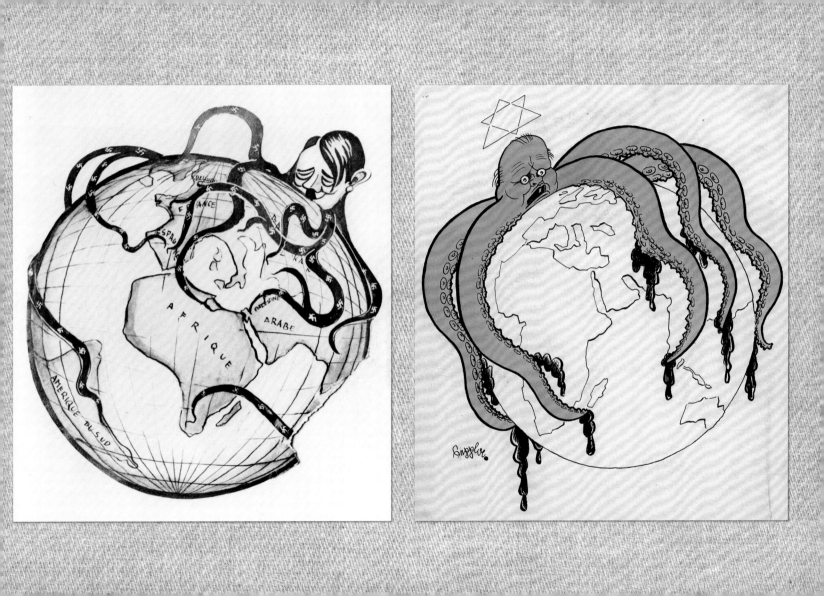

In the armistice with France, Germany had "solemnly declared . . . that it does not intend to use the French War Fleet . . . for its purposes in war." Hitler, however, was not renowned for keeping his promises. Moreover, British-French relations had often been strained, and some naval officers serving Marshal Pétain's collaborationist government (now established at the town of Vichy) might not be averse to employing their warships against their former ally. Of particular concern was the French Mediterranean Fleet, which, in tandem with the Italian navy, could greatly increase the threat to the British in that vital region. Thus, the British issued an ultimatum that the French must disarm or scuttle their Mediterranean warships. On July 3, 1940, after the French failed to comply, the British attacked. At the ports of Mers-el-Kébir and nearby Oran, Algeria, Britain's Gibralter-based Force H, under Vice Admiral Sir James Somerville, struck a French squadron commanded by Admiral Marcel Gensoul. In fifteen minutes, the British damaged two battleships, a battle cruiser, and a destroyer—and killed nearly thirteen hundred French sailors. This was "a hateful decision," Winston Churchill later wrote; in fact, it embittered many Frenchmen for decades. Yet Churchill believed it was necessary—and not only to prevent joint Vichy-French-Italian action. He viewed Mers-el-Kébir as "the turning point in our fortunes," for "it made the world [most especially, the Americans] realize that we were in earnest in our intentions to carry on."

ABOVE: *Oran*. Cartoon from a satirical German calendar, 1941.

RIGHT: *N'oubliez pas Oran!* ("Don't forget Oran!"). Color lithograph poster, France, between 1942 and 1945.

MARCH 18

1945 Escorted by 670 fighters, 1,250 U.S. bombers make the heaviest daylight raid on Berlin of the war, dropping three thousand tons of bombs.

After France fell, Britain faced the Axis alone. The British government and its top military commanders reasoned (and not without cause) that it would not be long before the Germans attempted an invasion of their island nation. In that case, what would the sixty thousand to seventy-five thousand Germans, Austrians, and Italians then living in Britain do? When the Germans invaded Norway, Vidkun Quisling had emerged to assist them (see March 8); and when the Germans had swept through the Low Countries and France, it was rumored that they were helped by a "fifth column" of spies and sympathizers. "The paltriest kitchen maid not only can be, but generally is, a menace to the safety of the country," former British ambassador to the Netherlands Sir Neville Bland wrote after fleeing the Continent. On June 25, 1940, under the threat of imminent invasion, the government interned all suspect aliens between ages eighteen and sixty—including thousands of Jewish refugees from Germany and many Italians who had lived in the country so long that they thought of themselves as British. Five thousand were held, behind barbed wire and under guard, in an unfinished housing development in Lancashire; fifteen thousand were interned on the Isle of Man. Some were deported to Canada—a dangerous journey that resulted in tragedy for one transport ship. On July 2, 1940, the *Arandora Star* was torpedoed by a U-boat. Nearly half the 1,190 German and Italian internees aboard drowned.

An armed sentry guards civilian aliens interned in a barbed-wire-enclosed township in the English northwest, June 1940.

MARCH 19

1942 U.S. Maj. Gen. "Vinegar Joe" Stilwell assumes command of the Chinese Fifth and Sixth armies in Burma—the first time in history Chinese troops have been led by a foreigner.

Since May 1938, when the U.S. Congress established the House Committee to Investigate Un-American Activities (HUAC), chaired by Texas Democrat Martin Dies, the committee had been overzealously investigating. In addition to focusing its attention on the American Communist Party and the German-American Bund (see February 10), HUAC quickly labeled 483 newspapers, 280 labor organizations, and 640 other groups "Communistic"—including the Boy Scouts and the Camp Fire Girls. As war came to Europe, HUAC increased pressure on Attorney General Frank Murphy to prosecute suspected subversives, despite Murphy's reminders that the Department of Justice had to refrain from actions that violated "the fundamental rights and privileges of free assembly, free opinion, and free speech." Yet Murphy also assured President Roosevelt, who was demanding a "no-nonsense approach to Un-Americanism," that he would demonstrate that the United States was "not a soft, pudgy democracy." Thus, on January 13, 1940, the FBI, acting under his orders, arrested seventeen members of a bitterly anti-Semitic and pro-Nazi organization called the Christian Front and charged them with planning, in the words of FBI director J. Edgar Hoover, to "knock off about a dozen congressmen" and "blow up the goddamned [New York City] police department." There was little hard evidence to support those charges, however. The jury that considered the case refused to convict the accused.

ABOVE: *Democracy . . . a challenge.* Color silk-screen poster published by the Chicago, Illinois, Federal Art Project, August 1940.

RIGHT: Christian Front membership card of Patrick Lawlor, 1940.

MARCH 20

1943   German officers make a second attempt (see March 13) to kill Hitler with a bomb. Hitler leaves the room before the bomb can be detonated.

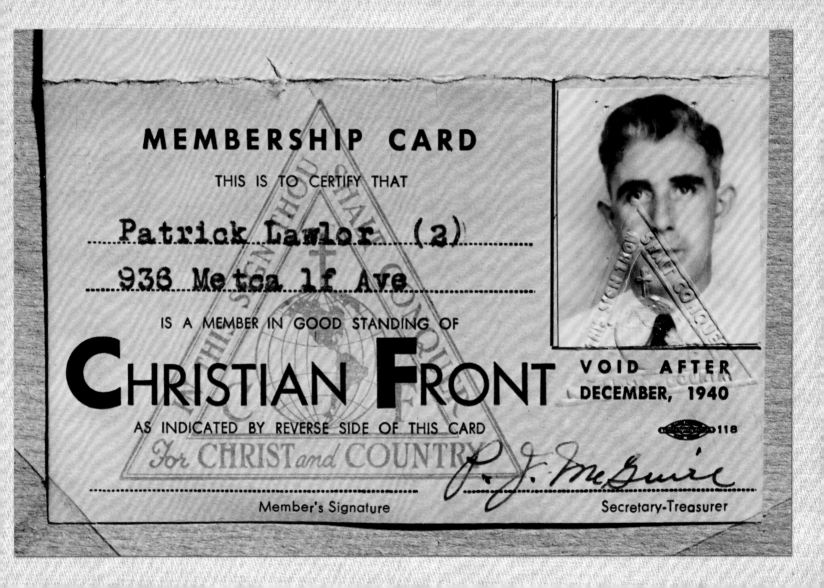

MEMBERSHIP CARD

THIS IS TO CERTIFY THAT

Patrick Lawlor (2)

938 Metcalf Ave

IS A MEMBER IN GOOD STANDING OF

CHRISTIAN FRONT

AS INDICATED BY REVERSE SIDE OF THIS CARD

For CHRIST and COUNTRY

VOID AFTER
DECEMBER, 1940

118

Member's Signature

Secretary-Treasurer

F our days after the British began the internment of Germans, Austrians, and Italians living in England (see March 19), President Roosevelt signed the U.S. Alien Registration Act (Smith Act), requiring the registration and fingerprinting of all aliens living in the United States. The act also streamlined deportation procedures and forbade any person to "knowingly or willfully advocate, abet, advise, or teach the duty, necessity, desirability, or propriety of overthrowing or destroying any government in the United States by force or violence." In this time of pressing threats, the measure sailed through Congress, despite questions about the encroachment on civil liberties—although some legislators, among them Democrat Emmanuel Celler of Brooklyn, supported the bill only "in fear of a worse one." During this first complete U.S. inventory of noncitizens, some five million aliens would eventually register (among them six hundred thousand Italians, two hundred sixty thousand Germans, and forty thousand Japanese)—under circumstances particularly structured to make them feel at ease. As Solicitor General Francis Biddle noted, they had all "seen Hitler register the Jews as a preliminary to stripping them of their rights." Current and future attorneys general Frank Murphy, Robert H. Jackson, and Biddle—who remembered the vigilantism and prosecutorial excesses of the World War I era—all opposed the bill. Throughout the war, there were only two prosecutions under the Smith Act.

LEFT: *Civil liberties in war times.* Color silk-screen poster published by the Iowa Federal Art Project, January 1940.

RIGHT: Political cartoon, probably pertaining to passage of the U.S. Alien Registration Act, June 29, 1940. Ink, opaque white, and blue pencil drawing by William Gropper (b. 1897).

MARCH 21

1942 With Allied troops under siege on the Bataan peninsula, General Jonathan Wainwright moves his headquarters to the heavily fortified island of Corregidor in Manila Bay.

On July 10, 1940, German aircraft based in France began a relentless aerial campaign against the lone undefeated European Ally. Germany's aim in the Battle of Britain was to destroy the Royal Air Force (RAF), ravage Britain's radar defenses and aircraft factories, and generally prepare the way for Operation Sealion, the invasion of the British Isles. An invasion force was assembling as Luftwaffe fighters and bombers began their campaign of destruction—which, Hermann Göring assured Hitler, would be successful in a matter of weeks. The RAF disabused him of that notion, however, putting up a stubborn defense, even as it took a terrible beating: By August 18, 106 British pilots had been killed, 208 fighter-aircraft had been destroyed, and replacement planes could not be secured quickly enough. Then, on August 25, the British bombed Berlin. An incensed Hitler ordered the Luftwaffe to abandon its original targets and concentrate on English cities, initiating what the British soon dubbed the Blitz. From September to November, civilians endured nights riddled with the sights, sounds, and smells of violent death, the wail of sirens, the dreadful flickering of burning buildings. As they soldiered on, the RAF regrouped and continued to pummel the attackers; on September 15, now Battle of Britain Day, they knocked down fifty-six Germans, losing twenty-three of their own. That was the turning point. Although raids continued, Hitler cancelled Operation Sealion—and began activating plans for a much larger operation in the east.

London smoldering during the Blitz, September 7, 1940.

MARCH 22

1945   U.S. forces achieve total surprise when they make a late-night crossing of the Rhine River at Oppenheim, south of Mainz.

On September 7, 1940, Britain's *Daily Telegraph* reported: "London was heavily raided during the evening, much damage was done and many fires caused, mainly in the East End. . . . To watchers in the center and west the whole eastern arc of the sky seemed full of fire." The Blitz had just begun (see March 22), and civil defense programs had become the first line of protection for millions of British civilians. Honed under extreme wartime conditions, Britain's civil defense program included circulating rafts of instructional and precautionary posters, distributing gas masks and Anderson bomb shelters (named for Minister of Civil Defense John Anderson), moving people, especially children, from cities to the greater safety of the country—and mobilizing millions of civilians. Members of the Home Guard patrolled coastlines, airfields, and factories and apprehended downed German flyers. Air raid wardens enforced blackout rules and helped in the aftermath of attacks. People of the Royal Observer Corps counted and reported the movements of enemy aircraft. "If it is a case of the whole nation fighting and suffering together," Churchill said in August 1940, "that ought to suit us, because we are the most united of all the nations, because we entered the war upon the national will and with our eyes open, and because we have been nurtured in freedom and individual responsibility and are the products, not of totalitarian uniformity but of tolerance and variety."

Two British civil defense posters, published between 1939 and 1941. *Children are safer in the country . . . leave them there* and *Look before you sleep* promoting a pre-bed safety check.

MARCH 23

 1944   New Zealand forces break off their costly attempt to take Monte Cassino, Italy.

CHILDREN
are safer in the country
. . . leave them there

PRINTED FOR H.M. STATIONERY OFFICE BY POSH & CROSS LTD., LONDON. (51/5237)

LOOK before you sleep

ALL WINDOWS AND INNER DOORS OPEN?

WATER IN BUCKETS?

WATER WATER

SAND IN BUCKETS?

SAND SAND

GAS MASK, CLOTHES AND TORCH HANDY?

GOOD NIGHT!

Printed for H.M. Stationery Office by Johnson, Riddle & Co., Ltd., Penge. S.E.20. 51-7979

In a speech on June 10, 1940, President Roosevelt condemned Italy's declaration of war against Britain and France that day and declared that the United States would "extend to the opponents of force the material resources of this nation." He further pledged that America would develop "the equipment and training equal to the task of any emergency and every defense." Ten days later the Burke-Wadsworth Selective Training and Service Bill was introduced in Congress. The brainchild of attorney and army veteran Grenville Clark, who had sparked the development of pre–World War I military training camps for business and professional men, the bill aroused enormous controversy—just as Roosevelt was embarking on another reelection campaign (see March 30). Opponents said that the proposed conscription was immoral, smacked of "dictatorship and fascism," and would subject American youths to "syphilis and slavery." As arguments flared at home, however, American newspapers began printing pictures of English cities ravaged during the Battle of Britain—a portent, perhaps, of future aerial attacks on U.S. cities. The Selective Service bill that passed on September 16 (during the height of the Blitz, see March 22) established a one-year draft system. All men between the ages of twenty and thirty-six were required to register, providing a pool from which inductees would be selected by lottery. By the middle of October more than sixteen million men had complied. This was the first peacetime draft in American history.

Gen. Lewis B. Hershey draws the last capsule from the goldfish bowl during the Selective Service lottery in Washington, D.C., October 15, 1940.

MARCH 24

1944 Maj. Gen. Orde Wingate, organizer of the Chindits and a leading proponent of irregular warfare, is killed in a plane crash in Burma.

By September 1940, Brigadier General Charles de Gaulle (see May 22), recently endorsed by Winston Churchill as the leader of all free Frenchmen, had developed a plan to lead elements of his still-small Free French force into French West Africa, which was aligned with the collaborationist Vichy government. Strategically located only seventeen hundred miles from the eastern tip of Brazil, and eight times larger than France, the colony was uncomfortably close to shipping lanes that the British used to sail around Africa after the Italian navy went *en garde* in the Mediterranean. Thus, the British agreed to support de Gaulle in "Operation Menace," an attempt to secure the well-protected port of Dakar (now in Senegal). On September 23–24, an estimated twenty-seven hundred Free French troops, forty-two hundred British troops and a British naval force arrived at their objective, where, before any shots were fired, a perhaps overconfident de Gaulle invited the Vichy governor, Pierre Boisson, to surrender. "France has confided Dakar to me," Boisson signaled defiantly, "and I shall defend it to the end." In the ensuing two-day battle, Vichy military forces sustained some damage, and about three hundred civilians were hurt—but the Allies suffered an embarrassing minor military defeat (dubbed "the Great Dakar F__k-up" by British troops). This unhappy beginning to de Gaulle's Free French command did very little to enhance the aloof French general's reputation with his British and American allies.

LEFT: One of twelve cartoons from a satirical German calendar, ridiculing the Allied failure at Dakar. Photomechanical print, 1941.

RIGHT: Cartoon published by the American interventionist "Fight for Freedom" group, underlining the strategic location of Dakar, c. 1940–41.

MARCH 25

1940 U.S. Air Corps contractors are authorized to sell modern army combat airplanes to anti-Axis governments under a "liberalized release policy."

"It may become possible to set up a nuclear chain reaction in a large mass of uranium, by which vast amounts of power and large quantities of new radium-like elements would be generated. . . . This new phenomenon would also lead to the construction of bombs, and it is conceivable . . . that extremely powerful bombs of a new type may thus be constructed." The idea of such a powerful new weapon, expressed in a letter signed by Albert Einstein that President Roosevelt received on October 11, 1939, led to the creation of the U.S. Advisory Committee on Uranium later that month—the first step on the road to U.S. development of the atomic bomb. Less than a year before, two scientists at Berlin's Kaiser Wilhelm Institute for Chemistry had become the first to achieve nuclear fission, and Einstein and many of his scientific colleagues feared that Hitler might be the first to develop a nuclear weapon. Though an ardent pacifist, the 1921 Nobel laureate knew the threat Hitler posed to the world and believed that threat should be countered. Einstein had witnessed firsthand the thuggery and corrosive anti-Semitism that accompanied Hitler's rise to power (Nazis had denounced his theories of relativity as "Jewish-Communist physics"), and when the Nazi leader was named chancellor in 1933, the scientist left Germany and accepted a position as a professor of theoretical physics at Princeton University. The Nazis promptly stripped him of his German citizenship. In 1940, he became a citizen of the United States.

Judge Phillip Forman hands Albert Einstein his certificate of American citizenship. Photograph by Al Aumuller, October 1, 1940.

MARCH 26

1938 With its military still mired in what was to have been a short war against China, the Japanese government passes the National Mobilization Bill, giving the government dictatorial powers over most areas of Japan's economic life.

1943 Second Lt. Elsie S. Ott, U.S. army nurse, becomes the first woman awarded a U.S. Air Medal for care she provided during a ten-thousand-mile aeromedical evacuation of five casualties from India to Washington, D.C.—her first airplane flight.

In September 1940, Italy's foreign minister, Count Galeazzo Ciano, traveled to Berlin for the signing of the Tripartite Pact between Italy, Japan, and Germany. In this ten-year military and economic agreement, the three main Axis powers pledged to "cooperate . . . in regard to their efforts in greater East Asia and regions of Europe . . . to establish and maintain a new order of things." "The pact is signed," Ciano wrote in his diary on September 27. "Japan is far away. Its help is doubtful. One thing alone is certain: that the war will be long." Articulate, ambitious, and having, at best, an intermittent relationship with scruples, Ciano alternately favored and was ambivalent toward Italy's alliance with the Germans. Like his father-in-law, Mussolini, he bristled at Hitler's increasingly pronounced habits of disregarding Italian counsel and keeping his chief ally in the dark before taking significant unilateral action. When Ciano had gone to Berlin in August 1939—that time to argue against the war with Poland for which Hitler was obviously preparing—German foreign minister Joachim von Ribbentrop had been polite but evasive. Hitler had listened, Ciano noted in his diary, "with a faraway and impersonal interest." Although the Italians weren't officially notified of the German invasion until it actually happened, Ciano correctly deduced on August 11 that, "even if the Germans were given more than they ask for they would attack just the same, because," he went on, "they are possessed by the demon of destruction."

Italian foreign minister Count Galeazzo Ciano with Mrs. Hermann Göring at the Göring country estate, Carinhall, probably in late September 1940.

MARCH 27

1942 British forces begin a costly overnight raid on the German naval facility at Saint-Nazaire, France, which destroys the only possible French coastal base of operations for the German battleship *Tirpitz*.

In October 1940, German troops entered Romania to secure the oil fields at Ploesti that were vital to both Germany and resource-strapped Italy. Although Mussolini had been aware that Hitler was contemplating such a move, he became livid when it actually took place without his being informed in advance and without Italian participation. Mussolini, too, had been considering a move of which Hitler was vaguely aware but which Il Duce knew the führer was not eager to have happen at this time. "Hitler always faces me with *faits accomplis*," he railed to his son-in-law, Italian foreign minister Galeazzo Ciano. "This time I will pay him back in his own coin. He will discover from the newspapers that I have occupied Greece. In this way the equilibrium will be reestablished." Launched on October 28, by way of Albania, the invasion of neutral Greece (which the Italians averred had unneutral ties to Britain) quickly descended into an Italian fiasco. Ill-prepared, poorly led, insufficiently equipped, and ill-supported Italian troops pushed forward—only to be pushed back into Albania by better disciplined, motivated, and equipped Greek forces. Meanwhile, on the night of November 11, British carrier-based planes heavily damaged the Italian fleet moored at Taranto. At the same time, Italian forces were not faring well in North Africa. Far from reestablishing equilibrium, Mussolini had created a situation that invited direct German military intervention in his Mediterranean realm—something he had long sought to avoid.

LEFT: Benito Mussolini delivering a speech, date unknown.

RIGHT: One of a set of Italian propagandist postcards. Color silk screen, published by the Ministry of Popular Culture, between 1939 and 1943.

MARCH 28

1939 The Spanish Civil War enters its final phase as Madrid falls to the fascist Nationalist forces of Francisco Franco.

« La Fanteria fu e sarà sempre la regina delle battaglie ».

MUSSOLINI

(Dal discorso pronunciato al Senato, il 30 Marzo 1938). — XI. 240 e 241.

Throughout 1940, increasingly worried Americans had been trying to parse the hosts of conflicting news reports and propaganda barrages that were flowing from the major combatants in Europe and Asia. On October 28, *Time* magazine published an article, "We Can Take It," that reported two views of the Battle of Britain. "London's ability to carry on under a continuous hail of bombs . . . without a roof over the heads of people, without sleep and with the slenderest food supplies, is not due to British ability to 'take it,'" the German SS publication *Schwarze Korps* sneered. "Rather, this England approaches death with sensual pleasure . . . [hoping] that, in dying, it may also drag its enemy into the abyss." At the same time, *Time* noted, the British released a seven-minute film, "London Can Take It," that graphically depicted what Londoners had been enduring—and stoutly refuted the idea that Britain was dying, with or without sensual pleasure. Commentary within the film (published later in booklet form) declared, "The sign of a great fighter in the ring is: 'Can he get up from the floor after being knocked down?' Britain does this every morning." Meanwhile, despite Hitler's promises to the contrary, German civilians were also being subjected to air raids, yet on a much smaller scale. "Every night the citizens [of Berlin] spend from four to five hours in the cellar," Italy's Count Ciano reported in his diary September 27, 1940. "Bomb damage is slight; nervousness is very great."

LEFT: Passersby reading headlines, including war news, posted in the street-corner window of the *Brockton Enterprise* newspaper office, Brockton, Massachusetts. Photograph by Jack Delano (1914–1997), December 1940.

RIGHT: People in northwest Berlin look at a crater that German authorities attributed to a British bomb dropped on the night of September 25–26, 1940.

MARCH 29

1942   Philippine guerrillas are organized as the Anti-Japanese People's Army under Communist Luis Taruc.

Bulletins from the war fronts vied with U.S. political news in the turbulent summer and fall of 1940. In June, as the French were capitulating, the Republicans nominated a former Democrat, attorney and businessman Wendell L. Willkie (1892–1944), to run against Franklin Roosevelt (officially nominated in July) in FDR's unprecedented campaign for a third term as president. Although he was a critic of Roosevelt's New Deal policies, particularly those affecting business, Willkie largely supported the president on foreign policy and on the need for defense preparedness—garnering criticism from Republican ranks that he was a "me too" candidate. As debate raged through the summer over the proposed Selective Training and Service Bill (see March 24), Willkie refused to make the smart political move and come out against it. "I would rather not win the election than do that," he said, adding that Selective Service was "the only democratic way in which to assure the trained and competent man-power we need in our national defense." Roosevelt won the November election—but Willkie received twenty-two million votes, the largest number received by a defeated candidate up to that time. The president then recruited him as a personal overseas emissary, and by 1943, Willkie had visited England, the Middle East, the Soviet Union, and China. In his subsequent book *One World*, he stressed the importance of international cooperation, and he urged the creation of an organization like the United Nations—which he did not live to see become a reality.

LEFT: *The Same Sweetheart in Every Port*. Drawing by Clifford Berryman (1869–1949), depicting FDR wooing a third term, March 7, 1940.

RIGHT: *For President Wendell L. Willkie*. Campaign poster attributed to F. A. Russo, 1940.

MARCH 30

1945 U.S. Sixth Division tanks break through German defenses north of Frankfurt.

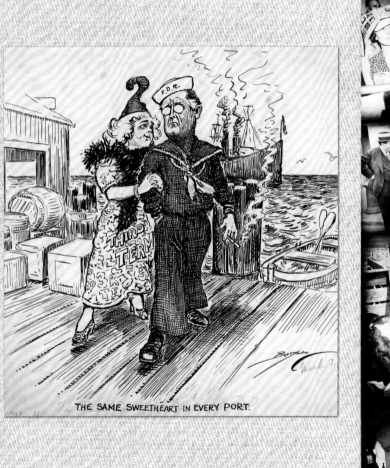

THE SAME SWEETHEART IN EVERY PORT.

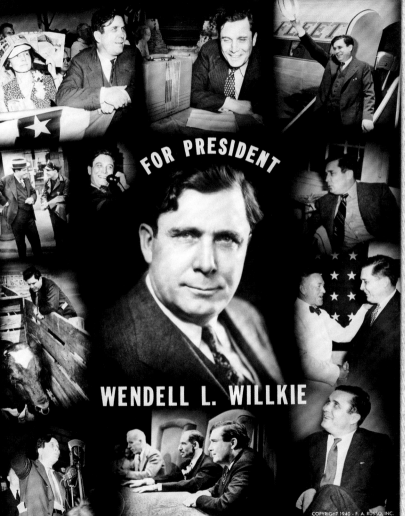

FOR PRESIDENT

WENDELL L. WILLKIE

COPYRIGHT 1940 - F. A. RUSSO, INC.

"On the crest of a wave of passion, prejudice and panic the President [Roosevelt] was carried into a third term of service," the English-language Japanese magazine *Japan Times* observed on November 14, 1940. "His will be the opportunity . . . to inaugurate a constructive policy of cooperation with Japan." The Roosevelt administration remained disinclined to frame such a policy, however, faced with Japanese movement into French Indochina and the continuing Sino-Japanese war. In August, Chinese Communist units had launched the "Hundred Regiments Offensive," hitting transport, mines, industry, and some of the fortified blockhouses the Japanese used to keep the Communists penned in the north. Though taken by surprise, the Japanese quickly recovered and, by late fall, had repelled the offensive. Yet the increasing aggressiveness of the Chinese Red Army, coupled with ongoing opposition from Nationalists and some freelance Chinese warlords, made it clear to Tokyo that Japan's "short" war in China would continue into another year. With resources tight and plans for expansion continuing, this prompted the formulation of a new policy. Promulgated early in 1941, "Outline Measures for a Protracted War in China" called for "acquiring from China all materials needed for Japan's mobilization." Although most Japanese forces had not previously been shy about taking what they wanted from the Chinese, this new directive meant that, in future, China would face even greater torment at the hands of the invader.

A Flash of the Spirit of Japan. Reproduction of a painting by Chisoku Sakurai, published in *Seisen Gafu* ("A Picture Album of the Holy War"), Tokyo, 1939.

MARCH 31

1942 As British troops occupy Cap Serrat, Tunisia, civilian authorities in Britain record the casualty statistics for the month of March from air raids at home: 973 killed, 1,191 wounded.

A Global Conflict: 1941

As 1941 began, Americans peered anxiously across their two shielding oceans at the wars raging in Europe and Asia. Although the United States was still determinedly isolationist, the Roosevelt administration was nudging the nation toward greater international involvement. "We must be the great arsenal of democracy," Roosevelt had said in his *Fireside Chat* of December 29, 1940. He pursued the topic in his annual address to Congress on January 6, initiating a debate on what was to become the U.S. Lend-Lease Program. Noting that the Allied nations now at war were growing short of resources, he declared, "We cannot, and we will not, tell them they must surrender merely because of present inability to pay for the weapons which we know

they must have." The United States must achieve a "swift and driving increase in our armament production," he continued, as part of a campaign to achieve a secure world founded on four essential freedoms: freedom of speech and expression; freedom of worship; freedom from want; and freedom from fear.

The country entered the first phases of what would become a massive transformation to a wartime economy. As the foundation of Henry Ford's immense sixty-seven-acre Michigan war-production facility began taking shape in March, the National Defense Mediation Board was established to settle labor disputes in defense industries. That same month, Congress established a Special Senate

APRIL 1

1941 The first four-thousand-pound bombs are dropped by RAF Wellingtons during an air raid on Emden, Germany.

Committee to Investigate the National Defense Program to root out profiteering, mismanagement, and other problems that might plague American industries as defense production rapidly expanded. To keep prices at manageable levels as war production boomed, the Office of Price Administration was established in April.

In Europe, the aerial assault on Britain continued, but at a less furious pitch, as the Germans transferred air and ground units to the east to prepare for a massive attack on the Soviet Union. First, however, Hitler had to shore up the Germans' southern flank by aiding his floundering Italian allies. In April, Luftwaffe groups and Wehrmacht columns, supported by a Hungarian army, swept into Yugoslavia and Greece. Just over two months later, with the Balkans relatively secure, a massive German force crashed across the Soviet border, beginning a blitzkrieg attack that Hitler was confi-dent would result in Stalin's capitulation well before winter. Meanwhile, combined German and Italian forces pursued a near-continuous seesaw campaign against British and Commonwealth troops in North Africa—and the costly Battle of the Atlantic raged on.

In the East, Japanese leaders bristled as the Roosevelt ad-ministration added to the list of items embargoed from ship-ment to Japan and, finally, froze all Japanese assets and closed the Panama Canal to Japanese shipping. On September 6, government officials, meeting in the Imperial Conference, decided that if diplomacy did not reverse America's policy of restricting Japan's access to vital resources, by early October, they would implement the "Southern Operation"—attacking British and American bases and securing the oil-rich Dutch East Indies. On December 7, 1941, this strategy was effected, and the Asian and European conflicts merged to become World War II.

Freedom of Speech *Freedom of Worship*

Freedom from Want *Freedom from Fear*

Ours to fight for: freedom of speech, freedom of worship, freedom from want, freedom from fear. Color poster by Norman Rockwell (1894–1978), 1943.

On January 21, 1941, Prime Minister Fumimaro Konoye addressed the seventy-sixth session of the Imperial Japanese Diet: "Japan is now confronted with an emergency unparalleled in her long history. The present world situation makes it urgent that she should . . . take appropriate measures centering on the establishment of a new order in Greater East Asia and placing emphasis on the settlement of the China Affair." The words "China Affair" cloaked a vicious war that was eating away at Japanese resources and killing millions of Chinese. As Konoye spoke, Japan's North China Area Army was engaged in a new offensive. Mounted primarily in retaliation for the Communists' Hundred Regiments campaign of the previous year (see March 31), the offensive was part of what its Chinese targets termed the "Three Alls Campaign" (kill all, burn all, destroy all), which aimed to smash Red Chinese bases so effectively that "the enemy could never use them again." Millions died, and millions more became refugees as Japanese troops swept through the countryside, burning and looting desperately needed food. At year's end, the approach taken in this brutal campaign became official policy. On December 3, Imperial Headquarters, Army, issued Order Number 575, directing its forces in China to "strengthen the containment of the enemy and destroy his will to continue fighting."

Shouting Banzai. Reproduction of a painting by Shysei Kobayakawa, published in *Seisen Gafu* ("A Picture Album of the Holy War"), Tokyo, 1939.

APRIL 2

1941 Anti-British general Rashid Ali overthrows the Iraqi government. In response, the British will land forces at Basra, repelling an attack by nine thousand Iraqis, and move on Baghdad, forcing Ali to flee the country.

1942 Planes of the U.S. Tenth Air Force fly their first missions in the China-Burma-India theater of operations.

In January 1941, as Japan tacitly supported Thailand in a brief clash with French forces in Indochina (forcing Vichy to cede territory to the Thais), a new U.S. ambassador arrived in Vichy. Admiral William D. Leahy, who had just completed service as governor of Puerto Rico, had been a trusted adviser to Assistant Secretary of the Navy Franklin Roosevelt (1913–20) and had also served under commander in chief Roosevelt as chief of naval operations (1937–39). His career as a military officer no doubt contributed to the respectful relationship he established with Marshal Philippe Pétain. Yet Leahy had been given an impossible task. By maintaining a presence in ostensibly neutral Vichy, the U.S. government hoped to influence Pétain and his cabinet to *remain* strictly neutral and to cooperate as little as possible with the Germans occupying the other two-thirds of France. Initially optimistic, Leahy was soon engulfed in the treacherous currents of Vichy politics—which included underground resisters, dedicated collaborationists, and the increasingly intolerant and isolated Pétain and his small trusted circle. Though Leahy retained his compassion for the hard-pressed French people, by October, after Pétain announced the cessation of parliamentary government, the ambassador wrote, "The present government of France is not essentially different from that of Nazi Germany." Recalled in April 1942, Leahy became Roosevelt's highly effective chief of staff.

William Daniel Leahy (center, right), American ambassador to Vichy France, presenting credentials to Mar. Philippe Pétain, January 8, 1941.

APRIL 3

1941 British Ambassador Sir Richard Stafford Cripps informs Joseph Stalin that German units are being deployed on the Soviet Union's western frontier in preparation for an attack.

Both France and Britain had significant colonial interests in the Mediterranean region. In early 1941, however, most French territories in the area remained loyal to Vichy. The British, meanwhile, were stoutly resisting Italy's best efforts to dislodge them from any of their Mediterranean holdings: The bastion of Gibraltar remained intact and combative; the strategically located and increasingly battered island of Malta remained a base for planes and submarines that disrupted Axis operations; and British and Commonwealth forces had not only protected Egypt and the Suez Canal, they had pushed the Italians back into Libya and captured the vital port of Tobruk. In February, Hitler sent Italy help in the form of Major General Erwin Rommel and a force soon named the Afrika Korps. Theoretically subordinate to the Italian high command, and definitely subordinate to his German commanders, Rommel proceeded to ignore both bodies' wishes that his combined German-Italian force maintain a chiefly defensive posture. In March, he began pushing the British back; by April, he reached Tobruk, where stubborn Australian defenders forced him to place the city under siege. That same month, British forces defeated a coup attempt in Iraq that Hitler supported by sending planes and supplies to neighboring Vichy-held Syria. Two months later, as Germany was on the verge of invading the Soviet Union, British and free French forces entered Syria and Lebanon—which, by July 14, were under Allied control.

General Italo Gariboldi (left), Italian governor of Libya, and General Erwin Rommel, commander of German units in North Africa, review troops of the Afrika Korps, 1941.

APRIL 4

1944   The Twentieth Air Force is activated in Washington, D.C.

When Britain entered World War II, it could still be said that "the sun never sets on the British Empire." Not including the sovereign dominions of Australia, Canada, the Irish Free State, New Zealand, and South Africa, British colonial holdings ranged from the Caribbean and the Atlantic; through Africa, the Mediterranean and the Middle East; to several Pacific islands and large areas of Southeast Asia. These colonies were critically important sources of strength, manpower, and resources as Britain faced the Axis. They were also bones of contention. In India, the jewel of the empire, a strong, multi-faceted, independence movement had taken root well before 1939. Its great moral leader, Mahatma Gandhi, though sympathetic to the Allies, maintained throughout the war his drive to achieve Indian sovereignty by means of peaceful protests; by the end of 1941, more than twenty-three thousand of his followers had been arrested. Indian nationalist Subhas Chandra Bose, meanwhile, had chosen another path; by January 1941, he had arrived in Germany to seek an alliance with Hitler (see May 8). At the same time, Muslim Indian leader Mohammad Ali Jinnah was calling for a separate state for Muslims, to be named "Pakistan." Despite this continuing domestic tumult (echoed in other British and French colonies), India contributed more than 2.5 million men to the Allied war effort; Indian soldiers were in the thick of combat in most theaters of the war.

LEFT: *Do you know that the colonies . . . ?* Color poster by Herrick, published by H. M. Stationery Office, between 1939 and 1941.

RIGHT: *What about India?* Color silk-screen poster by Maurice Merlin, published by the Michigan Federal Arts Project between 1941 and 1943.

APRIL 5

1941 In Moscow, Yugoslavian and Soviet representatives sign a treaty of friendship and nonaggression.

1945 Russia renounces the Russian-Japanese neutrality pact.

HERRICK

DO YOU KNOW THAT THE
COLONIES

produce over half the world's
rubber and a third of the tin:
that they are rich in sugar, tea,
coffee, cocoa and fruits: that
Colonial copper, gold and oil
are increasingly important.

THESE ARE THE SINEWS OF WAR

What about India?

India

"The heaviest effect of our operations against the English war economy has lain in the high losses in merchant shipping inflicted by sea and air warfare," Hitler wrote in his Directive Number 23, issued on February 6, 1941. "A further considerable increase is to be expected in the course of this year by the wider employment of submarines, and this can bring about the collapse of English resistance within the foreseeable future." By January 1941, the Allies had lost thirteen hundred merchant vessels, almost half of those to U-boats. Now fighting alone, the British were watching the reduction of their supplies with alarm. Heretofore, the ongoing contest in the Atlantic had been simply an economic warfare campaign; early in 1941, with the example of the Battle of Britain in mind, Winston Churchill told Admiral Sir Dudley Pound, "We have got to lift this business to the highest plane. . . . I am going to proclaim 'The Battle of the Atlantic.'" On March 6, he issued a Battle of the Atlantic Directive, emphasizing several tactics for combating this German offensive, and he formed the Battle of the Atlantic Committee. "The next four months," he predicted, "should enable us to defeat the attempt to strangle our food supplies and our connection with the United States." In fact, it was to take much longer. Yet, as the battle continued, one observation in Hitler's Directive 23 remained true: "The least effect of all (as far as we can see) has been made upon the morale and will to resist of the English people."

One of twelve cartoons from a satirical German calendar confiscated by U.S. military intelligence authorities. Photomechanical print, 1941.

APRIL 6

1941 Twelve hundred Luftwaffe planes support coordinated German attacks against Yugoslavia from Bulgaria, Romania, Austria, and Hungary. British troops enter Addis Ababa, Ethiopia—the first national capital liberated from the Axis.

F ive days after Churchill formed the Battle of the Atlantic Committee (see April 6), the U.S. Congress passed "An Act Further to promote the Defense of the United States, and for other purposes," authorizing the Lend-Lease Program. The idea for lending the British (and, later, other Allies) war matériel they could not immediately pay for grew out of a lengthy letter Churchill had written to Roosevelt on December 7, 1940, in which the prime minister declared, "The moment approaches when we shall no longer be able to pay cash for shipping and other supplies." Relaxing in the Caribbean after the 1940 election, Roosevelt examined the letter without saying much to his aides. "Then one evening," top adviser Harry Hopkins later wrote, "he suddenly came out with it—the whole program." The president introduced the lend-lease concept to the public in December and January (see April 1); introduction of the bill itself precipitated a stinging isolationist-versus-interventionist debate. Opponents called it a "war bill," decried the broad authority it gave the president, and condemned "humanitarian lollipopping all over the world." (To help counter the criticism, Roosevelt successfully pressured Britain to liquidate many of its few remaining assets to help pay for the construction of U.S. production facilities.) In the end, with polls showing that a majority of Americans favored helping Britain, the Lend-Lease Bill—amended to include some isolationist restrictions—passed by substantial majorities in both houses.

LEFT: President Franklin D. Roosevelt signs H. R. 1776, the Lend-Lease Bill, 1941.

RIGHT: Cases of TNT gunpowder shipped from the United States under Lend-Lease are stacked in a tunnel one hundred feet underground, dug out of solid rock in western England. U.S. Office of War Information photo, between 1941 and 1945.

APRIL 7

1941 The first British jet plane, a Gloster E28/39, is successfully test-flown.

"**S**omewhere over northern England an American flag has been waving its defiance at the totalitarian world since November, 1940," Byron Kennerly wrote in *The Eagles Roar!* (1942). "The flag marks the home base of the Eagle Squadron, RAF, the first all-American combat unit to see action in the second World War." As had been the case during World War I, some Americans chose to fight for the Allied cause before most of their countrymen were willing to face the prospect of war. In September 1940, the Royal Air Force established the first of three Eagle Squadrons (71 Squadron, to which Kennerly belonged); in May and August 1941, 121 and 133 Squadrons were created. The U.S. pilots, Kennerly reported, "were college students, engineers, construction workers, farmers, crop-dusting and commercial flyers. One was a stunt parachute jumper. All of them had two things in common. They loved to fly. They loved the freedom which flying symbolizes." At a heavy cost in casualties, the Eagle Squadrons compiled a proud combat record, continuing to fly with the RAF until the fall of 1942 when, at a change of command ceremony, most Eagles formed the Fourth Fighter Group of the U.S. Army Air Forces. "We of Fighter Command deeply regret this parting," chief of RAF Fighter Command Sholto Douglas said at the ceremony. "In . . . the past 18 months we have seen the stuff of which you are made. We could not ask for better companions with whom to see this fight through to a finish."

A group of U.S. pilots, members of the all-American Royal Air Force "Eagle Squadron," at an airfield "somewhere in England." (Left to right): Charles E. Bateman, San Gabriel, CA; William H. Nichols, San Carlos, CA; Stanley N. Kolendorski, Lakehurst, NJ; W. E. G. Taylor, New York City (squadron leader); Andrew Mamedoff, Thompson, CT; Eugene Q. Tobin, Los Angeles; Nathaniel Maranz, New York City; Luke E. Allen, Ignatio, CO; two unidentified men; Gregory A. Daymond, San Francisco; and Sam A. Mauriello, Astoria, NY. March 29, 1941.

APRIL 8

1942 About two thousand of the seventy-eight thousand Allied men defending Bataan escape to Corregidor. The U.S. Air Ferry Command begins vital supply flights over the Himalayas ("the Hump") to China.

On March 1, 1941, with American defense production heating up and Lend-Lease well on the way to approval (see April 7), the U.S. Senate established the seven-member Special Committee Investigating the National Defense Program. Charged with examining "the procurement and construction of supplies, materials, munitions, vehicles and facilities in connection with the national defense," it was to become one of the most effective investigative bodies in the Senate's history. It was popularly known as the Truman Committee, after its chairman, Missouri Democrat Harry S. Truman, who had suggested its creation. Earlier in the year, after receiving letters of complaint from his constituents, Truman had embarked on a ten-thousand-mile tour of military bases to check on the disposition of ten billion dollars in defense contracts that had been let in 1940. He returned outraged at the waste and inefficiency he encountered and disturbed that most contracts had been awarded to a handful of large companies. These were among the chief problems that the committee addressed when, on April 15, it embarked on years of highly effective hearings and on-site inspections. Truman won plaudits for honesty and determination, and the committee's work eventually drew a compliment from an early critic, U.S. Army Chief of Services and Supply General Brehon B. Somervell. The committee's examination of camp construction sites and other areas under his jurisdiction, Somervell said, had "saved the government $250 million."

Harry S. Truman , (center), with fellow Truman Committee members Homer Ferguson, Harold Hitz Burton, Thomas Terry Connally, and Ralph Owen Brewster, c. 1942.

APRIL 9

1940   Thirteen hundred German aircraft, including three hundred transport planes, take part in the invasion of Norway.

1945   British bombers sink the German cruisers *Admiral Scheer* and *Hipper* at Kiel.

"He who owns oil will own the world," French commissioner for oil Henry Bereger declared during World War I. The statement seemed even more apt during World War II, when the major combatants depended on huge fleets of oil-thirsty ships, planes, tanks, and transport vehicles to achieve their war aims. In the Far East, resource-poor Japan, no longer able to procure a ready supply of U.S. oil, was looking south, toward the oil-rich Dutch East Indies. In Europe, Germany was also thirsty for petroleum. German "oil commandos" (experts to get conquered European fields up and running again for the Reich) had accompanied the first waves of troops invading Poland, France, and the Low Countries. In spring 1941, the commandos were standing by to perform the same mission once Hitler abrogated his agreements with Stalin and the invading Wehrmacht overran the USSR's Caucasus oil fields. Beyond the Caucasus lay the vast oil resources of Iran and Iraq and the largely untapped riches of Saudi Arabia—all coveted by both Axis and Allies. In April and May 1941, British troops had defeated a coup attempt in Iraq that briefly installed pro-Nazi leader Rashid Ali as head of government. In neighboring Iran, the government of Shah Reza Pahlavi still maintained close ties with Germany. By the end of the year, both these nations would be host to large contingents of Allied troops charged with developing, maintaining, and protecting supply routes for oil and Lend-Lease supplies.

LEFT: *Fifty-fifty Again, Joe?* Ink, crayon, and opaque white drawing by Herbert Block ("Herblock"), May 2, 1941, when Germany and the USSR were still adhering to their mutual trade and nonaggression pacts.

RIGHT: Supplies from India and Lend-Lease. Map showing Allied supply-line routes, including those used to transport oil. *Illustrated London News*, November 22, 1941.

APRIL 10

1944 Soviet forces recapture the Black Sea port of Odessa from the Germans.

THE MIDDLE-EAST CAMPAIGN: A RELIEF MAP OF RAILROADS, HIGHWAYS, AND MAIN ROUTES OF ANGLO-AMERICAN SUPPLIES TO RUSSIA, CONVERGING ON THE CAUCASUS;

On March 12, 1941, Japanese foreign minister Yosuke Matsuoka departed Tokyo for a six-week trip to the German and Soviet capitals. An adept negotiator (known at home as the "talking machine"), he had done much to secure bases for Japan in northern French Indochina. He had also lived and been schooled in the United States and had derived from that experience the belief that the best way to keep the Americans from interfering in Japanese plans was to take a firm stance—and form strong alliances. On this trip, Matsuoka hoped to begin engineering a quadruple alliance among the three major Axis partners and the Soviet Union (despite quiet warnings from Japan's Berlin ambassador that Germany and the USSR might soon be at war). In Berlin, Matsuoka dominated his conversations with the usually more-loquacious Hitler—and evaded German pressure that Japan enter the war and wrest the strategic Chinese port city of Shanghai from British control. Shrugging off German foreign minister Joachim von Ribbentrop's negative response to a possible Japanese-Soviet alliance, he moved on to Moscow—just as German armies invaded the Balkans (see April 13), where the Soviets had extensive interests. "Now," Matsuoka exulted, "I have the agreement with Stalin in my pocket!" Matsuoka and Stalin signed the Japanese-Soviet Neutrality Pact on April 13, as Stalin was receiving German assurances that their Balkans campaign was directed against the British and constituted no threat to the Soviets.

Hitler and Hermann Göring greet Japanese foreign minister Yosuke Matsuoka during Matsuoka's visit to Germany, March 28, 1941.

APRIL 11

1940   In the second battle of Narvik, Norway, which begins today, the British sink seven German destroyers.

1945   Allied forces liberate survivors of the Buchenwald concentration camp.

Named U.S. ambassador to Japan in 1932, Joseph C. Grew was uniquely qualified for the role by training, empathy, and family connections. A career diplomat (and a classmate of President Roosevelt's at Groton and Harvard), the eloquent and aristocratic Grew was married to Alice Perry, who had lived in Japan and was a descendant of Commodore Matthew Perry. (The commodore's U.S. Navy squadron had sailed into Tokyo harbor in 1853, opening Japan to the outside world after more than two centuries.) The Grews formed fast friendships among the Japanese, as the ambassador did his best to counter the misperceptions that were widening the gulf between Japan and America. "I . . . incline to the opinion," he wrote in his journal on May 27, 1941, "that in his talks with me [Foreign Minister Yosuke Matsuoka] follows the carefully studied policy of painting the darkest picture of what will happen if the United States gets into war against Germany, probably in the mistaken belief that such tactics may serve to exert a restraining influence on American policy. Soon after Mr. Matsuoka took office he indicated that his platform would be that the United States could and should be intimidated into adopting an attitude of complete isolation with regard to both the Far East and Europe. That platform was implemented by the Three-Power [Axis] Alliance, which action not only failed to have the desired effect but was one of the major factors in stimulating the trend of American opinion away from isolationism."

LEFT: Joseph Clark Grew (1880–1965), U.S. ambassador to Japan, with his wife, Alice Perry Grew, photographed in San Francisco as they prepared to return to Japan on the *Yatbuta Maru*, 1936.

RIGHT: *View of the U.S. Capitol from Meriken kōkai nikki ryakuzu* ("Journal and Sketches from the Voyage to America"), chronicling the first Japanese diplomatic mission to the United States. Watercolor, 1860.

APRIL 12

1945 Franklin Delano Roosevelt dies at his retreat in Warm Springs, Georgia. Harry S. Truman becomes president of the United States.

議事堂

景色頗ル
江上眺望

アレキサンデリヤ

Initially considered by both Hitler and Mussolini to be one of Italy's prime areas for empire building, by early 1941 the Balkans had become a potential monkey wrench in German plans. Italian armies were faring poorly in their attempted conquest of Greece (see March 28); should they fail altogether, the Greeks might allow the British to establish bases on their soil, placing Hitler's forthcoming campaign against the Soviet Union in jeopardy. Hitler made both diplomatic and military preparations to assist Mussolini. On March 25, German pressure brought Greece's neighbor, Yugoslavia, into the Axis; two days later, a Yugoslavian coup took it out again. An enraged Hitler added a new objective to his Balkan campaign, telling his military commanders to "smash Yugoslavia militarily, and as a state." When the campaign began, on April 6, Luftwaffe attacks savaged the Yugoslavian capital of Belgrade and killed seventeen thousand civilians—the largest number killed in one day since the war began. At the same time, German troops slashed into southern Yugoslavia and northern Greece from Bulgaria. Despite furious resistance from the Greeks, and from British troops that had recently reinforced them, by April 24, both Yugoslavia and Greece had been forced to surrender. Nearly fifty-one thousand Allied troops managed to withdraw to Crete and Alexandria. Those on Crete would shortly be killed, captured, or forced to retreat again when the Germans staged Operation Mercury May 20–29, the first all-airborne invasion in history.

ABOVE: *The Greeks Have a Word—Courage.* Drawing by John R. McGaw, April 1941.

RIGHT: German units moving southward through Greece, despite heavy spring rains and muddy roads, April 1941.

APRIL 13

1941   With Rommel's forces encircling Tobruk, Winston Churchill assures Franklin Roosevelt that the British will not abandon North Africa—but they will need supplies from the United States.

As Greece began years of Axis occupation and the Wehrmacht ended its successful campaign on Crete (see April 13), the 41,673-ton German battleship, *Bismarck*, set sail on its first combat mission on May 18, 1941. It had been ordered to join Operation *Rheinübung*, a campaign against Allied convoys, but the British interrupted these plans. On May 24, the battle cruiser *Hood* and the battleship *Prince of Wales* located and engaged *Bismarck* and the heavy cruiser *Prinz Eugen* in the Denmark Strait, southeast of Iceland. It was a disastrous encounter—for the British. Shells from *Bismarck*'s great guns found the *Hood*'s magazines, and the ship disappeared in a fiery round of explosions; only three of its fifteen-hundred-man crew survived. *Prince of Wales* was badly damaged, but *Bismarck* had also been hit. Separating from *Prinz Eugen*, *Bismarck* headed toward occupied France for repairs. After an error-plagued 1,750-mile pursuit, the British caught up with *Bismarck* on May 26. Swordfish biplanes from the carrier *Ark Royal* scored hits that jammed *Bismarck*'s rudder as the battleship was turning, forcing it to sail in circles while the battleships *King George V* and *Rodney* and smaller warships moved in. On May 27, the British sank the *Bismarck*, which went down with all but one hundred of its two-thousand-man crew. The destruction of the newly launched pride of the German fleet made Hitler cautious in deploying his remaining capital ships—and reinforced the German navy's reliance on U-boats.

The German battleship *Bismarck* suffering the effects of a torpedo from the British crusier *Dorsetshire* (left background). Painting by Walter Zeeden, reproduced in *Bismarck*, published in Germany, 1950.

APRIL 14

1944 To help prevent word of the planned Allied invasion of France from leaking out, Britain sharply restricts diplomatic privileges.

At 3:15 A.M. on June 22, 1941, at the town of Koden, on the border between German-occupied and Soviet-occupied Poland, German sentries summoned their Soviet counterparts onto a bridge for a meeting. As the Soviets approached, the Germans let loose with machine guns—one of many small treacheries that preceded Operation Barbarossa, Hitler's long-planned massive blitzkrieg assault on the Soviet Union. By 5:30 A.M., when the German ambassador in Moscow presented the Reich's declaration of war to Foreign Minister Vyacheslav Molotov, three million Germans were hurtling across the USSR's borders, shoving aside weak Red Army defenses as the Luftwaffe shattered Russian planes before they could leave the ground and lacerated Soviet armor. For months, Stalin had been receiving reports that a German invasion was imminent; his reliable Tokyo-based spy, Richard Sorge, had even transmitted the correct date. Possibly because he believed the reports were a ploy to disrupt the Soviet-German alliance, Stalin refused to believe them. Now he, his unprepared armed forces, and millions of civilians in the paths of the three-pronged German assault were engulfed in a conflict that was marked, from the beginning, by near-bestial savagery. "The war against Russia cannot be fought in knightly fashion," Hitler had declared in a pre-invasion order. "The struggle is one of ideologies and racial differences, and will have to be waged with unprecedented, unmerciful and unrelenting hardness."

Nächtlicher Kampf ("Night Battle"). Halftone color photomechanical print of a painting by Walter Gotschke (1912–2000), 1941.

APRIL 15

1941 Roosevelt signs an executive order that will allow men to resign from the U.S. armed forces so that they can join the American Volunteer Group headed by Claire Chennault. Operating in China, the group will be more familiarly known as the Flying Tigers.

"**G**erman People! National Socialists! . . . For weeks constant violations of this frontier have taken place. . . . This has brought us to the hour when it is necessary for us to take steps against this plot devised by the Jewish Anglo-Saxon warmongers and equally the Jewish rulers of the Bolshevist center in Moscow. . . . At this moment a march is taking place that, as regards extent, compares with the greatest the world hitherto has seen."

Adolf Hitler
Proclamation on War with the Soviet Union, June 23, 1941

"**C**omrades! . . . By virtue of this war which has been forced upon us, our country has come to death-grips with its most malicious and most perfidious enemy—German fascism. . . . The enemy is cruel and implacable . . . thus the issue is one of life or death for the Soviet States, . . . there must be no room in our ranks for whimperers and cowards, for panic-mongers and deserters. Our people must know no fear in fight and must selflessly join our patriotic war of liberation, our war against the fascist enslavers."

Joseph Stalin
Radio address, July 3, 1941

LEFT: *A Modern Version of the Kilkenny Cats*. Drawing by Clifford Berryman (1869–1949), June 29, 1941.

RIGHT: Map showing the German plan of attack on the Soviet Union. Illustration from *A Graphic History of the War*, September 1, 1939 to May 10, 1942, published by the U.S. War Department, 1942.

APRIL 16

1942 The British government awards the George Cross—given only for the most valiant of deeds—to the entire island of Malta.

A MODERN VERSION OF THE KILKENNY CATS.

"No one has been a more consistent opponent of communism than I have," Churchill declared during a radio broadcast on June 22, 1941, "but all this fades away before the spectacle which is now unfolding." That spectacle was the German invasion of the Soviet Union (see April 15), then just a few hours old. "We shall give whatever help we can to Russia and to the Russian people," Churchill pledged. This was important on principle—and it was a practical necessity. The Nazis would not be satisfied with victory on the eastern front. If Hitler succeeded there, the prime minister said, "he will be able to bring back the main strength of his army and air force from the East and hurl it upon this island, which he knows he must conquer or suffer the penalty of his crimes." Both British and American military analysts shared Hitler's view that the Red Army was too weak to resist the Germans for long. Yet every day the Wehrmacht concentrated on its campaign in the east was a day the Western Allies would have to build their strength. The Soviets, meanwhile, were suffering devastating losses in men and machines, and they immediately acted on Churchill's pledge of assistance. On June 29, they presented to the British ambassador in Moscow a daunting list of matériel (including an impossible six thousand aircraft). As limited shipments began, the two countries signed an Agreement for Joint Action on July 12, pledging mutual assistance and affirming that neither would conclude a separate peace with the Germans.

An artist's conception of the first face-to-face meeting of Joseph Stalin and Winston Churchill. Color drawing by Edward Sorel (b. 1929), 1991.

APRIL 17

1944 A Seattle restaurant owner places an ad that reflects the desperate shortage of workers on the home front: "Woman wanted to wash dishes. Will marry if necessary."

In his June 22, 1941, speech pledging aid to the Russians (see April 17), Winston Churchill declared that the British would "bomb Germany by day as well as by night in ever-increasing measure . . . making the German people taste . . . the miseries they have showered upon mankind." Britain had been slow to adopt the concept of strategic bombing (aimed at the destruction of enemy war resources, such as civilian-manned factories and transportation), a reflection of the abhorrence of "terror bombing" that had prevailed during the interwar years. After the Low Countries and France fell and surviving Allied forces were pushed back into Britain, however, attitudes changed. In July 1940, as the Battle of Britain raged in England's skies (see March 22), Churchill wrote Minister of Aircraft Production Lord Beaverbrook, "We have no Continental army which can defeat the German military power . . . there is one thing that will bring . . . [Hitler] down, and that is an absolutely devastating exterminating attack by very heavy bombers from this country upon the Nazi homeland." A new factor entered the strategic calculus after the Soviet Union joined the war against Germany: Stalin insisted that the Western Allies take the pressure off his hard-pressed forces by opening a second front in the west. Yet, in 1941, a land assault against the Germans in western Europe was clearly impossible. For the time being, bombers would be the Allies' chief offensive weapon there.

Allied air offensive against Germany. Color poster published in Britain, c. 1940–41

APRIL 18

1945 One of America's most celebrated and beloved war correspondents, Ernie Pyle, is killed by Japanese fire on Ie Shima in the Ryukyu Islands.

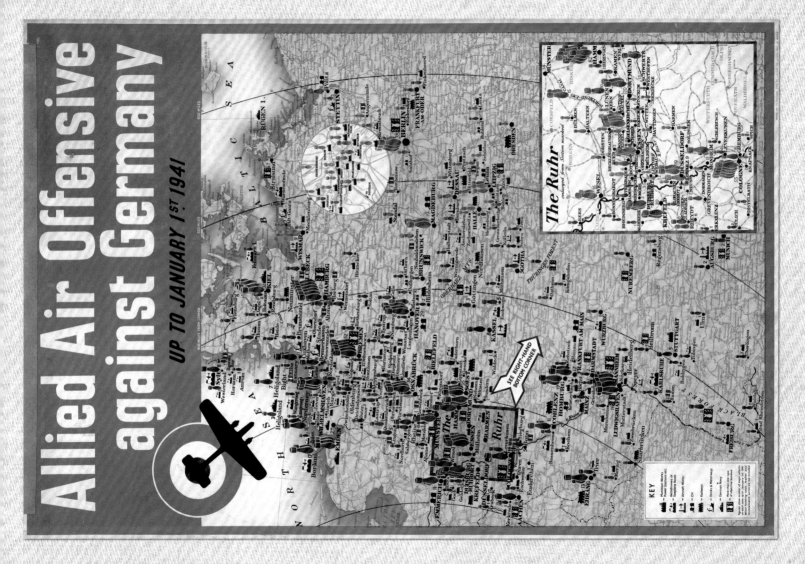

Japan's new ambassador to the United States, retired admiral Kichisaburo Nomura, assumed his duties in February 1941, as negotiations to resolve the growing differences between the two nations were proceeding along two sometimes-contradictory tracks. Informally (but with the covert assistance of the U.S. government), Catholic bishop James E. Walsh and Father James M. Drought had broached to Japanese contacts a proposal based on establishing a Japanese "Far Eastern Monroe Doctrine" and maintaining a stand against the "corroding social disease" of Communism. Meanwhile, Cordell Hull and his State Department staff continued official exchanges. Unbeknownst to the Japanese, the Americans were able to read Japan's "Purple" diplomatic code. Translations of intercepted messages into English were often faulty, however, a fact that contributed to the suspicions and confusion that plagued these diplomatic efforts. Events added to the tension: In July, after General Hideki Tojo's elevation to prime minister, the replacement of Foreign Minister Matsuoka with Admiral Teijiro Toyoda, and the movement of Japanese troops into southern French Indochina, the U.S. government froze all Japanese assets in America. By then, the debate within Japan over whether to expand to the north (involving a clash with the Soviet Union) or to move south (leading to a clash with the European colonial powers and the United States) had been decided in favor of the south. Yet war was not yet certain. Negotiations continued.

Japan's newly arrived ambassador to the United States, Adm. Kichisaburo Nomura (1877–1964), meets with U.S. Secretary of State Cordell Hull (1871–1955), February 1941.

APRIL 19

1943 Jews in the Warsaw ghetto begin a heroic but suicidal uprising.

On April 23, 1941, sixteen American conscientious objectors, among the six thousand jailed throughout the war for their refusal to serve in the military or in Civilian Public Service camps, refused to eat or work after their prison warden stopped them from supporting a national student strike for peace. Remaining a noncombatant nation was still the desire of most Americans, but since the fall of France in June 1940, support had been growing for such interventionist measures as Lend-Lease assistance. Throughout 1941, the verbal war between interventionist and isolationist groups continued. "When history is written," Charles Lindbergh argued in a speech before the America First Committee on April 23, "the responsibility for the downfall of the democracies of Europe will rest squarely upon the shoulders of the interventionists who led their nations into war uninformed and unprepared. . . . they have already sent countless thousands of young men to death in Europe." "To say that Hitler's defeat is essential to insure man's freedom is a cowardly and immoral position, unless we are willing to face the dangers and sacrifices others are suffering in this struggle for freedom," Episcopal bishop Henry W. Hobson of the interventionist Century Group stated that same month. The isolationist versus interventionist split was reflected in the mid-August vote that extended the Selective Service Act for one year. It passed in the House by only one vote.

LEFT: *Unter den Lindbergh*, a cartoon criticizing Charles Lindbergh's political views. Drawing by Rollin Kirby (1875–1952), October 7, 1941.

RIGHT: *Fall Planting*. Black ink drawing by Clarence Daniel Batchelor (1888–1977) depicting the ravages of World War II in Europe, as representatives of the U.S. "War Party" and "Peace Party" debate, November 1, 1941.

APRIL 20

1941 The Germans cut off Greek forces in Macedonia and Epirus. Greece is forced to capitulate to Axis forces.

The Selective Service and Training Bill that was enacted in September 1940 (see March 30) included the stipulation that "there shall be no discrimination against any person on account of race or color." The result of pressure that came primarily from the black press and organizations such as the Committee for Negro Participation in the National Defense and the NAACP, as well as from sympathetic whites, this provision did nothing to end racial discrimination in the segregated U.S. military. Yet it was part of a slow movement toward change. In 1940, Roosevelt promoted Benjamin O. Davis Sr. from colonel to brigadier general, making him the first African American general officer in the history of U.S. armed forces. Having worked his way up through the ranks (he enlisted as a private during the 1898 Spanish-American War), Davis continued his service throughout World War II, including a tour of duty in the European Theater of Operations. His son, Benjamin O. Davis Jr., graduated from West Point in 1936 and was commissioned in the infantry. At that time, African Americans were not allowed in the U.S. Army Air Corps. In 1941, the newly renamed U.S. Army Air Forces established a segregated fighter unit, whose pilots were to be trained at the Tuskegee Institute in Alabama. The younger Davis was among the first thirteen men to receive pilot training. He went on to command the Italy-based 332nd Fighter Group—and become the first African American general in the postwar U.S. Air Force.

ABOVE: Brig. Gen. Benjamin O. Davis Sr. somewhere in France. U.S. Army Signal Corps photograph c. 1944.

RIGHT: Capt. Benjamin O. Davis Jr. climbing into an advanced training plane at the flying school for African American air corps cadets, Tuskegee, Alabama. U.S. Army Air Forces photograph, January 1942.

APRIL 21

1942 President Roosevelt orders the seizure of all patents controlled or owned by nations at war with the United States.

"I must be at the side of Hitler in Russia as he was at mine in the war against Greece," Mussolini declared in June 1941. "The destiny of Italy is intimately bound up with that of Germany." In fact, by then, the destiny of Fascist Italy *depended* on Germany, whose armed forces had been required to rescue the Italians' flagging Greek and North African campaigns (see April 4, 13, 23). In East Africa, where the Italians had no German assistance, the British had taken Italian Somaliland in March and by August had secured nearly all of Ethiopia. In an effort to bolster Italian prestige, and to defend Italy's right to claim a share of eastern front spoils, Mussolini convinced a reluctant Hitler to include a sixty-thousand-man Italian force in his assault on the Soviet Union. Italy could ill afford to spare these men from the Mediterranean campaigns—yet, while visiting Hitler at his eastern headquarters in August, Mussolini pressed the führer to accept even more Italian troops. Hitler equivocated, his obvious lack of eagerness to accept Mussolini's latest offer was only one of the reasons Il Duce emerged from the meeting in less than good humor. Italy's foreign minister, meanwhile, had been worried about sending any troops at all. "I am concerned about a direct comparison between our forces and the Germans," Count Galeazzo Ciano wrote in his diary on June 26. "Not because of the men, who are, or may be, excellent, but because of their equipment. I should not like to see us play the role of a poor relation yet again."

Benito Mussolini, Hermann Göring, and Adolf Hitler with staff officers, probably near the führer's headquarters at Rastenburg, East Prussia, August 26, 1941.

APRIL 22

1941 Two thousand U.S. army reinforcements are sent to the Philippines. A joint U.S.– New Zealand Naval Command is established.

After two less-than-successful counterattacks against Rommel's German-Italian forces in North Africa—operations Brevity in May and Battleaxe in mid-June—the British high command sent General Sir Claude Auchinleck to assume command in the Middle East. On November 18, after intercepted German messages indicated that Rommel's forces had been weakened because of the campaign against the Soviet Union, reorganized British and Commonwealth forces launched Operation Crusader—a costly month-long series of armored clashes. Rommel's army (now designated Panzer Group Afrika) initially out-maneuvered and outgunned the British. But Rommel lost the advantage after he divided his forces to stage a raid into Egypt. Throughout his offensive, Allied bombers and submarines based on Malta had pummeled convoys bound from Italy to North Africa, causing an aggravated Rommel to dub the island the "scorpion of the sea." Now, with the resources that had made it through depleted and his supply lines stretched too thin, he was forced to withdraw across the Libyan province of Cyrenaica. By mid-December, he was back in El Agheila, where he had begun his offensive in March (see April 4). This setback led Hitler to appoint Field Marshal Albert Kesselring commander in chief south. Among the field marshal's principal duties: to "secure mastery of the air and sea in the area between Southern Italy and North Africa . . . and . . . paralyze enemy traffic through the Mediterranean."

German infantrymen advance toward the Egyptian border in North Africa, May 1941.

APRIL 23

1941 Charles A. Lindbergh speaks against U.S. involvement in the war at the first mass rally of the America First Committee in New York City.

1945 British troops enter Bremen, Germany.

While British submarines were sinking ships laden with supplies meant for Rommel in the Mediterranean (see April 23), German U-boats continued to prey on Britain-bound convoys in the Atlantic. The Lend-Lease Bill (see April 7) specifically prohibited the still-officially-neutral U.S. Navy from escorting convoys. Yet with the British and Canadian navies spread increasingly thin, shipping losses were mounting—and Roosevelt began exploring ways to circumvent that restriction. On April 10, employing creative logic to comply with Selective Service restrictions on where U.S. draftees might serve, he declared the remote Danish colony of Greenland part of the Western Hemisphere (and thus subject to the Monroe Doctrine) and announced its occupation by American forces. Two months later, he used similar logic to justify the occupation of the Danish territory of Iceland. U.S. Navy vessels could now extend their patrols to these two territories, both of which lay along convoy routes. After Roosevelt's meeting with Churchill at Argentia Bay, Nova Scotia (see May 1, 2), patrol duty included providing armed escort service to convoys as far as Iceland. Hitler still forbade his fuming naval commanders from doing anything to bring America into the war—yet clashes did occur between the two navies. On October 31, USS *Reuben James*, escorting eastbound convoy HX-56, broke in two and sank when a torpedo from German submarine U-552 exploded its magazine. Only forty-four of the ship's 159-man crew survived.

GIs disembark from U.S. Navy launches after a trip from the United States that was kept secret until the troops were out of danger from possible submarine action against the transports that brought them to this strategic Atlantic post, October 1941

APRIL 24

1941   Bulgaria declares war on Greece and Yugoslavia.

1945   Through a neutral go-between, SS chief Heinrich Himmler offers to surrender to Britain and the United States but not to the Soviet Union.

"If you attack us," Admiral Harold R. Stark said to Japanese ambassador Kichisaburo Nomura in 1941, "we will break your empire before we are through with you." The admiral's confidence was real, but, as U.S. chief of naval operations (August 1939–March 1942), Stark was also fully aware of what remained to be done to expand the navy by 70 percent, as authorized by passage of the Vinson Walsh Act in July 1940. A massive building program was under way, but the "two-ocean navy" wasn't scheduled to be operational until 1946. In the interim, the United States would have to husband its naval resources. Keeping Britain in the war—and the Royal Navy on patrol in the Atlantic—was therefore essential. Meanwhile, it was hoped that keeping the Pacific Fleet at Pearl Harbor, Hawaii, midway between the United States and Japan, would deter Japanese expansion in the Pacific. Yet in July the Japanese had occupied the whole of French Indochina, threatening the Dutch East Indies and the Philippines, and by November intelligence intercepts had made it clear that Japan was preparing for war. "Chances of favorable outcome of negotiations with Japan very doubtful," Stark cabled the Pearl Harbor and Philippines naval commanders on November 24. "This situation coupled with statements of Japanese Government and movements of their naval and military forces indicate in our opinion that a surprise aggressive movement in any direction including attack on Philippines or Guam is a possibility."

ABOVE: Adm. Harold R. Stark (1880–1972). U.S. Navy photograph, between 1935 and 1945.

RIGHT: U.S. Pacific Fleet maneuvers near Hawaii, September 1940.

APRIL 25

1943 A British officer, Comm. Robert Alexander Allan, leads a spectacularly successful gunboat/torpedo boat raid against a German convoy in Italian waters.

"**A**ir raid on Pearl Harbor. This is no drill." On Sunday, December 7, 1941, while bombs were still falling on U.S. ships in Hawaii, the first alerts that America had been brutally swept into war went out to the U.S. mainland and naval vessels at sea. At 7:55 A.M. the first of three waves of carrier-based Japanese fighters and bombers had screamed out of the sky and ravaged the unprepared U.S. Pacific Fleet, moored in close formation (see April 27). Part of a naval strike force commanded by Vice Admiral Chuichi Nagumo, the Japanese pilots were executing a plan developed by Admiral Isoroku Yamamoto on the assumption that a crippling blow to America's Pacific navy would keep the United States from effectively moving to counter Japan's southward expansion for at least two years. Yet the hugely destructive attack did not touch the fleet's three aircraft carriers, *Enterprise*, *Lexington*, and *Saratoga*, which were not at Pearl Harbor that morning; nor did the Japanese destroy Hawaii-based submarines. Moreover, because of delays, Ambassador Kichisaburo Nomura did not present Secretary of State Cordell Hull with Japan's war message until the raid was already in progress. Fury at Japanese perfidy in starting a war, "while carrying on peace negotiations," as the president told his cabinet that night, would do much to fuel the epic war effort that Americans would engage in over the next four years.

LEFT: *Admiral Yamamoto.* Ink and pencil drawing of Adm. Isoroku Yamamoto (1884–1943) by Arthur Szyk. *Time* magazine published this image on its cover December 22, 1941, under the heading "Japan's Aggressor: Admiral Yamamoto. His was the daring execution of a brilliant treachery."

RIGHT: Pearl Harbor. U.S. Navy map showing the location of American facilities and ships at Pearl Harbor, the headquarters of the U.S. Pacific Command, just before the Japanese attack on December 7, 1941.

APRIL 26

1945 U.S. troops on Okinawa meet furious Japanese resistance on the Maeda Escarpment, as, offshore, kamikaze (suicide) pilots maintain their costly assault on Allied naval vessels.

ARTHUR SZYK, N.Y. 1941.

0 — 1
STATUTE MILE

AKI

KALAUAO

Waiau Bank

PEARL CITY   East Loch

AIEA

Clipper
Base

PHOENIX

HOSPITAL SHIP
(SOLACE)

DETROIT

RALEIGH

NEVADA

CURTISS

ARIZONA

VESTAL

UTAH

TENNESSEE

W. VIRGINIA

TANGIER

FORD
ISLAND

MARYLAND

OKLAHOMA

HALAWA

CALIFORNIA

NEOSHO

MAKALAPA
CRATER

HELENA

NEW ORLEANS

OGLALA

SAN FRANCISCO

Submarine
Base

SHAW

HONOLULU

WAIPIO
PENINSULA

ST. LOUIS

DOWNES

Navy
Yard

PENNSYLVANIA

Puuloa
Station

CASSIN

Smoke and flames still covered the U.S. base at Pearl Harbor when Admiral Harold R. Stark sent instructions to all commanders in the Pacific area and Panama: "Execute unrestricted air and submarine warfare against Japan." Organizing the first air strike against Japan would take several months (see June 15), but U.S. submarines would be in Japanese waters by January. Meanwhile, Americans would put out the fires—and begin to honor the heroism displayed by so many who were caught in the surprise attack. "Praise the Lord and pass the ammunition," Chaplain Howell M. Forgy said, encouraging the men aboard USS *New Orleans* as they ducked incoming fire and loaded their guns. On the *West Virginia*, ship's cook Doris ("Dorie") Miller dragged his commanding officer out of the line of fire and manned a machine gun. Sailors braved heat and flame to pull men from the water, while the few airmen who managed to get their planes off the ground went after an entire Japanese strike force. The post-attack damage assessment was grim: Two battleships, *Arizona* and *Oklahoma*, were lost; two more were disabled; eleven other warships were sunk or severely damaged; 188 land-based U.S. aircraft were destroyed. The machines could be replaced, and the twelve hundred people who had been wounded could be rehabilitated. But the Japanese had taken 2,343 American lives. December 7, 1941, President Roosevelt told Congress and the nation the next day, was "a date that will live in infamy."

ABOVE: *Above and beyond the call of duty—Dorie Miller received the Navy Cross at Pearl Harbor, May 27, 1942.* Color poster by David Stone Martin. U.S. Government Printing Office, 1943.

RIGHT: American sailors attempt to contain the flames consuming the battleship USS *West Virginia*, December 1941.

APRIL 27

1941 The Germans occupy Athens.

1942 President Roosevelt places the American economy on a full war footing.

As night fell on Washington on December 7, 1941, people gathered across the street from the White House. Inside the president dictated the address he would make to Congress the next day, prepared for an emergency meeting of his cabinet that had been called for 8:30 P.M.—and received a phone call from Winston Churchill. "They have attacked Pearl Harbor," he said, in response to Churchill's inquiry. "We are all in the same boat now." Aides bustled in and out as more bulletins came in from Hawaii, each one bringing worse news than the last. When the cabinet assembled, Roosevelt told the shocked administration leaders what he knew of the attack and said that, for the time being, they should keep the extent of the damage done to the Pacific Fleet confidential. When congressional leaders joined the meeting, he gave them a less-detailed briefing and arranged to address Congress at 12:30 P.M. the following day. Meanwhile, at the local NBC radio studio, Eleanor Roosevelt became the first public figure to address the nation about the attack when she prefaced her regular Sunday-evening radio broadcast with reassuring words. "For months now the knowledge that something of this kind might happen has been hanging over our heads," she told her audience. "That is all over now and there is no more uncertainty. We know what we have to face and we know we are ready to face it. . . . Whatever is asked of us, I am sure we can accomplish it; we are the free and unconquerable people of the U.S.A."

The White House on the evening of December 7, 1941, as President Roosevelt confers with cabinet officials and congressional leaders.

APRIL 28

1945 Benito Mussolini is shot and killed by Italian partisans as he attempts to flee Italy.

A GLOBAL CONFLICT: 1941

On December 8, as the United States, Great Britain, Canada, New Zealand, and other countries declared war on Japan, the Japanese attacked the Philippine Islands, landed at the British colony of Malaya (Malaysia), occupied the International Settlement in Shanghai, China, placed Hong Kong under siege, and attacked Singapore, Guam, Midway, and Wake island. Three days later, Germany and Italy declared war on the United States. The wars in Asia and Europe had now merged into a world conflagration—one that was going all too well for the Axis. On December 22, Roosevelt, Churchill, and the U.S. and British chiefs of staff assembled in Washington, D.C., for their first strategic conference as allied combatants. Code-named Arcadia, the three-week conference established the Combined (American and British) Chiefs of Staff, to be headquartered in Washington; established a combined American-British-Dutch-Australian (ABDA) command; and framed the United Nations Declaration, announced to the world on January 1 (see May 2). The scene of stormy discussions, as well as accord (a characteristic of the special U.S./U.K. relationship throughout the war), ARCADIA also helped forge a closer relationship between Roosevelt and Churchill, who stayed at the White House throughout. Churchill later wrote of that visit, "I formed a very strong affection, which grew with our years of comradeship, for this formidable politician . . . whose heart seemed to respond to many of the impulses that stirred my own."

British military leaders at the White House during the Arcadia conference: (left to right) Admiral of the fleet Sir Dudley Pound; Air Chief Mar. Sir Charles Portal; Sir John G. Dill, retiring chief of the British imperial staff and soon to be Britain's military representative in Washington; Lt. Gen. Sir Colville Wemyss, an adviser, and Air Marshal Arthur Harris, December 27, 1941.

APRIL 29

1945 After designating Admiral Karl Dönitz his successor, Hitler marries his longtime companion, Eva Braun, in his Berlin bunker.

In October 1941, Americans recognized the importance of sustaining the Soviet Union in its war against Germany by including the USSR in the Lend-Lease Program. At the same time, the Soviets, having transported more than two thousand industrial plants out of the range of German bombers, were beginning to reestablish their own war production. Against prevailing beliefs, they were also maintaining their military defense—but at a terrible cost. Entire armies had been surrounded and destroyed; by December, the Germans had taken between two and three million military prisoners, whom they treated abominably. Mass murders were common—the Germans executed Jews, political officers, and partisans by the thousands. Still, Soviet resistance, and German miscalculations, had put Hitler's plan for speedy conquest well behind schedule. Moscow, he believed, was the key, and on October 2, the Germans launched Operation Typhoon, a massive assault that pushed to within sixty miles of the city. As the Germans closed in, they ran into Soviet defenses hastily created by soldiers and civilians commanded by Marshal Georgi Zhukov—and a frigid Russian winter. German equipment broke down; soldiers froze. A renewed assault on the Russian capital in November almost succeeded, but in the end, the Nazis were forced to halt. "The offensive on Moscow has ended," Field Marshal Heinz Guderian wrote in his journal on December 5. "All the sacrifices and efforts of our brilliant troops have failed. We have suffered a serious defeat."

LEFT: *Nashe delo pravoe; pobeda budet za nami*. ("Our cause is just; victory will be ours"). 1970 reprint of a 1941 color poster commemorating Soviet victory in World War II.

RIGHT: *Otstoem Moskvu* ("Defend Moscow"). 1970 reprint of a 1941 color poster commemorating Soviet victory in World War II.

APRIL 30

1945 The day after their marriage, Hitler and Eva Braun commit suicide in the führer's underground bunker in Berlin.

НАШЕ ДЕЛО ПРАВОЕ

ПОБЕДА БУДЕТ ЗА НАМИ

ОТСТОИМ МОСКВУ!

Interlude: Allies Versus the Axis

"If we are together nothing is impossible," British prime minister Winston Churchill told an American audience at Harvard University in 1943. "If we are divided all will fail." Since December 1941, the United States and Great Britain had, together, formed the head and heart of the United Nations alliance that, by the end of the war, included forty-five countries. Representatives of all the Allied governments endorsed eight principles, as set forth in the Atlantic Charter, which Churchill and President Franklin Roosevelt framed during a shipboard meeting off Newfoundland, August 9–12, 1941. Prominent among those principles was a determination to respect "the right of all peoples to choose the form of government under which they will live." The three central members of the Axis alliance—Germany, Japan, and Italy—shared an exactly opposite aim: All were engaged in ruthless campaigns to impose their rule on vast areas of the globe.

This simple differentiation of the two warring camps masks a volatile tangle of political motivations that marked every aspect of the war—including the formation of alliances: Hitler, who proclaimed Nazi Germany the defender of the purity and superiority of the so-called Aryan race, allied Germany with non-Aryan Japan. The Allied nations defending democratic principles included (after a brief Russo-German détente) the Soviet Union—whose government, under Stalin, bore much more

MAY 1

1937 President Roosevelt signs the "permanent" Neutrality Act, essentially banning the American government and American businesses from providing weapons or financial assistance to belligerent nations.

1940 President Roosevelt asks Italy not to enter the war.

striking similarities to the brutal Nazi regime than it did to any democratic body. Among the dozens of national groups comprising the Soviet Union, there were some that resented Russian-Communist domination so strongly that they allied themselves with the German invaders. In the Far East, some nationalists seeking independence from British and French colonial rule supported Japan—until they realized that the Japanese "new order" would not allow them the independence they sought. Other warring countries—from China and Burma to Yugoslavia and France—were riven by internal differences as they coped with Axis assaults and occupation.

Within the two warring alliances, military and political cooperation differed sharply not only in aims but in methods of operation. Axis leaders generally viewed their alliance as a propaganda tool and a means to further their individual military and political goals, rather than a means to implement an overall, mutually beneficial strategy. Allied cooperation was built on a much stronger base. Rooted in the special relationship between the United States and Great Britain, it was maintained by the Combined (U.S. and British) Chiefs of Staff Committee and by a series of strategy conferences. Allied aims were also bolstered by America's astonishing wartime industrial output and, after June 22, 1941, by the epic

struggle between Germany and the Soviet Union, which kept an estimated 60 percent of the Wehrmacht mired in the East.

There were many inter-Allied disagreements—even the close Anglo-American ties were occasionally strained. As the tide of war turned, the Soviet Union increasingly pursued its own imperatives, and by 1945, the first intimations of the Cold War were in the air. Yet, throughout, the principal Allied leaders agreed that Germany and Japan must be defeated *decisively.* "The militarists in Berlin and Tokyo started this war," Roosevelt declared in January 1942. "But the massed, angered forces of common humanity will finish it."

United we are strong, united we will win. Color lithograph poster by Henry Koerner, published by the U.S. Office of War Information, 1943.

On January 1, 1942, representatives of twenty-six Allied nations issued a Declaration by the United Nations, in which they resolved to cooperate "in a common struggle against savage and brutal forces seeking to subjugate the world." Citing "a common program of purposes and principles embodied in . . . the Atlantic Charter," they vowed "to defend life, liberty, independence and religious freedom, and to preserve human rights and justice in their own lands as well as in other lands." Allied leaders depicted here include, *Left to right, seated*: George II (Greece), Grand Duchess Charlotte (Luxembourg), W. Mackenzie King (Canada), Chiang Kai-shek, Roosevelt, Churchill, Stalin, Queen Wilhelmina (Netherlands), and Gen. Tiburcio Carias Andino (Honduras). *Standing, from left*: Haakon VII (Norway), Peter II (Yugoslavia), John Curtin (Australia), Peter Frasier (New Zealand), Wladyslaw Sikorski (Poland), Hubert Pierlot (Belgium), Eduard Benes (Czechoslovakia), Jan Smuts (South Africa), Fulgencio Batista (Cuba), Anastasio Somoza (Nicaragua), the Marquess of Linlothgow (viceroy of India), Elie Lescot (Haiti), Ricardo Adolfo de la Guardia (Panama), Manuel de Jesus Troncoso de la Concha (Dominican Republic), Rafael Guardia (Costa Rica), Maximiliano Martinez (El Salvador), Jorge Ubico (Guatemala), and Charles de Gaulle.

United Nations. Color drawing by Miguel Covarrubias (1904–1957), May 1942.

MAY 2

 1941 British troops occupy Basra and several Iraqi oil fields.

1945 Fighting in Italy ends with the unconditional surrender of one million German troops.

Centered on the ambitions of Hitler, Mussolini, and the militarists in Japan, the Axis alliance also included subsidiary members: Bulgaria, Hungary, Romania, the particularly brutal "Independent State of Croatia" (carved from Axis-occupied Yugoslavia), and the Slovak Republic (a portion of German-occupied Czechoslovakia). After its 1940 defeat by the Soviet Union (see February 28, March 3), Finland made a separate alliance with Germany—which it ended in September 1944, signing a new treaty with the Soviets. The government of Thailand entered a mutual defense pact with Japan in December 1941 (while a strong anti-Japanese insurgency began forming). Puppet governments (such as the one installed by Italy in neighboring Albania), nationalist groups who believed the Axis might free them from colonial domination, and collaborationists in Axis-occupied countries from France to China also supported the Axis. Yet one sympathetic and strategically located power, whose help Hitler coveted, insisted on remaining officially neutral—despite the führer's best efforts in the year of Germany's greatest triumphs. On October 23, 1940, at Hendaye, on the French-Spanish border, Spanish dictator Francisco Franco evaded, dodged, and ducked Hitler's arguments for nine hours—in a dull monotone that did nothing to soothe the führer's volatile temperament. "Rather than go through that again," the Nazi leader later growled to Mussolini, "I would prefer to have three or four teeth yanked out."

LEFT: *The New Order.* Drawing by Saul Steinberg (1914–1999), published in *American Mercury*, April 1942, with the caption, "Balance of Nations."

RIGHT: Caricature, in a six-of-clubs playing card motif, of Axis leaders Hirohito, Mussolini, and Hitler. Color halftone print by Antonio Arias Bernal (1914–1960), from *Album historico la II guerra mundial* ("Historical Album [of] World War II"), published between 1939 and 1945.

MAY 3

1938 Hitler begins a six-day state visit to Rome, during which he and Mussolini will pledge "eternal friendship."

1945 German forces in Hamburg surrender.

"We cannot wage this war in a defensive spirit," President Roosevelt said in January 1942. "As our power and our resources are fully mobilized, we shall carry the attack against the enemy." Yet full mobilization could not happen overnight, and the enemies' plans were uncertain. Strong homeland defense measures were imperative. Japan's initial assaults had raised fears of a possible West Coast invasion, and U.S. war planners were still wary of possible German/Italian thrusts into South America. Thus, American authorities expanded civil defense programs and bolstered coastal defenses that the nation had begun putting in place in the late 1930s. The military reinforced existing coastal artillery emplacements, expanded the U.S. Navy's unique fleet of airships (blimps) for coastal patrols, and laid submarine nets and minefields to protect important areas—from Casco Bay, Maine, New York Harbor, and Chesapeake Bay in the East, through Pensacola, Florida, Mobile Bay, Alabama, and Galveston, Texas, in the South, to San Francisco and other ports in the West. As reinforcements were dispatched to garrisons in Hawaii, Panama, the Caribbean, Iceland, and Greenland, the United States continued diplomatic and intelligence operations dedicated to strengthening defenses in South America—where Axis agents had been active since 1939.

Logistics of hemisphere defense, 1941. Map outlining a "citadel" defense of the area north of the Brazilian bulge. Published in Richard M. Leighton and Robert W. Coakley, *Global Logistics and Strategy, 1940–1943*, U.S. Department of the Army, 1955.

MAY 4

1942 The five-day Battle of the Coral Sea begins. The United States loses the aircraft carrier *Lexington* and 66 of 144 aircraft, but halts the Japanese advance in the Pacific.

LOGISTICS OF HEMISPHERE DEFENSE, 1941

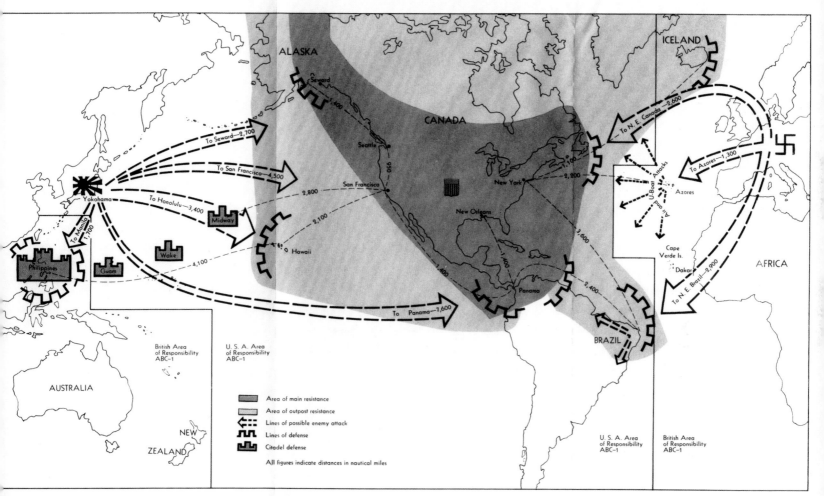

ICELAND

ALASKA

Seward

CANADA

Seattle

San Francisco

New York

New Orleans

Azores

AFRICA

Cape Verde Is.

Dakar

Philippines

Yokohama

To Seward—2,700

To San Francisco—4,500

To Honolulu—3,400

Midway

Wake

Guam

Hawaii

To Manila—1,700

2,800

3,100

4,100

To Panama—1,600

Panama

BRAZIL

To N. E. Canada—2,600

To Azores—1,300

To N. E. Brazil—2,900

3,600

2,400

U-Boat Attacks

Air and

2,900

2,200

1,100

British Area
of Responsibility
ABC–1

U. S. A. Area
of Responsibility
ABC–1

U. S. A. Area
of Responsibility
ABC–1

British Area
of Responsibility
ABC–1

AUSTRALIA

NEW

ZEALAND

Area of main resistance

Area of outpost resistance

Lines of possible enemy attack

Lines of defense

Citadel defense

All figures indicate distances in nautical miles

P 3

295038 O—55 (Face p. 51)

In his first inaugural address, in March 1933, Franklin Roosevelt pledged that, in foreign relations, he would "dedicate this Nation to the policy of the good neighbor . . . who respects his obligations and respects the sanctity of his agreements in and with a world of neighbors." As war approached, U.S. good-neighbor diplomacy increasingly emphasized measures for defending the Western Hemisphere against Axis incursions—whether economic, subversive, or military. The U.S. government was particularly interested in maintaining strong ties with the countries of Latin America. Germany had vastly expanded its economic interests in the region during the 1930s, and several nations were home to substantial German and Japanese communities—regarded by the United States and some Latin American governments as potential bases for anti-Allied sabotage and intelligence gathering. The danger from Axis activity was particularly acute, Secretary of State Cordell Hull wrote in his postwar memoirs, "in its indirect form of propaganda, penetration, organizing political parties, buying some adherents, and blackmailing others." Such Axis activities were effectively countered by Latin American intelligence agencies—and by agents of the U.S. Office of Strategic Services and the Federal Bureau of Investigation.

LEFT: *Strengthen good neighbor policy*. Silk-screen poster, created by the New York State Works Progress Administration's art program, 1941.

RIGHT: *Europe is Getting Hot! We've Got to Move to the Western Hemisphere*. Hitler, Goebbels, Göring, Himmler, and Spanish dictator Francisco Franco looking at a map of Nazi penetration into South America. Ink and pencil drawing by Arthur Szyk (1894–1951), 1944.

MAY 5

1945 Japanese kamikazes sink seventeen U.S. ships off Okinawa in twenty-four hours; 131 Japanese planes are destroyed.

"There is real purpose behind my seeing the president," Canadian Prime Minister Mackenzie King remarked in 1940 of his relationship with Franklin Roosevelt. "I can do more in one week spent to that end than might be accomplished in months by remaining at Ottawa." Always cordial, relations between the two North American leaders had grown closer as the threat from Nazi Germany increased. In August 1940, two months after the fall of France and while the RAF and the Luftwaffe were furiously dueling in the Battle of Britain (see March 22), Roosevelt invited King to meet him in Ogdensburg, New York, where the president was reviewing U.S. Army maneuvers. (Roosevelt was also noting how far the country had to go before even its relatively small preconscription army would be properly equipped: "We are using broomsticks for machine guns and rain pipes for mortars," Major General Clifford Powell of the Forty-fourth Division informed him at Ogdensburg.) The meeting with King, which also included U.S. secretary of war Henry Stimson, took place in a railway car and lasted far into the night. "It has been agreed," they announced the following day, "that a Permanent Joint Board on Defense shall be set up at once by the two countries. . . . It will consider in the broad sense the defense of the north half of the Western Hemisphere." The joint board—cementing a formal defensive pact between the still-neutral United States and a country at war—was formed and began meeting almost immediately.

President Franklin D. Roosevelt, Prime Minister W. L. Mackenzie King of Canada, and U.S. Secretary of War Henry L. Stimson at Lisbon, New York, not far from Ogdensburg, where they concluded the joint defense agreement, August 1940.

MAY 6

1942   In the Philippines, Corregidor surrenders; the Japanese take sixteen thousand Filipino and American prisoners. U.S. commander Jonathan Wainwright writes: "We have done our best, both here and on Bataan, and although beaten we are still unashamed."

"We're the battling bastards of Bataan, . . . " Allied soldiers in the Philippines sang in 1942, ending their song: "And nobody gives a damn." U.S. war leaders gave more than a damn but, so soon after Pearl Harbor, they were unable to send any substantial help to the American and Filipino forces trying to hold out on this important Pacific Theater base. A U.S. territory since 1898, a commonwealth since 1934, the Philippines was slated to become completely independent on July 4, 1946. By February 1942, however, survival itself was at issue. The Japanese were advancing so fast that Philippine president Manuel Quezon was forced to leave to establish a government-in-exile in Washington, D.C. Shortly thereafter, Roosevelt ordered General Douglas MacArthur, commander of Allied forces in the Philippines, to withdraw to Australia, leaving General Jonathan Wainwright in command. In April, as Allied defenses on the Bataan peninsula crumbled (and Allied prisoners suffered the horrors of the Bataan Death March), the Japanese began so unrelenting an artillery and aerial bombing assault on Wainwright's headquarters, the island of Corregidor in Manila Bay, that the island's topography was altered. "They are piling the dead and wounded in our tunnels," an army telegrapher signaled home. "The jig is up." Forced to surrender on May 5, Wainwright signaled Roosevelt: "With profound regret and with continued pride in my gallant troops I go to meet the Japanese commander."

ABOVE: Manuel Quezon (1878–1944), president of the Philippines, November 1942.

RIGHT: *Corregidor.* Drawing by Lute Pease (1869–1963), 1942.

MAY 7

1945 Germany signs an unconditional surrender to the Allies at Reims, France.

ROLL OF HONOR

CORREGIDOR

LutePease

The conflict they initiated in December 1941, the Japanese government declared, involved "liberation of East Asian peoples from the aggression of America and Britain" and "the establishment of a genuine world peace and the creation of a new world culture." Such statements, bolstered by Japanese propaganda campaigns, appealed to many nationalist groups throughout East Asia, many of which sent representatives to Tokyo in November 1943 for a Greater East Asia Conference. "One billion people of Greater East Asia," José Laurel, president of the Japanese-occupied Philippines said as the conference opened, "how could they have been dominated, a great portion of them particularly by England and America?" Virulent Indian nationalist Subhas Chandra Bose, "head of state" of the Axis-affiliated Provisional Government of Free India that had recently declared war on Britain and the United States, addressed a later session: "For India there is no other path but the path of uncompromising struggle against British imperialism. . . . Compromising with Britain means to compromise with slavery, and we are determined not to compromise with slavery any more." The next year, elements of Bose's Indian National Army—a minuscule force of thirteen thousand compared with the 2.5 million Indians who mobilized for the Allies—took part in the Imphal Offensive, a costly and unsuccessful Japanese push into India. Subsequently reduced to making propaganda broadcasts, Bose died in a plane crash in August 1945.

LEFT: In this piece of Japanese propaganda, Japanese soldiers save a Filipino from waters infested with "American imperialism" and "racial prejudice." Reproduction of a drawing, 1943–45.

RIGHT: Subhas Chandra Bose (1897–1945), November 10, 1941.

MAY 8

1945 The war in Europe is declared to have ended. Prime Minister Churchill and President Truman proclaim "V-E Day."

Arrested by the British in 1939, Indian nationalist Subhas Chandra Bose (see May 8) escaped to Afghanistan and gradually made his way to Germany, arriving there in January 1941. He stayed for two years, was treated well, but received little help in his campaign for Indian independence. Thus, when the Japanese invited him to return to East Asia to head the "Free India" movement, he accepted, making the difficult trip around the warring world by submarine. The German vessel U-180 took him as far as the Indian Ocean south of Madagascar—an area in which, under an agreement the three major Axis powers signed in January 1942, all their navies could operate. There Bose transferred to the Japanese submarine I-29, while two Japanese officers, some military equipment, and gold were transferred to the U-180 for transport to Germany. Such German-Japanese naval cooperation was not unusual. German vessels refueled the I-29 on a later mission, when it sailed to occupied France for an exchange of supplies and information; Japan allowed German surface raiders to make repairs and restock supplies in Japan or in Japanese-held territories and let the Germans establish a few small naval outposts in Asia; and Germany gave Japan two U-boats. By mid-1943, however—despite a murderous March in which U-boats located all North Atlantic convoys, attacked half of them, and sank 108 ships—the Battle of the Atlantic was finally turning in favor of the Allies, and the Germans had no U-boats to spare.

A German U-boat attacking an English vessel. Reproduction of a painting by Adolf Bock (1890–1968). From a portfolio published in Berlin, c. 1944–45, and confiscated by U.S. military intelligence authorities.

MAY 9

1945 The German garrison on the Channel Islands surrenders, and the British reclaim their only home territory occupied by the Germans during the war.

Deutsches U-Boot versenkt englischen Frachtdampfer

"**O**ur killings of the U-boat . . . have this year greatly exceeded all previous experience," Winston Churchill reported in a speech to a joint session of the U.S. Congress on May 19, 1943, that broadly surveyed the progress of the war. Churchill and his top military advisers had come to Washington for a two-week strategy session in the wake of Allied victory in North Africa and the stunning German defeat at Stalingrad (see August 7, 16). The American and British leaders, their advisers, and the Combined Chiefs of Staff considered a list of proposed operations for 1943–44, major logistical problems, and measures to keep long-suffering China in the war. Their major disagreements centered on British-proposed operations around the Mediterranean, which the Americans viewed as much less vital than preparing for a full-scale invasion of France. (The British, American Secretary of War Stimson growled to his diary, seemed to be "straining every nerve to lay a foundation throughout the Mediterranean for their own empire after the war is over.") Some differences were left unresolved as the two Allies jointly prepared for the hard fighting that lay ahead. "The enemy is still proud and powerful," Churchill told Congress. "He still possesses enormous armies, vast resources, and invaluable strategic territories. War is full of mysteries and surprises. A false step, a wrong direction, an error in strategy, discord or lassitude among the Allies, might soon give the common enemy power to confront us with new and hideous facts."

Winston Churchill addressing a joint session of Congress, May 19, 1943.

MAY 10

1940 Britain launches its first strategic bombing raid on Germany. German forces invade the Low Countries and France.

espite occasional resentments and sometimes-heated disagreements, the special relationship between the United States and Britain remained strong throughout the war, a fact reflected in the smooth operation of the Combined Chiefs of Staff Committee (CCS; see April 29). Headquartered in Washington, CCS comprised the U.S. Joint Chiefs of Staff (JCS) and the British Joint Staff Mission, which represented Britain's Chiefs of Staff Committee (COS) and kept in close touch with that body—at crucial times on an hourly basis. Chaired by JCS chairman Admiral William D. Leahy, the CCS met every week while in Washington, with additional meetings during the major Allied strategy conferences. It also oversaw a network of organizations, including the Combined Intelligence Committee, the Combined Meteorological Committee, and the Combined Civil Affairs Committee. To simplify operations, the two nations divided the world into three major areas: The United States assumed principal responsibility for the Pacific area (including the Americas, China, Australia, New Zealand, and Japan, but excluding Sumatra and the Malay Peninsula); Britain took the lead in the Indian Ocean and the Middle and Near East (receiving material aid from the United States, which had access to bases in India and routes to China); while the two powers shared responsibility for Europe and the Atlantic. Applied with a great deal of flexibility, this proved an effective operational framework.

American and British chiefs of staff in conference in the Anfa Hotel, Casablanca, Morocco. Left of the conference table (from foreground): Adm. Ernest J. King, USN; Gen. George Marshall, USA; Lt. Gen. "Hap" Arnold, USAAF; Gen. John R. Deane, unidentified, and Gen. Albert Wedemeyer. Right of the table (from foreground): Field Mar. John Dill, Air Chief Mar. Sir Charles Portal, Gen. Sir Alan Brooke, Adm. Sir Dudley Pound, Lord Louis Mountbatten, and Gen. Sir Hastings Ismay.

MAY 11

1940 British bombers attack the German city of Mönchengladback (considered the first major attack by either side against a "population center").

"The Americans are so helpless that they must fall back again and again upon boasting about their matériel," Nazi propaganda minister Joseph Goebbels taunted. "Their loud mouths produce a thousand airplanes and tanks almost daily, but when they need them they haven't got them." The taunt was monumentally ill-founded. American war production, which began in earnest after the fall of France, surged to astounding levels after the Japanese attack on Pearl Harbor. Civilian automobile production was put on hold while auto plants produced Jeeps, planes, and tanks. Shipyards manufactured vessels of all shapes and sizes. Businesses large and small added unusual items to their production rosters (for a time, some U.S. piano makers also manufactured parts for military gliders). Many of these items made their way, via Lend-Lease, to other Allied nations, which needed not only war matériel, but basic supplies as well. U.S. farmers, still recovering from the Great Depression and the environmental disaster of the Dust Bowl, dug in and raised record crops, striving to make America the breadbasket of the war-ravaged world. Private citizens organized dozens of groups, such as Polish War Relief, Bundles for Britain, and British War Relief, to knit, sew, and send clothing and other items to refugee communities and to other Allied countries that, unlike the United States, were in the direct line of Axis fire.

LEFT: Girl in the ruins of a house, Battersea, England. Photograph by Toni Frissell (1907–1988), January 1945.

RIGHT: *Home Front.* Lithograph by Jolán Gross-Bettelheim (1900–1970), 1942–43.

MAY 12

 1941 — German aircraft begin operations out of Iraqi and Syrian bases.

1943 — Gen. Jürgen von Arnim surrenders all Axis forces in North Africa; the Allies take 238,243 German and Italian soldiers prisoner.

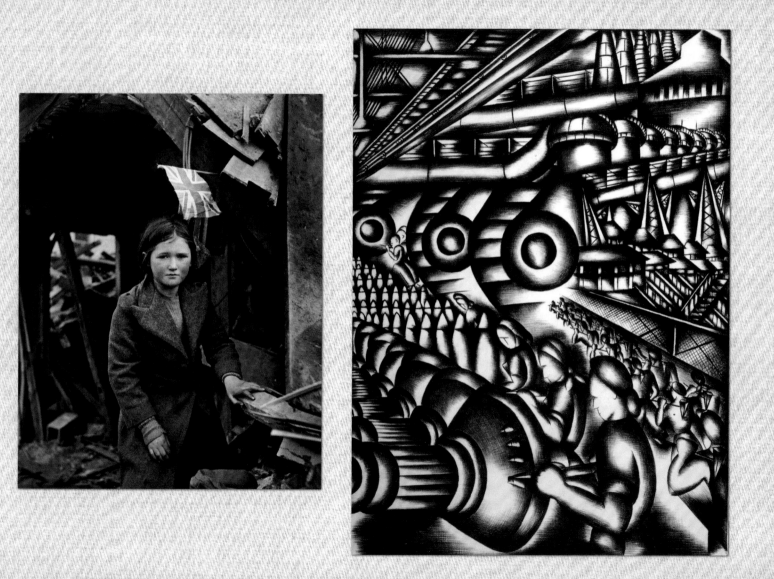

As the United States became the hub of an elaborate global Allied transport system, the American merchant marine expanded from a prewar complement of fifty-five thousand mariners manning a modest fleet that included many near-obsolescent ships to a service of more than 215,000 mariners and the world's largest merchant fleet. At the same time, the burgeoning U.S. Army Air Forces developed an Air Transport Command that became a mainstay of Allied logistics—and a larger operation than all commercial U.S. airlines combined. American, British, Commonwealth, and other United Nations merchant and military transport services together comprised one of the most potent Allied weapons of the war, keeping people and goods moving despite Axis attacks, foul weather, and impossible terrain. Fending off enemy planes, U.S. transport pilots flying over the "Hump" to get badly needed supplies from India to China threaded their way through fifteen-thousand-foot-high windswept Himalayan ridges, a treacherous route they called the "Aluminum Trail" because of all the planes that crashed along the way. Other air routes ranged from Brazil, through Africa, to Iran, where supplies were transferred to trains and trucks to reach the Soviet Union (from early 1943, U.S. troops ran the southern sector of the Iranian State Railway). Meanwhile, convoy after convoy braved multiple dangers to reach destinations from Murmansk to Karachi, Bombay to Brisbane.

American Transoceanic Supply, 1942–43, map published by Richard M. Leighton and Robert W. Coakley, *The United States Army in World War II: Global Logistics and Strategy, 1940–1943.* Office of the Chief of Military History, Department of the Army, 1955.

MAY 13

1938 U.S. Congress passes legislation making November 11 a federal holiday. Armistice Day honors the sacrifices of those who fought the Central Powers in the Great War and the armistice that ended the carnage.

1940 German paratroopers land in northeast France, part of the larger German offensive; Liege falls.

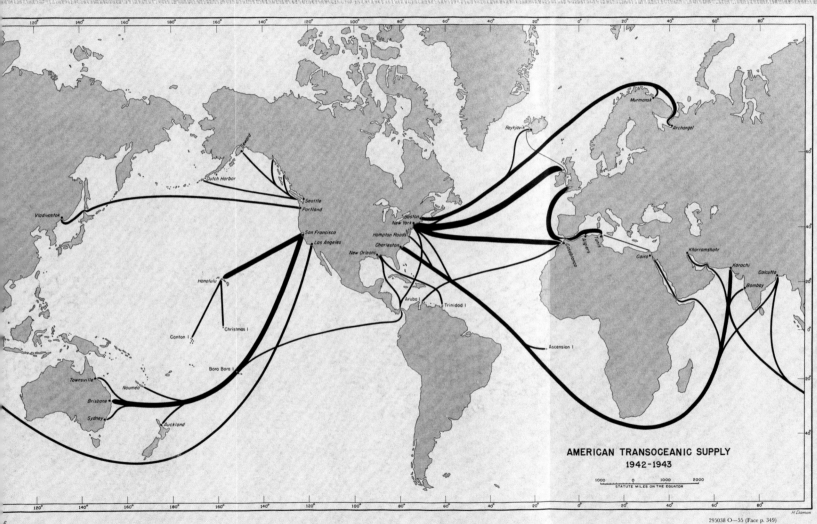

AMERICAN TRANSOCEANIC SUPPLY
1942-1943

1000   0   1000   2000
STATUTE MILES ON THE EQUATOR

Murmansk
Archangel
Reykjavik
Boston
New York
Hampton Roads
Charleston
New Orleans
Aruba I.
Trinidad I.
Algiers
Tunis
Casablanca
Cairo
Khorramshahr
Karachi
Calcutta
Bombay
Ascension I.

Dutch Harbor
Seattle
Portland
San Francisco
Los Angeles
Vladivostok
Honolulu
Canton I.
Christmas I.
Boro Bora I.
Townsville
Noumea
Brisbane
Sydney
Auckland

5

295038 O—55 (Face p. 349)

H. Damon

The Americans flying supplies across the "Hump" (see May 13) were part of a broad effort to sustain Chiang Kai-shek's Chinese Nationalists in the bitter war they had been fighting against the Japanese since July 1937. Before the United States entered the war, American aid was chiefly in money and goods. Yet one U.S. combat unit arrived to help the Chinese before Pearl Harbor. The American Volunteer Group (AVG) was the brainchild of retired U.S. Army officer Claire Chennault, who had been a military adviser to Chiang since 1937. Nicknamed the "Flying Tigers," the group began training at the British air base in Toungoo, Burma, in September 1941, and saw its first action against the Japanese in December. By summer 1942, AVG had been re-designated and incorporated into Chennault's China Air Task Force; later it became the U.S. Fourteenth Air Force (which included a composite wing comprising both U.S. and Chinese pilots). Close to both Chiang and Madame Chiang, Chennault constantly butted heads with General Joseph Stilwell, Chiang's American chief of staff and chief of all American forces in the China-Burma-India Theater. Chennault believed air power could be the chief deciding factor in the war; Stilwell believed that ground forces were essential—and he spent a great deal of effort attempting to properly train and equip Chinese army units. The Chiangs, eager to preserve the Nationalist army for the anticipated civil war with Mao Tse-tung's Communists, generally sided with Chennault.

LEFT: *This American drives the Jap from Chinese skies* (title translated from the Chinese). Color poster/leaflet, by the U.S. Office of War Information, 1945.

RIGHT: Gen. Claire Chennault (right) with the chief of U.S. Army Air Forces, Gen. Hap Arnold, c. 1944.

MAY 14

1940 Peruvian police finally end two days of anti-Japanese riots. U.S. intelligence agents in the country report: "The fear of . . . anti-Japanese riots will in all likelihood prove a great deterrent to sabotage attempts on the part of the Japanese community."

1942 The U.S. Women's Army Auxiliary Corps (WAAC) is established by legislation. In 1943, it will become the Women's Army Corps (WAC), an integral part of the army.

On June 22, 1941, as Chennault was recruiting U.S. pilots for service in China (see May 14), Germany attacked the Soviet Union, shocking the unprepared Red Army—and emphatically validating the thrust of U.S. diplomatic relations with the USSR over the previous two years. When the Soviets signed a pact with the Third Reich in August 1939, the Roosevelt administration assumed, as Secretary of State Cordell Hull later wrote, "that Russia and Germany would not become full allies, and that Hitler had not abandoned his ambitions with regard to Russia." The possibility that the USSR might still be drawn into the Allied struggle against the Third Reich led the Americans to react with restraint to the Soviets' subsequent military actions in Poland and Finland (see February 25, 28, March 3). Yet, after the German invasion placed the Soviets on the Allied roster (and Churchill immediately pledged all possible British aid), Roosevelt was initially cautious in his statements of U.S. support, knowing that he had to convince the public and Congress to assist the Communist dictatorship. The administration's assertion that "Any defense against Hitlerism will hasten the eventual downfall of the present German leaders" helped persuade some—but left many others unmoved. "It is ridiculous," the *Chicago Tribune* fulminated editorially, "that sane men should have the slightest faith that . . . the supreme monster . . . Bloody Joe . . . who brought on the war by selling out the democracies, will not sell them out again and make another deal with Hitler."

LEFT: *Little Goldilocks Riding Hood*. Ink, crayon, and opaque white drawing by Herbert Block ("Herblock," 1909–2001), 1939.

RIGHT: *What! No horns?* Drawing by Edwin Marcus (1885–1961), November 24, 1943.

MAY 15

1941 Vichy French leader Mar. Philippe Pétain confirms a recent meeting between Adm. Jean François Darlan and Hitler. This new evidence of collaboration provokes a warning from the United States, which seizes eleven French ships then in American ports.

1944 The first groups of 380,000 Hungarian Jews are deported to concentration camps, where 250,000 of them will die.

In July 1941, Roosevelt dispatched his most trusted adviser, Harry Hopkins, to Moscow to assess the Russians' determination and capacity to hold out against the savaging Wehrmacht. An astute observer so able to pierce through confusions that Churchill had dubbed him "Lord Root of the Matter," Hopkins returned from the USSR impressed with Stalin's resolve and in favor of extending all possible aid. Convincing Congress and the nation—and expanding production enough to meet both U.S. military needs and American obligations abroad—remained daunting problems (see May 15). Yet U.S. Army Chief of Staff George Marshall and Chief of Naval Operations Harold Stark, both leery of parting with matériel their own forces needed, understood the USSR's strategic importance and, in September, supported "the effective arming of Russian forces." Some public support for extending Lend-Lease to the USSR was expressed with the verbal equivalent of holding the nose: "Let's not pretend that there is anything sweet-smelling about the commies," a Scripps-Howard newspaper editorial declared. "Give them guns, tanks, planes—but keep on saying: 'Don't call me brother.'" After the Japanese attack on Pearl Harbor and the subsequent German and Italian declarations of war, the Soviets could call the Americans "Ally," however. The United States, Britain, China, and the USSR soon became known as the "Big Four" of the United Nations alliance—although the Soviets maintained their neutrality pact with Japan.

We will cut off all roads to the evil enemy, he will not escape from this noose! Color propaganda poster by Kukryniksy, published in Moscow, 1942.

MAY 16

1941   Iceland formally severs its ties to German-occupied Denmark and becomes an independent nation.

1945   U.S. Marines are badly mauled in an attack on Sugar Loaf Hill on Okinawa. They will take the hill on May 18.

The Soviet war effort was complicated by the multiethnic character of the Soviet Union, by political fears and repression within the armed forces, and by Stalin's ruthlessness and his early failure to heed solid military counsel. Yet the Red Army not only survived early battle disasters that cost millions of lives, it was transformed, in the midst of the most brutal combat, into a huge and effective fighting machine. In part this was because Stalin learned to trust and give leeway to some of his most talented commanders, including Konstantin Rokossovsky—who survived imprisonment during the Great Terror (see February 17) to become a pivotal figure in several hallmark Soviet victories. The wartime service of another Soviet general took an opposite course. A hero of the battle of Moscow (1941), Andrei Vlasov had been untouched by the Terror and was one of Stalin's favorites. Dispatched to the Volkhov Front south of besieged Leningrad in March 1942, Vlasov turned implacably against Stalin after the Germans destroyed his cut-off and ill-supplied army— a defeat he blamed on his commander in chief. Captured by the Germans in July, Vlasov agreed to head the Russian Liberation Army (ROA), a small force of anti-Stalinist Russian prisoners of war, and thereafter devoted himself to establishing a noncommunist Russian state. Vlasov's three-year collaboration with the Germans in pursuit of that impossible dream led to his execution for treason in 1946.

ABOVE: Andrei Vlasov (1901–1946).

LEFT: Members of Andrei Vlasov's ROA (Russian Liberation Army), c. 1942.

RIGHT: Mar. Konstantin Rokossovsky (1896–1968), on right, USSR, c. 1945.

MAY 17

1938 Faced with Axis threats in China and Europe, the U.S. Congress—though still isolationist—passes the Naval Expansion Act of 1938, which authorizes a 23 percent increase in the number and tonnage allowances of the navy's warships.

1945 In the last surface naval battle of the war, five British destroyers sink the Japanese cruiser *Haguro*, in the Malacca Strait, near Indonesia.

"If we don't stand on the side of Japan, the [Tripartite] pact is politically dead," Hitler told his foreign minister, Joachim von Ribbentrop, in December 1941, as Japan insisted that Germany join Japan in its war on the United States. Hitler had previously been determined to keep the Americans out of the European war. Now he was inclined to do as the Japanese asked—but for his own reasons, the chief one being, he told Ribbentrop, "that the United States is already shooting at our ships" (see April 24). It was not unusual for supporting his allies to come second in Hitler's reckoning; both he and his partners were primarily interested in building their own empires. On December 11, after the führer announced to a cheering Reichstag that Germany and the United States were at war, the three major Axis nations signed a pact pledging their "unshakable determination not to lay down arms until the joint war against the United States and England reaches a successful conclusion," each signatory vowing not to sign a separate peace. This was followed, on January 18, 1942, with an agreement dividing the world into "Zones of Operation" and calling for "mutual liaison." That call went largely unanswered, however, as demonstrated by a meeting between German and Japanese officers on February 13. The German army's chief of operations, General Alfred Jodl, went into the meeting under instructions not to allow the Japanese to participate in any German operations or to learn of German plans.

Japanese and German officers inspect the Maginot Line at Schoenenbourg, France, September 26, 1940.

MAY 18

 1940 German forces capture Antwerp, Belgium and reach Amiens, France.

 1944 In Italy, Monte Cassino falls to the Allies after a bitter four-month struggle.

Strategically placed, politically and economically unstable—and the site of rich oil fields—Romania was an important factor in Third Reich calculations for acquiring *lebensraum* in the east. As political and military triumphs increased German power, the Romanian government fell more deeply into the Third Reich's orbit, even acquiescing in German-engineered political settlements of geographic disputes with Hungary, Bulgaria, and the USSR that, by September 1940, resulted in the loss of nearly one-third of its territory. In the wake of these settlements, Romania's King Carol abdicated in favor of his teenage son, Michael—but first he appointed General Ion Antonescu prime minister. Romanian minister of war since 1932, and a friend of Hitler's, Antonescu established his own fascist dictatorship (in the process crushing a rival fascist organization, the Iron Guard, with which he had once been allied). Although he maintained Romanian sovereignty, Antonescu threw Romania's doors wide open to increased German influence. Almost immediately, German troops moved into the country to train and rebuild the Romanian military—and to safeguard the country's oil fields. (These fields were also vital to Italy; the German move incensed Mussolini and fed his disastrous decision to invade Greece. See March 28.) Antonescu later committed Romanian forces to eastern front combat—with devastating consequences. In the fighting around Stalingrad alone, the Soviets slaughtered two Romanian armies.

Field Mar. Hermann Göring and Gen. Ion Antonescu, leader of Germany's Axis ally Romania, at the Belvedere Palace in Vienna, 1941.

MAY 19

1941 The U.S. War Department establishes the nucleus of a European theater command called SPOBS (Special Observers Group) in London, under Maj. Gen. James E. Chaney.

1944 It is publicly revealed that the Germans have executed forty-seven RAF officers who were recaptured after escaping from a POW camp—an event that will later be commemorated in the American film *The Great Escape*.

On July 1, 1940, William C. Bullitt, U.S. ambassador to recently defeated France, reported to Washington on his recent conversation with Camille Chautemps, an adviser to Marshal Philippe Pétain. "He said that Pétain, [General Maxime] Weygand and [Pierre] Laval intended to abolish the present French Constitution and to introduce a semi-dictatorial state . . . The model would be probably the German Constitution when Hindenburg had been President and Hitler Chancellor. Pétain would be Hindenburg and Laval would be Hitler." This proved to be a semiaccurate prediction. Named vice premier and Pétain's designated successor on June 25, Laval designed Vichy's collaborationist policies. He arranged the October 23, 1940, meeting with Hitler at which Pétain alarmed the U.S. government by declaring Vichy's "support, within the limits of its ability, [for] the measures which the Axis Powers may take" to defeat England (which, a few months before, had attacked the French fleet at Oran). Yet relations between the two Vichy leaders were increasingly volatile. In December, Pétain dismissed Laval. Fourteen months later, in April 1942, he brought Laval back—and invested him with unprecedented authority. As that occurred, the Americans recalled their ambassador (and the U.S. journal the *Nation* termed Laval's reappearance "a minor Pearl Harbor"). Vichy-U.S. relations deteriorated further after Laval declared, during a radio broadcast in June, "I wish for a German victory." (See March 18, April 3)

LEFT: Mar. Henri Philippe Pétain (1856–1951), date unknown.

RIGHT: *In the Saddle*, a caricature of Vichy France leader Pierre Laval (1883–1945). Color drawing by Edwin Marcus (1885–1961), between 1940 and 1945.

MAY 20

1941 An entire invasion force is deployed from the air for the first time: Twenty-three thousand German paratroopers invade Crete.

After France fell, some French leaders wished to retreat to the French North African colonies of Morocco, Algeria, and Tunisia and continue the struggle against Germany from there. Yet colonial North African governors remained loyal to Vichy; and Marshal Pétain was determined to keep a firm hold on those colonies and preserve their neutrality. With British forces battling Italians and Germans farther east, in Libya and Egypt, the U.S. government trod a delicate line in this area. It supported the British war effort (including the British attack on the French fleet at Oran and the abortive Anglo–Free French assault on Dakar, French West Africa), yet maintained cordial diplomatic ties with Vichy's North African governors. (Meanwhile, the Roosevelt administration remained noncommittal toward other French African colonies, such as Chad, that had declared allegiance to de Gaulle's Free French movement.) America's entry into the war, and continuing Soviet pressure on its allies to open a second front in the West, precipitated a final U.S.-Vichy rift. After heated debate, the British and Americans chose French North Africa as the site of their first major combined operation. On November 8, 1942, the largest amphibious invasion force in history to that time landed at Casablanca in Morocco and Algiers and Oran in Algeria. After an initial storm of resistance, Vichy French forces agreed to an armistice— which was immediately denounced by the Pétain-Laval government (see May 22, June 28).

Map showing Operation Torch landings in North Africa, November 1942, published by the Center for Military History in *Algeria-French Morocco* (pamphlet in "The U.S. Army Campaigns of World War II" series).

MAY 21

1941 A German submarine sinks the American freighter *Robin Moore* in the South Atlantic. British warships sink Axis troop transports carrying reinforcements to Crete; 2,300 German troops are killed.

1945 A British patrol arrests Heinrich Himmler, head of the German *Schutzstaffel* (SS) and the dreaded Gestapo.

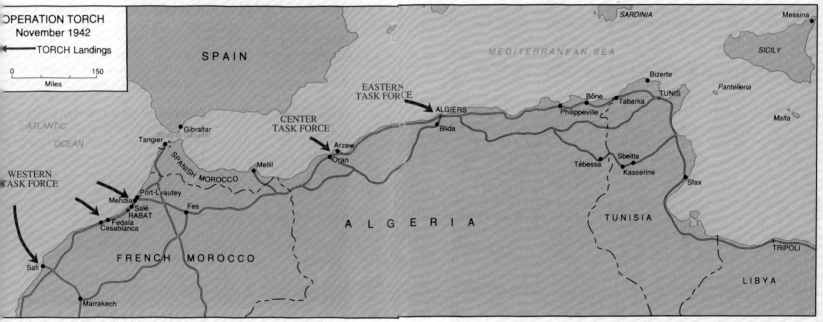

OPERATION TORCH
November 1942

← TORCH Landings

0 ——— 150
Miles

SPAIN

Gibraltar

Tangier
Strait of Gibraltar

SPANISH MOROCCO

ATLANTIC OCEAN

WESTERN TASK FORCE

Port-Lyautey
Mehdia
Salé
RABAT
Fedala
Casablanca

Fes

Safi

FRENCH MOROCCO

Marrakech

Mellil

CENTER TASK FORCE

Arzew
Oran

ALGERIA

EASTERN TASK FORCE

MEDITERRANEAN SEA

ALGIERS
Blida

Bône
Philippeville

Bizerte
Tabarka
TUNIS

Tébessa

Sbeïtla
Kasserine

TUNISIA

Sfax

SARDINIA

SICILY

Messina

Pantelleria

Malta

TRIPOLI

LIBYA

"I agree with you that de Gaulle will be an irritant, and his movement must be kept out," Churchill wrote Roosevelt on September 14, 1942, as the Allies planned Operation Torch. "We do not yet know what the local generals will do." After winning Churchill's endorsement as Free French leader in 1940, General Charles de Gaulle quickly won Vichy's enmity (and condemnation to death in absentia) by making radio broadcasts from London calling for French resistance. Yet he also proved to be aloof and uncompromising with his allies, irritating the British and occasionally angering the Americans. The September 1940 debacle at Dakar (see March 25) might have been due to the fortunes of war; but the Roosevelt administration viewed de Gaulle's wild-card intervention in the Western Hemisphere in December 1941—when the general sent four warships to secure the French-Canadian islands of Saint-Pierre and Miquelon—as wholly unwarranted. As Torch proceeded, de Gaulle conducted his own African operations: His Free French troops pushed Vichy forces out of Libreville, Gabon, while de Gaulle issued proclamations and ordinances that effectively declared his political independence from Britain. Meanwhile, U.S. agents secretly contacted General Henri Honoré Giraud, a French hero after his escape to Vichy from German captivity. The Americans believed Giraud would be the best man to lead Vichy French forces in North and West Africa back into the Allied fold once Operation Torch had been successfully completed.

LEFT: President Roosevelt and French general Henri Honoré Giraud (1879–1949), at Casablanca, Morocco. U.S. Army Signal Corps photo, January 1943.

RIGHT: Free French leader Charles de Gaulle (1890–1970), is welcomed to Chad by Félix Éboué (1884–1944), governor general of French Equatorial Africa, c. 1943.

MAY 22

1939 The Berlin-Rome-Tokyo-Axis becomes a reality when Germany and Italy forge the Pact of Steel, pledging to come to each other's aid in case of war.

Roosevelt to Churchill, December 26, 1942: "I think it would be best for de Gaulle to postpone visit here [Washington]. This will give Symbol a chance to clear situation first." Churchill to Roosevelt, December 28: "I strongly favor a meeting between de Gaulle and Giraud . . . before rivalries crystallize." "Symbol" was the code name for the forthcoming Allied conference, held in Casablanca, Morocco, January 14–24, 1943. Both de Gaulle and Giraud attended, first meeting separately with Roosevelt and Churchill, who strenuously urged them to cooperate, then shaking hands briefly for the benefit of the press. Rivalry between them had already crystallized, however; de Gaulle would prevail as Free French leader by the end of the year. Less fundamental differences existed between the American and British military chiefs, who debated strategy at fifteen meetings during Symbol. More thoroughly prepared with arguments (and backup information they had brought with them on their "floating file cabinet," HMS *Bulolo*), the British won more extensive commitments in the Mediterranean Theater than the Americans would have liked. "We came, we listened, and we were conquered," conference participant Major General Albert C. Wedemeyer later wrote. In fact, the parties compromised. There would be no compromise with the Axis, however. At the concluding press conference, Roosevelt announced that the Allies would only accept the enemies' *unconditional* surrender.

President Roosevelt and Prime Minister Churchill talk to war correspondents at the conclusion of the Allied conference at Casablanca, Morocco. U.S. Army Signal Corps photo, January 1943.

MAY 23

1940   The Germans occupy Boulogne, Amiens, and Arras, France.

1945   In Allied captivity, Heinrich Himmler commits suicide.

In December 1941, the first Japanese units pushed into the British dominion of Burma, a vital conduit of supplies from India to China. By mid-1942, they had occupied all but the remotest northern regions of the country—and both regular and irregular forces comprising Britons, Americans, Chinese, Indians, Gurkhas, and Burmese had begun a long campaign to oust them. The first American unit arrived in the area in June 1942. Detachment 101 of the Office of Strategic Services, initially led by Major Carl Eifler, recruited fighters among Anglo-Burmese soldiers and Burmese refugees in India and trained them at an old British tea plantation in Assam. Detachment leaders then took small groups of the trained recruits behind Japanese lines to wreak as much havoc as possible—and to contact other prospective guerrillas, particularly the formidable Kachin tribesmen. With the assistance of Kachin-speaking Catholic missionary Dennis MacAllindon, 101 officer William C. Wilkinson built a force of some seven hundred guerrillas and a network of agents; his colleague Vincent Curl joined forces with Kachin guerrilla leader Zhing Htaw Naw. Later joined by British guerrilla-war expert Orde Wingate and his Chindit irregulars and the U.S. commandos known as Merrill's Marauders, Detachment 101 fighters operated in Burma until July 1945, gathering intelligence, spotting targets for the China-based U.S. Tenth Air Force, rescuing downed Allied flyers, and generally harassing, and occasionally engaging in all-out battles with, the Japanese.

Sgt. James Fletcher of Atlanta, Georgia (left foreground), and Pvt. John Davenport Jr. of Goldsville, S.C., lead a group of Kachin scouts as they cross a stream in northern Burma. Photograph by Frank Cancellare, 1944.

MAY 24

1941 The British battle cruiser *Hood* is sunk during a classic naval duel with the German battleship *Bismarck* and the destroyer *Prinz Eugen*. Only three of its crew of 1,419 survive.

When Joseph Stilwell, Chiang Kai-shek's American chief of staff and the U.S. military commander in the China-Burma-India Theater, led two Chinese divisions into Burma in 1942, they performed poorly. This was in part because they were also receiving orders from Chiang, who was too distant to appreciate the battle situation and had no wish to risk units he would have preferred to have kept at home (where he continued to husband resources for the anticipated postwar battle with Chinese Communists). Immediately after retreating from Burma, Stilwell wrote Chiang a memo that advocated sweeping changes in the Nationalist forces—including a new command system. Yet two years later, it was painfully clear that few improvements had been made. In April 1944, when the Japanese launched a major campaign, Chiang's troops rapidly gave way. The Japanese were moving "virtually at will," intelligence reports informed the frustrated Stilwell. "The Chinese have shown only slight evidence of either plan or capability." In some cases, Chinese troops refused to fight. In others, such as around the city of Hengyang, they fought with amazing valor—but without much support from Chiang (or from Stilwell, who, at the time, was concentrating on Burma). "All that flesh and blood could do the Chinese soldiers were doing," U.S. correspondent Theodore White reported from the scene, "but they had no support, no guns, no direction. They were doomed." Hengyang fell to the Japanese on August 8.

Rushing the Enemy's Position. Reproduction of a painting by Syusei Kobayakawa, published in *Seisen Gafu* ("A Picture Album of the Holy War"), Tokyo, 1939.

MAY 25

1945 The U.S. Chiefs of Staff set November 1 as the date for the invasion of Japan.

Operation Ichigo, the campaign that Japan launched in China in April 1944 (see May 25), had the ultimate goal of forcing China out of the war and included several interim objectives: controlling major transportation routes, improving communication—and destroying the bases from which Major General Claire Chennault's Fourteenth Air Force launched air strikes. The biggest single Japanese offensive of the war, it reached peak ferocity in June as Allied troops were fighting in Normandy (see September 12 and 13) and involved a half-million men, eight hundred tanks, more than twelve thousand motorized vehicles, and more than seventy thousand horses. It also prompted a spike in the existing rancor between Stilwell and Chennault; Chennault believed his air force could smash Ichigo, *if* Stilwell would give him more planes and supplies—something neither Stilwell nor Chief of Staff George Marshall in Washington was willing to do. At the same time, Chiang was pressuring Stilwell to transfer men from Burma to China at a crucial point in the Burma campaign. "The crazy little bastard [with] that hickory nut he uses for a head," Stilwell railed to his diary, condemning Chiang's "usual cockeyed reasons and idiotic tactical and strategic conceptions." Meanwhile, Ichigo continued; by October the Japanese had captured all but three of the Allied air bases in southeast China. That month, Chiang finally won his long contest with "Vinegar Joe." (See May 27.)

RIGHT: The resources Japan poured into the Ichigo offensive meant increased misery for Chinese civilians who had already suffered through nearly seven years of war. Here, firemen cope with the effects of Japanese incendiary bombs, c. 1938–1944.

MAY 26

1942 Britain and the Soviet Union sign a twenty-year treaty of alliance in which both parties pledge to "act in accordance with the two principles of not seeking territorial aggrandizement for themselves and of non-interference in the internal affairs of other States."

"I think I am fully aware of your feelings regarding General Stilwell," Roosevelt wrote to Chiang Kai-shek in July 1944. "Nevertheless . . . I know of no other man who has the ability, the force and the determination to offset the disaster which now threatens China . . . I recommend . . . that you . . . charge him with full responsibility and authority for the . . . direction of the operations required to stem the tide of the enemy's advances." The president's note preceded a flurry of American diplomatic activity, including visits to Nationalist territory by presidential emissaries Donald Nelson and Patrick Hurley and a political/military mission that established relations with the Communist Chinese. Yet in mid-September, Chiang and Stilwell remained at odds, the Japanese were still gaining ground—and Roosevelt telegraphed Chiang, insisting he immediately place Stilwell "in unrestricted command of all your forces." That message, Chiang said, was "the greatest humiliation I have been subjected to in my life," and he reacted with cold fury. Telling Hurley in person that he was tired of Stilwell's insults, he cabled Roosevelt that Stilwell was unfit. It was clear he was not going to yield, and on October 12, Hurley recommended that Stilwell be replaced; on October 19, as Stilwell wrote in his diary, the "AXE FELL." His replacement, expert war planner Albert C. Wedemeyer, was a firm yet tactful officer who had served in China in the 1930s and, like Stilwell, spoke Chinese.

LEFT: Gen. Joseph W. Stilwell (1883–1946), c. 1945.

CENTER: Chiang Kai-shek (1887–1975). Drawing by Miguel Covarrubias, between 1920 and 1957.

RIGHT: Lt. Gen. Albert C. Wedemeyer (1897–1989), March 16, 1945.

MAY 27

1941 President Roosevelt declares an unlimited national emergency in the United States: "The war is . . . coming very close to home." The German battleship *Bismarck* is sunk by two British battleships; only 110 of the two-thousand-man crew survive.

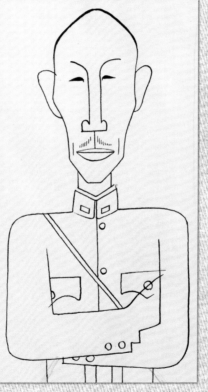

A roiling political and military battlefield, China was also a staging area for clandestine operations in neighboring French Indochina. The Japanese controlled the area via the existing French colonial government, a system described by Vietnamese nationalist leader Ho Chi Minh in a March 1945 report to the U.S. Office of Strategic Services (OSS): "The Japanese become the real masters. The French become kind of respectable slaves. And upon the Indo-Chinese falls the double honor of being not only slaves to the Japanese, but also slaves of the slaves—the French." By 1944, Ho, as head of the Communist-oriented League for the Independence of Vietnam (Viet Minh), was working with, around, or in spite of Chinese, British, Free French, and American intelligence groups, both to defeat the Japanese and to establish a basis for Vietnam's national sovereignty. In the summer of 1945, he and his lieutenant, Vo Nguyen Giap, welcomed a seven-member American OSS group to their headquarters in north Indochina. The "Deer Team" lived with, equipped, and trained Viet Minh fighters—just as the war was ending. Although some Deer Team members, and other Americans in the region, were leery of Ho's ideology, most were impressed by the man and his organization. After witnessing an independence demonstration in Hanoi, OSS officer Archimedes Patti wrote on September 2, 1945: "From what I have seen these people mean business. The French will have to deal with them. For that matter we will all have to deal with them."

Members of the U.S. Office of Strategic Services "Deer Team." Team leader Allison Thomas stands at center; to his right are Ho Chi Minh and Deer Team second-in-command René Défourneaux; to his left, Vo Nguyen Giap. Medic Paul Hoagland (far right) tended the ailing Ho when the team first arrived in Vietnam. Ho would later be an adversary to Americans during the Vietnam War (1959–75). Photograph, c. August 1945.

MAY 28

1945 British Fascist and wartime radio propagandist for the Nazis, William ("Lord Haw-Har") Joyce is captured by Allied troops. He will be tried, convicted, and executed for treason.

The Nazis "have always planned on a split of the Allies," U.S. Army chief of staff George C. Marshall wrote on March 1, 1945. "They never . . . calculated that the Allies could continue to conduct combined operations with complete understanding and good faith." Like other American war leaders, Marshall had emerged optimistic from the February 4–11, 1945, Allied conference at Yalta. Questions regarding the nascent United Nations Organization, Soviet entry into the war against Japan, the treatment of defeated Germany, and the fate of eastern Europe were settled to the general satisfaction of the U.S. delegation—although Admiral William Leahy, chairman of the Joint Chiefs of Staff, remained skeptical of Russian intentions. He believed that the terms agreed to at Yalta might "make Russia the dominant power in Europe, which in itself carries a certainty of future international disagreements and prospects of another war." The British were also worried. But their influence with the United States had waned as American power increased—and American objections to European colonialism strengthened. "This is the age of the Big Two," a March 1945 American analysis of postwar security declared. "Only the Soviet Union will have a power position comparable to that of the United States. . . . Soviet Russia is a power whose good intentions must be assumed until there is incontrovertible evidence to the contrary." Even as the analysis circulated in Washington, the Soviets began violating Yalta accords.

Winston Churchill, Franklin D. Roosevelt, and Joseph Stalin, with their staffs, pose during the Allied conference at Yalta, Crimea, February 1945.

MAY 29

1942 Two days after SS commander for Czechoslovakia Reinhard Heydrich is severely wounded by partisans in an assassination attempt near Prague, Joseph Goebbles blames Jewish terrorists for the attack.

During the Allied conference at Yalta (see May 29), Roosevelt's physical condition alarmed some observers, among them Churchill's doctor, Lord Moran: "The President . . . has all the symptoms of hardening of the arteries of the brain in an advanced stage, so that I give him only a few months to live," he wrote in his diary. "But men shut their eyes when they do not want to see, and the Americans here cannot bring themselves to believe that he is finished." Moran's prognosis proved correct. On April 12, 1945, Roosevelt died at his "little White House" retreat in Warm Springs, Georgia, of a cerebral hemorrhage. News of his death traveled swiftly around the world, reaching two of the president's sons, John and FDR Jr., on duty on separate ships in the waters off Okinawa, where a costly battle was raging. Conferring by radio, they decided against going home, Franklin Jr. saying: "Let's clean it up out here, first." At the White House, their mother placed a consoling arm around Harry S. Truman as he learned that he had become the thirty-third president of the United States. "I then asked them what I could do," Truman recorded, "and she said, 'What can we do for you?'" Though he felt like "the moon and stars and all the planets had fallen on me," Truman reassured the Allies that he would maintain Roosevelt's war policies and announced in his first speech that the United States would continue to insist on the unconditional surrender of Germany and Japan.

The Gold Star, mourning the death of Franklin D. Roosevelt. Drawing by Edwin Marcus (1885–1961), April 15, 1945.

MAY 30

1942 California Japanese American Fred Korematsu, who had plastic surgery to avoid being sent to a relocation camp, is arrested. He later agrees to let his case be used as a test of the government's evacuation decree.

Less than a month after Roosevelt's death, and five days after Hitler committed suicide in his underground bunker in besieged and ravaged Berlin, an emissary from the new German head of state, Admiral Karl Dönitz, arrived at the headquarters of General Dwight D. Eisenhower, Supreme Commander Allied Expeditionary Force, to negotiate terms of surrender. Eisenhower refused to negotiate. In line with Allied policy, he demanded unconditional surrender on all fronts, and the Germans complied, signing the surrender papers in separate ceremonies before the Western Allies on May 7 and the Soviets on May 9. Four Allied powers—the United States, Britain, the Soviet Union, and France—then implemented occupation procedures that had been devised over the preceding eighteen months by the European Advisory Commission and confirmed at the Yalta conference. As these events unfolded—and fighting continued in Asia—delegates from around the world were concluding a two-month meeting in San Francisco, where they fashioned the charter of a new organization, the United Nations. "Tomorrow we shall separate and return home," U.S. Secretary of State Edward Stettinius Jr. told the assembly on June 26. "But in this Charter we will carry to our Governments and to our peoples an identical message of purpose and an identical instrument for the fulfillment of that purpose. . . . This Charter is a compact born of suffering and of war. With it now rests our hope for good and lasting peace."

ABOVE: *A Tale of Two Cities.* Drawing by Edwin Marcus (1885–1961), April 1945.

RIGHT: Secretary of State Edward R. Stettinius Jr., standing at the rostrum, opens the San Francisco Conference, 1945.

MAY 31

1945 Two teams established by President Truman begin separate searches for an alternative to dropping the atomic bomb that might similarly prevent the huge number of anticipated casualties of an American invasion of the Japanese mainland.

Axis Ascendant: 1942

In 1942, the Allies were on the defensive, trying to strengthen and mobilize even as they continued to reel from blow after devastating blow. This bitter year took a dreadful toll: Axis forces killed or imprisoned millions of civilians and soldiers, engulfed strategically important military bases and entire land masses, and destroyed millions of tons of equipment. From the Philippines to Singapore to their continuing battle for China, Japanese armed forces exhibited a terrible ruthlessness. But their cruelties were far exceeded by German brutality in Europe.

On January 20, in a villa in the pleasant Berlin suburb of Wannsee, fifteen high-ranking Nazis approved security chief Reinhard Heydrich's plan for the "Final Solution" of the "Jewish question"—the systematic mass murder of an entire people. In the Soviet Union, mass murders were already in progress: One of the worst massacres of the previous year had occurred outside Kiev, when the Germans slaughtered more than thirty thousand Jewish men, women, and children at a place called Babi Yar. This year, with the Red Army still defying Hitler's prediction that it would quickly collapse, the German campaign remained vicious. In the spring, after a battle that took more than one hundred thousand Soviet lives, the Wehrmacht captured the Crimean port city of Kerch on the peninsula between the Sea of Azov and the Black Sea. Some three thousand soldiers, nurses, and civilians from Kerch, trapped on the peninsula, took refuge in a nearby

JUNE 1

1942 Mexico declares war on Germany, Italy, and Japan. The Nazis order all Jews in France and Holland to wear Star of David identification badges.

1954 In the wake of World War II and the Korean War, President Dwight D. Eisenhower signs legislation changing the name of the November 11 day of commemoration from Armistice Day to Veterans Day.

maze of caves and tunnels. The Germans hurled explosives into the caves and released gas in the tunnels. Very few Soviets escaped; over agonizing months, most died from German attacks or starvation. They never tried to surrender; they had learned the character of their enemy.

"Conquered nations in Europe know what the yoke of the Nazis is like. And the people of Korea and of Manchuria know in their flesh the harsh despotism of Japan," Roosevelt said in a February 23 radio broadcast. "All of the people of Asia know that if there is to be an honorable and decent future for any of them or for us, that future depends on victory by the United Nations over the forces of Axis enslavement. . . ."

"Our first job," he continued, "is to build up production"— but Axis victories had made that more difficult, cutting off normal avenues for procuring rubber and other resources. As compensatory measures were developed, the United States joined other Allied nations in imposing strict rationing: Limits were placed on the consumption of items from coffee to gasoline, and few sartorial frills were allowed (men's suits could not have cuffs, pleats, or patch pockets). Across the nation, people collected scrap metal to be turned into implements of war. Shipbuilding increased, plane production started to soar—and, by the hundreds of thousands, Americans joined the armed forces.

"From Berlin, Rome, and Tokyo we have been described as a nation of weaklings—'playboys'— who would hire British soldiers, or Russian soldiers, or Chinese soldiers to do our fighting for us," Roosevelt told the American people. "Let them repeat that now. Let them tell that to General MacArthur and his men. Let them tell that to the sailors who today are hitting hard in the far waters of the Pacific. Let them tell that to the boys in the flying fortresses. Let them tell that to the Marines."

Avenge December 7. Color poster by Bernard Perlin (b. 1918), published by the U.S. Office of War Information, 1942.

In his annual message to Congress in January 1942, President Roosevelt paid tribute to the U.S. Marines of the First Defense Battalion, who had mounted a heroic defense of Wake atoll, an American possession since 1899. Comprising tiny Wake, Peale, and Wilkes islands, the atoll occupied a strategic location: About two thousand miles west of Hawaii, it was a potential fueling base for U.S. B-17s and might also be used to launch reconnaissance flights over the Japanese base on Kwajalein, some six hundred miles due south. The marines and about a thousand civilian contractors had just finished building an airfield and fortifying the islands when bombing attacks began on December 7, 1941. Three days later, the Japanese attempted a landing. Holding their fire until the last minute, the marines (reinforced by a few civilian volunteers) repelled the landing force, sank two destroyers, damaged two cruisers and several troop transports, and inflicted seven hundred casualties. Two weeks later, they were confronted with a much larger armada, including *Hiryu* and *Soryu*, two of the aircraft carriers that had attacked Pearl Harbor. The marines fought hard, inflicting heavy casualties, before superior numbers forced their surrender. Marines, navy personnel, and many civilians were then taken prisoner—and they were not treated gently. Japanese navy lieutenant Toshio Saito later ordered the beheading of two marines and three sailors, apparently chosen at random, as "revenge" for the casualties inflicted by Wake Island's defenders.

Wake—America's beach of bayonets. Color poster commemorating the heroism and sacrifices of U.S. Marines on Wake Island. Published c. 1942.

JUNE 2

1942 The Germans begin reprisals for the fatal Czech Resistance attack on SS deputy commander Reinhard Heydrich, executing 131 Czech civilians.

1943 Pope Pius XII appeals to combatants to apply the "laws of humanity" in air warfare.

WAKE - AMERICA'S BEACH *of* BAYONETS

Quotation from President Roosevelt's Message to the Congress on the···
State of the Union, Jan. 6, 1942.

 HERE WERE ONLY SOME FOUR HUNDRED
UNITED STATES MARINES·WHO·IN THE
HEROIC AND HISTORIC DEFENSE OF WAKE
ISLAND·INFLICTED SUCH GREAT LOSSES
ON THE ENEMY· SOME OF THESE MEN WERE
KILLED IN ACTION AND OTHERS ARE NOW PRISON-
ERS OF WAR·WHEN THE SURVIVORS OF THAT
GREAT FIGHT ARE LIBERATED AND RESTORED TO
THEIR HOMES· THEY WILL LEARN THAT A HUN-
DRED AND THIRTY MILLION OF THEIR FELLOW
CITIZENS HAVE BEEN INSPIRED TO RENDER
THEIR OWN FULL SHARE OF SERVICE *and* SACRIFICE."

433 PB

MCPB 105750 9-17-42 15M.

As American losses to the Japanese mounted in the Pacific, Admiral Karl Dönitz, commander of Germany's submarine fleet, launched Operation *Paukenschlag* ("Drumbeat"), sending U-boats into American waters off Bermuda, in the Caribbean and the Gulf of Mexico, and along the Atlantic seaboard. All three areas proved to be fertile hunting grounds: Most merchant ships, carrying tin and bauxite for U.S. armaments, or fuel from the Dutch oil refineries in Aruba, still sailed alone, rather than in convoys. By the end of the year, the Germans had sunk 337 Allied ships in the Caribbean alone. Despite mounting losses, Americans were extremely slow to institute blackout polices along the eastern seaboard. U-boats could easily target ships silhouetted against the glowing coastal lights. One U-boat, hovering outside glittering New York Harbor in January, sank eight ships in twelve hours. On the night of April 10, U-123, running on the surface off Jacksonville, Florida, used its deck gun to set SS *Gulfamerica* ablaze. Its captain, Reinhard Hardegen, then watched tourists pour out of well-lit hotels and restaurants into the eerie light shed by the sinking tanker. "A burning tanker, artillery fire, the silhouette of a U-boat," he wrote in his log, "how often had that been seen in America?" By the fall, America had seen quite enough and imposed more effective eastern seaboard defenses—including tighter blackout discipline and a "bucket brigade" system of escorting merchantmen from port to port.

INSET: *Blackout means black*. Color silk-screen poster by the Oakland, California, Federal Art Project, issued by the Oakland Defense Council, between 1941 and 1943.

RIGHT: Two nighttime photographs of the New York City skyline taken from across the Hudson River before (top) and during (bottom) a trial blackout, March 1942.

JUNE 3

1942   Japanese carrier-based aircraft bomb Dutch Harbor and Fort Mears in Alaska.

1943   A German submarine mines waters off Halifax, Nova Scotia.

While German U-boats retained the upper hand in the Battle of the Atlantic, in the Mediterranean, German Field Marshal Albert Kesselring, newly arrived Commander-in-Chief South, directed the Luftwaffe to concentrate its attentions on the British island of Malta, from which Allied submarines and planes had been pummeling Axis convoys. As Axis supply problems in North Africa dramatically decreased, Hitler rejected Mussolini's proposal to invade the island. Yet that provided little relief to the Maltese. Subjected to unrelenting air attacks, they were also nearly cut off from much-needed supplies that could be brought in only by ship. In June, Axis air and U-boat attacks decimated a convoy (code-named Vigorous) attempting to reach the island from Alexandria, Egypt. In August, the Allies tried again with Operation Pedestal: A convoy of fourteen freighters, under heavy escort, sailed toward Malta from Gibraltar. It, too, came under fierce attack—more than half the freighters were sunk. But the forty-two thousand tons of food and fuel the surviving ships delivered, all carefully rationed, allowed the long-suffering Maltese to survive. Meanwhile, Malta's striking power was gradually reinforced: Aircraft were flown in from May through December, many of them long-range torpedo planes. By November these planes, Allied submarines, and mines had pushed Axis shipping losses to an all-time high of 77 percent.

ABOVE: Field Mar. Albert Kesselring (1887–1960), February 2, 1942.

RIGHT: Some citizens of the island of Malta in one of the island's many makeshift shelters, 1942 or 1943.

JUNE 4

1942 The Battle of Midway begins; this decisive U.S. victory, which costs Japan heavily in aircraft carriers, planes, and pilots, marks a turning point in the war in the Pacific.

1944 Bad weather causes Gen. Eisenhower to postpone D-Day to June 6.

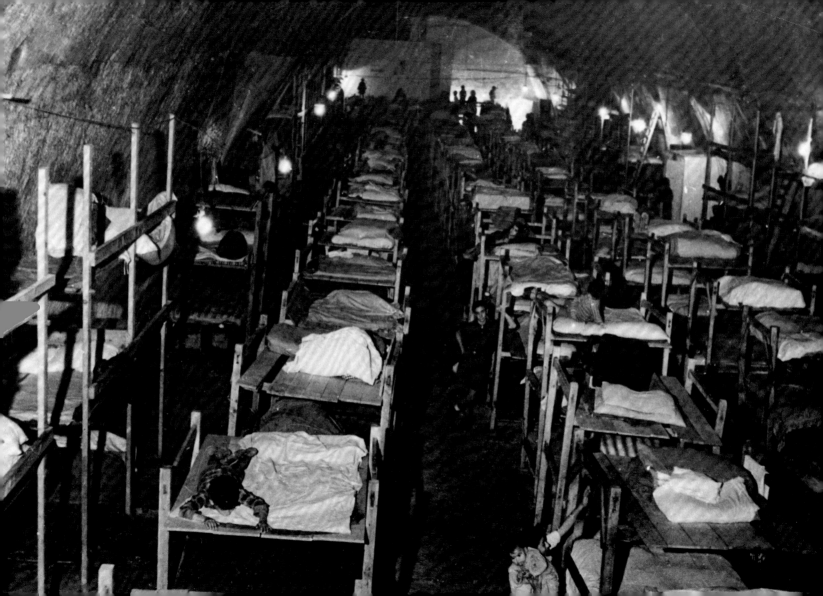

On January 11, 1942, the Japanese Imperial Army took Kuala Lumpur, in the British colony of Malaya, after a spectacular campaign that forced British troops into a pell-mell retreat down the Malay Peninsula. "The confusion was unbelievable," British army engineer Ronald Searle later reported. "In the suffocating tropical heat, among abandoned equipment, filth, smoke, blood and rubble . . . [I felt] my skin blister as we plunged through the flaming ruins of the villages we were burning. . . . Meanwhile the Japanese moved forward to chop into small pieces all the wounded that had to be left behind." The British were retreating to a prime Japanese target. Singapore, Japanese officer Masanobu Tsuji wrote, was "Britain's . . . eastern gate for the defense of India and the northern gate for the defense of Australia." At the southern tip of the peninsula and connected to the mainland by a causeway, the diamond-shaped island was plagued by ill-placed fortifications and defended by soldiers who were either battered from their recent retreat or new and insufficiently trained. General Tomoyuki Yamashita's assault, launched late on February 8, quickly pushed forward to Singapore City, which was crowded with terrified civilians. Low on food and water and believing that further resistance would be futile, the British commander, General Arthur Percival, surrendered unconditionally on February 15. Singapore's fall, Churchill said, was "the worst disaster and largest capitulation in British history."

ABOVE: *Keep calm and carry on*. Color poster published in Britain between 1939 and 1941.

RIGHT: Women and children line up at the port of Singapore to be evacuated from the city, shortly before the Japanese overrun it. British Press Service photograph, 1942.

JUNE 5

1942 The United States declares war on Bulgaria, Hungary, and Romania. An explosion at an ordnance plant in Elmwood, Illinois, kills forty-nine civilian workers.

As Japanese armies swept through southern Asia (capturing rubber plantations, oil fields, and other resources badly needed by the imperial war machine), they suffered from logistic support that, throughout the war, ranged from poor to abysmal. No combat force could long continue achieving its objectives unless its frontline "teeth" were supported by a briskly reactive logistic "tail"—a bit of military anatomy that extended from quartermaster troops on the front lines to rear-echelon supply depots and home-front factories. "If quartermasters and civilian officials are left to take their own time over the organization of supplies," German field marshal Erwin Rommel said, "everything is bound to be very slow. . . . This can lead to frightful disasters when there is a man on the other side who carries out his plans with greater drive and thus greater speed." In North Africa, Rommel's intermittent supply crises stemmed mostly from blowing sand and Allied action against his supply lines. In the Soviet Union, German logistics had to overcome not only enemy action and bouts of appalling weather, but poor initial planning by the high command; vast distances and odd Soviet railroad gauges; and a hodgepodge of vehicles and weapons brought together for the massive campaign that provided huge maintenance and resupply challenges. Americans studied Axis logistic problems as they built their own system to supply Allied troops in a global war (see May 13).

Scheme of Army Supply System and *German Use of Military Supplies*, two charts from U.S. Coordinator of Information Monograph No. 5, *The German Supply Problem on the Eastern Front* (conclusions and summary), April 4, 1942.

JUNE 6

1944   D-Day. Allied forces begin their invasion of France.

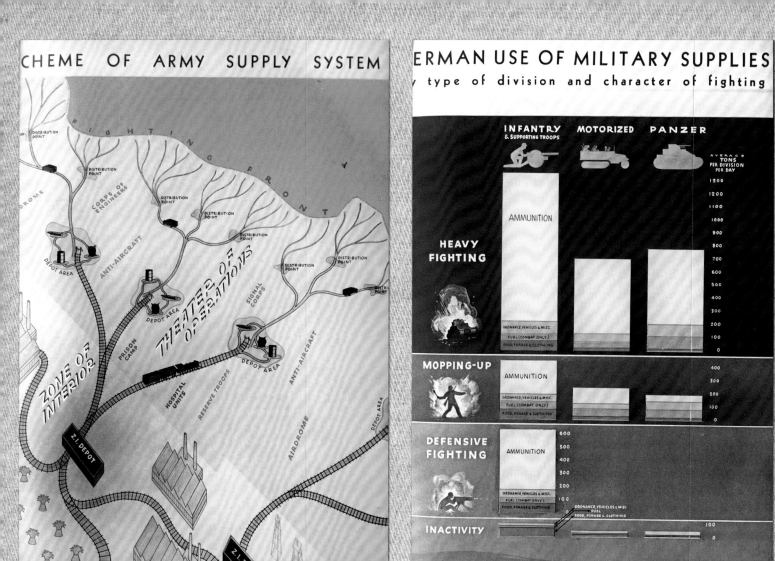

Head of the Nazi Ministry of People's Enlightenment and Propaganda since 1933, Joseph Goebbels proved singularly adept at the "art" of black propaganda—defined by American Office of Strategic Services propagandist Edmond Taylor as "essentially calumny and provocation, the age-old crafts of tyrant and conspirator." With his ministry in full control of all communications media, and making masterful use of the twentieth-century technologies of radio and film, Goebbels launched campaigns against Allied morale while filling the media at home with twisted, seductive interpretations of events. "It is not enough to reconcile people more or less to our regime," he stated. "We would rather work on people until they are addicted to us." Despite his best efforts, he was having no luck at all reconciling Britain to the Nazi worldview. ("The English can stand a lot of beating before they become rebellious and notice things," he noted in his diary on April 14, 1942.) Both the British and the Americans lampooned and refuted Axis propaganda via their own organizations, often bolstered by commentary in the civilian press, which remained comparatively unrestricted. As Gardner Cowles Jr., head of the U.S. Office of War Information's domestic program, noted, "intelligent, informed, and honest criticism of government programs and policies is an indispensable part of the service of a free press to a free people in war."

LEFT: *Wir brechen Englands tyrannei* ("We're breaking England's tyranny"). Color German propaganda poster, 1941.

RIGHT: Cover of *Collier's* magazine, January 17, 1942, with an illustration by Arthur Szyk lampooning Axis propaganda efforts. Goebbels is caricatured at the extreme right; the other figures (left to right) are Göring, Himmler, and Hitler.

JUNE 7

1940 French bombers attack Berlin.

1942 Two days after landing on the western Aleutian island of Kiska, the Japanese occupy Attu, beginning the only Axis occupation of North American territory.

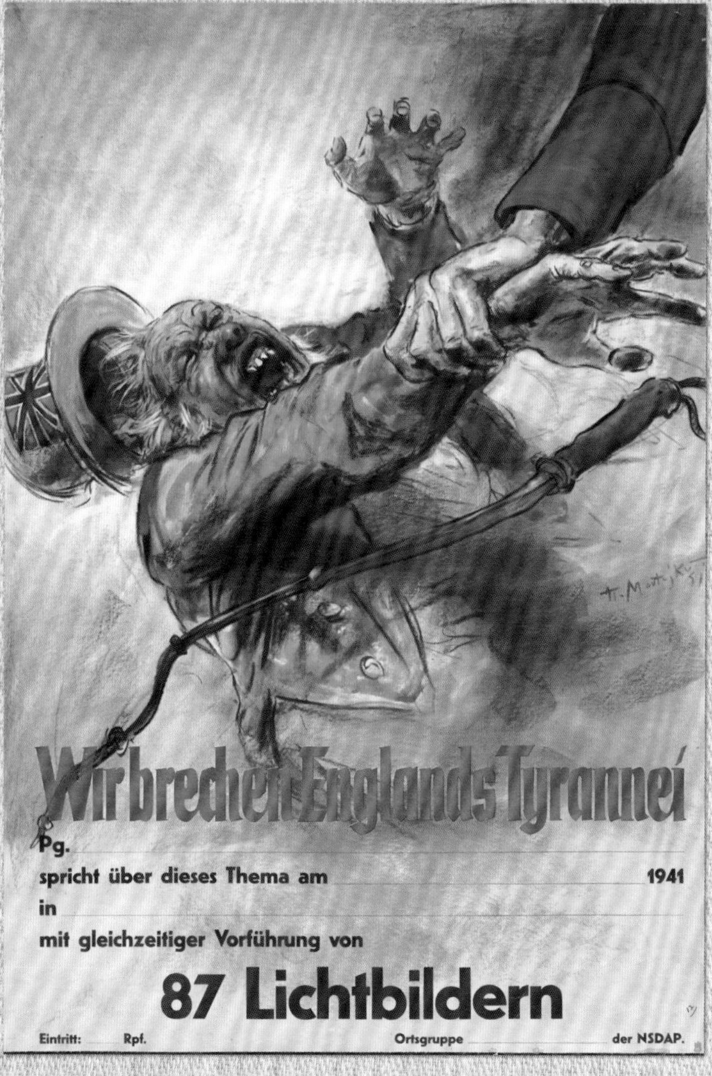
Wir brechen Englands Tyrannei
Pg.
spricht über dieses Thema am 1941
in
mit gleichzeitiger Vorführung von
87 Lichtbildern
Eintritt: Rpf. Ortsgruppe der NSDAP.

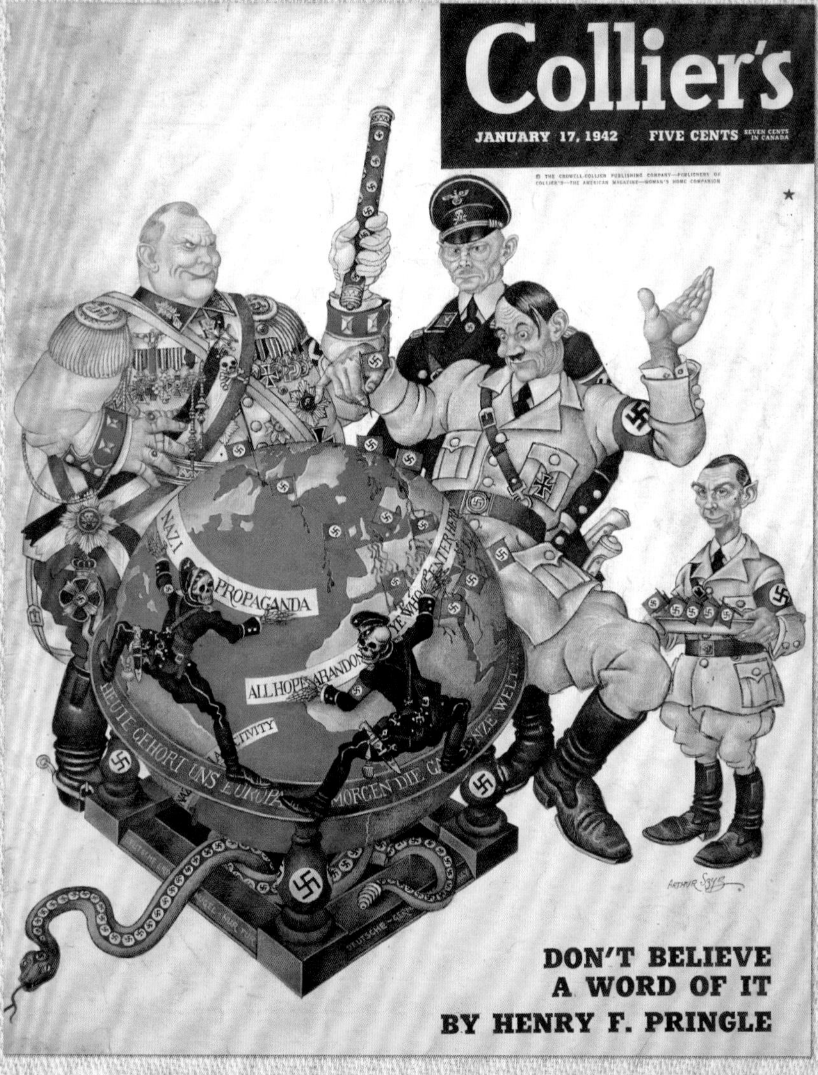
Collier's
JANUARY 17, 1942 FIVE CENTS SEVEN CENTS IN CANADA
© THE CROWELL-COLLIER PUBLISHING COMPANY—PUBLISHERS OF COLLIER'S—THE AMERICAN MAGAZINE—WOMAN'S HOME COMPANION
NAZI
PROPAGANDA
ALL HOPE ABANDON
HEUTE GEHÖRT UNS EUROPA MORGEN DIE GANZE WELT
DON'T BELIEVE
A WORD OF IT
BY HENRY F. PRINGLE

While the Roosevelt administration streamlined its propaganda, intelligence, and information efforts in 1942 by, among other measures, creating the Office of War Information (see June 7), U.S. military commanders concentrated on building up their armed services. The massive and speedy expansion of the U.S. Army from a force that, in 1940, numbered fewer than three hundred thousand men into an army capable of waging a multifront war was soon plagued by shortages in housing and equipment—and from failure in its administrative structure. In March 1942, the General Headquarters (GHQ) that had been established in July 1940 as the central control for army expansion was abolished during a reorganization that established three major army components: Ground Forces, Air Forces, and Service Forces. This restructuring considerably eased the process of expansion. Yet even as the army inducted and trained new troops, top commanders debated many questions. Among the most vexing was how many combat divisions would be needed. Initial estimates, made under the assumption that the USSR would be conquered or would make a separate peace with the Germans, placed the number at 213 (nearly 3.2 million frontline ground troops, backed up by support troops and a vast array of equipment). As Soviet armies continued to tie down 60 percent of the German army, this was gradually reduced until commanders settled on what became known as the "ninety-division gamble."

LEFT: Front page of the *Washington Daily News*, January 6, 1942.

RIGHT: A U.S. Army formation on parade. Frame enlargement from the U.S. Army Signal Corps film *The Japanese Soldier*, 1942.

JUNE 8

1941 Australian, Indian, and Free French troops under British command invade Syria and Lebanon and are quickly involved in bitter fighting with Vichy forces comprising Tunisians, Algerians, and Senegalese under Vichy French officers.

The Washington Daily News

Index

Dial Year—No. 53   Two Cents   Entered as Second Class Matter at D. C. Post Office

HOME EDITION

TUESDAY, JANUARY 6, 1942

Weather

2¢

F. D. TELLS CONGRESS:
ARMY TO FIGHT EVERYWHERE & GO TO BRITAIN

Says U. S. War Plan Includes:

In 1942 . . .

60,000 Planes & 45,000 Tanks

8 Million Tons of Shipping

20,000 Anti-Aircraft Guns

In 1943 . . .

125,000 Planes & 75,000 Tanks

10 Million Tons of Shipping

35,000 Anti-Aircraft Guns

COST 56 BILLION THIS YEAR

(Story on Page 2, Text on Page 5.)

Although the U.S. Selective Service Act of September 1940 contained an antidiscrimination provision (see April 21), within the armed services, segregation of black from white was not interpreted as discrimination. Nevertheless, separation of the races often resulted in blatant discrimination against African American servicemen in housing, transportation, recreational facilities, blood banks ("black" blood was maintained separately from "white" blood)—and duty assignments. "Half a million Negroes are now bearing arms in the service of their country," Dwight Macdonald of the March on Washington Movement wrote in a pamphlet titled *The War's Greatest Scandal: Jim Crow in Uniform*. "In return for their patriotism, the Negroes of America have been jim-crowed into segregated regiments and used largely as servants and laborers . . . a doctrine of 'White Supremacy' which is simply Hitler's 'Nordic Supremacy' in Cracker lingo has become the official policy of the American armed forces." Political pressure, wartime manpower requirements, and concern over racial tensions slowly led to some improvements. By the end of the war, thousands of African American soldiers had served proudly on the front lines, among them components of the Ninety-second and Ninety-third divisions, fifty-three platoons of African American volunteers who served with the First and Seventh Armies in Europe, and members of the famed 332nd Fighter Group (see September 6).

Training for war. Color silk-screen print by William H. Johnson (1901–1970), 1941 or 1942.

JUNE 9

1941 To prevent disruption of fighter aircraft production by striking workers, U.S. soldiers with fixed bayonets seize the North American Aviation plant in Inglewood, California. The strikers soon return to work.

W.H.Johnson.

This is the reason that I want to fight
Not 'cause everything's perfect, or everything's right
No, it's just the opposite; I'm fightin' because
I want a better America, and better laws
And better homes, and jobs, and schools
And no more Jim Crow, and no more rules, like
"'You can't ride on this train 'cause you're a Negro.'"
"'You can't live here 'cause you're a Jew. . . .'"
So, Mr. President
We got this one big job to do,
That's lick Mr. Hitler and when we're through
Let no one else ever take his place
To trample down the human race.
So what I want is you to give me a gun
So we can hurry up and get the job done!

— Excerpt from "Dear Mr. President," a song composed by folk
singer (and World War II soldier) Pete Seeger (b. 1919), 1942

American soldiers en route to the
New York port of embarkation,
between 1942 and 1945.

JUNE 10

1940 Italy declares war on France and Britain. The following day, Italian aircraft attack French bases in Tunisia and Corsica as well as British installations on the strategically located island of Malta.

1944 A German SS company murders all the inhabitants—some six hundred men, women, and children—of the French village of Oradour-sur-Glane, near Limoges.

"A black day for the enemy side," Joseph Goebbels wrote in his diary on April 11, 1942. "The Americans must admit they have evacuated Bataan. They now have nothing more to defend in the Philippines except Corregidor. The whole United States is in a dither. The hero's halo they gave MacArthur is fading. We are naturally going to seize upon this opportunity. This big shot, whom New York only a few days ago still tried to sell as the outstanding genius of the century, will now be unmasked completely by our propaganda." General Douglas MacArthur was not "unmasked" nor particularly perturbed by the Goebbels propaganda machine. In April 1942, he was immersed in frustration and tragedy, watching from afar as Japanese forces relentlessly broke the resistance of the Allied units cut off in the Philippines. On Roosevelt's orders, MacArthur had established new headquarters in Australia, where he publicly vowed to the people he had left behind, "I shall return." Meanwhile, a PT-boat squadron commanded by Lieutenant Commander John D. Bulkeley, who had spirited MacArthur away from Corregidor ("that bold buckaroo," the general had dubbed him), was raising American home-front morale with stinging attacks on Japan's vastly superior naval forces in Philippine waters. By May, however, the last Allied bastions of Bataan and Corregidor had fallen. As Americans mourned this latest loss, the few Allied fighters who had escaped to the Philippine countryside began organizing guerrilla warfare (see also May 7).

ABOVE: Gen. Douglas MacArthur. U.S. Army photograph, August 24, 1945.

RIGHT: Last stand on Luzon. Map showing the Bataan Peninsula-Corregidor-Manila area, where Allied forces made their last stand before surrendering to the Japanese in May 1942. U.S. Army Signal Corps/Office of War Information, March 1943.

JUNE 11

1942 German submarines begin mining U.S. waters, dropping mines off Boston Harbor, Delaware Bay, and the Delaware capes; the mines sink three ships off the capes shortly thereafter.

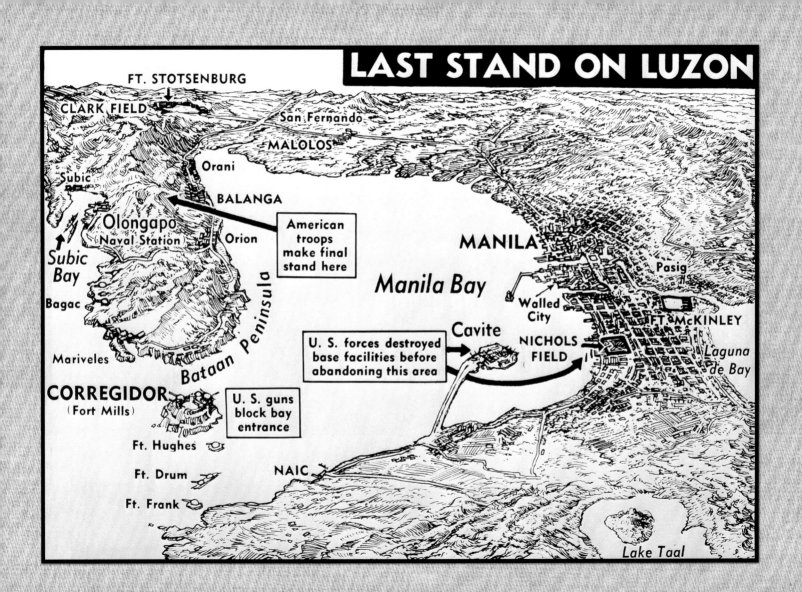

LAST STAND ON LUZON

FT. STOTSENBURG

CLARK FIELD

San Fernando

MALOLOS

Orani

Subic

BALANGA

Olongapo
(Naval Station)

Orion

Subic
Bay

American
troops
make final
stand here

MANILA

Pasig

Bagac

Manila Bay

Walled
City

FT. McKINLEY

Mariveles

Bataan Peninsula

Cavite

U. S. forces destroyed
base facilities before
abandoning this area

NICHOLS
FIELD

Laguna
de Bay

CORREGIDOR
(Fort Mills)

U. S. guns
block bay
entrance

Ft. Hughes

Ft. Drum

NAIC

Ft. Frank

Lake Taal

In the months after the Japanese attack on Pearl Harbor, U.S. authorities took into custody 9,121 enemy aliens the FBI had previously identified as particular threats to national security—including 5,100 Japanese. Still, Attorney General Francis Biddle declared that he was "determined to avoid mass internment, and the persecution of aliens that had characterized the First World War." Yet fears and rumors of Asian spies and sabotage soon began to spread, leading to a heated and often ugly debate about interning Japanese Americans (all of whom, the attorney general of Idaho said, should "be put in concentration camps for the remainder of the war. We want to keep this a white man's country"). Finally Biddle was compelled to agree that "enemy aliens" should be evacuated from sensitive areas. On February 19, 1942, President Roosevelt made this possible by signing Executive Order 9066, authorizing the creation of U.S. military zones, "from which any or all persons may be excluded." The order ultimately led to the internment of more than one hundred thousand West-Coast Japanese and Japanese Americans—about two-thirds of whom were U.S. citizens. Deprived of their property, the internees were taken first to such temporary "detention camps" as hastily refitted racetrack stables, then to one of ten more permanent "relocation camps," where they were forced to live behind barbed wire, watched over by armed guards. (See July 5, August 9)

ABOVE: A Japanese American boy with one of the troops sent to evacuate his family from Bainbridge Island, Washington, 1942.

RIGHT: A Japanese American family and the pastor of the Bainbridge Island Japanese church under guard in the back of a truck during their evacuation from the island, 1942.

JUNE 12

1944 The arrival of U.S. Special Task Air Group One in the Russell Islands in the South Pacific marks the first deployment of an American guided missle unit to a combat area. Two days later, the first German V-1 rocket bombs fall on England.

Post–Pearl Harbor anti-Japanese feeling was amply reflected in American propaganda —which sometimes included venomous caricatures. Even the swastika-wearing personification of the Axis in this poster urging greater war production has a demonic Asiatic mien. As the government and private companies produced hosts of (usually less dramatic) posters on the same theme, federal agencies established to oversee production and pricing proliferated. Faced with consequent problems, in January 1942, Roosevelt signed an executive order under which two existing agencies, the Supply Priorities Allocation Board and the Office of Production Management, were subsumed by the newly created War Production Board (WPB), which seemed intended to be *the* overall agency for directing war mobilization and federal procurement. The man Roosevelt tapped to head WPB, former Sears, Roebuck executive Donald Nelson (1888–1959), was initially a popular choice. But Nelson was quickly caught in bureaucratic and philosophical jousts that pointed out the actual limits of his authority and the weaknesses in his conciliatory management style. By the summer, Secretary of the Interior Harold Ickes was writing, "Nelson is the failure that many were afraid that he would be but hoped that he wouldn't be." The embattled Nelson stayed on the job for another two years. Meanwhile, in May 1943, Roosevelt established the Office of War Mobilization headed by James F. Byrnes— whose influence quickly eclipsed Nelson's.

ABOVE: Donald M. Nelson, chairman of the U.S. War Production Board. Photograph between 1940 and 1946.

RIGHT: *Let's not be next on Axis's crime table—Produce more for victory.* Color poster by G. Lawson produced for the General Motors Corporation, 1942.

JUNE 13

1942 On what will become known as "Black Saturday," the British Eighth Army in North Africa loses most of its armor in a devastating ambush by Rommel's forces near El Adem.

1944 Germany begins launching V-1 rocket bombs against England.

Americans, Hermann Göring reportedly said, could produce razor blades but not artillery. Throughout the war years, Americans proved him extraordinarily wrong as they manufactured 372,000 artillery pieces, twenty million small arms, six million tons of bombs, 2.5 million trucks, 102,000 armored vehicles, and more than three hundred thousand assorted warplanes. Among these were tens of thousands of bombers, including the famed B-17 "Flying Fortress" heavy bomber and the even heavier B-29, used to drop atomic bombs on the Japanese cities of Hiroshima and Nagasaki (see October 26, November 25). Among U.S. medium bombers, the problem-plagued B-26 (which pilots dubbed the "Widow-maker") was extremely unpopular, while the B-25 "Mitchell" won pilots' praise. Designed in 1938, B-25s were first produced in February 1941. Several months later, five B-25s were on the list of items Roosevelt offered as initial aid to the Soviets. The Russians, however, "were already displaying their peculiar methods of doing business," U.S. Army Air Forces chief Henry ("Hap") Arnold later reported. "In their endeavor to get the best we had, they immediately started voicing the opinion . . . that none of our airplanes were any good. They did not want any B-25's or B-26's; the only plane they wanted was the B-17." At the time, none of the planes were available in great quantities. As of April 1942, the army had accepted delivery of only five hundred B-17s and an equal number of Mitchells.

Employees at North American Aviation's outdoor assembly line in Inglewood, California, rush a B-25 "Mitchell" bomber to completion. Photograph by Alfred T. Palmer (1906–1993), October 1942.

JUNE 14

1940 German troops march into Paris; the French government implores the United States for aid. Russian troops invade Lithuania.

1944 Charles de Gaulle makes a triumphant return to France.

Modified B-25s were the aircraft of choice for the first U.S. bombing raid on Japan. This daring enterprise, undertaken to bolster American morale while damaging morale in Japan, called for sixteen of the usually land-based bombers to take off from an aircraft carrier, hit the cities of Kobe, Nagoya, Yokosuka, Yokohama, and Tokyo, then land farther west in China. After special training on short takeoffs, mission commander Lieutenant Colonel James H. ("Jimmy") Doolittle, his men, and their planes boarded the USS *Hornet*, which then joined Admiral William ("Bull") Halsey's Task Force 16. On April 18, 1942, *Hornet* sighted and quickly sank a Japanese boat. Yet, fearing the vessel might have had time to radio a report, Halsey decided to launch the bombers immediately—some eight hundred miles from Japan rather than the planned four hundred. Tension rose as the airmen, none of whom had actually taken off from a carrier before, watched Doolittle rev up for takeoff while the big ship bobbed like a bottle in tremendous seas. Then his plane surged off the deck as *Hornet* rose to the top of a wave. "The engines of three other ships were warming up, and the . . . turbulent sea made additional noise," B-25 pilot Ted Lawson later wrote. "But loud and clear above those sounds I could hear the hoarse cheers of every Navy man on that ship." Loaded with both high-explosive and incendiary bombs, the planes completed their mission, shaking civilian confidence and enraging the Japanese high command. (See also June 16.)

ABOVE: Maj. Gen. James H. Doolittle (1896–1993). U.S. Army Signal Corps photo, 1943.

RIGHT: Japan and the Coast of China, map depicting the "Doolittle Raid" of April 18, 1942, published in *Thirty Seconds over Tokyo*, Capt. Ted Lawson's account of the raid, 1943.

JUNE 15

1941 Vichy France issues a decree limiting the rights of Jews.

1944 U.S. Marines invade Saipan; U.S. B-29s, flying from China, attack Japan, the first U.S. raid there since the 1942 Doolittle raid.

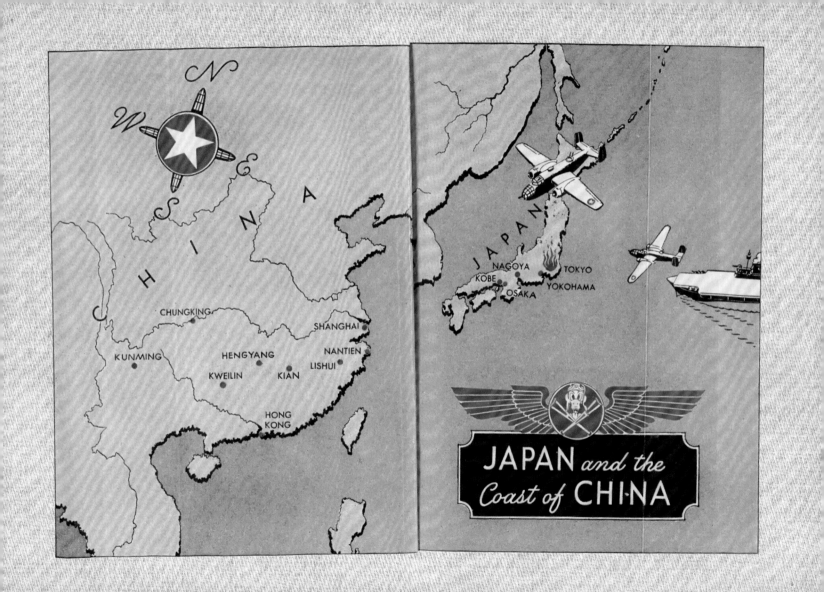

JAPAN *and the* Coast *of* CHINA

Flying on fumes after their April 18, 1942, raid on Japan (see June 15), the sixteen B-25s crewed by Doolittle's eighty raiders headed toward prearranged landing points in China. Overtaken simultaneously by night and bad weather, and with no ground navigational aids to assist them, they could not locate their landing fields. Fifteen of the planes crash-landed in China and one landed at a Soviet air base north of Vladivostok. Seventy-two of the raiders survived: Of the eight picked up by Japanese patrols, one died in prison, four were released after the war—and three were eventually executed, further enraging the American public. The Japanese also punished those who helped or were suspected of helping the American flyers. In May, the high command dispatched fifty-three battalions to destroy airfields and execute Chinese in the provinces where the planes landed. Over the following four months of terror, as many as 250,000 Chinese people were killed. This orgy of revenge was one more on a long list of Japanese atrocities, demonstrations of savagery that effectively negated, for most Chinese, Japan's "Asia for Asians" propaganda—although the propaganda continued throughout the war. "The Chinese people are, it goes without saying, our friends," an Imperial Japanese Government release stated in July 1944. "What Japan earnestly desires is to bring to consummation a permanent relationship of good neighborliness and friendship between Japan and China."

LEFT: *Honourable Persuasion: I'm Sure You'd Like to Repeat After Me, 'Asia for the Asiatics Alone!'* Photoprint of a linecut by E. H. Shepard, 1938.

RIGHT: *A Poster for Pacification Propaganda*. Reproduction of a painting by Eijiro Suzuki, published in *Seisen Gafu* ("A Picture Album of the Holy War"), Tokyo, 1939.

JUNE 16

1941 All German and Italian consular, information, and tourist officers and staff are ordered to be withdrawn from the United States by July 10, for engaging in activities of "an improper and unwarranted character."

As the Japanese launched their campaign of reprisal in China (see June 15, 16), a Japanese fleet moved toward Port Moresby, the capital of Papua, an Australian colony comprising the southeastern quarter of New Guinea. If the Japanese gained a foothold there, they would be within air-strike range of Australia. Alerted by intelligence, Allied command sent a task force to stop them. A first tentative clash occurred at Tulagi, an island just north of Guadalcanal in the Solomon chain. After planes from the U.S. carrier *Yorktown* attacked a newly arrived Japanese occupation force and its naval support, the opposing naval strike forces began to hunt for each other. This culminated in the two-day Battle of the Coral Sea—the first naval battle in history in which the vying fleets were never in visual contact. On May 7, aircraft from the *Yorktown* and USS *Lexington* sank the small Japanese carrier *Shoho*. In fierce fighting the next day, with planes crisscrossing the two hundred miles separating their fleets, *Yorktown* was damaged and the *Lexington* was lost. After the firing stopped, both sides claimed victory. Hitler believed the Japanese: "After this new defeat, the United States warships will hardly dare to face the Japanese fleet again," he crowed. Yet the Battle of the Coral Sea was, in fact, a strategic victory for the Allies, who had forestalled Japan's Port Moresby operation. Moreover, damage the Allies inflicted on the Japanese carriers *Zuikaku* and *Shokaku* prevented their participation in the pivotal Battle of Midway a month later.

Death of the Shoho. Color reproduction of a painting by Robert Benney (1904–2001), c. 1944.

JUNE 17

1940 In the wake of German success in France, the British declare: "We have become the sole champions now in arms to defend the world cause."

"We have decided to storm and occupy Diégo Suarez," Churchill wrote South Africa's prime minister Jan Smuts on March 24, 1942, "as arrival of Japanese there would not be effectively resisted by the Vichy French and would be disastrous to the safety of our Middle East convoys." The site of a large French navy base, Diégo Suarez lay at the northern end of the island of Madagascar, a French colony in the Indian Ocean off the southeast coast of Africa, that had been loyal to Vichy since the British attack on the French Fleet at Oran (see March 18). British intelligence knew that the Germans had been urging Japan to establish a base on the island, and, not long after Churchill's message, the Japanese navy had become stingingly active in the eastern Indian Ocean. Thus, on May 5, the British launched Operation Ironclad—the first Allied invasion, and Britain's first major amphibious operation of the war. Landing with heavy naval support, a force comprising British, British East African, and South African troops met strong initial resistance. By May 7, however, the French had retreated from Diégo Suarez, which was, originally, Britain's sole objective. However, the confirmed presence of at least one Japanese submarine in the area, the South African government's insistence that the Allies secure the island's other ports, and the Vichy governor's adamant refusal to surrender led to additional action (September 10–November 5) that secured the whole island. Thereafter, the Free French controlled Madagascar.

LEFT: The front cover of Eric Rosenthal's 1944 book *Japan's Bid for Africa* shows one Japanese tentacle reaching for Diego Suarez, at the northern tip of Madagascar.

RIGHT: After securing the naval base at Diego Suarez, Madagascar, Allied troops inspect damage inflicted on defending Vichy-French air defenses by their own naval aircraft during the invasion, 1942.

JUNE 18

1945 U.S. Tenth Army commander Lt. Gen. Simon Bolivar Buckner Jr.—son of the Confederate Civil War general—is killed by a Japanese shell on Okinawa.

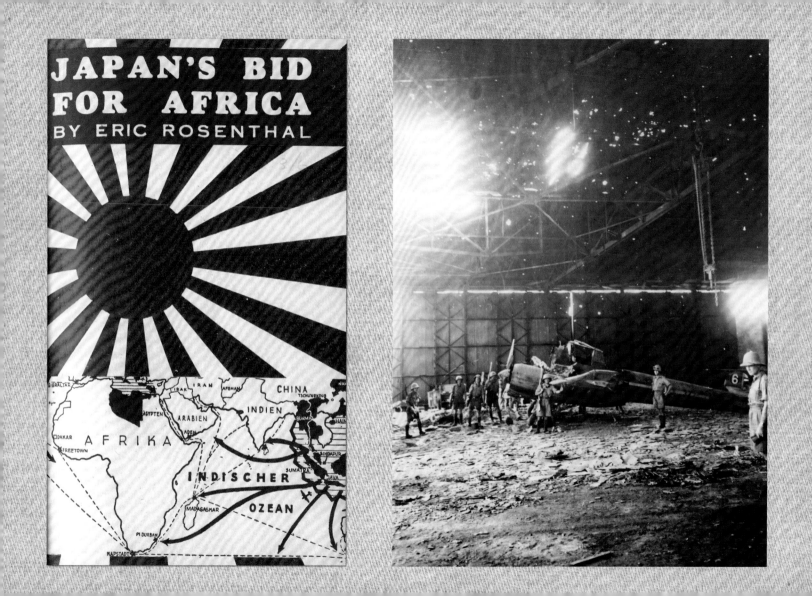

The thwarted try for Port Moresby and the British landing on Madagascar were small negative aberrations within Japan's overall victorious sweep in spring 1942. In the British dominion of Burma, the Japanese campaign was proceeding so well that Chiang Kai-shek's chief of staff, Joseph Stilwell, leading two Chinese divisions that Chiang had reluctantly dispatched to help the British, wrote to his wife on April 16: "We are about to take a beating, I think." Only four days later he hastily scrawled in his diary, "Disaster at Loikaw. 55th [Chinese Division] completely smashed. . . . Phone wires all cut. Are the British going to run out on us? *Yes*." A Japanese breakthrough at Lashio precipitated a massive Allied withdrawal to India—the longest retreat in the history of the British army. Some officers got out by air, but Stilwell declined to be rescued. He was determined to stay with his rapidly disintegrating Chinese force (whose officers responded to distant Chiang more readily than they took Stilwell's orders) and get them to India. But everything went wrong. In the end, the general led only a hardy band of 114 Chinese, Malayan, Burmese, British, and American civilian and military refugees out of Burma. Their epic 140-mile, twenty-day march across the mountains to India earned Stilwell plaudits as a hero— in America, if not in China. "Stilwell deserted our troops," Chiang said, angry that the general had not even attempted to keep him informed of his movements. "I doubt if he knows the importance of military discipline."

Some of the band of Americans, Burmese, Chinese, Indians, Britons, and Anglo Indians who participated in U.S. Maj. Gen. Joseph Stilwell's march out of Burma in 1942 take the ten minutes of rest Stilwell allowed every hour. U.S. Army photograph, 1942.

JUNE 19

1944 The two-day Battle of the Philippine Sea begins. In this decisive victory, U.S. forces will sink three Japanese aircraft carriers and destroy 426 aircraft.

As Stilwell was leading his small band out of Burma (see June 19), U.S. intelligence intercepted and deciphered messages that revealed a Japanese plan to take Midway atoll, in the northwestern Hawaiian Islands. Admiral Isoroku Yamamoto (architect of the attack on Pearl Harbor) devised his elaborate plan for the battle with one chief objective in mind: a decisive victory over the U.S. Pacific Fleet. Even forewarned, the Americans were at a huge disadvantage. Yamamoto's forces were far larger and included four of Japan's eight heavy aircraft carriers, *Akagi*, *Hiryu*, *Kaga*, and *Soryu*. The American force included three carriers, *Enterprise*, *Hornet*, and *Yorktown*—the last having just undergone hasty repairs after being damaged in the Battle of the Coral Sea (see June 17). On June 4, the second day of the Battle of Midway, one U.S. air attack group was badly mauled; but a second air attack damaged three of the four Japanese carriers so badly they had to be scuttled. Planes from the remaining carrier, *Hiryu*, took *Yorktown* out of the battle (it was finished off by a Japanese submarine); then planes from *Enterprise* fatally wounded *Hiryu*. The battle concluded with Midway still in American hands and Yamamoto's fleet bereft of carriers. The Japanese navy's first major defeat, Midway was a blow from which it would never recover. "Pearl Harbor," U.S. Pacific Fleet commander Chester Nimitz declared, "has now been partially avenged."

ABOVE: Vice Adm. Nobutake Kondo (1886–1953) commanded the Midway Assault Group, one of four components in Yamamoto's battle plan. Reproduction of a painting by Eiza Okuse published in *Seisen Gafu* ("A Picture Album of the Holy War"), Tokyo, 1939.

RIGHT: Battle of Midway: A Japanese bomber scores a direct hit on the carrier USS *Yorktown*, June 1942.

JUNE 20

1940 A Japanese military mission arrives in Vietnam; the area of Tonkin—adjacent to China—is opened to Japanese military control

"This is the moment for me to send you my heartiest congratulations on the grand American victories in the Pacific [Coral Sea and Midway], which have . . . altered the balance of the naval war," Churchill wrote Roosevelt on June 13, 1942. Four days later, Churchill and some of his military chiefs flew to the United States to discuss pressing problems. Among the foremost was the deteriorating Allied position in North Africa, where Field Marshal Erwin Rommel's German-Italian forces had been pushing British and Commonwealth troops steadily back. On June 21, Churchill was in Roosevelt's White House study when a secretary entered and handed the prime minister a telegram: Rommel had taken the vital port city of Tobruk, Libya, which had become a focal point for British morale as it held out for months against an Axis siege. The thirty thousand men of the city's garrison were now prisoners of war. As Churchill absorbed the unhappy news, Roosevelt asked what the United States could do. "Give us as many Sherman tanks as you can spare," the prime minister said, "and ship them to the Middle East as quickly as possible." Roosevelt consulted Army Chief of Staff George Marshall—who was struggling to properly equip his own growing force. "It is a terrible thing to take the weapons out of a soldier's hands," Marshall said. But he agreed that this was an emergency. Very quickly, three hundred of the latest-model Sherman tanks and one hundred self-propelled artillery pieces were on their way to North Africa.

The harbor at the much-contested Libyan port city of Tobruk, which fell to the Germans, June 21, 1942.

JUNE 21

1941 Japanese submarine I-25 surfaces off the coast of Oregon and fires on Fort Stevens, slightly damaging a baseball field.

While Rommel was closing in on Tobruk (see June 21), an RAF plane left England to drop two Czech resistance fighters by parachute into their occupied country. Jan Kubis and Josef Gabeik were men with a mission. They had come to assassinate Heinrich Himmler's chief deputy, Reinhard Heydrich, whom historian William Shirer has described as an "icy-eyed . . . policeman of diabolical cast, the genius of the 'final solution.'" On May 27, the two Czechs mortally wounded their target. His death on June 4 sparked massive reprisals, the Nazis eventually murdering an estimated five thousand people. The most infamous episode in this retributive slaughter occurred on June 9, when ten truckloads of Nazi Security Police surrounded the Czech village of Lidice and the nearby hamlet of Lezaky. Every man, woman, and child of these villages, some five hundred souls, suffered for Heydrich's death. The Germans immediately shot all the men and boys older than sixteen, plus a few women. They transported all but four of the surviving women to Ravensbrueck concentration camp, where fifty-two of them died. (The other four women, all pregnant, were allowed to deliver their babies, whom the Nazis then killed, before being sent on to Ravensbrueck.) The younger children were sent to a separate concentration camp (where a few were selected to be raised as Germans). Finally, using fire and dynamite, the Germans erased Lidice itself from the face of the earth.

ABOVE: Reinhard Heydrich (1904–1942).

RIGHT: German soldiers with the victims of one of their mass executions as they destroy the town of Lidice, Czechoslovakia, June 1942.

JUNE 22

1941 Germany and its Axis partners launch a massive attack on the Soviet Union along an eighteen-hundred-mile front from the Arctic to the Black Sea.

1942 The first V-mail is sent from New York to London.

"We were disappointed at not breaking Rommel's front last week though heavy losses were inflicted upon him in bitter fighting," Churchill wrote Roosevelt on July 27, 1942. "We have far heavier reinforcements approaching and far better communications than he has and marked superiority in the air." With Tobruk in Axis hands (see June 21), Rommel had advanced into Egypt, thrusting toward the vital Suez Canal. Repulsed by the British when he attacked their defensive line at El Alamein in early July, Rommel then faced a logistic and tactical dilemma: He had only thirty-six operable tanks and, with Malta-based planes again hitting Axis convoys, he was low on fuel and other supplies. On July 17, he wrote his wife: "The enemy is using his superiority, especially in infantry, to destroy the Italian formations one by one, and the German formations are much too weak to stand alone. It's enough to make one weep." After attacking and counterattacking through the rest of July, both sides had paused to regroup when, on August 15, Field Marshal Bernard Law Montgomery arrived in North Africa. Assuming command of the British Eighth Army, he moved quickly to raise the morale of his dispirited troops. "No more maneuvers," he said. "We will fight a battle." The furious battle they fought at Alam El Halfa at the end of August forced Rommel to withdraw. Two months later, the British sent Rommel's forces reeling back into Libya at the second Battle of El Alamein—one of the turning points of the entire war.

LEFT: Field Mar. Bernard Law Montgomery (1887–1976). U.S. Signal Corps photograph, June 15, 1944.

RIGHT: German and Italian signposts in Tobruk, Libya, point to former Axis offices. U.S. Army Signal Corps photograph, c. 1942–43.

JUNE 23

1941 Hungary declares war on the Soviet Union.

On August 7, 1942, nineteen thousand U.S. Marines landed on Guadalcanal and four other islands in the Solomon group, launching the first major U.S. ground offensive of the war. The struggle for Guadalcanal introduced American fighting men to the no-quarter combat of soul-shaking viciousness that would characterize the long Pacific theater campaign. "I have never heard or read of this kind of fighting," the ground force commander, Major General Alexander A. Vandegrift, reported to the Marine Corps commandant in August. "These people refuse to surrender. The wounded will wait till men come up to examine them, and blow themselves and the other fellow to death with a hand grenade." Vandegrift's marines had other pressing problems. After a bitter defeat at the battle of Savo Sound, August 8–9, the navy pulled back, leaving the ground force low on critical supplies— and without air support until Marine aircraft landed at the island's hastily repaired airstrip on August 20. Land combat and naval battles roiled on into the fall, the American situation becoming so tenuous that Southwest Pacific theater commander Douglas MacArthur warned Roosevelt, "If we are defeated in the Solomons . . . the entire Southwest Pacific will be in gravest danger." Additional troops were rushed to the island, Roosevelt interceded to ensure additional warships were sent to the South Pacific, and by December the Americans had gained the upper hand—though more hard fighting lay ahead.

Marines battle Japanese troops on Guadalcanal. Drawing by a former marine F. Miller (first name unknown), date unknown.

JUNE 24

1942 — Maj. Gen. Eisenhower assumes command of U.S. forces in the European Theater.

1943 — Broadcasting from Tokyo, pro-Axis Indian leader Subhas Chandra Bose calls for an armed uprising by Indians against the British.

On August 8, 1942, as American marines were beginning their struggle on Guadalcanal (see June 24), U.S. authorities executed six German agents at the District of Columbia jail. The Germans had begun their fatal journey four months before, when they started training at a Nazi sabotage school for a mission to America, code-named Operation Pastorius. On June 13, a submarine landed George Dasch, Ernest Burger, Heinrich Heinck, and Richard Quirin on a beach near Amagansett, Long Island. Four days later, another submarine deposited Edward Kerling, Werner Thiel, Herman Neubauer, and Herbert Haupt at Ponte Vedra Beach, Florida. The men were under orders to destroy critical facilities such as bridges, railroad stations, and aluminum processing plants. Yet within ten days, and before they had done any damage, all eight were in government hands. A vigilant coastguardsman who had encountered the Long Island group and thought it suspicious alerted authorities. Yet it was George Dasch who aborted the mission by turning himself and his fellows in. After a swift trial by a military tribunal (July 8–August 4)—and a habeas corpus appeal to the Supreme Court by seven of the agents (*Ex Parte Quirin*)—all eight were found guilty and sentenced to death. (Roosevelt commuted Dasch's sentence and that of Burger, who had colluded in Dasch's actions.) The near-instant collapse of Operation Pastorius discouraged the Germans from attempting any more such sabotage missions to the United States.

German saboteurs caught and tried in the United States. Top, left to right: Herman Neubauer, Heinrich Heinck, Werner Thiel, Edward John Kerling; bottom, left to right: Richard Quirin, Herbert Hans Haupt, George Dasch, Ernest Peter Burger. August 8, 1942.

JUNE 25

1943 Jews in the ghetto of Czestochowa in Poland begin an uprising that is swiftly and ruthlessly suppressed.

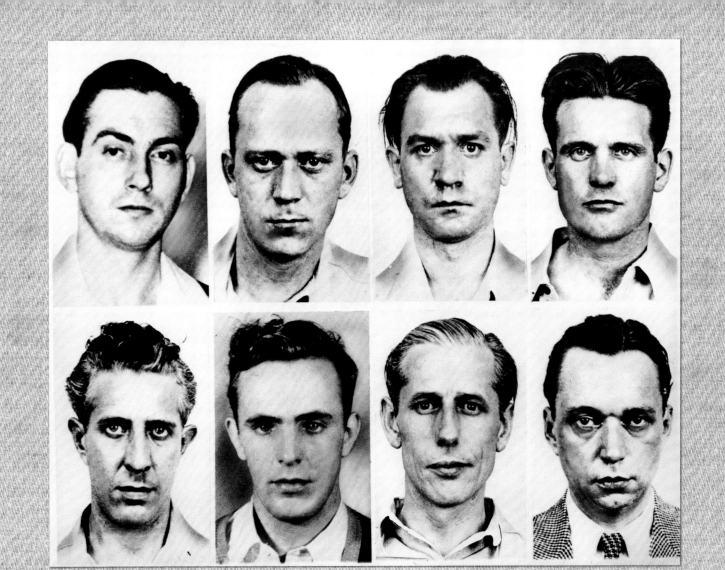

"The greatest Commando operation of the war so far was carried out to-day, when Allied forces attacked Dieppe and fought for nine hours on French soil," Britain's *Daily Telegraph* reported on August 19, 1942. "It was a combined operation in every sense of the term, with British, Canadian, American and Fighting French troops taking part. The American troops were having their baptism of fire in Europe in the present war." Sixty U.S. Army rangers were with the five thousand Canadians, one thousand Britons, and a few Free French troops who embarked on this elaborate raid. Code-named Operation Jubilee, it was undertaken to raise morale in occupied France, demonstrate the western Allies' resolve to the Soviet Union, and test coastal defenses and amphibious landing tactics. When the *Daily Telegraph* reported "The attack took the enemy by surprise," however, it was stretching the truth. Germans discovered the assault force before the landings, defenders on the beach set up a deadly crossfire, and the raid deteriorated from there. By 9 A.M. the situation was grievous, and commanders issued the order to withdraw. The returning raiders were far fewer in number: Nearly 50 percent of the landing force remained behind, either killed or taken prisoner. The covering RAF units had lost more than a hundred planes. Whether these heavy losses were worth the major lesson the Allies learned from the venture—that heavy bombardment must precede any major landing—is still being debated.

ABOVE: Map depicting the Dieppe raid, published in *The Daily Telegraph Story of the War, September 1941–December 1942*, 1943.

RIGHT: Allied troops return from the raid on Dieppe, France, August 1942.

JUNE 26

1942 Germany announces it will begin unrestricted submarine warfare off the East Coast of the United States.

1945 In San Francisco, delegates to the United Nations organizational conference sign the United Nations Charter.

On Sunday, August 23, 1942, six hundred German planes appeared over Stalingrad, a vital manufacturing and transport center on the Volga River and a city that Stalin had ordered held at all costs. By nightfall, this model city of parks and apartment buildings had been reduced to heaps of flaming rubble. There had been action this year all along the thousand-mile eastern front: The Wehrmacht's Army Group North still held Leningrad under siege; Army Group Center, which had been halted in front of Moscow, launched operations to smash Red Army units that threatened its line. Yet Hitler directed that the main thrust of action would be in the oil-rich south, and Stalingrad was one of the führer's principal objectives. As the German Sixth Army under General Friedrich Paulus closed in, Stalin poured reinforcements into the city, shifted Marshal Georgi Zhukov from Moscow to Stalingrad, and put General Vasily Chuikov in charge of the city's defenses. In mid-September the vicious ground fighting began; before it was over more than a million men would be dead. "The heavy casualties, the constant retreat, the shortage of food and munitions, the difficulty of receiving reinforcements . . . all this had a very bad effect on morale," Chuikov later wrote. "Many longed . . . to escape the hell of Stalingrad." But at the end of the year, after storms of offensives and counteroffensives, the Red Army was still holding—while Paulus's Sixth Army, freezing cold and low on vital supplies, was in trouble. (See August 7)

Stalingradskaia Pereprava, ("Crossing the River at Stalingrad"). Reproduction of a painting by V. K. Dmitrievskii, c. 1958.

JUNE 27

1941 In the Soviet Union, the encircled city of Minsk falls to the Germans, who take three hundred thousand prisoners. In the battle for the city the Germans destroy three Soviet armies and badly maul two others.

Relentlessly pressed by the Germans, Stalin relentlessly pressed his Western Allies to open a second front, thus forcing Hitler to transfer troops from the Soviet Union to meet the new threat. The abortive raid on Dieppe (see June 26) had proved how unprepared the Allies were to stage a landing in western Europe in 1942, yet some major operation was imperative. By late summer, the British and American high commands had decided to mount Operation Torch, the invasion of northwest Africa (see May 21). An earlier Anglo American agreement specified that the Mediterranean region was primarily a British responsibility. However, since most invasion troops were to be American, the British asked for an American commander. On November 8, an invasion force comprising 670 vessels and about sixty-five thousand men under the command of Lieutenant General Dwight D. ("Ike") Eisenhower faced some 120,000 Vichy French troops when they launched assaults at Casablanca in Morocco, and Algiers and Oran in Algeria. The Allies took Algiers the first day, but they faced stiff resistance around Oran and Casablanca (landing site for General George Patton's Western Task Force). The resistance did not last long; by November 11, Eisenhower and the Vichy French commander in chief, Admiral Jean François Darlan (who happened to be in Algiers during the invasion), had negotiated an armistice. There were now two Allied forces in North Africa—and Rommel's army, retreating toward Tunisia, was between them.

U.S. troops battle snipers in a street skirmish, Algiers, Algeria, November 1942.

JUNE 28

1943 Launching their summer offensive, the Germans begin an immense eastern front clash; the battle of Kursk causes two hundred thousand Soviet and fifty thousand German casualties in the first ten days of fighting.

"**H**itler . . . has not built up any illusions on the French desire to fight," Italian foreign minister Galeazzo Ciano, meeting with Hitler in Munich, wrote in his diary on November 9, as Anglo American forces moved into North Africa. He also noted Hitler's "definite point of view: the total occupation of France." German troops quickly swept into the previously unoccupied Vichy territory—provoking one major act of resistance. Admiral Jean Laborde, commander in chief of the Vichy French navy, ordered his men to scuttle the vessels moored at Toulon: Seventy-seven ships (half the tonnage of the French navy) were rendered useless to the Reich. As German troops also seized control of the French colony of Tunisia, former Vichy French soldiers farther west expanded the ranks of Free French forces. These troops became new beneficiaries of the "arsenal of democracy." A month before Operation Torch, a clandestine meeting at Cherchel, Algeria, between U.S. general Mark Clark and a representative of General Henri Giraud (see May 22) engendered an American pledge "to furnish the French forces with arms and modern equipment." After Torch and throughout the rest of the war, the United States fully equipped and trained eight French divisions in North Africa, trained and partially equipped three more in France, provided matériel for nineteen air squadrons, and helped rehabilitate the French navy. Yet as 1942 ended, the question of the overall leadership of Free French forces remained open.

American troops present arms as French soldiers march past. Oran, Algeria, December 1942.

JUNE 29

1940   Congress passes the Alien Registration Act, requiring all alien residents in the United States over the age of fourteen to register and to divulge their occupational status and political beliefs.

"I am sure you are keeping my wife's official business to the minimum," Roosevelt wrote to Churchill on October 24, 1942. "I would appreciate it if you would let me know occasionally how things are going with her." Three days before, Eleanor Roosevelt had embarked on an official visit to Britain, where she proceeded to awe Britons and Americans alike with her energy and probing interest in everything from war damage to women's war employment. "Mrs. Roosevelt has been winning golden opinions here from all for her kindness," Churchill reported to the president. "I did my best to advise a reduction of her program and also interspersing it with blank days, but I have not met with success and Mrs. Roosevelt proceeds indefatigably." Visiting American troops (including her son Elliott), the first lady insisted on climbing into a B-17 so that she could get a feel for what each crew member did; noted rising tensions between southern white soldiers and African American troops who were dating white English girls; and managed to arrange, via General Eisenhower, for soldiers to be issued woolen socks to replace the thin cotton socks they were wearing (which promoted blistering when they marched). "Every soldier I see is a friend from home," she wrote in her newspaper column, "and I want to stop and talk with him whether I know him or not. When I find we really have some point of contact, it gives me a warm feeling around the heart for the rest of the day."

On a goodwill tour of Great Britain, First Lady Eleanor Roosevelt pauses to talk with an American soldier. Photograph by Toni Frissell, November 1942.

JUNE 30

1941 At a Liaison Conference this day, Japanese military and civilian officials finally decide the ongoing debate about whether to expand north by attacking the USSR or south, moving into British, Dutch, and American Pacific holdings. Their decision to go south is formally confirmed on July 2.

1943 Allied forces launch Operation Cartwheel, involving amphibious operations against Japanese-held islands in the southwest Pacific.

Interlude: Total War

"This whole nation of one hundred and thirty million free men, women and children is becoming one great fighting force," President Roosevelt said in a radio address in October 1942. "Some of us are fighting the war in airplanes five miles above the continent of Europe . . . and some of us are fighting it in mines deep down in the earth of Pennsylvania or Montana . . . all of us can have that deep and permanent inner satisfaction that comes from . . . playing an honorable part in the great struggle to save our democratic civilization."

World War II was a "total war" fought not only by front-line armed forces, but also around the globe by "home-front" civilians who provided economic, industrial, humanitarian, and scientific support. This massive effort disrupted patterns of life, even in the United States, which, unlike other major combatants, was not subjected to bombing raids. Millions of people migrated to war production centers. Women worked at jobs previously reserved for men. Everyone got involved: Young people collected rubber and scrap metal; older people staffed civil defense organizations; even convicts were pressed into service. New opportunities opened for minorities and colonial peoples—but opportunity was often tempered by continuing prejudice. "In some communities, employers dislike to employ women," Roosevelt noted. "In others they are reluctant to hire Negroes. . . . We can no longer afford to indulge such prejudices or practices."

JULY 1

1941 Under German occupation, Parisians this month are limited to one pound of meat per week (if available) and one pound of bread per day.

Racial struggles, wage worries, and opportunism did not vanish during the war years, but they were vastly overshadowed by the struggle to achieve victory. "From New York City to Frisco Bay, We're speedin' up production everyday," Pete Seeger declared in his 1942 song "Deliver the Goods." "And every time a wheel goes around, It carries Mr. Hitler to the burying ground."

Stealing food and war matériel from occupied countries, Mr. Hitler had been slow to insist on total mobilization at home. By 1943, however, he agreed to support a total war plan suggested by his chief propagandist, Joseph Goebbels, who launched the program at a rally in February. "Are you determined to follow the Führer through thick and thin in the struggle for victory," he challenged the assembled crowd, "and to accept even the harshest personal sacrifices?"

Five months later an estimated forty-five thousand Germans living in the major port and industrial center of Hamburg were killed in the war's first firestorm, ignited by Allied incendiary bombs on the hot, dry night of July 27 (see August 23). Flying to and from Hamburg, Allied air units used a new and extremely effective radar-defeating device, code-named "Window," to flummox German air defenses and reduce the airmen's own high casualty rate. Comprising bundles of metal strips, this device was among the simplest of the many innovations produced by both sides in the ongoing technological and scientific "war" raging behind the front lines. In 1944 and 1945, Hitler unleashed his "terror weapons," the V–1 and V–2 rockets. In 1945, scientists in the United States produced the most terrible new weapons of all. The use of atomic bombs against two Japanese cities in August 1945 ushered in the Nuclear Age—in which it became possible for total war to lead to the total destruction of humankind.

Are YOU doing all you can? Color poster published by the General Cable Corporation, 1942.

"Our paratroops made a great name for themselves in this war," an anonymous writer trumpeted in Japan's 1942 English-language publication, *Victory on the March: A Pictorial Record of the War of Greater East Asia* (see July 10). "Navy 'chutists descended upon Menado, in the Celebes, on January 11 and on Kupang, Timor, on February 20 and the army 'chutists fell on Palembang, in Sumatra, February 24, and . . . carried out their objects to perfection. Composed of picked men, they represent the strongest fighters in the services." World War II was the first conflict in which paratroops were deployed in battle—initially by the Axis. Their effectiveness stunned the Allies, although they were well aware of interwar developments: The Red Army had staged some spectacular jumps in the 1930s, and by 1940, the Italians had organized two understrength airborne divisions. The Germans improved on lessons learned from both those sources and were the first to use paratroops in battle, successfully deploying them in the assault on Norway and again during the Wehrmacht's sweep through the Low Countries and France. As worried British civilians envisioned Nazi paratroopers descending through English skies, Churchill ordered the formation of British paratroop units. Across the Atlantic, the Americans were doing the same. U.S. paratroopers first saw action during Operation Torch (see May 21, June 28) and were essential to U.S. and combined operations through the end of the war. The Japanese, meanwhile, did not follow up on their early airborne-operation successes.

Paratroops at Palembang. Painting by Goro Tsuruta reproduced in the Japanese propaganda publication *Victory on the March,* 1942.

JULY 2

1940 Hitler issues sealed orders for the invasion of Great Britain (Operation Sealion).

D evelopment of airborne assault forces; procurement of new and better weapons, aircraft, and ships; the care and feeding of millions of troops, prisoners, and refugees—all these required vast sums of money. To raise it, combatant countries taxed citizens and businesses, went into debt, courted inflation by printing more money, and sought donations of valuable commodities, as in Nationalist China's "Offer Gold to the State" campaign. (Axis governments, most particularly Germany's, augmented these methods with theft.) Most major combatants also sold war bonds, none more successfully than the United States. The U.S. Treasury began selling "Victory Bonds" in May 1941— and a certain Franklin D. Roosevelt was among the first purchasers. Throughout the war years, the War Finance Committee in the Department of the Treasury supervised eight major bond campaigns, all of them accompanied by blizzards of publicity coordinated by the War Advertising Council. The media donated hundreds of millions of dollars in print, radio, and billboard advertising; bond posters were ubiquitous; and bond rallies all over the country featured bands, auctions, competitions, and appearances by celebrities. Beginning in 1942, paying for bonds became much easier: buyers could simply elect to have the costs deducted from their paychecks via the Payroll Savings Plan. By the end of the war, Americans had purchased $157 billion in bonds, exceeding government goals by more than $50 billion.

A photomural designed by the Farm Security Administration promotes the sale of defense bonds in New York City's Grand Central Station. Photograph by Arthur Rothstein (1915–1985), 1942.

JULY 3

1945 The Allies take over their zones of occupation in Berlin.

One group of Americans contributed a substantial amount of money to the war effort even before U.S. war bond drives began (see July 3). In 1940, after passage of the Selective Service Training Bill (see March 24, April 21), the General Council of the Klamath Tribe donated $150,000 to the federal government, which was to use the money to establish an army-run defense training camp on the Klamath reservation. After Pearl Harbor, American Indian tribes continued their financial support for the war effort. At the same time, men of many American Indian nations joined the armed services: A total of 21,767 eventually served in the army, 1,910 in the navy, 874 in the marines, and 121 in the Coast Guard. Some American Indian women served in the Women's Army Corps and the Navy WAVES. Like the ten thousand American Indians who had served in World War I, this new generation compiled a proud record. One distinctive contribution to battlefield service echoed their forefathers' service in the earlier war. Men of the Comanche, Choctaw, Creek, Menominee, Chippewa, and Hopi nations served as "code talkers" throughout the campaign to liberate Europe from *posah-tai-vo* (Comanche for "crazy white man," a.k.a. Adolf Hitler), using their complex and unfamiliar languages to stymie Germans attempting to eavesdrop on Allied communications. On the other side of the world, four hundred Navajo U.S. Marine code talkers participated in every marine assault in the Pacific campaign, most notably at Iwo Jima.

Freedom's Warrior—American Indian. Lithograph by Charles Banks Wilson (b. 1918), between 1941 and 1943.

JULY 4

1941 — Tito (Josip Broz) announces a Communist resistance movement in Yugoslavia: the "Partisans." It is the first use of a term that will become common during the war.

"**M**ost of us desire to be treated in the same way as all other Americans, both as to sacrifices and benefits," delegate Sim Togasaki said during a conference of the Japanese American Citizens League (JACL) in the summer of 1942. "Even though we have gone through so much, I am confident that most of us are willing to forget and forgive, and join the Army and fight for our country and our future." JACL national secretary Mike Masaoka agreed with Togasaki. Although his own family had been forced behind the barbed wire of the Manzanar relocation facility (see June 12), Masaoka strongly advocated extending the draft to Nisei (second-generation) men in the camps. Before that occurred, however, the U.S. government formed a trial segregated volunteer unit, the 442nd Regimental Combat Team. Masaoka was among its first members—and he was joined by five of his six brothers (one, Hank, later transferred to the paratroops). Deployed to Italy, France, then Italy again, the 442nd became the most decorated American unit of its size in World War II, fighting hard and paying so heavily in casualties it was nicknamed the Purple Heart Battalion. Some of those Purple Hearts went to the Masaokas: Tad was wounded but returned to the front; medic Ike was hit so severely rescuing wounded men he was listed as 100 percent disabled; Ben was killed during the 442nd's stunning rescue of another U.S. battalion cut off by the Germans; and Mike was grazed by shrapnel during his vain search for Ben's body.

Four Masaoka brothers (left to right): Ben, Mike, Tad, and Ike. U.S. Army Signal Corps photograph, April 1944.

JULY 5

1945 Gen. Douglas MacArthur announces the liberation of the Philippines.

embers of the 442nd Regimental Combat Team (see July 5) were not the only Japanese Americans in uniform. Americans of Japanese descent also served with the U.S. Army Military Intelligence Service, garnering information by translating, monitoring Japanese-language radio broadcasts, and interrogating prisoners of war. Intelligence gathering was just one aspect of wartime covert operations, which ranged from research and analysis to sabotage and subversion. Initially, the United States had some catching up to do in this underground realm, so in July 1941 Roosevelt appointed the much-decorated World War I veteran William "Wild Bill" Donovan coordinator of information (COI) to help centralize and develop American clandestine operations. In 1942, COI became the Office of Strategic Services (OSS) and, under Donovan's aggressive leadership, mounted effective operations in the Mediterranean Theater, Asia, and Europe. In Germany, meanwhile, Admiral Wilhelm Canaris headed the Third Reich's military intelligence and counterintelligence organization, the Abwehr, overseeing a worldwide espionage network. His enthusiasm and authority lessened, however, as his disenchantment with Hitler grew. At the same time, Hitler grew disenchanted with the Abwehr, which harbored too many officers of suspect loyalties. The Nazis arrested Canaris after the July 20, 1944, attempt to assassinate the führer, although the admiral was not involved in the plot, and the Abwehr fell under Heinrich Himmler's control.

LEFT: Maj. Gen. William J. Donovan (1883–1959), November 7, 1950.

RIGHT: Adm. Wilhelm Canaris, born 1887, executed by the Nazis, April 9, 1945.

JULY 6

1944 Vice Adm. Chuichi Nagumo, who commanded the Pearl Harbor attack force and led the carrier strike force during the Japanese defeat at the Battle of Midway, commits suicide on Saipan.

Covert operations (see July 6, October 18) included hundreds of underground newspapers run by resistance organizations in occupied countries—such as *Combat* in France, *La Libre Belgique* in Belgium, and *Action de la Gueux* in Holland. Produced and distributed at terrible risk, these publications penetrated the fog of Axis propaganda, raised morale, and kept the idea of freedom alive. In the United States, the idea of freedom is most potently expressed in the Declaration of Independence and the Constitution. During World War II, these seminal documents were in the custody of the Library of Congress, which conveyed them to the safety of Fort Knox, Kentucky, after the Japanese attack on Pearl Harbor—along with other cultural treasures, including the Lincoln Cathedral copy of the Magna Carta, which was in the United States for the 1939 World's Fair (see February 24). "This conflict is not a conflict which can be won by arms alone, for it is not a conflict fought for things which arms alone can conquer," Librarian of Congress Archibald MacLeish stated in June 1942. "It is a conflict fought for men's convictions—for the things which lie beneath convictions—for ideas. The war of arms might end in victory . . . , and the war might still be lost if the battles of belief are lost—above all if the battle to maintain the power and authority of truth and free intelligence were lost—if the confidence of men in learning and in reason and in truth were broken and replaced by trust in force and ignorance and superstition."

LEFT: Archibald MacLeish (1892–1982), Librarian of Congress, 1939–44, c. 1942.

RIGHT: *All out for defense of democracy, Informed Opinion Counts.* Color silk-screen poster published by the New York State WPA Art Program, 1941.

JULY 7

1937 An incident at the Marco Polo Bridge, near Peking, sparks what will become a full-scale, nearly eight-year war between Japan and China.

1941 U.S. Marines occupy Iceland, Trinidad, and British Guiana, which will allow the British to withdraw and redeploy the forces they have stationed in those countries.

Maintaining the free flow of ideas and keeping the public informed, while also preserving morale and restricting information that might be of use to the enemy, constituted a wartime challenge for the Allied democracies. On December 19, 1941, Roosevelt issued Executive Order 8985, establishing the U.S. Office of Censorship (USOC), and appointed as its director former Associated Press executive Byron Price. "Society has hit upon but three basic methods of controlling publication," Price stated. "One is the method of rigid government compulsion, . . . One is a compromise procedure, under which enforcement is largely voluntary, but with a strictly worded statute hovering in the background. The third is a system of self-discipline under the leadership of the government, but with no statutory sanction and no penalty." Totalitarian countries practiced the first method, Britain the second, and the United States the third. In addition to supervising the examination of communications coming from or going abroad, Price's office developed, published, and periodically updated codes of wartime practices for radio broadcasters and the press and enlisted volunteer editors and publishers to explain these guidelines to local media. Much was left to individual discretion: newspapers and radio stations themselves decided whether to submit a story to the censors before publication or broadcast. The system worked: USOC issued a few cautionary letters but publicly cited only one paper for a code violation.

LEFT: *"Censored" let's censor our conversation about the war.* Color silk-screen poster published by the WPA War Services of Louisiana, sponsored by the Federal Art Project, between 1941 and 1943.

RIGHT: Byron Price (1891–1981), director of the U.S. Office of Censorship, 1941–45. Photograph, 1941.

JULY 8

1941 B-17s are flown in combat for the first time, by the RAF in an attack on Wilhelmshaven, Germany.

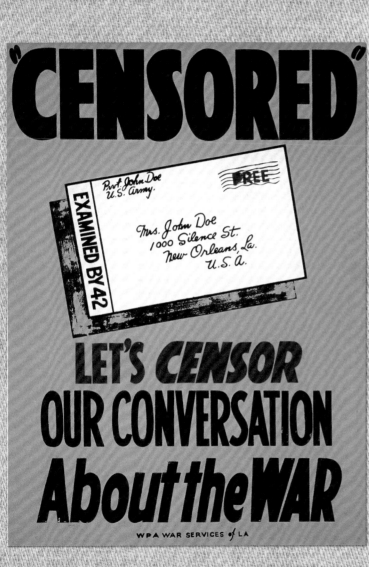

"CENSORED"

EXAMINED BY 42

Pvt. John Doe
U.S. Army.

FREE

Mrs. John Doe
1000 Silence St.
New Orleans, La.
U.S.A.

LET'S CENSOR
OUR CONVERSATION
About the WAR

WPA WAR SERVICES of LA

On December 7, 1941, CBS Radio's London-based correspondent Edward R. Murrow was in the White House, giving President Roosevelt his assessment of the morale of the British people after two years of war, when news arrived of the Japanese attack on Pearl Harbor. Because he considered what the president subsequently told him about the extent of the damage to be privileged, Murrow did not report the information to the public. By then, the stern-faced newscaster had become the voice of the European war to a vast American radio audience. "This is London," he would begin, and his listeners would hear air raid sirens and explosions in the distance as he continued that evening's account. Mixing "hard news" items with descriptive features, Murrow brought U.S. audiences closer to the front lines. In 1943, he went on an RAF raid over Berlin and later reported on his experience: "Berlin was a kind of orchestrated Hell—a terrible symphony of light and flame." In Berlin, an expatriate American was engaging in a far different kind of broadcasting. Mildred Gillars, dubbed "Axis Sally" by American troops, practiced the dark art of "black propaganda," interspersing familiar recorded songs with anti-Semitic and anti-Roosevelt screeds, seductive patter, and sometimes dramatic attempts to shatter Allied troops' morale, including her role in the radio play *Vision of Invasion*: "D [in D-Day] stands for doom . . . disaster . . . death." After the war, American authorities arrested, tried, and convicted Gillars of treason.

LEFT: Edward R. Murrow (1908–1965), CBS correspondent, at his typewriter in wartime London. Photograph between 1939 and 1945.

RIGHT: Mildred Gillars "Axis Sally" (1900–1988) 1946.

JULY 9

1944   Saipan is secured by U.S. forces.

As 1942 came to an end, Japan's Asahi Shimbun Publishing Company released *Victory on the March: A Pictorial Record of the War of Greater East Asia*, an English-language publication with a decidedly propagandistic bent: "Our war and peace aims are identical," its anonymous author wrote. "They lie in the complete elimination from Greater East Asia of the selfish predatory imperialism of the Anglo-American Powers and in the establishment of conditions of peace and security which would enable our peoples each to find their proper place in the new order of cooperative and harmonious existence." The magazine included a chart purporting to be an accurate tally of the destruction Japanese imperial forces had wrought on the Allies to date. Whether or not its numbers were exaggerated, 1942 had been a near-devastating year for the Allies. Despite terrible and continuing losses, they had taken the offensive at Guadalcanal and in North Africa (see May 21, June 24, 28), and war production was surging—yet at the end of the year, resources were still spread perilously thin. "We are learning to ration materials," Roosevelt told Americans in October, "and we must now learn to ration manpower." There were two major objectives: "to select and train men of the highest fighting efficiency needed for our armed forces" and "to man our war industries and farms with the workers needed to produce the arms and munitions and food required by ourselves and by our fighting allies to win this war."

Brilliant war results of the Imperial Japanese Army and Navy over one year period from December 8, 1941, to December 7, 1942. Chart from the Japanese propaganda publication Victory on the March, *1942.*

JULY 10

1940 The French parliament votes itself out of existence, giving Mar. Pétain dictatorial powers; Pétain will be named chief of the French state the next day.

BRILLIANT WAR RESULTS OF THE IMPERIAL JAPANESE ARMY AND NAVY OVER THE YEAR PERIOD FROM DECEMBER 8, 1941, TO DECEMBER 7, 1942

AS ANNOUNCED BY THE IMPERIAL HEADQUARTERS

BATTLESHIPS:
SUNK: 9
HEAVILY DAMAGED: 7

CALIFORNIA TYPE · CALIFORNIA TYPE · ARIZONA TYPE · OKLAHOMA TYPE · MARYLAND TYPE · UNCONFIRMED TYPE · UNCONFIRMED TYPE
UNCONFIRMED TYPE · TEXAS · NORTH CAROLINA · MARYLAND · PENNSYLVANIA · NEVADA · PENNSYLVANIA · UNCONFIRMED TYPE

SUNK: 2
HEAVILY DAMAGED: 2

PRINCE OF WALES · REPULSE · WARSPITE · QUEEN ELIZABETH

AIRCRAFT CARRIERS: (INCLUDING AIRCRAFT TENDERS)
SUNK: 10
HEAVILY DAMAGED: 4

LEXINGTON · YORKTOWN · WASP · ENTERPRISE · HORNET · UNCONFIRMED TYPE
SARATOGA · UNCONFIRMED TYPE · UNCONFIRMED TYPE · NEW LARGE TYPE · NEW MEDIUM TYPE · UNCONFIRMED TYPE · UNCONFIRMED TYPE

LANGLEY
SUNK: 1
HERMES

HEAVY AND LIGHT CRUISERS:
SUNK: 33
HEAVILY DAMAGED: 15

OTHER CRUISERS SUNK OR DAMAGED INCLUDE UNIDENTIFIED HEAVY OR LIGHT TYPES

ASTORIA · HOUSTON · PORTLAND · SAN FRANCISCO · WICHITA · ASTORIA · AUGUSTA
ASTORIA · OMAHA · AUGUSTA
ASTORIA · MARBLEHEAD · NORTHAMPTON · SAN FRANCISCO

SUNK: 9
HEAVILY DAMAGED: 3

EXETER · LONDON · CORNWALL
HOBART · AUSTRALIA · ACHILLES
HOBART · AUSTRALIA · UNCONFIRMED TYPE
ARETHUSA · LEANDER · ARETHUSA

SUNK: 4
HEAVILY DAMAGED: 1

DE RUYTER · TROMP · JAVA · JAVA · TROMP

SUNK: 12
HEAVILY DAMAGED: 5

SUNK: 4

DESTROYERS:
SUNK: 32
HEAVILY DAMAGED: 18

SUBMARINES:
SUNK: 93
HEAVILY DAMAGED: 58

SPECIAL SERVICE SHIPS:
SUNK: 4
HEAVILY DAMAGED: 2

GUNBOATS:
SUNK: 5
HEAVILY DAMAGED: 6

TORPEDO BOATS:
SUNK: 2
HEAVILY DAMAGED: 1

MINE SWEEPERS:
SUNK: 2
HEAVILY DAMAGED: 1

OTHER WARSHIPS:
SUNK: 18
HEAVILY DAMAGED: 34

MINE LAYERS:
SUNK: 2
HEAVILY DAMAGED:
CAPTURED: 1

CAPTURED: 1

CAPTURED: 5

CONVERTED WARSHIPS:
SUNK: 2
HEAVILY DAMAGED: 1

UNCONFIRMED TYPES OF WARSHIPS:
SUNK: 1
HEAVILY DAMAGED: 3

CAPTURED: 2

AIRPLANES:
SHOT DOWN OR DESTROYED: OVER 3,798
(EACH UNIT=10)

TRANSPORTS:
SUNK OR DAMAGED: 416
GROSS TONNAGE: 2,240,000 TONS

CAPTURED: 503
GROSS TONNAGE: 220,000 TONS

IN SOUTHERN REGIONS AND ALEUTIANS:

ENEMY TROOPS ENGAGED: APPROX. 600,000

TAKEN PRISONER: APPROX. 303,000

ENEMY DEAD ABANDONED: APPROX. 51,000 (EACH UNIT=10,000)

WAR TROPHIES TAKEN:

GUNS OF VARIOUS TYPES: 3,620 (EACH UNIT=1,000)

HEAVY AND LIGHT MACHINE GUNS: 11,300 (EACH UNIT=1,000)

OTHER ARMS: 206,000 (EACH UNIT=10,000)

TANKS: 1,440 (EACH UNIT=100)

AUTOMOBILES: 31,700 (EACH UNIT=1,000)

RAILWAY ENGINES AND CARRIAGES: 12,200 (EACH UNIT=1,000)

AIRPLANES: GRAND TOTAL... 1,959
SHOT DOWN: 731 · DESTROYED: 993 · CAPTURED: 235 (EACH UNIT=10)

WARSHIPS AND TRANSPORTS:
SUNK OR HEAVILY DAMAGED: 104 (EACH UNIT=10)

IN CHINA:

ENEMY TROOPS ENGAGED: APPROXIMATELY 3,600,000

NUMBER OF ENGAGEMENTS: APPROX. 25,000

PRISONERS TAKEN: APPROX. 123,000 (EACH UNIT=10,000)

ENEMY DEAD ABANDONED: APPROX. 280,000 (EACH UNIT=10,000)

WAR TROPHIES TAKEN:

GUNS OF VARIOUS TYPES: 846 (EACH UNIT=1,000)

OTHER ARMS: 159,100 (EACH UNIT=10,000)

HEAVY AND LIGHT MACHINE GUNS: 3,200 (EACH UNIT=1,000)

AUTOMOBILES: 129 (EACH UNIT=100)

RAILWAY ENGINES AND CARRIAGES: 208 (EACH UNIT=1,000)

AIRPLANES: SHOT DOWN, DESTROYED AND CAPTURED: 118 (EACH UNIT=100)

First among the four production goals President Roosevelt included in his January 1942 annual message to Congress was "To increase our production rate of airplanes so rapidly that in this year . . . we can produce sixty thousand planes . . . This includes forty-five thousand combat planes." Through December 1942, American aircraft manufacturers produced 47,836 military aircraft; in 1944, production more than doubled, to 96,318, including 35,003 bombers. The four-engine Consolidated Aircraft B-24 "Liberator" was among the most dependable of these expressions of American air power, proving ideal not only for long-range bombing sorties, but also for maritime patrol, antisubmarine work, reconnaissance, and transport of both cargo and personnel. As of June 1942, however, the U.S. Army Air Forces had received only 500 of the 18,188 Liberators that would eventually fly. To reach that wartime total, Consolidated employees, like workers in other American war industries, accepted the challenge implicit in Roosevelt's January address: "Production for war is based on men and women—the human hands and brains which collectively we call labor. Our workers stand ready to work long hours; to turn out more in a day's work; to keep the wheels turning and the fires burning 24 hours a day and 7 days a week. They realize well that on the speed and efficiency of their work depend the lives of their sons and their brothers on the fighting fronts."

Workers at the Consolidated Aircraft Corporation plant in Fort Worth, Texas, where they build B-24 "Liberator" bombers. Photograph by Howard R. Hollem, October 1942.

JULY 11

1940 The Luftwaffe assures Gen. Franz Halder, chief of the German Army General Staff, that it can eliminate the RAF within a month.

"There shall be no discrimination in the employment of workers in defense industries or government because of race, creed, color, or national origin, . . ." In signing Executive Order 8802 on June 25, 1941, President Roosevelt was responding to pressure from such prominent African Americans as A. Philip Randolph and Mary McLeod Bethune. Confronted by blatant discrimination in defense industry hiring ("We have not had a Negro working in 25 years," Standard Steel told one civil rights organization, "and do not plan to start now"), they had organized the March on Washington Movement, which had planned to bring one hundred thousand protesters to the nation's capital, marching under the slogan, "We loyal Negro American citizens demand the right to work and fight for our country." The executive order, and the Fair Employment Practices Committee established under it, prevented the march. It did not prevent racial tensions from boiling over, however, as the percentage of defense industry jobs held by African Americans increased from 3 percent in 1942 to 8 percent in 1945. In 1943, 242 violent racial clashes took place in forty-seven cities; in Detroit and Harlem, a total of thirty-nine people were killed. Eleanor Roosevelt worried that such bitter convulsions, springing from discrimination against one group of citizens, put Americans "on a par with Nazism which we fight, and makes us tremble for what human beings may do when they . . . let themselves be dominated by their worst emotions."

Americans all. Color poster published by the U.S. Government Printing Office, 1942.

JULY 12

Britain and the Soviet Union sign a mutual assistance treaty in Moscow.

NIENCIEWISCZ

DU BOIS

COHEN

LAZARRI

HRDLICKA

SANTINI

SCHMIDT

WILLIAMS

AMERICANS ALL

KELLY

"...it is the duty of employers and labor organizers to provide for the full participation of all workers without discrimination because of race, creed, color, or national origin."

Franklin D. Roosevelt

WAR MANPOWER COMMISSION • WASHINGTON, D. C.

In Allied countries, national figures such as Eleanor Roosevelt and Britain's Queen Elizabeth (whom Hitler dubbed "the most dangerous woman in Europe") set high standards for wartime resolve and comportment. Millions of less-celebrated women more than lived up to those standards, both in civilian war work and in the armed forces. In 1941, Britain became the first country to conscript women into military service with the passage of the National Service Act. Yet most of the approximately 450,000 women in the British armed forces remained volunteers—as were all 272,000 women in the U.S. Women's Army Corps (WAC), the Women Appointed for Voluntary Emergency Service (WAVES), the Women's Coast Guard Reserve (SPARS), the U.S. Marines, and the Women's Airforce Service Pilots (WASP). While many of these women came under fire, none were permitted to serve as front-line soldiers. The Red Army did not have that restriction: Some Soviet women served as combat pilots, tank commanders, and snipers. Others marched with infantry units that pushed the Wehrmacht back into Germany. In the Third Reich some women were involved in war production, and volunteer female *Helferinnen* ("helpers") were integrated into every branch of the military, serving in such support roles as translators and radar operators. Yet the Nazi Party stressed childbearing as each woman's principal duty. "In my state," Hitler said, "the mother is the most important citizen."

LEFT: *Are you a girl with a star-spangled heart? Join the WAC now!* Color poster by Bradshaw Crandell, published by the U.S. Army Recruiting Publicity Bureau, 1943.

RIGHT: *Hilf auch du mit!* ("You can help, too!") Color poster by Theo Matejko, published in Germany, c. 1941.

JULY 13

1945   Italy declares war on Japan.

Are you a girl with a
Star-Spangled heart?

JOIN THE WAC NOW!

THOUSANDS OF ARMY
JOBS NEED FILLING!

Women's Army Corps
United States Army

Hilf auch Du mit!

"**A** definitely encouraging trend has been a breakdown . . . of the prejudices against certain types of women workers," U.S. Secretary of Labor Frances Perkins reported in 1942, noting that some four million American women were then employed in war industries. The first female cabinet member, Perkins had organized a mid-December 1941 Washington conference of U.S. industry and labor leaders—including John L. Lewis, head of the Congress of Industrial Organizations and president of the United Mine Workers of America—to help assure that disputes between management and labor would not impair American war production. After exhausting negotiations, all parties pledged that there would be no wartime strikes or lockouts and that disputes would be settled by negotiation. "The pledges were kept," Perkins later reported, "if imperfectly." A major imperfection occurred early in 1943, when Lewis led his low-paid coal miners out on strike after mine owners refused them a two-dollar-a-day wage increase. But coal was vital to the war effort. Some congressmen demanded Lewis be indicted for treason; the army's official newspaper, *Stars and Stripes*, snarled, "John L. Lewis, damn your coal-black soul." On June 25, as polls showed that Lewis had become the most unpopular man in the country, Congress passed, over Roosevelt's veto, the War Labor Disputes (Smith-Connally) Act, which gave the president broad powers to combat labor problems during the war.

LEFT: John L. Lewis (1880–1969), president of the United Mine Workers (left) testifying before the Truman Committee on war production, March 26, 1943.

RIGHT: Frances Perkins (1880–1965), U.S. Secretary of Labor, 1933–45. Photograph by the Keystone View Company, 1918.

JULY 14

1941 German authorities close all Christian Science churches in the Reich and confiscate their property.

Opening jobs in agriculture and defense industries to women, minorities, and others who had previously been denied them did not entirely solve wartime labor shortages. Like other Allied countries, the United States employed prisoners of war (POWs) in jobs that were allowed under the provisions of the Geneva Conventions. About half the 425,000 Axis POWs held within U.S. borders worked at nonmilitary jobs, mostly in agriculture. Americans in federal prisons were sometimes employed in war-related work as well— although some would not participate for reasons of conscience. The World War II federal prison population included more than six thousand conscientious objectors (COs) who not only refused induction into the armed services, but also refused to support the war by performing alternate service in the 152 Civilian Public Service (CPS) camps around the country. More than thirty-seven thousand COs did serve in those camps, working as conservationists and forest-fire fighters, running rural medical clinics, and engaging in agricultural experiments. Other COs performed dangerous service as medical guinea pigs, as doctors sought remedies for some of the exotic diseases felling Allied troops in remote theaters of war. COs who worked in mental health facilities sometimes found appalling conditions— which they partially remedied by instituting nonviolent methods of patient care. Meanwhile, they began a campaign that fostered postwar reforms.

Inmates of California's San Quentin Prison help distribute eight million ration books, 1943.

1943 U.S. aircraft down forty-five of seventy-five attacking Japanese planes in the Solomon Islands, with only three American losses; hereafter, the Japanese will severely limit their daylight attacks.

"**A** Liberty Ship was launched [yesterday] in [the] record time of 26 days," Henry J. Kaiser told workers at his Richmond, California, shipyards in August 1942. "Today you have . . . established a new [record] of 24 days. . . . I am told by our boys that tomorrow's record of less than 18 days will be established within the next few months." The most celebrated American entrepreneur of the World War II era, Kaiser operated under the motto "Find a need and fill it"—and the Allies had a desperate need for ships. Using prefabrication and assembly-line techniques rather than the painstaking craftsmanship usually employed in shipbuilding, welding rather than riveting the vessels together, seven Kaiser shipyards built nearly a third of the 2,710 no-frills "Liberty" cargo vessels that the Allies put into wartime service. While admirers dubbed Kaiser "Sir Launchalot," competitors who adopted Kaiser shipbuilding techniques were slower to appreciate the benefits he extended to his workers, including day-care facilities and a groundbreaking health-care plan. These were fully appreciated by Kaiser employees, however, who accepted the boss's challenge and managed to shave their Liberty-ship construction time to seventeen days. (They built one ship, the SS *Robert E. Peary*, in only four. Launched in November 1942, the *Peary* saw service in both the Pacific and European theaters of operation and was among the vessels supporting the invasion of Normandy in June 1944.)

ABOVE: Henry J. Kaiser (1882–1967), 1962.

RIGHT: Nine Liberty cargo ships at the outfitting docks of the California Shipbuilding Corporation's Los Angeles yard, nearly ready to be delivered to the U.S. Maritime Commission, December 4, 1943.

JULY 16

1937 The German government opens a concentration camp at Buchenwald; initially, it holds political prisoners.

Liberty and other cargo ships carried thousands of 70- to 127-ton U.S. locomotives and many railroad cars overseas during the war to keep vital railways operating from Britain to the liberated Philippine Islands. American railway equipment augmented captured stock on the railroad from Casablanca to Tunis in North Africa, which played an important part in the buildup of men and supplies for the invasion of Sicily and southern Europe. Millions of long tons (2,240 pounds each) of Lend-Lease locomotives and other cargo were also shipped to the Soviet Union by northern-route convoys and by land via the Persian Corridor, through Iran. In 1944, as Allied bombers dropped more than eight thousand tons of bombs on French railways to prevent them from carrying German reinforcements once the D-Day landings began (see September 12, 13), the Allies were also stockpiling a thousand U.S.-built locomotives and twenty thousand railroad cars all around Britain. After Allied troops secured a foothold in Normandy in early June, ships transported American and British railroad equipment to France—where the first official Allied railroad run took place between Cherbourg and Carentan on July 11, 1944. Meanwhile, on the U.S. home front, the Office of Defense Transportation worked to coordinate use of railways by civilians and federal agencies, including the military. And demand could be heavy: In 1942, the movement of one armored division between camps required sixty-nine trains comprising 2,221 cars.

LEFT: A laboratory assistant at the Chicago and Northwestern Railroad works at a precision balance. Photograph by Jack Delano (1914–1997), December 1942.

RIGHT: Locomotives in the Chicago and Northwestern railroad shops. Photograph by Jack Delano, December 1942.

JULY 17

1944 In Normandy, Field Mar. Erwin Rommel is seriously wounded when his car is strafed by an Allied airplane.

"The spire of Coventry Cathedral today stood as a sentinel over the grim scene of destruction below, following a dusk-to-dawn raid on the town, which the Nazis claimed was the biggest attack in the history of air war," Britain's *Guardian* newspaper reported on November 16, 1940. "The famous Cathedral is little more than a skeleton." The Battle of Britain was raging, and the Luftwaffe had zeroed in on the midland city of Coventry, home to a fourteenth-century cathedral, reportedly as a reprisal for a British bombing raid on Munich. "The whole city was ringed with leaping flames," one witness reported after incendiary bombs gutted the cathedral and laid waste to the city center. The "Coventry Blitz," as this night came to be known in England, would shortly be eclipsed by much more destructive raids as the air war continued to escalate—so rapidly that strategy was sometimes dictated by the limitations of technology. Originally, Britain intended to strike at German strength in occupied Europe by the use of "precision" bombing. However, reliable technology for delivering bombs precisely on target did not exist in the early 1940s. This was amply verified by a 1941 British study (the Butt Report) that showed that only 30 percent of RAF bombs were falling within five miles of their targets (only 10 percent, in the smoke-filled Ruhr industrial area). This became a major factor in Britain's increasing embrace of "area" bombing—the targeting of entire urban or industrial areas.

LEFT: *Pilot of a Ju [junkers] 88 [bomber]*. Plate from the sketchbook of German artist Hans Liska, published in 1942.

RIGHT: Prime Minister Winston Churchill walks with a guard and members of the Anglican clergy through the ruins of Coventry Cathedral, which was bombed by the Germans in 1940. Photograph, January 23, 1942.

JULY 18

1944   Gen. Hideki Tojo is removed as Japanese premier, war minister, and army chief of staff due to military reverses in the Pacific.

"The attack on Coventry, . . . seemed to the enemy so successful," Chief Marshal Sir Arthur Harris reported in his postwar memoir, *Bomber Offensive*, "that they proposed to make it a standard of all bombing and call any city 'Coventrated' if it had endured similar damage." Coventry's industries were back in operation within two months, he noted, but "there were special circumstances which led us to believe that production would not recover so quickly in Germany." As Head of RAF Bomber Command (February 1942–September 1945), "Bomber" Harris wholeheartedly embraced the British high command's decision to concentrate on area bombing (see July 18). Precision bombing was, at that time of limited technological resources, an "abstract theory," he wrote, that failed to take into account "the practical impossibility of hitting . . . factories, by day because of the German air defense, and by night because we could not find them in the dark." Daylight raids having proved too costly in RAF men and machines, the British concentrated on night bombing raids. When Major General Carl Spaatz arrived in Britain in May 1942 to activate the U.S. Eighth Air Force, he represented the American determination to concentrate on specific targets during daylight raids. By 1943, the two Allied air forces developed a joint around-the-clock bombing campaign: The USAAF bombed by day, the RAF by night. Meanwhile, Spaatz proved to be, in the words of his driver, Kay Summersby, "the hardest working man in the whole U.S. Army Air Forces."

LEFT: Air Ch. Mar. Sir Arthur ("Bomber") Harris (1892–1984). Photograph by Maurice Constant, c. 1940.

RIGHT: Maj. Gen. Carl Spaatz, commanding general, U.S. Army Air Forces, Europe (left), and Brig. Gen. Ira C. Eaker. U.S. Army Signal Corps photograph, c. 1942.

JULY 19

1941 Churchill launches the "V for Victory" campaign in Europe during a midnight radio broadcast. "The V sign is the symbol of the unconquerable will of the occupied territories and a portent of the fate awaiting Nazi tyranny." (In French, the "V" stands for *Victoire*; in Dutch, for *Vryheid*, or "freedom.")

In 1944, General Henry "Hap" Arnold, chief of U.S. Army Air Forces, and Assistant Secretary of War Robert Lovett determined, as Arnold reported in his postwar memoir, *Global Mission*, that they needed "an accurate, unbiased analysis of the effects of our bombing . . . Was strategic bombing [aimed at enemy resources] as good as we thought it was? Or were we carried away by our own bomber-mindedness?" The United States Strategic Bombing Survey, established that November, comprised eleven hundred civilians, military officers and enlisted men; headquartered in London, the group closely followed the troops after the D-Day landings, examining damage, evaluating documents, and interviewing thousands of Germans. The resulting voluminous study of the European air war (a separate study later evaluated the air war against Japan) includes the following statement in its summary report: "The great lesson to be learned in the battered towns of England and the ruined cities of Germany is that the best way to win a war is to prevent it from occurring." United Service Organizations (USO) artist Mimi Korach Lesser conducted a much less formal survey as she visited hospitals and army camps in 1945: "As we approached Germany signs of war became more apparent," she later wrote, "but it was not until we crossed the border that the true effect of Allied bombing was seen. Towns were destroyed, leveled to the ground in many instances. There was only silence with not a human or animal to be seen."

Bombed buildings, Aachen, Germany. Watercolor by American USO sketch artist Mimi Korach Lesser, April 15, 1945.

JULY 20

1944   One of the German army's anti-Nazi officers, Col. Count Claus von Stauffenberg, makes an unsuccessful attempt to assassinate Hitler with a bomb. He and other collaborators will be executed.

To avoid being easily targeted by enemy bombers, both sides made creative use of the art of camouflage. Americans used it even on the home front, where there proved to be little real danger of aerial attack. Yet in 1940, with most of Continental Europe occupied by the Germans and Britain under unrelenting assault by the Luftwaffe, air raids on the U.S. mainland did not seem such a remote possibility. Schools and military bases began offering classes in industrial and military camouflage; Americans developed new nongloss camouflage paints (more likely to fool cameras); tested colors to see which most effectively blended in various terrains; and tested nets for disguising artillery emplacements and mechanisms for raising and lowering the nets. Among the most elaborate home-front manifestations of this surging interest in camouflage were the fake neighborhoods and small towns built of plywood and chicken wire that were erected atop aircraft factories on the West Coast after Japan attacked the United States. Studded with petite plywood houses, rubber cars, and artificial plants, these pseudosuburbs qualified as "spoofs"—a British term for elaborate deceptions that involved extensive use of decoys and dummies. During the Battle of Britain, British "spoofers" created hundreds of fake docks, factories, shipyards, and supply depots to draw thousands of tons of enemy bombs. Their decoy airfields, lit at night, were so effective they drew more Luftwaffe bombs than the real RAF bases.

Camouflage class at New York University, New York City. Photograph by Marjorie Collins, March 1943.

JULY 21

1944   U.S. forces land on Guam.

Essential in many areas behind the lines, camouflage (see July 21) was also crucial for front-line soldiers. In the Pacific Theater in 1942, Japanese snipers easily zeroed in on the government-issued white T-shirts of the American troops—until the Yanks began using the juice of berries or the tannin of tree bark to camouflage their clothing. (Olive-drab clothes reached Pacific Theater units in 1943.) But in this no-holds-barred, technology-intensive war, even the best camouflage could not prevent physical wounds that ranged from slight to ghastly. The most terrible wounds often inspired the development of new medical techniques, such as the experimental reconstructive surgery British plastic surgeon Archibald McIndoe used to treat severely burned RAF airmen. As his dauntless patients formed the "Guinea Pig Club" in July 1941, the United States Army was expanding its Medical Corps, which eventually included forty-seven thousand physicians, fifteen thousand dentists, fifty-seven thousand nurses, and more than six hundred thousand technicians, aid men, and other specialists. After the United States entered the war, the Medical Corps established "chains of evacuation" suited to each area of operation and saved approximately ninety-six out of every one hundred wounded who reached army hospitals. It also developed an elaborate rehabilitation system for patients with neuropsychiatric disorders ("combat fatigue"), which affected 18.7 percent of all U.S. Army patients evacuated to the United States between 1942 and 1945.

A class observes as two U.S. Army medical students attempt to diagnose a leg injury under the supervision of a surgeon at Bellevue Hospital, an affiliate of the New York University medical school, as part of the army's specialized training course, c. 1944.

JULY 22

1942 The same day they begin the "resettlement" of Jews from Warsaw, the Germans open the concentration camp in Treblinka.

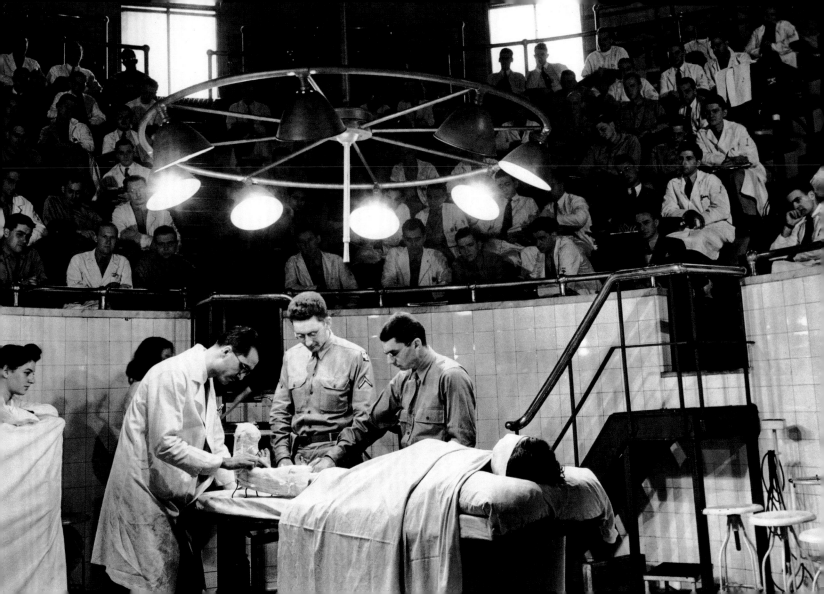

"Our eastern campaign has cost us three million casualties," Third Reich propagandist Joseph Goebbels wrote in his diary on November 2, 1943. "At some point or other we simply must try to get out of this desperate bloodletting. Otherwise we are in danger of slowly bleeding to death in the East." To help treat the German soldiers who suffered in the desperate bloodletting that Hitler had initiated on the eastern front—and additional casualties in the west, after the Allied D-Day landings—the Nazis drafted more and more women, ages fifteen to sixty, as auxiliary nurses. Irma Krueger, conscripted at age fifteen, later remembered: "Normally we auxiliaries—all girls in our teens—would arrive at our old school about seven in the morning. The wounded would already be there, packed into the gymnasium by the hundreds. . . .they were stripped naked on the straw, covered with lice for the most part, . . . We would help them the best we could . . . Then the sprinklers in the ceiling would be turned on, and if the wounded were lucky, lukewarm water would descend upon them, cleaning them up a little. If they were unlucky it would be cold, because there was a shortage of fuel. Then they would scream. . . . Thereafter the doctors would be operating all day long, their rubber boots and aprons a bright red with blood, and our old school janitor, Herr Schmitz, would be back and forth all the time, carrying sawed-off limbs under his arms to be burned in the school incinerators. . . . It was a terrible time."

Captured German nurses in the custody of U.S. military police (far right). Photograph, Europe, c. 1944–45.

1942   A German submarine mines the main approaches to the Mississippi River.

On August 28, 1939, four days before the Wehrmacht invaded Poland and well before the German government began conscripting teenagers to be auxiliary nurses (see July 23), Germany instituted rationing on the home front, issuing color-coded cards for different foods and for items such as clothing and soap. The following January, Britain followed suit. "Our country is dependent to a very large extent on supplies of food from overseas," a government leaflet reminded Britons at a time when U-boats were sending too many supply ships to the bottom of the sea. Rationing was common to all the major combatants, as were drives to collect scrap metal, rubber, and other materials that could be recycled and used in war production. Americans collected thousands of tons of needed materials, including car and bicycle tires, aluminum pots, tinfoil, and tin cans. "I remember jumping on the tin cans to flatten them and . . . peeling the foil off my dad's cigarette packs to roll up into a ball to donate to the war effort," wrote Gerard Quinn, who was a child during the war. Unlike Quinn, Britons all too often could simply look up, to the vapor trails of dogfighting aircraft, to understand the importance of scrap metal drives. As Lady Reading, head of the Women's Voluntary Service, told a radio audience: "Very few of us can be heroines on the battle-front, but we can all have the tiny thrill of thinking as we hear the news of an epic battle in the air, 'Perhaps it was my saucepan that made a part of that Hurricane [fighter aircraft].'"

LEFT: *Salvage scrap to blast the Jap*. Color poster by Phil von Phul, produced by the Washington WPA Federal Art Project, c. 1942.

RIGHT: *Americans! Share the meat as a wartime necessity*. Color poster published by the U.S. Government Printing Office, Washington, D.C., 1942.

JULY 24

1943 RAF aircraft use "window" decoy tinfoil for the first time, to confuse German radar in a raid on Hamburg.

Americans!

SHARE THE MEAT

as a wartime necessity

To meet the needs of our armed forces and fighting allies, a Government order limits the amount of meat delivered to stores and restaurants.

To share the supply fairly, all civilians are asked to limit their consumption of beef, veal, lamb, mutton and pork to 2½ lbs. per person per week.

YOUR FAIR WEEKLY SHARE

Men, women and children over 12 yrs. old . . . . **2½** *Pounds per week*

Children 6 to 12 yrs. old . . . . **1½** *Pounds per week*

Children under 6 yrs. old . . . . **¾** *Pound per week*

You can add these foods to your share: liver, sweetbreads, kidneys, brains and other variety meats; also poultry and fish.

HELP WIN THE WAR!

Keep within your share

FOODS REQUIREMENT COMMITTEE
War Production Board

Claude R. Wickard
Chairman

OWI Poster No. 10   Additional copies may be obtained upon request from the Division of Public Inquiries, Office of War Information, Washington, D. C.

"Food is a munition of War," the British Food Ministry declared in broadcasts and on posters, "Don't Waste It!" As rationing in Britain increased, and milk and eggs joined the already lengthy list of controlled food items, in many parts of the Soviet Union food all but disappeared in the chaos and destruction that followed the German invasion. "We get five spoonfuls of soup in the morning," one Soviet soldier complained in 1941. "We're hungry all day." Both German and Soviet armies requisitioned or stole livestock and food stocks, and prices for what was left soared: "We spend twenty rubles a day on half a liter of milk [about one U.S. pint] for [infant son] Kolya," Natalya Taranichev wrote to her soldier husband early in 1943. "If we took that milk away from him, we'd be condemning him to complete emaciation." The Chinese were suffering similar deprivations, compounded by a terrible famine in 1943—the same year a famine killed more than a million people in India. As food became an important element of Lend-Lease shipments, Americans found ways to preserve foodstuffs longer and pack more into smaller spaces: New packaging was developed for cheese and evaporated milk, and beef, vegetables, eggs, and milk were shipped in dehydrated form. In one of the war's most constructive uses of instruments of destruction, some bombers being ferried from America to Britain carried packages of concentrated vitamins that were distributed free to children under two years of age.

ABOVE: *These hands are vital to victory.* Color poster, 1943.

RIGHT: *Our allies need eggs. Your farm can help.* Color silk-screen poster by Herbert Bayer (1900–1985), published by New York City WPA War Services between 1940 and 1943.

JULY 25

1943 Allies prepare to invade Italy; Italian generals and politicians overthrow Mussolini.

OUR ALLIES NEED EGGS

YOUR FARM CAN HELP

herbert bayer

Rural Electrification Administration, U. S. Department of Agriculture

"Perhaps the most difficult phase of the manpower problem is the scarcity of farm labor," Roosevelt declared on October 12, 1942. "[T]he people are trying to meet it as well as possible. In one community that I visited a perishable crop was harvested by turning out the whole of the high school." During the war, more than a million experienced U.S. farmworkers entered the armed forces or took defense industry jobs. Farmers grappling with how to raise more food with less manpower turned to new technology and tried combining small farms into larger, more commercial operations. Yet they still needed farmworkers. An August 1942 agreement between the U.S. and Mexican governments brought a total of three hundred thousand Mexican temporary farm laborers to the United States. These new hands augmented the efforts of existing volunteer farm labor groups—such as the Women's Land Army and the Victory Farm Volunteers (for youth from eleven to seventeen years of age)—all of which were reorganized under the U.S. Crop Corps in 1943. Most of the other major combatants also counted labor shortages among their agricultural problems. In Germany, the labor problem was partially alleviated by drafting boys between the ages of fourteen and eighteen and women between the ages of seventeen and twenty-five for one-year periods of agricultural work. Until late in the war, Germans also had another recourse: They could eat food stolen from the people of occupied countries.

LEFT: *Be a victory farm volunteer in the U.S. Crop Corps—See your principal.* Color poster, published by the U.S. Department of Agriculture, 1943.

RIGHT: *Jugend dient dem Führer* ("Youth serves the Führer"). Color poster celebrating the Hitler youth organization, published in Berlin by the Press und Propagandaamt der Reichsjugendführung, c. 1941.

JULY 26

1945 In a post-VE-Day election, Winston Churchill is ousted as British prime minister.

World War II involved many more species than *Homo sapiens* (the human race). Both Axis and Allies enlisted animals in the war effort. Wehrmacht divisions that crashed across Soviet borders in June 1941 included more than seven hundred thousand horses, used mostly to pull supply wagons and artillery. Soviet horses also pulled loads—but they charged into combat, too: By January 1, 1942, there were seven Soviet cavalry corps and eighty-two cavalry divisions. Other horses, mules, and donkeys saw service in the jungles of Burma, the rugged interior of Sicily, and many other places unfriendly to motorized vehicles. Elephants did their bit in the China-Burma-India Theater, as did camels, which were also employed in the Middle East. Dogs were on duty almost everywhere. American combat canines carried messages and sniffed out enemy cave emplacements in the Pacific Theater and transported GIs by sled in Alaska and Greenland. German medics harnessed both dogs and, in the far north, reindeer to transport injured men and medical supplies. Pigeons carried messages; trained hawks hunted message-carrying pigeons. Even "civilian" species that were ordinarily remote from battlefields sometimes ran afoul of the war. In his 1943 book, *The Pacific Is My Beat*, correspondent Keith Wheeler reported: "There are more whales than submarines in the Pacific, but whales and submarines produce the same reaction in a destroyer's sound detection gear. This is a terrible war for whales."

ABOVE: *A Military Dog* Reproduction of a painting by Tomoji Mikami, published in Seisen Gafu ("A Picture Album of the Holy War"), Tokyo, 1939.

RIGHT: Soviet soldiers construct a river crossing near a destroyed bridge as a horse team pulls a caisson across. Photograph by Evgenii Khaldei (1917–1997), 1945.

JULY 27

1942   From Osaka, Gen. Hideki Tojo calls on Australia to surrender.

Keith Wheeler's *The Pacific Is My Beat* (see July 27) was one telling drop in an ocean of wartime literature that encompassed factual reports, fiction, poetry, and the blatant propaganda that was most prevalent in the tightly monitored Axis regimes. Japan's intensive overseas propaganda efforts (see June 16, July 2, 10) were matched at home by the activities of the Japanese Literary Society, which dedicated one of its "literary patriotic rallies" to "the study of . . . books on the extermination of America and Britain." To counter the Japanese, both Chinese Communist and Nationalist writers, when not warring with each other, dedicated themselves to *k'ang-chan*, or a "war of resistance"—a literary campaign echoed in the similarly pressed Soviet Union, where writers of all genres mobilized to help defeat the German invader (which had a well-oiled literary war machine of its own). On the quieter U.S. front, readers preferred nonfiction, ranging from Richard Tregaskis's gripping *Guadalcanal Diary* (1943) to army cartoonist Bill Mauldin's collection of illustrated writings, *Up Front* (1945). In Britain, where both fiction and nonfiction flourished, the nation's war experience was also revealed in stunning poems, from Dylan Thomas's "A Refusal to Mourn the Death, by Fire, of a Child in London," to soldier, poet, and war casualty Keith Douglas's electrifying "How to Kill": "Now in my dial of glass appears / the soldier who is going to die. . . . How easy it is to make a ghost."

LEFT: Cover of *The Yellow Nazis* by Stanton Hope, a propagandistic attempt "to provide some first-hand close-up views of the Japanese mind and scene." Published in London by W. H. Allen & Co., Ltd., 1942.

RIGHT: Cover of *Japan gegen USA und England* ("Japan against the USA and England") by Karl Heinz Norweg. Published in Leipzig by W. Conrad & Co., 1943.

JULY 28

1941   The Japanese government freezes all American, British, and Dutch assets.

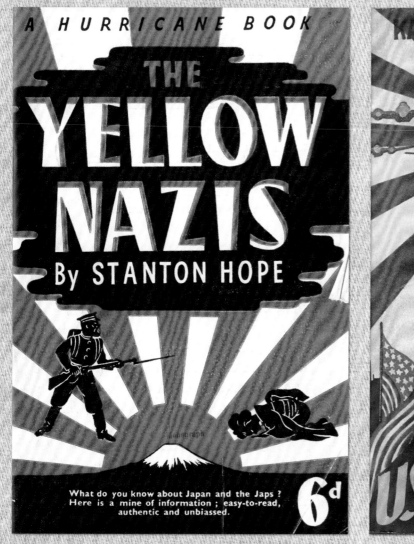

A HURRICANE BOOK

THE YELLOW NAZIS

By STANTON HOPE

6d

What do you know about Japan and the Japs?
Here is a mine of information; easy-to-read,
authentic and unbiased.

KARL HEINZ NORWEG

JAPAN

gegen

USA und ENGLAND

"Film," Joseph Goebbels said in 1934, "is one of the most modern and far-reaching means of influencing the masses." Most major combatants agreed and mustered their film industries to aid the war effort, bolster home-front morale, and in the case of the Axis powers, win support (or at least acquiescence, in occupied nations). Feature films, such as Britain's *In Which We Serve* and Hollywood's *Thirty Seconds over Tokyo*, the story of the 1942 Doolittle raid on Japan (see June 15, 16), and documentary features such as Germany's *Victory in the West* and Japan's *Victory of the East*, were often preceded in movie theaters by newsreels, generally enhanced by dramatic music and narration. Audiences in both Britain and the United States watched Movietone news, and Americans also favored "March of Time" newsreels created by Henry Luce's Time, Inc. On the other side of the conflict, the Japan Motion Picture Company (Nippon Eigasha) produced news films for home-front audiences, but also created versions in Chinese, Tagalog, Thai, Malay, French, and English. By 1943, with war reverses mounting, German "newsreels," produced under Goebbels's supervision, had become so freighted with obvious propaganda that not even German audiences believed them. People lingered outside theaters while the newsreels were onscreen, waiting for the features to start—a practice Goebbels stopped by issuing an order that no one would be allowed to enter a theater once the newsreel had begun.

LEFT: *To hell with Hitler*. Color poster advertising a popular comedy film (released in Britain as *Let George Do It*) starring British entertainer George Formby, 1940.

RIGHT: *War Newsreel Drawing a Full House*. Reproduction of a painting by Shunsui Higashimoto published in Seisen Gafu ("A Picture Album of the Holy War"), Tokyo, 1939.

JULY 29

1944   The German ME 163 becomes the first jet aircraft to be used in combat.

At 5:30 A.M. on July 16, 1945, U.S. Army cameramen filmed a raging explosion in the desert near Alamogordo, New Mexico. After a blinding flash that sent the detonation-site temperature soaring to ten thousand times hotter than the surface of the sun, a huge, radioactive cloud billowed into the sky. The United States had successfully completed the ultra-secret "Manhattan Project" by detonating the first atomic bomb. "There floated through my mind a line from the *Bhagavad-Gita*," the project's head scientist, J. Robert Oppenheimer, later wrote: "'I am become death: the destroyer of worlds.'" In utmost secrecy, the U.S. government had embarked on the atom-bomb project, fearing that Hitler's scientists would develop the devastating weapon first (see March 26). By 1944, however, German atomic research had faltered, and Hitler was relying instead on *Vergeltungswaffen*, or "retaliation weapons." Developed under the supervision of engineer Wernher von Braun, these "V-weapons" included the V–1 pilotless flying bombs that began crashing into Britain in June 1944 and the more advanced and powerful V–2 rockets, first launched against Allied targets later that year. Although frightening and destructive (they caused tens of thousands of casualties), these new weapons did not inspire the terror that Hitler hoped for. Their major impact was on postwar rocket development—in which von Braun played a leading role in the U.S. space program.

LEFT: J. Robert Oppenheimer (1904–1967), date unknown.

RIGHT: Wernher von Braun (1912–1977), between 1950 and 1970.

JULY 30

1942 The U.S. Women's Naval Reserve (Women Appointed for Voluntary Emergency Service, or WAVES) is established.

"The Near East, cradle of human civilization, now plays a major role in a world-wide war to save civilization. Ethiopia was one of the first of the United Nations to fight in World War II . . . provoked by Mussolini's treacherous invasion. Her fight against overwhelming modern armament is legendary."

"Iraq, a progressive Arab stronghold, is one of the Allies' most important sources of oil."

"Iran, another Near Eastern ally, set the stage for a vital step toward victory—the first meeting of President Roosevelt, Prime Minister Churchill, and Marshal Stalin, in November 1943. From this historic meeting grew the Allies' master blueprint for winning the war and erasing Fascism from the face of the earth. . . . "

"Forged in the fire of resistance to Fascism, the world-fraternity of 'United Nations' has opened a new chapter in history—a chapter that will live in international unity and cooperation long after Fascism is forgotten. . . . In *United* Allied action lay the key to Axis defeat!"

—Excerpts from *The United Nations at War*, 1944

Ethiopia—Iraq—Iran. One of twenty-four plates from *The United Nations at War*, produced by Charles A. Long Jr., Inc. for the Dixie Cup Company. Gift to the Library of Congress and the people of the United States from Charles A. Long Jr., Inc., 1944.

JULY 31

1942 A German submarine lays mines off Charleston, South Carolina.

UNITED NATIONS AT WAR··· ETHIOPIA – IRAQ – IRAN

ETHIOPIA–Seasoned Regulars now on duty

IRAQ–Native troops aid British

IRAN–Oil for the Fighting Front

The Tide Begins to Turn: 1943

"Today, in the midst of a great war for freedom, we dedicate a shrine to freedom." President Roosevelt said on April 13, 1943. It was Thomas Jefferson's two hundredth birthday, and Roosevelt was presiding over ceremonies inaugurating the Jefferson Memorial near the National Mall in Washington, D.C. In honor of the occasion, one of Jefferson's greatest accomplishments, the Declaration of Independence, had been retrieved from its wartime repository at Fort Knox, Kentucky, and placed on display for one week. "Thomas Jefferson believed, as we believe, . . . that men are capable of their own government, and that no king, no tyrant, no dictator can govern for them as well as they can govern for themselves," Roosevelt said. "He believed, as we believe, in certain inalienable rights. He, as we, saw those principles and freedoms challenged. He fought for them, as we fight for them."

As Roosevelt spoke, two Allied armies were on the verge of defeating German-Italian forces in North Africa; the Germans were still suffering the effects of their crushing defeat at Stalingrad; and the Japanese were feeling the sting of Allied resistance from Burma to New Guinea and the Solomon Islands. By July 28—after Allied forces had swept out of liberated North Africa, taken Sicily, and begun what was to become a long and bloody campaign to push German forces out of Italy—the president was able to declare in a *Fireside Chat*, "The first crack in the Axis has come." But

---

AUGUST 1

1943 Japan declares Burma's independence. The government in Rangoon under Dr. Ba Maw immediately declares war on Britain and the United States. One year later, an anti-Japanese Burmese faction will form a government in India.

the tide was only beginning to turn. The United States and Britain were still unable to satisfy Stalin's demand for a full-scale invasion of Western Europe, which they now planned to stage in 1944. Meanwhile, they continued to concentrate on the Combined Bomber Offensive. This round-the-clock strategic bombing campaign, costly in Allied lives, pummeled Axis war industries and vital resources—and, in July, sparked a ghastly firestorm in Hamburg, Germany.

At the same time, the Germans proceeded with the systematic slaughter of millions of unarmed people in extermination camps, ran factories with slave labor, and ruthlessly stamped out any resistance to their regime, including a month-long uprising in the Warsaw Ghetto that began on April 19. In the East, the Japanese continued to tout the Greater East Asia Co-Prosperity Sphere—while engaging in the brutal mistreatment of both military and civilian prisoners of war. All the Axis governments were ravaging occupied territories: In Greece, where vicious guerrilla warfare was building, a French consul wrote in February of "the plundering of every living thing by the invaders in order to make the population die of hunger." But it was not only Axis plundering that resulted in starvation. In both India and China that year, catastrophic famines took

millions of lives.

The number of battlefield deaths continued to rise. In the United States, a September issue of *Life* magazine included the first photographs of U.S. war dead to be seen on the home front, as the government sought to prepare the American people for greater sacrifices ahead. "The war is now reaching the stage where we shall all have to look forward to large casualty lists—dead, wounded and missing," the president told a radio audience on December 24. "War entails just that. There is no easy road to victory. And the end is not yet in sight."

In the face of obstacles—COURAGE. Color recruiting poster by Jes Wilhelm Schlaikjer, published by Brown & Bigelow/U.S. War Department, 1943.

In January 1943, Field Marshal Bernard Montgomery's British troops were pushing Field Marshal Erwin Rommel's Axis forces westward from Egypt, through Libya, into the southern section of the Vichy French protectorate of Tunisia. At the same time, Allied forces newly established in western North Africa after Operation Torch (see May 21, June 28) were moving east from Algeria into Tunisia—where a German force under General Jürgen von Arnim had seized control of the central and northern sectors. In Tunisia, the Allies aimed to capture the ports of Bizerte and Tunis and to secure vital mountain passes, thus preventing Rommel from linking up with von Arnim. They had limited initial success. On January 30, von Arnim's panzers defeated the Free French at the Faid Pass. Three weeks later, Rommel's forces caused more than six thousand casualties as they smashed through American positions at the Kasserine Pass. German high command disagreements caused Rommel's momentum to falter, and within a few days his forces withdrew through the pass—leaving more than forty-three thousand brutally effective land mines in their wake. In this explosive atmosphere, U.S. Army private Peter Sanfilippo clung to the moments he could spend with his paints; here he depicts light aircraft used for reconnaissance, patrol, and rescue operations: "I felt truly gifted that my painting offered such a hopeful diversion," he later wrote. "When creating, a peaceful and serene mind prevails. The horrors of war shall not overtake me."

Piper Cub. Watercolor painting by PFC Peter Sanfilippo, Battery C, 633rd Field Artillery, U.S. Army, Setif, Algeria, 1943.

AUGUST 2

1942 Romania declares war on Nicaragua and Haiti.

"There will be a commotion in this country if it is discovered that I have flown across any old seas," Roosevelt wrote to Churchill on December 11, 1942. "However, . . . I have just about made up my mind to go along with the African idea—on the theory that public opinion here will gasp but be satisfied when they hear about it after it is over." In realizing the "African idea"—traveling to the Allied conference in Casablanca, Morocco (see May 23)—Roosevelt became the first sitting U.S. president to visit Africa, the first to travel overseas during wartime, and the first since Abraham Lincoln to visit an active war zone. He was not the first Roosevelt to visit North Africa that year, however. Naval gunnery officer Franklin D. Roosevelt Jr. had recently won a commendation during Operation Torch (see May 21, June 28), when he participated in a sea battle off Casablanca that historian Samuel Morison characterized as "an old-fashioned fire-away Flannagan." Another Roosevelt son, Elliott, a U.S. Army Air Forces officer whose air reconnaissance squadron had also participated in Torch, greeted his father in Casablanca, where he served as the president's temporary military aide. (Roosevelt's other sons, John and James, were on active duty in other theaters.) Prevented for security reasons from visiting front-line troops after the conference, the president traveled by car to Rabat, Morocco, where he lunched with twenty thousand soldiers of the Fifth Army and inspected the Ninth Infantry Division before it departed for the front.

ABOVE: The four Roosevelt sons: Elliott, James, Franklin Jr., and John, c. 1941–46.

RIGHT: Riding in a jeep driven by Sgt. Oran Lass of Kansas City, Missouri, President Roosevelt reviews American troops in Casablanca, Morocco. U.S. Army Signal Corps photograph, January 1943.

AUGUST 3

1940   Italian forces invade British Somaliland in East Africa.

1944   Incurring heavy losses, Allied troops capture Myitkyina, Burma.

While Allied leaders were meeting in Casablanca (see August 3), the long campaign to take Guadalcanal in the Solomon Islands was coming to a close. Grit and stubborn determination had kept U.S. ground forces going during the first harrowing months, when they had insufficient naval, air, and logistic support (see June 24). After U.S. naval reinforcements arrived, American and Japanese fleets engaged in a series of clashes in November 1942, and slowly and painfully, the Americans at sea and on land secured the advantage. Unable to replace the vessels they were losing—and thus no longer capable of supporting their men on the ground—at the end of January 1943 the Japanese ordered their surviving troops to withdraw from the island, which they accomplished in daring night operations in early February. Major General Alexander M. Patch and his U.S. ground forces—which had grown to more than fifty thousand marines and infantrymen—had won the Battle of Guadalcanal. The cost had been dear: More than seven thousand Americans had been killed or were missing; Japanese dead numbered more than twenty-two thousand. The savage encounter had been a revelation to American commanders: "There is no question of our being able to defeat [the Japanese]," General George C. Kenney wrote to U.S. Army Air Forces chief, General "Hap" Arnold, "but the time, effort, blood and money required to do the job may run to proportions beyond all conception."

ABOVE: *Devil Dog Days*. Drawing by LeBaron Coakley, 1942.

RIGHT: Lt. Gen. Millard F. Harmon (center), commander of army forces, South Pacific area, consults with Gen. Alexander Patch (left), commander of ground action on Guadalcanal, and Maj. Gen. Nathan F. Twining, commander of Aircraft, Solomon Islands. U.S. Army Air Forces photograph, 1943.

AUGUST 4

1944 British forces reach the outskirts of Florence, Italy, where Wehrmacht units have destroyed all the bridges in the city except the celebrated fourteenth-century Ponte Vecchio.

Among the men suffering—and helping others endure—the razor-sharp kunai grass, snakes, mosquitoes, sickness, and combat on Guadalcanal was U.S. Army Chaplain Terence P. Finnegan, who received a Bronze Star for his meritorious service. Finnegan was one of 11,778 Protestant, Catholic, and Jewish chaplains who served in the wartime U.S. Armed Forces, comforting the wounded and dying, counseling the troubled, and conducting religious services in every conceivable atmosphere. Unlike German chaplains, who were constrained by Nazi Party rules and political officers, American and other Allied chaplains were able to give their principal allegiance to their beliefs and to the human souls in their charge. Many made the ultimate sacrifice. In the dark morning hours of February 3, 1943, U.S. chaplains George Fox, Alexander Goode, John Washington, and Clark Poling were aboard the transport ship *Dorchester* when it was torpedoed by German submarine U-223 in the icy waters near Greenland. In the frantic minutes before the ship sank, carrying 672 of the 902 men on board to their deaths, they saved many lives. "I could hear the chaplains preaching courage," survivor William B. Bednar reported. "Their voices were the only thing that kept me going." The four chaplains gave their own life preservers to men who had none, then linked arms on the listing deck and prayed as the ship took them down. Survivor John Ladd later said: "It was the finest thing I have seen or hope to see this side of heaven."

LEFT: *Honoring the Four Chaplains.* Cover of a commemorative program, 1943.

RIGHT: *Men with God.* Reproduction of a painting by Robert Benney, one of a series of paintings created between 1939 and 1945 under the auspices of Abbott Laboratories depicting the activities of the U.S. Army Medical Department.

AUGUST 5

1940 The U.S. Chief of Naval Operations establishes general ground rules for the exchange of scientific and technical information with a British mission named after its senior member Sir Henry Tizard.

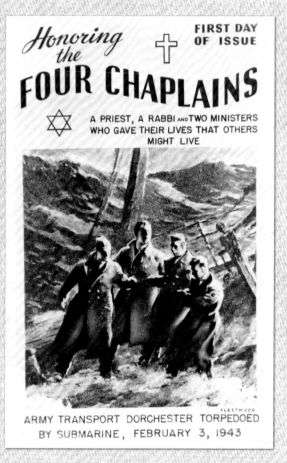

Honoring the **FOUR CHAPLAINS**

FIRST DAY OF ISSUE

A PRIEST, A RABBI AND TWO MINISTERS WHO GAVE THEIR LIVES THAT OTHERS MIGHT LIVE

ARMY TRANSPORT DORCHESTER TORPEDOED BY SUBMARINE, FEBRUARY 3, 1943

MEN WITH GOD—ROBERT BENNEY

The Corps of Chaplains (see August 5) was one of many components in the U.S. Army Service Forces (ASF) commanded by Lieutenant General Brehon Somervell. Adopting the motto "The impossible we do at once, the miraculous may take a little longer," the ASF provided the massive administrative and logistic support needed by a huge army fighting a global war. It included the Army Medical Department, the Corps of Engineers, the Quartermaster Corps, the Transportation Corps, and the Signal Corps (which was responsible for communication, including photographing V-mail). Before army units could be deployed they had to be properly trained and organized. That was the job of Lieutenant General Lesley J. McNair's Army Ground Forces (AGF), which became, in 1942–43, the largest single command in the army as the United States prepared to field more than ten times the number of combat divisions it had before the war. A peripatetic and hands-on general, McNair placed particular emphasis on effective leadership. "Your knowledge and personal example must inspire as well as teach your men," he told one graduating class of young officers. "I have seen too often in this emergency the two infallible signs of utter lack of leadership: reading from the book, and turning things over to the sergeant while the officer tries to look important." But if the officer does his job: "The Army's peerless soldiers will follow you, believe in you, trust in you, need you, and fight for you." (See September 20)

LEFT: *Reach your boy overseas by V-mail* (letters transferred to film overseas, then printed out on lightweight photo paper for delivery at home). Color poster by Jes Wilhelm Schlaikjer, produced by the U.S. Government Printing Office, 1942.

RIGHT: Secretary of War Henry L. Stimson (1867–1950), at left, with Lt. Gen. Lesley J. McNair (1883–1944), center, and Lt. Gen. Brehon Somervell (1892–1955), right. U.S. Army Signal Corps photograph, December 24, 1942.

AUGUST 6

1943 Destructive Allied air raids prompt a partial evacuation of Berlin.

1945 At 8:15 A.M., the U.S. B-29 *Enola Gay* drops an eight-thousand-pound atomic bomb, nicknamed "Little Boy," on Hiroshima, Japan.

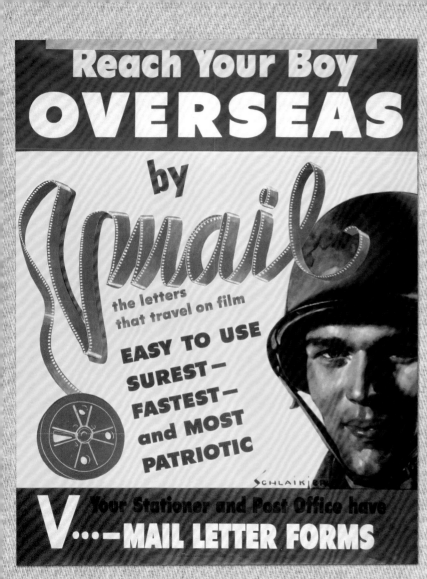

Reach Your Boy OVERSEAS by mail

the letters that travel on film

EASY TO USE
SUREST —
FASTEST —
and MOST PATRIOTIC

SCHLAIKJER

Your Stationer and Post Office have
V····—MAIL LETTER FORMS

"Let me thank you for your friendly congratulations on . . . the successful annihilation of the encircled enemy troops near Stalingrad," Stalin cabled Churchill in February 1943. By the end of January, after three months of savage fighting in and near that vital city, the Soviets had isolated and surrounded two separate pockets of exhausted Axis forces (see June 27). On January 31 (the day Hitler promoted him to field marshal), the Axis field commander, Friedrich Paulus, surrendered himself and the men in one pocket—an act that his führer contemptuously described as less than "what a weakling of a woman can do." Although Hitler ordered the troops in the other pocket to fight to the last man, they surrendered two days later. More than six hundred thousand Axis soldiers (Germans, Romanians, Italians, Hungarians, and Croatians) had been killed in the battle; more than a million Soviets had been killed or wounded. The German defeat at Stalingrad was a turning point of World War II. Hitler would reach no farther into the Soviet Union, and the Red Army acquired a new sense of its burgeoning power. ("Imagine it," one Soviet soldier wrote home, "the Fritzes [Germans] are running away from us!") Very shortly, the Soviets would begin an offensive that would—slowly, and at terrible cost—push Axis armies off Soviet soil. Meanwhile, some one hundred thousand Axis prisoners they had taken at Stalingrad in January began a forced march to camps in Siberia. Only about five thousand of them would survive the war.

LEFT: Axis prisoners who have been issued a loaf of Russian bread. Photograph by Georgii Zel'ma (1906–1984), 1943.

RIGHT: Newspaper map showing the Red Army's 1943 offensive.

AUGUST 7

1942 U.S. forces in the Pacific take the offensive for the first time in the war with the invasion of Guadalcanal in the Solomon Islands.

SEPT. 22, 1943

| 0 | 100 | 200 | 300 Miles |

RAILROADS
LONG ISLAND DRAWN TO SAME SCALE

FINLAND
FINLAND WAVERS

GULF OF
BOTHNIA

ALAND IS.   Turku (Abo)
Hango   Helsinki
Stockholm   GULF OF FINLAND
HIIUMAA   Tallinn
OESEL   ESTONIA   Lake
                        Peipus
           Riga   Pskov   Staraya
LATVIA   Russa   Demyansk
Memel   Velikie
LITHUANIA   Dvinsk   Polotsk
Konigsberg Kaunas   Vitebsk
EAST   Wilno   Smolensk
PRUSSIA   Orsha
           Minsk   Mogilev
Bialystok   WHITE   Bryansk
Warsaw   RUSSIA   Gomel
           PRIPET MARSHES
POLAND   Chernigov
Brest Litovsk
                    Kiev
RUSSO-GERMAN   Zhitomir   UKRAINE
BORDER AT   Lwow   Lubny
START OF   (Lemberg) Poltava
NAZI ATTACK   Berdichev Cherkassy
JUNE 22, 1941
HUNGARY   Krivoi Rog Dnepropetrovsk
                   Nikolaev
INCIPIENT REVOLT IN
RUMANIA; HUNGARY REFUSES   Odessa
HITLER MORE TROOPS
Arad   RUMANIA
Brasov
TRANSYLVANIAN ALPS   Galatz
IRON   Ploesti   MOUTHS OF
GATE   Pitesti   THE DANUBE
        Bucharest   Constanta
                   BLACK SEA

SOLDIERS SHOW ADVANCE LINE
OF RUSSIAN OFFENSIVE
SEPTEMBER 22, 1943

Leningrad   Vologda
Volkhov
Tikhvin
MARSHES
Bologoye   Kalinin   Yaroslavl   Kazan
Kalinin
Rzhev   Moscow   Gorki
Borodino
Vyazma   Kaluga   OKA
         Tula   Ryazan   Penza
                          Michurinsk   Saratov
Orel   U.S.S.R.
Kursk   Voronezh   LINE OF FARTHEST
RUSSIANS RETAKE   DON   GERMAN ADVANCE
CHERNIGOV SEPT. 21   Belgorod   1941, 1942
Sumy   Kharkov   Kupyansk
         Izyum   DONETS   Kamensk   Stalingrad
CAPITAL OF UKRAINE   Lozovaya   VOLGA
WITHIN STRIKING
DISTANCE OF RED ARMY   DNIEPER
RUSSIANS WITHIN FEW
MILES OF DNEPROPETROVSK
Zaporozhe   Taganrog   Rostov   MANYCH
Mariupol   Elista
SEA OF
AZOV   Tikhoretsk   Kropotkin
Melitopol   Armavir
Kerch   Krasnodar
CRIMEA   Maikop   Georgievsk   Mozdok
Simferopol   Novorossiisk   Tuapse   GROZNY
Sevastopol   CAUCASUS   Ordzhonikidze

Kuibyshev

Kirov

VOLGA

A month after Axis armies capitulated at Stalingrad (see August 7), a sixteen-ship Japanese convoy carrying supplies and reinforcements left Rabaul on the island of New Britain and sailed toward New Guinea, where Allied forces had been battling the Japanese since March 1942. Forewarned by intelligence, the Allies precipitated the Battle of the Bismarck Sea, a two-day aerial assault on the convoy that sank four Japanese destroyers and all eight troop transports. Only about 850 of the 4,500 Japanese reinforcements lived to reach the island—but Japan later sent more. As fighting on New Guinea continued (Japanese forces there did not surrender until September 1945), the Allies had the able assistance of New Guinea natives, who transported supplies and wounded soldiers, served as scouts, and provided other essential services. Around the globe, many people within Axis-occupied nations chose either to actively assist or actively resist their conquerors. Some kept their options open as they sought to further their own political objectives. This was true in Yugoslavia, where Communist guerrilla leader Josip Broz, generally known as Tito, fought Germans, Italians, and rival Yugoslav political factions; conducted ultimately unsuccessful negotiations with the Germans in early 1943 (when his partisan forces had suffered reverses and the Germans feared an Allied invasion); and finally emerged, with Allied support, as head of Yugoslavia's provisional government in 1945.

ABOVE: Josip Broz ("Tito") (1892–1980), 1948.

RIGHT: People of New Guinea enjoy a short rest period with Allied troops at a forward-area Young Men's Christian Association (YMCA) facility. Official Australian Commonwealth photograph, March 1943.

AUGUST 8

1940   U.S. aircraft production reaches a rate of five hundred per month.

1945   Russia declares war on Japan.

In January 1943, the U.S. War Department announced the formation of a new all-Japanese-American combat unit and reserved fifteen hundred places in it for Hawaiians. Ten thousand volunteered—eager to prove, as some declared to the military governor of the islands, "We know but one loyalty and that is to the Stars and Stripes." There were no relocation camps in Hawaii, but there was discrimination. Soon after the attack on Pearl Harbor, Japanese Americans who had been serving in the Hawaiian Territorial Guard had been discharged as "enemy aliens." Even students serving in the Reserve Officer Training Corps (ROTC) were discharged. (They promptly formed the nonmilitary "Varsity Victory Volunteers.") In April 1943, Hawaiians selected for the new combat unit were sent to Camp Shelby, Mississippi, where they joined a smaller group of mainland Japanese Americans, most of whom had been recruited from relocation camps. At first, the two groups did not get along: The mainlanders called the Hawaiians "Buddaheads" (from a pidgin term meaning "pigheaded"); Hawaiians called the mainlanders "Katonks" (after the sound their heads made hitting the floor during fistfights). Understanding increased after the Hawaiians were taken to visit the arid, inhospitable camps in which the mainlanders' families were still incarcerated, and soon the two groups were forged into one of America's proudest and most formidable fighting units—the 442nd Regimental Combat Team. (See July 5)

A group of 110 men from the village of Aiea, Hawaii, crowd in the Selective Service Board No. 9 in Waipah to volunteer for the U.S. Army's recently formed combat regiment comprising American citizens of Japanese ancestry. U.S. Office of War Information photograph, March 1943.

AUGUST 9

1945 An American B-29, nicknamed *Bockscar*, drops the second and final atomic bomb used in the war; the target is Nagasaki, Japan.

The Hawaiian tradition of interracial amity devolved into suspicion and prejudice against local Japanese Americans after the attack on Pearl Harbor (see August 9). Yet economic considerations argued against establishing internment camps in Hawaii as was done on the mainland's West Coast. Almost one-third of Hawaii's population was of Japanese ancestry and, after Pearl Harbor, labor was instantly at a premium. "Anyone who could tell the difference between a hammer and a saw was classified as a skilled carpenter," author James H. Shoemaker wrote in 1946 of wartime Hawaii. "A man who could handle a wrench immediately became a plumber." The situation was eased only a little by the gradual arrival of eighty-three thousand civilian workers from the mainland—a small percentage of the more than fifteen million Americans who relocated during the war, most to find better employment near military bases and industrial centers. In 1943, war production peaked, the economy threatened to overheat—and Roosevelt reacted by issuing a "hold-the-line" order to stabilize wages and prices. "We are determined to see to it that our supplies of food and other essential civilian goods are distributed on a fair and just basis—to rich and poor, management and labor, farmer and city dweller alike," he had said in his January State of the Union address. "We Americans intend to do this great job together. In our common labors we must build and fortify the very foundation of national unity—confidence in one another."

ABOVE: *Our home front "task force!"* Color poster by Fred Little Packer (1886–1956), published by the "Victory-builders" Division, Bressler Editorial Cartoons, 1944.

RIGHT: Workers at the Chattanooga Stamping and Enameling Company form a "V" for Victory outside their defense plant. Office of War Information photograph between 1941 and 1946.

AUGUST 10

1944 is complete.

Japanese resistance ends on Guam; the American conquest of the Marianas

In 1943, as Allied prospects improved—and as prices rose faster than wages—some two million Americans violated the "no-strike" pledge that unions had made when the United States entered the war and staged 3,800 walkouts. Most were "wildcat" actions unsanctioned by union leaders. Yet four major strikes by almost a half million low-paid coal miners were led by United Mine Workers president John L. Lewis. Although the government finally negotiated a contract that the miners accepted, Lewis was castigated by many political leaders and vilified by much of the press for damaging the war effort—an accusation also hurled at striking rank-and-file members of other unions. "The most important thing in this war is to preserve the system of government that we have," one striking New York aviation worker responded, "and among other things, the procedure for adjudicating union troubles." Congress was not moved by that argument. Determined to prevent more wartime strikes, it passed the War Labor Disputes (Smith-Connally) Act on June 25. The act ordered that there be a thirty-day cooling off period before workers in a non-war-related plant could strike; established criminal penalties for those convicted of urging war workers to strike; and gave the president the power to seize war plants when strikes and lockouts threatened to halt production. Once the government assumed control, as it did with about four dozen privately owned defense firms, workers were not permitted to strike. (See July 14)

The First Strike Vote [after passage of the Smith-Connally Anti-Strike Act]. Drawing by Clifford Berryman (1869–1949), August 4, 1943.

AUGUST 11

1940   Italians begin a four-day battle that will force British and South African troops to yield the Tug Argan Pass in British Somaliland.

While civilian workers worried over the progress of the war and kept a cautious eye on inflation and wages, they and everyone else on the home front coped with shortages (see July 24, 25). To ease strains caused by food rationing in the United States, Secretary of Agriculture Claude Wickard had suggested that Americans plant "Victory gardens," and by 1943 an estimated 20.5 million gardens had taken root in backyards and in public spaces, such as Copley Square in Boston. "Gardens will help, too. Weed 'em and reap for victory," was one of many slogans that decorated the pages of *The Wartime Cook Book: 500 Recipes, Victory Substitutes and Economical Suggestions for Nutritious Wartime Meals*, which included other tips as well as rationing-sensitive recipes: "READ EVERY LABEL . . . even those of brands that are old friends. Every manufacturer will be affected by shortages just as is the individual and alternatives will be used. The label will tell you whether these are what you want to feed your family. . . . To remind Americans how comparatively lucky they were, *The Wartime Cook Book* also included a page of photos taken in France in 1942, with the caption: "In France today, $^{7}/_{10}$ ounce of cheese for meatless days or a thin slice of meat loaf, 3½ ounces bread, Lima beans and 2 small apples with 5½ ounces wine are called a meal."

ABOVE: Cover illustration from *Sugarless Recipes: Aids for Housewives in Solving Sugar Rationing Problems*, by Ruth Odell. Published by the Washington [D.C.] Service Bureau, 1942.

RIGHT: Front and back covers of *The Wartime Cook Book: 500 Recipes, Victory Substitutes and Economical Suggestions for Nutritious Wartime Meals*, edited by Ruth Berolzheimer and Edna L. Gaul, published by Consolidated Book Publishers, Inc., Chicago, 1942.

AUGUST 12

1945   Soviet troops advance into northern Korea and invade southern Sakhalin Island.

506

THE WARTIME COOK BOOK

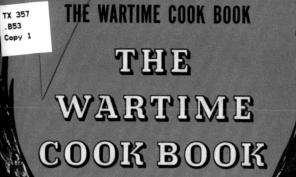

THE WARTIME COOK BOOK

NOTHING COUNTS · BUT VICTORY!

500 Recipes, Victory Substitutes and Economical
Suggestions for Nutritious Wartime Meals

In the Warsaw Ghetto, the Nazis allotted residents a food ration of only about three hundred calories a day—far below what is necessary for a human to survive. An area that had been sealed off from the rest of the city since 1940, the ghetto housed hundreds of thousands of Jews from Warsaw and other Polish cities in horribly crowded conditions that, coupled with the basely inadequate rations, encouraged the rapid spread of disease. Yet ghetto residents proved tremendously resilient: To fight starvation they planted small gardens wherever one might survive and, despite being closely guarded, developed a black-market trade with people beyond the wall. In 1943, they faced their most terrible challenge. By that time, the Germans had deported some three hundred thousand people from the ghetto to the Treblinka death camp, and those left behind had learned of the mass killings there. They formed resistance organizations that, in January, repulsed German troops sent in to remove more ghetto residents. When the Germans entered the ghetto again on April 19, resistance flowered into a full-scale rebellion now known as the Warsaw Ghetto Uprising—despite impossible odds. "What are we and our force against an . . . army, against tanks and armored cars," resistance fighter Simha Ratajzer wondered, "while we have only revolvers and, at best, grenades in our hands." They held out against the Germans for more than a month. Jews who survived the uprising were sent either to forced-labor camps or to their deaths at Treblinka.

German soldiers guard prisoners taken during the Warsaw Ghetto uprising, 1943.

AUGUST 13

1942 In the midst of anti-British rioting in India, several factories producing war materials are closed by strikes.

1945 The Mongolian People's Republic declares war on Japan.

In April 1943, as the Germans were preparing to enter the Warsaw Ghetto (see August 13), American intelligence deciphered a message sent in the Japanese naval code that detailed Admiral Isoroku Yamamoto's itinerary for the following five days. Commander in chief of the Japanese Combined Fleet, Yamamoto had been a chief architect of the December 1941 surprise attack on Pearl Harbor. Despite his later defeat at the Battle of Midway (see June 20), Americans still regarded him as Japan's most formidable naval commander, and U.S. Secretary of the Navy Frank Knox ordered that Yamamoto's aircraft be intercepted and destroyed. On April 18, sixteen American P-38 fighter aircraft flew the four hundred miles from recently secured Guadalcanal (see June 24, August 4) to Bougainville in the Solomon Islands on this deadly mission, which was timed to the second. As the U.S. planes approached the island, two Japanese bombers and six fighter escorts appeared. The Americans shot down three fighters and the two bombers, killing Yamamoto. The admiral's ashes were returned to Japan, where the Imperial Rule Assistance Association declared that the Japanese now had "a greater spirit to fight against our enemy, America and Britain. Let us march in line in one united body . . . so that the spirit of the late Fleet Admiral may be kept alive." On May 31, *Time* magazine reported quite another reaction by an unnamed "veteran of Pacific service: 'The only better news would be a bullet through Hitler.'"

ABOVE: Adm. Isoroku Yamamoto (1884–1943), 1942.

RIGHT: *Mitsubishi Navy 'G1' Bomber* (*Betty*), the type of plane in which Yamamoto was flying on April 18, 1943. Reproduction of a painting by Charles H. Hubbell, published by Thompson Products, Inc., Cleveland, Ohio, 1946.

AUGUST 14

1941   The United States and Britain issue the Atlantic Charter, which delineates "certain common principles . . . on which they base their hopes for a better future for the world."

1945   Japan agrees to surrender unconditionally.

CHARLES H. HUBBELL

Mitsubishi Navy "01" Bomber (Betty) — Japanese

SPAN—82 FT.   LENGTH—65 FT.   HEIGHT—16 FT.   CREW—8   TOP SPEED—330 M.P.H.   RANGE—2500 MILES

CEILING—30,000 FT.   ARMAMENT—1 CANNON, 5 MACHINE GUNS   BOMB LOAD—4000 LBS.

ENGINES—TWO MITSUBISHI "KASEI" 1800 H.P. 14-CYL. TWIN-ROW RADIALS

As U.S. pilots shot down Admiral Yamamoto's plane in the Solomon Islands (see August 14), two Allied armies were closing in on Axis forces in Tunisia, North Africa. After Rommel had withdrawn through the Kasserine Pass (see August 2), he had joined his rearguard forces and turned east to deal with Field Marshal Bernard Montgomery's British Eighth Army. Montgomery had discovered Rommel's intent via intelligence, however, and ordered his men to dig in around the town of Medenine, where they repulsed multiple Axis assaults. Ill and discouraged, Rommel turned command over to General Jürgen von Arnim and returned to Germany, leaving North Africa for good. While von Arnim extricated his men from a British trap and withdrew deeper into Tunisia, U.S. Army private Peter Sanfilippo depicted, in both picture and words, a "German anti-tank convoy . . . on the receiving end of an American 'Martin-Marauder' air attack." Caught on "a militarily constructed utility bridge" set against "the great span of the flat Tunisian terrain," the antitank contingent did not stand much of a chance. Nor did the larger Axis force, once Montgomery's army and the Allied units advancing from the west linked up. Together, they pushed von Arnim's German and Italian troops back to Tunis and Bizerte, taking both those cities, and more than two hundred thousand prisoners, on May 12. With those victories, North Africa was securely in Allied hands.

Enemy Under Attack.
Reproduction of a watercolor painting by PFC Peter Sanfilippo, Battery C, 633rd Field Artillery, U.S. Army, Bizerte, Tunisia, 1943.

AUGUST 15

1943 After a two-week bombing campaign, U.S. troops land on Kiska, one of two Aleutian Islands occupied by the Japanese during the 1942 Battle of Midway. The GIs find the island deserted; the Japanese had evacuated at the end of July.

1945 The Allies proclaim V-J Day. Emperor Hirohito goes on the radio for the first time to order all Japanese to lay down their arms.

With the surrender of Axis forces in North Africa in mid-May 1943 (see August 15), the siege of the island of Malta ended, and Allied fleets gained effective control of the Mediterranean. Meanwhile, past the Straits of Gibraltar, the Battle of the Atlantic was reaching its turning point. U-boat losses were steadily mounting as the Germans, whose U-boat Enigma codes were being read by the Allies, faced innovative U.S. and British technologies as well as more compact and faster aircraft carriers of the CVE or "escort" class. By the end of May, the Germans had lost one hundred U-boats in five months, and Admiral Karl Dönitz, commander in chief of the German navy, withdrew his submarines from the Atlantic. Now on the offensive, Allied subs and both carrier- and land-based aircraft stepped up attacks on German vessels in the North Atlantic, damaging the German battleship *Tirpitz* in September, and striking a German convoy and sinking forty thousand tons of shipping in October. A month later, the North Atlantic was also the site of a successful American experiment in racial integration when the weather ship USS *Sea Cloud* took up station there. *Sea Cloud*'s crew included both black and white seamen, as well as several African American officers. This success did not lead to widespread integration in the coast guard or navy. Nor did it mitigate the racial troubles that intermittently marred the American war effort (see August 17, 18).

LEFT: A United States flag waves over the deck of an escort carrier. U.S. Navy photograph, July 6, 1943.

RIGHT: U.S. Navy men: Oliver Murray, cook third class; Ned N. Holmes, cook second class; and Johnnie Fraction, steward's mate first class, on Guam. U.S. Navy photograph, c. 1945.

AUGUST 16

1942 U.S. Army Air Corps planes see their first action in North Africa.

1945 Gen. Prince Toshihiko Higashikuni becomes prime minister of Japan and forms a cabinet to arrange for surrender.

"The domestic scene is anything but encouraging," Eleanor Roosevelt wrote in her "My Day" column of June 20, 1943. "[I]t gives one a feeling that, as a whole, we are not really prepared for democracy." Throughout the year, festering resentments within the segregated U.S. armed forces resulted in race riots at military bases in Mississippi, Georgia, California, Texas, and Kentucky. Among civilian war workers, racial tensions had also increased as more blacks crowded into cities and found jobs in previously all-white factories (see July 12). The year had already seen race riots in Los Angeles, California; Mobile, Alabama; and Beaumont, Texas. They were all eclipsed by a riot that erupted in Detroit hours after the first lady completed her June 20 column. Beginning with fights between white and black teenagers at a popular amusement park, violence quickly spread to other parts of the city. Before it was over, twenty-five black and nine white people were dead and nearly seven hundred people had been injured. Some in the press blamed the riot on the first lady, whom the *Jackson Daily News* assailed for "personally proclaiming and practicing social equality at the White House and wherever you go." Intensely aware of the buildup of tensions, Mrs. Roosevelt had suggested a conference between white and black leaders to help avert just the sort of bloodshed for which she was being blamed. "Detroit," she wrote to a friend, "should never have happened."

Eleanor Roosevelt speaks into the microphone at radio station WOL, Washington, D.C., during a broadcast devoted to African Americans. U.S. Office of War Information photograph by Roger Smith, 1943.

AUGUST 17

1940 Germany announces a "total blockade" of Britain.

1943 The battle for Sicily ends with Allied success.

The Detroit riots (see August 17) occurred less than two weeks after days of violent clashes convulsed Los Angeles. Surrounded by military bases, the city was also home to more than two hundred and fifty thousand people of Mexican descent, many of whom were among the young jazz aficionados who adopted special attire known as "zoot suits." The fact that the jazz and zoot suit crowds tended to ignore social strictures against racial intermingling exacerbated existing tensions between white servicemen and Mexican American youths. The immediate cause of the violence was a fight on May 30 in which one sailor was badly injured. On June 3, fifty sailors, armed with clubs and other makeshift weapons, went looking for revenge. In the following days, they were joined by hundreds of others—sailors, soldiers, and civilians—who did not confine their targets to zoot suiters: "Street cars were halted while Mexicans, and some Filipinos and Negroes, were jerked out of their seats, pushed into the streets, and beaten with sadistic frenzy," a 1943 study of the violence reported. "If the victims wore zoot-suits, they were stripped of their clothing and left naked or half-naked on the streets. . . . A Negro defense worker, wearing a defense-plant identification badge on his workclothes, was taken from a street car and one of his eyes was gouged out with a knife." Finally, military authorities intervened and declared Los Angeles off-limits to servicemen, and the violence subsided.

LEFT: A man identified as Frank Tellez, wearing a zoot suit, June 11, 1943.

RIGHT: U.S. armed forces personnel with wooden clubs range the streets during the zoot suit riots in Los Angeles, 1943.

AUGUST 18

1943 Gen. Hans Jeschonnek, chief of the Luftwaffe General Staff, commits suicide, apparently because Hitler blames him for Allied air successes. The Germans will announce that he died of a stomach hemorrhage.

W hile governors and mayors coped with war-related problems affecting their states, in Washington, political partisanship was on the rise. Throughout the year the Seventy-Eighth Congress, a more conservative body than its predecessor, eviscerated some New Deal agencies, abolished others, and tussled with the Roosevelt administration over a variety of issues, including subsidies and the increase in farm prices. ("The New Deal has messed up the whole farm situation," the chairman of the Senate Agriculture Committee complained in April. "I hope a tornado blows along in 1944 and sweeps every New Dealer from Washington.") Still, as the two-party system and the democratic process continued to function in the usual cantankerous fashion, the central focus at both ends of Pennsylvania Avenue remained on winning the war. Democrat Roosevelt, who had brought prominent Republicans Henry Stimson and Frank Knox into his war cabinet in 1940, acknowledged this—and effectively bade farewell to the New Deal—during a December 1943 news conference: "How did the New Deal come into existence? It was because there was an awfully sick patient called the United States of America . . . [which] was suffering from a grave internal disorder. . . . And they sent for the doctor." By 1943, however, "Dr. New Deal" had done its job. The economic agonies caused by the Great Depression had largely been remedied, and the chief medic now had to be "Dr. Win-the-War."

LEFT: *To speak up for democracy, read up on democracy.* Color poster published by the WPA, published between 1935 and 1943.

RIGHT: *What This Country Needs Today is a New Declaration of Interdependence.* Drawing by Clifford Berryman (1869–1949), July 4, 1943.

AUGUST 19

1942 About six thousand Canadian and British raiders land at Dieppe, France. They are repulsed after nine hours, suffering heavy casualties. The P-51 Mustang fighter plane makes its combat debut during the battle.

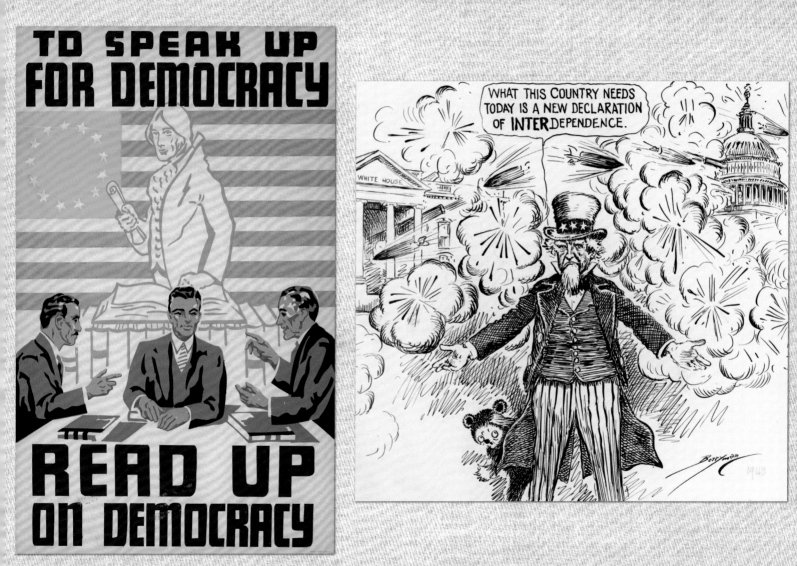

Balancing attention to domestic politics with inter-Allied diplomacy and war planning, in May 1943 Roosevelt made an unsuccessful attempt to set up a meeting with Stalin. He included in his message a U.S. intelligence estimate that "Germany will deliver an all-out attack . . . this summer . . . against the middle of your line." In fact, Hitler's target was a Red Army salient (a bulge into German-held territory) near Kursk, an important railroad junction. Already alerted by his own intelligence sources, Stalin set Red Army units, partisans, and civilians furiously to work preparing elaborate defenses around Kursk, and the Soviets were well prepared when, on July 5, the Wehrmacht launched Operation Citadel. Over the following week, two million men and more than six thousand tanks collided in one of the largest land battles in history. Ferocious artillery barrages, tactical bombing runs, and aerial dogfights swirled around the ground fighting as the Germans smashed their way forward, pinching in the sides of the salient and threatening to cut off and destroy a Soviet tank army. Soviet commander Georgi Zhukov rushed in reinforcements, and the ensuing clash, July 12, involving some eighteen hundred tanks, was the largest tank battle of the war. At the end of the day, bodies and shattered tanks littered the shell-ravaged battlefield. Both sides had been terribly battered, but by July 13 the Soviets had prevailed. The Germans began to retreat—with the Red Army hard on their heels.

Untitled color drawing from a sketchbook of German war correspondent Hans Liska (b. 1907), published in Berlin, 1944.

AUGUST 20

1944   Red Army troops cross the Danube into Romania.

While full-scale armored warfare raged on Europe's eastern front, in Burma, the Allies concentrated on irregular warfare throughout 1943. In February, British guerrilla warfare expert Orde Wingate led his "Chindit" long-range penetration group on Operation Longcloth, its first foray behind enemy lines. "If we succeed, we shall have demonstrated a new style of warfare to the world . . . and brought nearer the day when the Japanese will be thrown bag and baggage out of Burma," Wingate wrote at the outset. Supplied by air, the Chindits made hit-and-run thrusts at enemy forces in the north of the country during a difficult and costly four-month campaign: One thousand men, out of the original force of three thousand, were lost. Yet the campaign boosted British morale and taught the military valuable lessons about air support. It also captured the fancy of Winston Churchill, who asked to meet Wingate—and was so impressed, when he did, that he took Wingate to the Allied conference in Quebec that August. Wingate emerged from the conference with a promotion and additional resources. Moreover, his presence inspired the Americans to build their own long-range penetration group. The 5307th Composite Unit (Provisional), led by Brigadier General Frank D. Merrill, was established in September— but it would be months before "Merrill's Marauders" were fully trained and ready for the singular challenges of irregular jungle warfare (see May 24).

ABOVE: Gen. Frank D. Merrill (1903–1955) c. 1994.

LEFT: Sick and wounded members of British guerrilla warfare expert Orde Wingate's "Chindit" raiders returning to British lines after campaigning behind Japanese lines in Burma. Photograph, June 1943.

RIGHT: *Unconditional Surrender, Save Burma.* Illustration by American folk artist John F. Kratky, 1943.

AUGUST 21

1942 President Roosevelt restates the principle that officials of occupying powers will be held responsible for war crimes against civilian populations.

1944 The Dumbarton Oaks International Peace and Security Conference opens in Washington, D.C.

THE TIDE BEGINS TO TURN: 1943

As the Wehrmacht's Operation Citadel fell apart on the eastern front (see August 20), Hitler withdrew some of the surviving panzer units from his battered armies there and sent them to reinforce Axis troops facing a new assault in the Mediterranean. The Allied invasion of Sicily (Operation Husky) was one of the largest landing operations of World War II. The attack began late on July 9 with paratroop and glider landings—during which strong winds and inexperience claimed hundreds of Allied lives, as many gliders missed their targets and landed in the sea. On July 10, under the gloom of foul weather, ground commander General Sir Harold Alexander's Fifteenth Army Group landed on the southeastern part of the island; General George Patton's U.S. Seventh Army came ashore along the Gulf of Gela; and General Bernard Montgomery's British and Canadian Eighth Army disembarked south of Syracuse. The British quickly took Syracuse, but the Americans faced worse weather and stiffer resistance—which was overcome with the help of naval gunfire. After a delay while his men protected Montgomery's left flank, Patton led his troops north toward Palermo, which on July 22, became the first major European city the Allies liberated. Patton and Montgomery then raced northeast, to secure the port of Messina. Patton arrived first, on August 17; but a hundred thousand German and Italian troops had already escaped to the Italian mainland, where the Allies would face many of them again.

During the invasion of Sicily, an American munitions ship explodes after being hit by a German bomb. U.S. Army photograph by Lt. Robert J. Longini, Gela, Sicily, July 11, 1943.

AUGUST 22

1942 After losing five of its ships to German U-boats, Brazil declares war against Germany and Italy.

1944 French, American, and Algerian forces begin their final assault on Marseilles, France.

While Allied forces were fighting to secure Sicily (see August 22), farther north in Europe, British and American air forces continued the round-the-clock Combined Bomber Offensive. This harrowing campaign, in which Americans bombed by day and the British by night, took a heavy toll on Allied planes and airmen—while wreaking fearful destruction below. One important target, the major port and industrial center of Hamburg, Germany, was hit particularly hard between July 24 and August 3, ten days of relentless punishment that the Germans later referred to as "the catastrophe." The worst devastation occurred on the hot, dry night of July 27, when the incendiary bombs that poured out of RAF bombers ignited separate fires that quickly roared together, greedily devouring everything flammable and creating a savage firestorm before which local firefighters were helpless. An estimated forty-five thousand people were killed that night; nearly one million were left homeless. "The streets were covered with hundreds of bodies," Hamburg's police commissioner later reported. "Mothers with children, men young and old, burned, charred. . . . Shelters presented the same picture, even more gruesome . . . since it showed here and there the last desperate struggle against a merciless fate." Hamburg was the first but would not be the only German city to suffer through a firestorm. As was true during the Battle of Britain, however, even these terrible raids did not destroy civilian morale.

LEFT: During a night raid, the Royal Air Force drops four-thousand-pound and eight-thousand-pound explosive bombs and smaller incendiaries on the city of Hamburg, Germany, 1943.

RIGHT: U.S. B-17 "Flying Fortresses" pound the port of Hamburg, Germany, as smoke from previous attacks hangs over the city. U.S. Army Air Forces photograph, August 1943.

AUGUST 23

1944 French resistance forces begin taking over the administration of Paris as U.S. and French troops are blocked in their advance toward the city near Versailles.

The beginning of the catastrophe in Hamburg (see August 23) coincided with a sea change in Italy, where people had grown increasingly restive as Mussolini fell more deeply under German sway and the Allies made steady gains in the Mediterranean. With Italy now facing the prospect of an American invasion, members of Mussolini's government (including his son-in-law, Count Galeazzo Ciano), some military leaders, and Italy's king first confronted and then deposed and arrested Il Duce on July 24 and 25. Former chief of the Italian general staff Marshal Pietro Badoglio formed a government that, throughout August, attempted to assuage the Germans while conducting secret negotiations with the Allies. "Badoglio, our most bitter enemy, has taken over the government," Hitler said on July 25. Shocked at the abruptness of Mussolini's fall, he sent reinforcements to Italy to prepare for the Allied invasion—and to prevent further treachery. On September 3, the first Allied units landed at Reggio, at the toe of the Italian boot. September 8, on the eve of the main assault at Salerno, General Eisenhower's headquarters announced that Badoglio's government had signed an armistice. Badoglio, the king, and others involved in deposing Mussolini immediately decamped to the Allies—without warning their subcommanders or troops. Hundreds of thousands of Italian soldiers became prisoners and slave laborers of the Germans. Thousands who resisted the Wehrmacht were murdered after they were captured.

LEFT: *Italy Surrenders—And It's Unconditional!* Drawing by Willard Wetmore Combes (b. 1901), 1943.

RIGHT: Invasion of Italy, September 1943. Map from *Naples-Foggia*, pamphlet in The U.S. Army Campaigns of World War II series, Center for Military History.

AUGUST 24

1943   Hitler appoints SS Chief Heinrich Himmler reichminister of the interior.

1945   In Vietnam, Emperor Bao Dai abdicates.

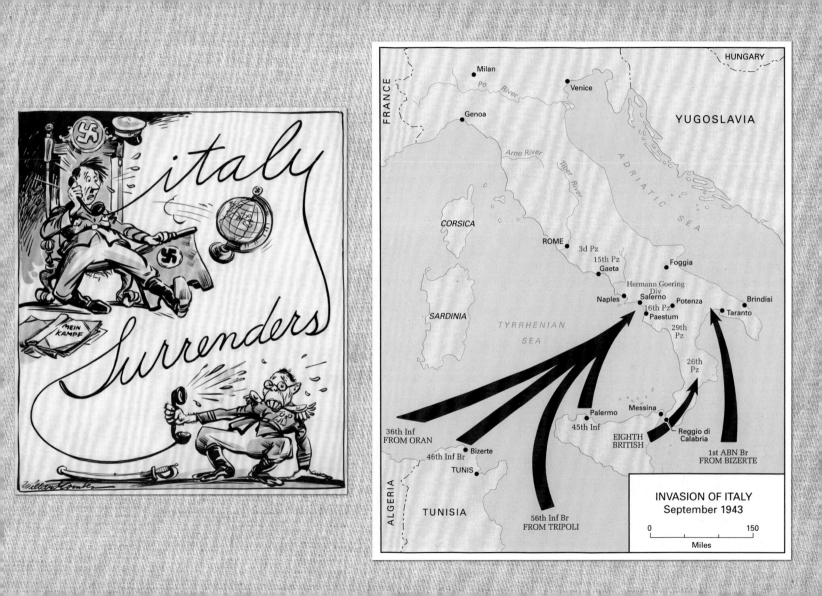

Operation Avalanche, the main Allied landing at Salerno, Italy, was so strongly hit by German resistance that by September 12, the Wehrmacht had pushed U.S. general Mark Clark's Anglo-American Fifth Army back toward the water. With naval support and the timely arrival of reinforcements, however, Clark's troops were able to regroup and push inland—as the British Eighth Army under Bernard Montgomery moved slowly northward from Reggio. The Italian campaign soon proved to be a grueling, muddy slog hindered by difficult mountainous terrain, wide rivers, unfriendly weather—and Germans determined to fight for every inch. "The country is shockingly beautiful, and just as shockingly hard to capture from the enemy," American war correspondent Ernie Pyle wrote in mid-December. "I know you folks back there [in the United States] are disappointed and puzzled by the slow progress. . . . Our men will get to Rome all right. There's no question about that. But the way is cruel. Right this minute some of them are fighting hand-to-hand up there in fog and clouds so dense they can barely see each other—one man against another. No one who has not seen this mud, these dark skies, these forbidding ridges and ghostlike clouds that unveil and then quickly hide your killer, has the right to be impatient with the progress along the road to Rome." As Pyle wrote, the Allies were being held up by a harsh winter—and by a formidable line of German fortifications known as the Gustav Line.

German soldiers march British and American prisoners of war captured at Netturno through Rome. Presse-Hoffmann photograph, c. 1944.

1941 British and Russian troops invade Iran.

1944 French and U.S. troops liberate Paris.
Romania declares war on Germany.

So haben sie sich den Einzug in Rom nicht gedacht

Englische und amerikanische Kriegsgefangene aus dem Kampfraum von Netturno marschiereren unter Sicherung deutscher Soldaten durch Rom

K-Aufn. Vack   63641   Presse-Hoffmann

In September 1943, as Allied troops were beginning their long fight to reach Rome (see August 25), *Life* magazine published a picture of three dead American soldiers, unidentifiable (their faces could not be seen) and lying exactly as they had fallen at Buna Beach, New Guinea, in February. This was the first such picture of American war dead to be published on the home front. Its carefully considered release stemmed, in part, from the Roosevelt administration's growing conviction that people on the home front, so far removed from the front lines, were becoming complacent, and too many were not wholeheartedly backing the war effort. Early in the year, Office of War Information staff had suggested that withholding graphic images of the costs of war encouraged the public to believe that "some get hurt and ride smiling in aerial ambulances, but that none of them get badly shot or spill any blood." In May, *Newsweek* printed photographs of wounded troops "to harden home-front morale . . . [by] letting civilians see photographically what warfare does to men who fight." Similarly, the editors of *Life* addressed their readers about the first image of GIs killed in battle: "Why print this picture anyway of three American boys, dead on an alien shore? The reason is that words are never enough. . . . [T]he words do not exist to make us see, or know, or feel what it is like, what actually happens."

LEFT: *To America's honored war dead.* Color poster by C. R. Miller, sponsored by the Think American Institute, published by Kelly-Read & Co., Rochester, New York, 1943.

RIGHT: The bodies of three dead American soldiers killed in a Japanese ambush lie on Buna Beach, New Guinea, February 1, 1943. Photograph by George Strock, published in *Life* magazine September 20, 1943. Courtesy of Getty Images.

AUGUST 26

1944 While Charles de Gaulle is attending services at Notre Dame Cathedral after the liberation of Paris, collaborationists and German soldiers in civilian dress fire at him from the church balcony. They miss de Gaulle but wound many others.

TO AMERICA'S HONORED WAR DEAD

They died protecting individual liberty and opportunity...Let's live for that same principle.

The same week Americans were confronted by the first picture of U.S. war dead (see August 26), singer Kate Smith, who had made Irving Berlin's song "God Bless America" a national phenomenon, raised almost $40 million during an eighteen-hour radio marathon. Smith was one of many international artists and entertainers, within and outside the military, who devoted time, energy, and emotion to supporting the war effort and bolstering the morale of their armed forces. Stage and screen stars dispatched by the Shochiku film company visited Japanese troops in the field. Germany's troop entertainment office developed an elaborate menu of programs, even including "decadent" American jazz. Soviet musicians lifted the spirits of battered Red Army troops. Singer Vera Lynn, comedienne and singer Gracie Fields, and expatriate American entertainer Josephine Baker helped keep British and commonwealth armed forces spirits high; and Americans Bob Hope and Mickey Rooney were prominent among the Allied entertainers who visited troops near the front lines. One of the first U.S. entertainers to volunteer for overseas tours, singer Jane Froman was severely injured in February 1943 when the airliner carrying her troupe crashed into the Tagus River in Portugal. Struggling to recover, Froman finally kept her date with American GIs during a three-month tour of the European Theater in 1945, while she was still on crutches.

LEFT: A bomb-damaged building in Algiers serves as the box tier for some of the American soldiers attending an army band concert in the North African base city. Photograph September 1943.

RIGHT: Jane Froman (1907–1980), c. 1948.

AUGUST 27

1940 The U.S. Congress authorizes a one-year call-up of the National Guard. In Africa, the Free French take control of Cameroon. They will take Brazzaville the next day.

On October 11, 1943, William Averell Harriman took the oath as the new U.S. ambassador to the Soviet Union. He immediately departed for Moscow, where he plunged into a round of meetings and negotiations that culminated in Roosevelt's first face-to-face meeting with Stalin. As a preliminary, British, American, and Soviet diplomats met in Moscow (October 18–November 7), where the Soviets continued to press for an American invasion of western Europe the following spring; avoided discussing growing problems surrounding the postwar disposition of Poland; and reluctantly agreed to acknowledge Chiang Kai-shek's Nationalist Chinese government as a "Great Power." The Chinese ambassador was thus allowed to sign the "Joint Four-Nation Declaration" issued during the conference. "Long strides forward have been made by the conference," Harriman wrote Winston Churchill on November 3, "but if it is not wisely followed up, we can get knocked back on our heels . . . inclusion [of the Soviets] in the next military conference, and the manner in which they are dealt with, are of inestimable importance." At the subsequent Allied strategy conference in Tehran, Iran (November 28–December 1), Roosevelt and Stalin got along well. "I am sure that it was an historic event," the president wrote Stalin afterward, "in the assurance not only of our ability to wage war together but to work in the utmost harmony for the peace to come." (See May 29).

LEFT: U.S. envoy William Averell Harriman (1891–1986) shakes hands with Joseph Stalin. Photograph, c. 1943.

RIGHT: Soviet color poster, 1943.

AUGUST 28

1944 French and American troops occupy Marseille, France.

1945 Japanese forces in Burma formally surrender in Rangoon. The first Allied personnel, U.S. Army Air Forces technicians, arrive at an airbase near Tokyo.

Самед на смерть идет, чтоб не погиб Семен,
Собою жертвует Семен за жизнь Самеда...
Пароль их „Родина" и лозунг их „Победа"!

As Roosevelt, Churchill, and the Combined Chiefs of Staff prepared for Allied strategy conferences in Cairo, Egypt (November 23–December 1, with Chiang Kai-shek) and Tehran, Iran (with Stalin, see August 28), the U.S. Fifth Fleet, Second Marine Division, and Twenty-seventh Infantry Division approached Makin and Tarawa atolls in the Gilbert Islands. In Operation Galvanic, part of the U.S. Central Pacific Campaign, Makin fell with relatively few casualties. Tarawa was another matter. Well dug in, the Japanese were little affected by the pre-assault bombardment and took full advantage of the opportunities presented by the Americans' initial problem-plagued assault. Landing craft snagged on the coral reef well off the beach, forcing marines to wade ashore through chest-high water under heavy fire. Waterlogged weapons misfired or broke, many officers were killed, and the men who made it to the beach were pinned down. "We crawled on our bellies through the sand because to stand up meant a quick death," marine corporal Robert Johnsmiller later remembered. "A Japanese hand grenade landed next to me. Alerted by my buddy to 'roll,' I quickly moved my body as it went off. I . . . was bleeding [he would lose an eye], but I ignored the pain and continued on." More and more marines waded ashore under fire. Eventually the weight of numbers made it possible for them to push inland—their every step contested by Japanese who preferred death to surrender.

LET'S GO GET 'EM!
U.S. MARINES

ABOVE: *Let's go get 'em! U.S. Marines.* Color recruiting poster, 1942.

RIGHT: Map of Tarawa Island, drawn by Corporal James George Brown, U.S. Army Air Forces, c. 1943.

AUGUST 29

1943 Germans seize the Danish king. In retaliation, Danes scuttle their own fleet, destroying twenty-nine ships to prevent them from falling into German hands.

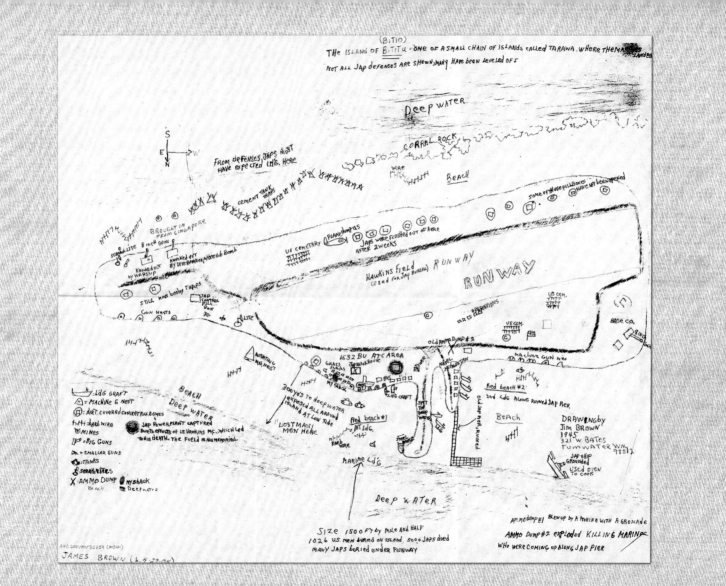

The Japanese high command had designated Tarawa the principal bastion in Japan's outer line of Pacific defense and instructed the five thousand troops there to "withstand assault by a million men for a hundred years." The defenders had prepared to do just that, erecting elaborate defenses including underwater obstacles on the beach approaches, mines, pillboxes, concrete blockhouses, and artillery. The fire they poured into the first waves of the American landing force, as men struggled to wade ashore from grounded landing craft (see August 29), left the landing site choked with wreckage and bodies. But the Japanese were also hit hard: Fire from U.S. naval guns and from the marines who had made it to shore smashed their communications and, by dusk, had killed half the garrison. On day two of the battle, the tide rose, landing craft were able to get tanks and artillery to the island, and the battered Americans began to push forward. The night of November 22, surviving Japanese hurled themselves at American lines in nerve-shattering "banzai" charges—that had little effect on the battle's outcome. By noon the next day, the Americans had secured Tarawa. The blood expended to take that obscure atoll profoundly shocked people in the United States: More than a thousand Americans had been killed, thousands more had been wounded. Only seventeen Japanese soldiers had survived.

LEFT: Untitled drawing by Donald Lester Dickson, U.S. Marine Corps, c. 1943–45.

RIGHT: Two Japanese Imperial Marines who killed themselves rather than surrender. U.S. Marine Corps photograph, Tarawa, 1943.

AUGUST 30

1937 As fires rage in Shanghai, where fierce fighting continues between Chinese troops and Japanese invaders, Dr. Wellington Koo presents China's case before the League of Nations.

1945 The U.S. First Marine Division and the army's Eleventh Airborne Division arrive in Japan to begin the Allied occupation.

The four-day agony that was the Battle of Tarawa (see August 30) occurred as a much longer struggle was beginning some fifteen hundred miles to the southeast, in the Solomon Islands. Bougainville, the largest island in the chain—and the place where American aircraft had shot down Admiral Isoroku Yamamoto in April (see August 14)—was the last major obstacle between advancing Allied forces and the major Japanese base at Rabaul, New Britain. Nearly sixty thousand Japanese were hidden in Bougainville's vast tangle of vines and mud, but most were deployed far from Empress Augusta Bay, where the initial force of fourteen thousand U.S. Marines came ashore November 1. As the marines dug in against light opposition, their naval support engaged and defeated a Japanese fleet in the Battle of Empress Augusta Bay, one of several naval and air clashes that swirled around the island during the first few months of the Bougainville campaign. By December, Allied air power (including planes from new airstrips on Bougainville) had effectively neutralized Rabaul; thousands more American troops had arrived on Bougainville (the Fourteenth Army Corps had replaced the marines); and the Japanese commander on the island, Lieutenant General Hyakutake Haruyoshi, was planning his first major offensive, launched in March 1944. Determined to make the Allies pay for every foot they advanced, Haruyoshi did not surrender with the surviving twenty-three thousand men of his force until August 1945.

U.S. Marines slog through the muddy terrain on Bougainville. U.S. Marine Corps photograph, November 4, 1943.

AUGUST 31

1939 Germany cuts communications with Warsaw. Anticipating the outbreak of war, Britain begins evacuations from London.

The Allies Close In: 1944

President Roosevelt's grim 1943 Christmas Eve message about casualties to come (see August 1) was followed by costly Allied offensives in 1944. In January, an amphibious landing at Anzio, Italy, quickly bogged down on the beach, where British and American troops were cut off and harassed by a growing force of German defenders. From Saipan to the Battle of the Philippine Sea, bitter struggles punctuated the slow Allied progress in the Pacific Theater, while British- and American-led forces made equally painful progress in new offensives they launched in Burma. In the Soviet Union, the Red Army finally broke the German ring around Leningrad—and learned grim details of the city's two-and-a-half-year siege. As supplies were used up or destroyed by artillery fire, people ate rats, sawdust, anything that might be digestible, as they held out against an enemy that had murdered so many Soviet civilians and prisoners of war. "In the worst part of the siege," one survivor remembered, "Leningrad was in the power of the cannibals." By the time Soviet forces broke through, more than 640,000 people in the city had starved to death.

Around the world, the furious air war continued—and in Britain and America bursts of home-front debates followed the destruction of Italy's Monte Cassino in February and the continuous rain of bombs on German population centers. Smaller conflicts continued to fester within the larger war: Thousands perished in battles between rival factions in oc-

SEPTEMBER 1

1939 War erupts in Europe as Germany invades Poland.

1943 As a catastrophic famine engulfs Bengal, India, the British chiefs of staff call for emergency measures so that "efficient prosecution of the war against Japan by forces based in India" can continue.

cupied Yugoslavia. In newly liberated Greece, right-wing and left-wing groups began a savage civil war. The British intervened: Fearing they would lose their influence in the Eastern Mediterranean to the Soviet Union, they interned thousands of suspected left-wing sympathizers—one of the first intimations of the coming "Cold War."

At the same time, partisans and Allied intelligence agents continued to fight an underground war against Axis forces in occupied countries. In France, Resistance units helped prepare for the coming Allied invasion, while American troops slated to be among the first waves of assault troops poured into Britain. On June 6, a huge invasion force hit Normandy's beaches. "From the standpoint of our enemy we have achieved the impossible," Roosevelt told Americans in a *Fireside Chat* on June 12. "We have broken through their supposedly impregnable wall in Northern France. . . . We have established a firm foothold and are now prepared to meet the inevitable counter-attacks of the Germans . . . we all pray that we will have far more, soon, than a firm foothold."

Fighting their way inland, the Allies pushed Wehrmacht forces back at such a rate that the British Joint Intelligence Committee predicted all German resistance might end by the first of December. Hitler had a different idea. "It is essential

to deprive the enemy of his belief that victory is certain," he told his generals on December 12. "We must allow no moment to pass without showing the enemy that, whatever he does, he can never reckon on [our] capitulation. Never!" On December 16, 250,000 German troops smashed through the Ardennes Forest in bitterly cold Belgium and Luxembourg, their massive counterattack trapping thousands of stunned American soldiers.

Over There. Drawing by Edwin Marcus (1885–1961), June 11, 1944.

During the late-1943 Allied conference at Teheran, Iran (see August 28), Stalin had asked Roosevelt who had been selected to head Operation Overlord, the 1944 Allied invasion of western Europe. The Soviet dictator was not pleased when Roosevelt replied that the invasion's commander had not yet been chosen. "Stalin made it plain," American envoy Averell Harriman later reported, "that until the supreme commander was appointed he could not take seriously the promise of a cross-Channel invasion." Roosevelt promised Stalin fast action—and kept his word. The logical choice, U.S. Army chief of staff General George Marshall, could not be spared from the Joint and Combined Chiefs of Staff. Thus, on December 7, 1943, during a stopover in Tunisia, Roosevelt informed General Dwight D. Eisenhower, Allied commander in the Mediterranean Theater, that he was to head Overlord. "Eisenhower is the best politician among the military men," the president later told his son James. "He is a natural leader who can convince other men to follow him, and this is what we need . . . more than any other quality." The British had utmost confidence in Eisenhower and were happy with the choice. In January 1944 supreme command in the Mediterranean passed to British field marshal Sir Henry Maitland Wilson. The new Mediterranean commander assumed responsibility for a plan designed to break the stalemate at the Gustav Line in Italy and get Allied armies moving toward Rome.

LEFT: Gen. Dwight D. Eisenhower (left), Gen. Harold Alexander (second from left), and Prime Minister Winston Churchill meet somewhere in the Mediterranean area, early in 1944.

RIGHT: Field Mar. Henry Maitland Wilson (1881–1964), c. 1944.

SEPTEMBER 2

1939 As British bomber squadrons are deployed to France, Ireland proclaims its neutrality.

1945 Japan officially surrenders in ceremonies aboard the USS Missouri, anchored in Tokyo Bay.

As part of the new Allied offensive in Italy, General Mark Clark's Fifth Army was ordered to capture the town of Cassino and Monastery Hill (Monte Cassino), a formidable outpost overlooking the Liri Valley, gateway to Rome—and the site of an ancient Benedictine monastery filled with irreplaceable treasures. Securing this objective took more than four months, cost some 120,000 Allied casualties, and ignited a controversy that lasted for years when Allied bombers destroyed the monastery. On January 22, ten days after the first assault at Cassino, the Allies launched Operation Shingle, an amphibious landing on the west coast of Italy, behind the Gustav Line. Sailing from Naples, Allied forces secured the towns of Anzio and Nettuno and pushed several miles inland. Then General John P. Lucas halted to consolidate the beachhead; German reinforcements arrived; and the invasion devolved into a harrowing four-month German siege before the Allies were able to break out. Lieutenant Deloris Buckley, a nurse with the Ninety-fifth Evacuation Hospital at Anzio, was treating patients when a German aircraft pursued by a British Spitfire jettisoned its bombs. "There was a mighty roar. . . . My whole body went numb. . . . I saw blood spurting through a pair of holes in my thigh. . . . Gert Morrow lay on the floor, unconscious and bleeding to death. Blanche Sigman, our charge nurse, a woman we all adored, was killed outright. . . . In all, the single blast killed and wounded twenty-eight doctors, nurses and patients."

LEFT: *Hit on an Ammunition Dump*, Monte Cassino, Italy. Watercolor painting by PFC Peter Sanfilippo, 1944.

RIGHT: The wreckage of an evacuation hospital on the Anzio beachhead, near Nettuno, Italy. U.S. Army photograph, 1944.

SEPTEMBER 3

1939 Britain, France, India, Australia, and New Zealand declare war on Germany.

1941 Russian POWs become the first victims of a new German method of "exterminating" prisoners at Auschwitz: poison gas.

THE ALLIES CLOSE IN: 1944

While Allied forces were slugging it out with the Germans in Italy (see September 3), the Red Army was pushing the Wehrmacht back along the eastern front. In January (the month they broke the German siege of Leningrad, see September 1), the Soviets crossed into eastern Poland; in June, they crossed the border with Finland, whose troops had supported the Wehrmacht in the north. (After agreeing to an armistice with the Soviets in September, the Finns initiated the Arctic War, a campaign to drive German troops out of their country.) In August, after reequipping and reinforcing at a rate the Germans could no longer match, the Red Army began a summer offensive into Romania; in September, they were in Bulgaria and on the Hungarian Plain. In Poland, they were closing in on Warsaw. Within the city, the Germans were contending with an uprising, part of a general revolt by the Polish Home Army, a resistance force loyal to the non-Communist London-based Polish government-in-exile. While Heinrich Himmler dispatched German reinforcements to the Polish capital with orders to crush the rebellion in the most brutal fashion, the Red Army paused well short of the city—for both military and political reasons: The army outside Warsaw was anticipating a clash with the Wehrmacht, and Stalin (who was harboring a rival Polish government-in-exile) was not eager to see non-Communist Poles gain ground. After sixty-three bloody days, the Germans smashed the Warsaw rebellion.

Soviet map showing the progress of the Red Army during 1944, published by Tsentral'nyi Dom Sovetskoi Armi Imei M. V. Frunze.

SEPTEMBER 4

1941 The U.S. destroyer *Greer* is attacked by a German submarine it has been tracking, 175 miles from Iceland.

1944 British forces enter Antwerp, Belgium.

ГОД РЕШАЮЩИХ ПОБЕД

В славную боевую летопись нашей Родины навечно записан великий подвиг советского народа и его воинов, совершенный под руководством Коммунистической партии в годы Великой Отечественной войны. Ярчайшей страницей этой летописи является 1944 год — год решающих побед над фашистскими захватчиками. Советские Вооруженные Силы обрушили на врага могучие последовательные удары, в результате которых гитлеровцы были изгнаны из пределов нашей страны.

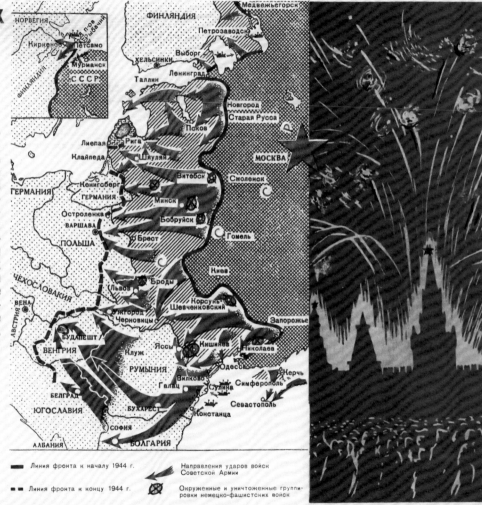

— Линия фронта к началу 1944 г.

⬛ ⬛ ⬛ Линия фронта к концу 1944 г.

➤ Направления ударов войск Советской Армии

Окруженные и уничтоженные группировки немецко-фашистских войск

2

"The Red Army has . . . liberated more than three-quarters of occupied Soviet land from the German-fascist yoke. The aim now is to clear the whole of our land from the fascist invaders. . . . But our tasks cannot be confined to the expulsion of the enemy troops from our Motherland. The German troops now resemble a wounded beast which is compelled to crawl back to the frontiers of its lair—Germany—in order to heal its wounds. But a wounded beast which has retired to its lair does not cease to be a dangerous beast. To rid our country and the countries allied with us from the danger of enslavement, the wounded German beast must be pursued close on its heels and finished off in its own lair. . . . Obviously this task . . . can be accomplished only as a result of the joint efforts of the Soviet Union, Great Britain and the United States of America. . . . In honor of the historic victories of the Red Army on the front and to mark the great achievements of the workers, collective farmers and intellectuals of the Soviet Union in the rear, today, on the day of the world festival of the working people . . . a salute of twenty artillery salvos shall be fired in Moscow, Leningrad, Gomel, Kiev, Kharkov, Rostov, Tbilisi, Simferopol, [and] Odessa. . . . Death to the German invaders!"

—Joseph Stalin, Order of the Day, No. 70
May 1, 1944

The Eighth Guard of the army of Gen. Vasily Chuikov marches through the streets of Odessa, Ukraine, in the Soviet Union. Photograph by Georgii Zel'ma (1906–1984), April 10, 1944.

SEPTEMBER 5

1939   The United States declares its neutrality.

1944   Ninety days after the Normandy landings, nearly 2.1 million Allied soldiers are ashore in France.

THE ALLIES CLOSE IN: 1944

Among U.S. air units providing air cover for the Allies at Anzio, Italy (see September 5), was the Ninety-ninth Fighter Squadron, commanded by Colonel Benjamin O. Davis Jr. (see April 21), the first group of African American "Tuskegee Airmen" to see active combat duty. In the Mediterranean Theater since mid-1943, the Ninety-ninth was eventually combined with other all-black squadrons to form the 332nd Fighter Group, also headed by Davis. Supremely effective in performing their principal mission—escorting bombers of the Fifteenth Air Force on missions ranging from Italy to Germany—the men of the 332nd won the sometimes-grudging regard of their white colleagues and the name *schwarze vogelmenschen* (black birdmen) from respectful German adversaries. Meanwhile, new pilots were being prepared at Tuskegee, Alabama, where the director of flight training, Lieutenant Colonel Noel Parrish, was sometimes able to relieve the tensions inherent in training at a strictly segregated base by arranging morale-boosting visits from stars such as singer Lena Horne. In the navy, meanwhile, a long and often acrimonious struggle to allow black women to enlist in the WAVES began to achieve positive results when Secretary of the Navy James V. Forrestal recommended on July 28, 1944, that African Americans be trained in the WAVES on an integrated basis—a move strongly supported by WAVES director Mildred H. McAfee.

LEFT: Lt. Col. Noel Parrish (right), director of training at the Tuskegee Army Flying School, joins his fliers in welcoming singer Lena Horne (first row, center), between 1942 and 1945.

RIGHT: Capt. Mildred H. McAfee, USN (1900–1994), director of the WAVES. U.S. Navy photograph, c. 1943.

SEPTEMBER 6

1939 South Africa declares war on Germany.

On February 20, 1944, while the Red Army was pushing the Werhmacht off Soviet soil (see September 4 and 5), in western Europe the Allies embarked on Operation Argument (unofficially dubbed "Big Week"), an intensive six-day air campaign that especially targeted factories and other facilities involved in aircraft production. Collaborating with the RAF (which bombed at night), the U.S. Eighth and Fifteenth air forces, flying by day, undertook the bulk of the attacks. They paid a heavy price; the Germans shot down 226 American bombers. But the Luftwaffe paid even more dearly. As the bombers dropped nearly twenty thousand tons of bombs on their targets, they and their long-range fighter escorts—including the especially formidable P-51—downed hundreds of German planes and killed many experienced and irreplaceable Luftwaffe pilots. This marked a turning point in the air war in Europe. "When at the end of 1943 and the beginning of 1944, I was able to get the long-range fighters to the Eighth Air Force, the long-legged P-47s, P-38s, and most notably, the P-51s, the Luftwaffe was finished," U.S. Army Air Forces commander Hap Arnold later wrote. "For the rest of that year there were rough battles, but after the great week of February 20th . . . in which both sides figure the back of the German Air Force was broken, the outcome was never in doubt."

An Allied bomber returns to its base in England from a mission over occupied Europe. Office of War Information photograph, c. 1944.

SEPTEMBER 7

1940 The Germans begin their most destructive air raids on London.

1941 Two hundred RAF bombers stage a four-hour night raid on Berlin.

As the Allies struck at the German Reich, their forces in the Far East were making slow progress across the Pacific toward Japan. In the Central Pacific, the year began with an assault on Kwajalein, the world's largest atoll and one of thirty-two making up the Marshall Islands. The plan for this amphibious operation, code-named Flintlock, called for troops to land only on Kwajalein island (assigned to the army's Seventh Infantry Division) and the linked islands of Roi and Namur (Fourth Marine Division). To avoid a repeat of the carnage at Tarawa (see August 29, 30), aircraft stationed on new bases in the recently secured Gilbert Islands, carrier-based navy planes, and naval artillery bombarded the objectives before the January 31 landings. Before the troops were sent in, "frogmen" from newly formed Underwater Demolition Teams scouted for hidden obstacles and marked landing craft lanes, and the soldiers and marines hit the beach with potent firepower, including many automatic weapons and flamethrowers. The marines met light resistance on Roi and somewhat heavier opposition on Namur. The army had to fight briskly for four days before securing Kwajalein—even though almost half the 8,600-man Japanese garrison on the three islands had perished in the preassault bombardments. Most others died in the fighting. The Americans took only 265 prisoners, all but 100 of whom were Korean laborers. American casualties included 372 killed and 1,582 wounded.

LEFT: Men of the Seventh Infantry Division break out their rations during the battle for Kwajalein, in the Marshall Islands, February 3, 1944.

RIGHT: *Save your cans—help pass the ammunition.* Color poster by McClelland Barclay, published by the U.S. War Production Board between 1939 and 1945.

SEPTEMBER 8

1943 The Allies announce Italy's surrender.

1944 The first V–2 rocket hits London—on the same night years of blackout restrictions had ended. The lights will go out again for a while as Londoners cope with these new weapons they dub "Bob Hopes" (because one must Bob down and Hope for the best).

SAVE YOUR CANS
Help pass the Ammunition

McCLELLAND BARCLAY USNR

PREPARE YOUR TIN CANS
FOR WAR
1 REMOVE TOPS AND BOTTOMS
2 TAKE OFF PAPER LABELS
3 WASH THOROUGHLY
4 FLATTEN FIRMLY

SALVAGE DIVISION, WAR PRODUCTION BOARD

Each Allied offensive meant an influx of seriously wounded patients, sent first to field hospitals, then ultimately to hospitals in the United States. Through 1943, volunteer Virginia Claudon had worked in the physical therapy department of Ream General Hospital in Palm Beach, Florida. ("Never before," she later wrote, "had I witnessed such bodily destruction.") After learning of her fiancé's death in Africa, she requested overseas duty with the Red Cross and was undergoing rigorous training in the United States in 1944 while the Allies engaged in a three-pronged campaign in Burma. As part of this offensive, the American raiders known as "Merrill's Marauders" (see August 21) cooperated with Chinese Nationalist troops and Orde Wingate's "Chindit" irregulars to take the Hukawng Valley in the north and then secure the important transport center of Myitkyina—all aimed at allowing completion of the Ledo Road, a new ground route for supplies to reach China. By August, Myitkyina was in Allied hands. After Claudon arrived in the China-Burma-India Theater several months later, she became "a G.I. Jill in answer to Tokyo Rose." In addition to her nightly fifty-five-minute radio broadcast to Allied troops, she ran a Red Cross Club and gave presentations (including a popular one on etiquette). She also sang, danced, and acted in shows, including a version of the Broadway musical *Call Me Mister*—which her troupe presented in a large open-air theater in Calcutta that the GIs had dubbed "Monsoon Square Garden."

LEFT: American Red Cross volunteer Virginia Claudon (Allen) preparing to make one of her "GI Jill" radio broadcasts to Allied forces in the China-Burma-India Theater, c. 1945.

RIGHT: Allied soldiers near a bridge, somewhere in the China-Burma-India Theater. Photograph by T5 Sigmund S. Bialosky, 1891st Aviation Engineer Battalion, U.S. Army, c. 1943–45.

SEPTEMBER 9

1939 Luftwaffe commander Hermann Göring states that Berlin will never be subject to aerial attack.

1942 Iran declares war on Germany.

Burma, India, and China were all affected by two separate and uncoordinated Japanese offensives in 1944. The first began in March, when the two hundred thousand men of Lieutenant General Renya Mutaguchi's Fifteenth Army invaded mountainous eastern India from Burma. Their primary objective: to disrupt Allied plans for a new incursion into Burma by seizing the British supply base at Imphal. (The inclusion of the collaborationist Indian National Army in the invasion-force ranks signified a lesser objective—stimulating an Indian revolt against the British colonial regime.) By mid-April the Japanese had besieged Imphal, as well as Kohima, a town commanding Imphal's supply lines. As Imphal withstood the siege, reinforcements helped break the Japanese ring around Kohima, from which the Japanese fell back toward Imphal, fighting for every bit of ground before conceding it to the pursuing British. By July, with both their objectives still well out of reach and the monsoon season upon them, the Japanese retreated to Burma. The disastrous Imphal Offensive disintegrated as Japanese forces in China were rapidly gaining ground in another operation. The Ichi-Go campaign (see May 25, 26) took place at a time when many Nationalist Chinese were chafing under Chiang Kai-shek's repressive government—unhappiness the Japanese sought to exploit in a precampaign propaganda blitz, with little success. Though not a disaster, Ichi-Go, too, ultimately failed in its major objectives.

On the Firing Line. Reproduction of a painting by Kakuzo Seno, published in *Seisen Gafu* ("A Picture Album of the Holy War"), Tokyo, 1939.

SEPTEMBER 10

1939   Canada declares war on Germany.

1943   German troops march into Rome; Germans disarm Italian troops in southern Italy.

While the Japanese were engaged in two new campaigns in the China-Burma-India Theater (see September 10), Allied troops in Italy achieved two important objectives: On May 18, Polish troops under General Wladyslaw Anders secured Monte Cassino, ending a costly struggle that had begun four months before. Meanwhile, the Allied forces that had been stuck on the beach at Anzio fought their way through the besieging Germans and met up with the rest of General Mark Clark's Fifth Army on May 25. (See September 3.) Violating orders from General Sir Harold Alexander to head toward Valmontone, where his army would be able to cut off retreating Wehrmacht units, Clark took all but one division of the Fifth Army directly to Rome, securing the city June 5. Alexander may not have been pleased (much of the German Tenth Army did escape through Valmontone), but Romans were ecstatic: "Every Allied armored car, every soldier, every vehicle, every gun made a royal progress through the streets between crowds whose rapturous attentions became positively embarrassing," British *Daily Telegraph* correspondent L. Marsland Gander reported. "They showered roses on the cars and leant out of the windows of five-and six-story buildings, cheering and waving Italian, American and British flags." The international attention Clark gained when he led the liberation of the first European capital from the Axis was quickly eclipsed, however, by a long-awaited event on the Channel coast of France (see September 12).

LEFT: On July 4, 1944, American troops in Rome raise the U.S. flag that had flown over the Capitol in Washington, D.C., December 8, 1941.

RIGHT: Lt. Gen. Mark W. Clark (1896–1984), commanding general of the U.S. Fifth Army, c. 1943.

SEPTEMBER 11

1940 Buckingham Palace and St. Paul's Cathedral are damaged in the London Blitz.

1945 President Harry S. Truman approves a brief proposal written by Secretary of War Stimson and Secretary of the Navy Forrestal the previous day: "It is recommended that 'World War II' be the officially designated name for the present war."

THE ALLIES CLOSE IN: 1944

On the morning of June 6, 1944, German soldiers looking out of their bunkers on the coast of Normandy, France, saw a fearful apparition through the lifting mist: Allied warships, as far as the eye could see. D-Day of Operation Overlord, the first giant step in the liberation of Nazi-occupied Europe, had arrived. More than 156,000 Allied ground troops, 11,590 aircraft, and 6,400 warships and landing craft were poised to break through 70,000 German troops and a terrible array of coastal defenses recently improved under the expert direction of Field Marshal Erwin Rommel. Artillery and machine gun fire raked through the air as the first assault waves headed toward the sixty-mile swath of Normandy coastline between Le Havre and Cherbourg that the Allies had divided into five beaches, code-named Sword, Juno, Gold, Omaha, and Utah. Off Utah Beach, young naval officer Tracy Sugarman maneuvered his landing craft toward the sector where he was to drop the troops he and his crew were carrying in. "Utah Beach was a deadly tapestry of chaos and carnage," he later remembered. "[T]he soldiers would attempt to run through the surf, sagging with the sodden weight of their gear. Desperately they searched the nightmarish clutter of the beach, looking for their outfits . . . fires continued to burn. The boom of detonating mines made us wince. . . . Jesus," he said to himself that night, as the Allies fought to keep their toehold in France, "we survived D-Day."

LEFT: *Self-portrait for June, Normandy, 1944*. Oil painting by Ltjg. Tracy Sugarman, U.S. Navy (b. 1921), 1944.

RIGHT: *On the Way to the LST 523 to Pick up Survivors*. Watercolor and white pencil drawing by Ltjg. Tracy Sugarman, 1944.

SEPTEMBER 12

1939   The Czechs form an army of exile in France.

1943   Ninety German glider-borne troops rescue Mussolini from imprisonment in Abruzzi, Italy.

THE ALLIES CLOSE IN: 1944

As the D-Day invasion began, the Allies broadcast a message from Dwight D. Eisenhower, Supreme Commander, Allied Expeditionary Force: "People of Western Europe: A landing was made this morning on the coast of France by troops of the Allied Expeditionary Force. . . . I call upon all who love freedom to stand with us now. Together we shall achieve victory." At that time, victory was by no means assured. On the landing sector that came to be known as "Bloody Omaha," where Americans faced the crack German 352nd Infantry, landing craft foundered on sandbars; Allied naval artillery sometimes hit friendly troops on the beach; many wounded drowned in the rising tide; and tanks released too soon from cargo vessels wallowed in the surf and could not provide covering fire. Only about a third of the men in the initial assault even got to the shore. Private First Class Jesse Beazley, twenty-one, was among the more fortunate and later remembered: "[S]oldiers . . . were begging for help. . . . I seen them with their face half blowed off and some of them with their intestines hanging out, and they'd just look at you with a pitiful look because you couldn't do nothing for them. . . . There was mortar shells coming in on us, artillery shells coming in on us, machine gun fire, everything imaginable, right on you." Eisenhower had prepared another message, accepting responsibility if the invasion failed. But on all five beaches, his international force held on, regrouped, and began to move forward.

D-Day Rescue, Omaha Beach. Photograph by Walter Rosenblum, 1944.

SEPTEMBER 13

1940 In the first major offensive of the North African war, five Italian divisions cross into Egypt from Libya and attack a British frontier post.

1943 Chiang Kai-shek is named president of China for a three-year term.

"On D+1 we started to organize the chaos left from the initial assault of D-Day," American naval officer Tracy Sugarman wrote in a postwar memoir. "It was bedlam, a cacophony of roarings and rattlings and screaming winches." A prominent feature of the bedlam: "the clanking of tanks and the groaning of bulldozers as the Seabees tore out the sand to build a causeway for all the armor that was panting to come ashore." A naval construction force established in January 1942, the Seabees (named for the initial letters in the words *construction battalion*) undertook their heaviest combat construction duties in the Pacific Theater, where they generally hit the beaches with the first assault waves. But the Atlantic was also their beat. During the Normandy landings, army combat engineers and Seabees who landed with the first waves blew gaps in the maze of shoreline obstacles the Germans had planted, cleared paths through minefields, and performed dozens of other jobs essential to the success of the invasion—all while under the same heavy fire as everyone else and while trying not to harm their own troops. (Engineers found it impossible to clear some German shore defenses because infantrymen were using them for cover.) From D-Day+1, army and navy engineers, still under fire, built pontoon causeways, docking facilities, piers, and breakwaters; operated special ferries; and organized the landing areas to keep men and supplies moving onto the beaches—and from there, inland.

ABOVE: *Enlist with the "Seabees."* Color recruiting poster for U.S. Navy engineers, between 1942 and 1950.

RIGHT: American troops come ashore at Normandy via a prefabricated harbor constructed of "spud pierheads" on steel pontoons, and floating roadways. U.S. Army Signal Corps photograph, June 1944.

SEPTEMBER 14

1939 Germany suffers its first naval loss of the war when British Royal Navy destroyers sink the submarine U-39.

Among its many other duties, the U.S. Army Corps of Engineers prepared millions of copies of tens of thousands of maps. Most of these assisted in, and record the progress of, combat operations. But this map, created in 1945, tells the story of one tank battalion during the Normandy Campaign. Accompanying text (not shown) contemplates the depth of meaning behind what might seem to some a lighthearted pictorial history: "We know about the terror, the grief, the violence, the hatred, the pride, and the bitterness of battle. But when we talk about the 743d and what we did, we will laugh and speak fondly, as these drawings do. The rest is too deeply buried in us for words and pictures. . . . We landed 20 minutes before H-Hour, the first American tanks in the invasion, leading the beachhead assault. This little blue ribbon [the Presidential Unit Citation, shown at right] is a symbol of a 16 hour battle on a thin strip of sand, with a furiously fighting German army in front of us and with the waters of the English Channel in back of us. . . . We punched out an exit . . . and with elements of the Rangers and the 29th and 1st Infantry Divisions, established an apron of Allied-held land from which the tedious and terrible hedgerow fighting of Normandy was developed. This sheet shows our part in that fighting. . . . It is a picture of the land we were in and some of the details of why we were there and what we did and what was done to us. It is a part of what is behind another . . . symbol—the Normandy Campaign Battle Star."

ABOVE: The Presidential Unit Citation ribbon and the Normandy Campaign Battle Star, both awarded to the 743rd Tank Battalion. Details from the map.

RIGHT: Normandy: D-Day: The Invasion and the first 48 days of action with the 743rd Tank Battalion in France [detail]. Commemorative map created by the 667 Engineers, U.S. Army, April 1945.

SEPTEMBER 15

1942 The U.S. aircraft carrier *Wasp* is torpedoed and sunk by a Japanese submarine near Espiritu Santo, Vanuatu.

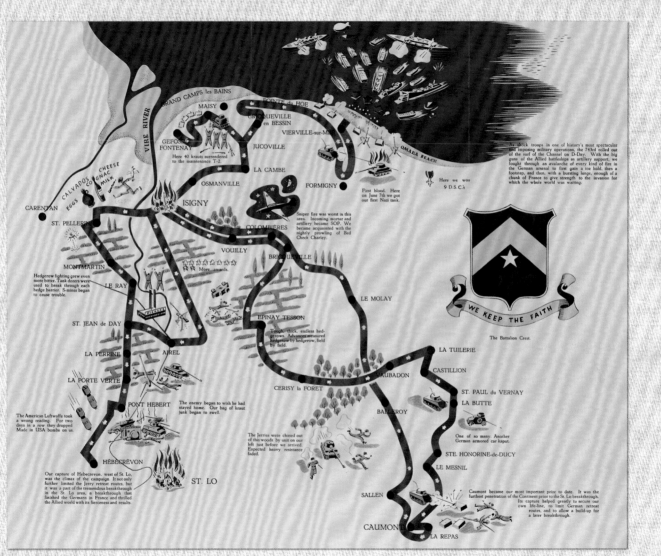

While the Allies secured the Normandy beachhead, Allied forces in the Central Pacific were on the doorstep of the Marianas, a chain of islands that included three U.S. objectives: Saipan, Guam, and Tinian. Holding these islands would give the U.S. Navy bases to support the anticipated offensive in the Philippines and provide the Allies with airfields from which bombers could reach the Japanese home islands. On June 15, eight thousand U.S. Marines assaulted Saipan, moving ashore under heavy fire from guns hidden in rocky cliffs, caves, and other natural fortifications that the preassault bombardment had not significantly weakened. Despite heavy casualties, they advanced slowly inland—while an army division that had been held in reserve, the Twenty-seventh Infantry, joined the fight. A brutal slugfest, the battle for Saipan lasted more than three weeks and caused more than 13,000 American casualties (more than 3,100 killed). It also included, on the night of July 6–7, the largest banzai charge of the war, one of such stunning ferocity that it temporarily breached American lines. GIs were even more shaken at the toll the fighting took on civilians—especially as the battle ended on July 9. That day, surviving Japanese soldiers—and hundreds of civilian men, women, and children—killed themselves rather than be taken prisoner, even as horrified Americans tried to stop them. More than twenty thousand Japanese civilians, and most of the thirty-thousand-man Saipan garrison perished during the battle.

LEFT: *Saipan, 1944*. Photograph by W. Eugene Smith (1918–1978), 1944.

RIGHT: *Tank Ambulance at Saipan*. Reproduction of a painting by Robert Benney, from the Abbott Laboratories Collection, 1945.

SEPTEMBER 16

1940 The U.S. Congress approves the Selective Training and Service Act, the first peacetime conscription program in U.S. history.

1941 Near Kiev, more than a half million Russians surrender to the Germans. Treated brutally, many will die in captivity.

ROBERT BENNEY

Four days after U.S. Marines landed on Saipan in mid-June (see September 16), much of their naval support moved off to meet a new threat as the Japanese launched Operation A-Go to reinforce troops in the Marianas and destroy U.S. naval power in the area. "The fate of the Empire depends on this one battle," Japan's chief of naval operations, Admiral Soemu Toyoda, declared as he ordered A-Go to begin. Vice Admiral Jisaburo Ozawa then led the First Mobile Fleet out of the Philippines and initiated the largest carrier battle of the war. In the Battle of the Philippine Sea, Admiral Raymond Spruance, commander of the U.S. Fifth Fleet, and Vice Admiral Marc Mitscher, who led the fleet's main fighting arm, Task Force 58, had an ace up their sleeves: Philippine guerrillas had secured a copy of the A-Go plan. Thus, in preliminary engagements, U.S. forces sank most of Ozawa's submarines and plastered the Japanese bases on Guam and Tinian, which Ozawa had planned to use as rearming and refueling stations. On June 19, U.S. radar detected the attack formations of Ozawa's carrier-based aircraft. Rising to meet them, U.S. pilots downed nearly three hundred Japanese planes in what fast became known as "the Great Marianas Turkey Shoot." Before fighting ended on June 21, the Americans also sank three Japanese carriers—including Ozawa's flagship, *Taiho*. The admiral survived to tender his resignation. "I am more responsible for this defeat than Admiral Ozawa," Toyoda said, and refused to accept it.

ABOVE: Adm. Raymond A. Spruance, U.S. Navy (1886–1969), April 1944.

LEFT: Adm. Soemu Toyoda (1881–1957). Reproduction of a painting by Goro Tsuruta, published in *Seisen Gafu* ("A Picture Album of the Holy War") 1939.

RIGHT: Adm. Marc A. Mitscher, U.S. Navy (1887–1947), on board USS *Lexington*, June 1944.

SEPTEMBER 17

1939 Red Army troops enter Poland and occupy territory that had been specified under a secret provision of the agreement reached between the Soviet and German governments the previous month.

1944 Twenty thousand Allied troops land behind German lines in the Netherlands. Operation Market Garden will be a costly failure.

The Battle of the Philippine Sea and the extended fighting on Saipan (see September 16, 17) delayed the assaults on the other U.S. objectives in the Mariana Islands for nearly a month. The battle to retake the American territory of Guam began on July 21; three days later, U.S. troops hit the beach on Tinian. Tinian was secured by August 1; the fighting on rugged, vegetation-shrouded Guam went on more than a week longer. Marines under General Roy S. Geiger and the soldiers of the Seventy-seventh Infantry Division under General Andrew D. Bruce grew to admire and depend on one another's skills as they endured enemy artillery barrages, were battered by fire from hidden defensive positions, suffered banzai charges, and grappled with Japanese soldiers in desperate hand-to-hand fighting. On Guam, as on Saipan, civilians were present, and some became casualties. But far from being terrified of their liberators, the people of Guam knew Americans well and welcomed them with open arms—particularly those whom the Japanese had imprisoned and abused over their two-and-a-half-year occupation. On August 10, General Geiger declared that the battle was at an end (although some Japanese soldiers, who retreated into the hills, did not come out until 1972). Guam was back in American hands and would be transformed into a major base for U.S. operations. The cost was heavy: nearly eight thousand American casualties, including some two thousand men killed. (See September 20)

A U.S. Navy corpsman gives a drink to a wounded marine on Guam. U.S. Navy photograph, July 1944.

SEPTEMBER 18

1943 Abandoned by the Germans, Sardinia, Italy, surrenders to a small British force that lands in two motorized torpedo boats.

While U.S. forces in the Central Pacific were securing their three objectives in the Mariana Islands (see September 16, 17), in Normandy, the Allies were poised for Operation Cobra, a plan to break out of the Cotentin Peninsula, site of the D-Day landings, and push into the heart of France. On July 24, American troops near the war-ravaged town of St. Lô (secured six days earlier after fierce fighting) waited for American bombers to soften their way forward by hitting the German lines. Correspondent Ernie Pyle was with them and later reported what happened: "As we watched, there crept into our consciousness a realization that windrows of exploding bombs were easing back toward us . . . instead of gradually forward, as the plan called for. Then we were horrified by the suspicion that those machines, high in the sky and completely detached from us, were aiming their bombs at the smokeline on the ground [intended to mark their target]—and a gentle breeze was drifting the smokeline back over us! . . . We dived [for cover]. . . . There is no description of the sound and fury of those bombs except to say it was chaos. . . . The feeling of the blast was sensational." American bombs dropped by inexperienced crews killed twenty-five American soldiers. During another try the next day—even after U.S. troops were moved back a thousand yards—another 111 GIs were killed. Enraged infantrymen began calling the USAAF the "American Luftwaffe." (See September 20)

Devastated St. Lô, France. Photograph by Andrew Lopez (1918–1970), August 8, 1944.

SEPTEMBER 19

1941 Kiev surrenders to the Germans, who suffered 350,000 casualties taking the city.

1944 In the Netherlands, Allied troops are trapped in Arnhem.

"It is to be noted that the front lines of [war] maps are simply where the infantryman is," Lieutenant General Lesley J. McNair declared in 1943. "It is true that he is supported magnificently by artillery and air, but this support is behind and above him. There is nothing in front of him but the enemy." As head of the Army Ground Forces (AGF, see August 6), McNair was ultimately responsible for training and organizing the infantry for war—and he fulfilled this responsibility with exceptional diligence. When his AGF combat observers disagreed over some matters in 1943, McNair traveled to the front in Tunisia to make his own evaluation and brought back the knowledge he had been seeking—as well as wounds from a German artillery shell. In July 1944, he turned the AGF over to General Ben Lear and went to France to assume a front-line command—while his son, Colonel Douglas McNair, headed for combat duty in the Pacific. Observing the start of Operation Cobra outside St. Lô (see September 19), General McNair was killed by a misdirected American bomb—the first three-star general in American history to be killed in combat. Twelve days later, Colonel McNair was killed in a gunfight with Japanese soldiers on Guam (see September 18). At home, Mrs. Lesley J. McNair quietly moved out of military quarters and into a small apartment, took a job with the State Department, and continued her volunteer work—writing of her husband: "He never asked a soldier to do what he would not do."

Lt. Gen. Lesley J. McNair, commander, Army Ground Forces, with his son, Col. Douglas McNair, Mrs. Douglas McNair (seated left) holding Bonny Clare McNair, and the general's wife, Mrs. Lesley J. (Clare Huster) McNair, 1944.

SEPTEMBER 20

1939 The RAF and the Luftwaffe fight their first air engagement over Aachen, Germany.

In August 1944, news of Allied progress in France sparked an uprising by the people of Paris against the formidable German garrison occupying their city: twenty thousand troops, including some Waffen SS armored units. Initially, there was little violence: On August 10 (nine days after the Polish Home Army began the uprising in Warsaw, see September 4), railroad workers went on strike. On August 15 (the day Allied forces landed in southern France), the police struck as well, barricading themselves in their headquarters. A day later, the postal workers followed suit (except those responsible for the telephone system, who kept it operating for the benefit of the rebellion). Sporadic street fighting began on August 19. As the French flag played in the breeze over police headquarters, and policemen inside sang the "Marseillaise," Parisians built barricades in the streets or took to the rooftops and sniped at every German that crossed their sights. Meanwhile, Swedish diplomat Raoul Nordling convinced the German garrison commander, General Dietrich von Choltitz, not to destroy the city by following Hitler's orders to fight for it stone by stone. By this time, Charles de Gaulle had returned to France, established a provisional government at Bayeux, and was in touch with the people of Paris. His agents cautioned them that the Allies would not reach the city until the second week of September. Yet the Paris uprising itself accelerated that schedule. (See September 22)

Éveil du Peuple de Paris ("Parisians Awake!"). Photograph by Beaugers, reproduced in *Paris de 19. au 26 Août 1944*, 1945

SEPTEMBER 21

1939 President Roosevelt calls a special session of Congress to repeal the arms embargo provision of the U.S. Neutrality Act.

1943 The U.S. House of Representatives (with the Senate concurring) passes the Fulbright Resolution, "favoring the creation of appropriate international machinery with power adequate to establish and to maintain a just and lasting peace" and favoring U.S. participation.

THE ALLIES CLOSE IN: 1944

On August 23, after the British Broadcasting Corporation (BBC) reported that the Parisians were liberating their city themselves (see September 21), the Supreme Allied Commander in Europe, General Dwight D. Eisenhower, and U.S. Third Army commander George S. Patton released Lieutenant General Philippe Leclerc's Second French Armored Division from the Third Army to officially free the French capital. Leclerc (the nom de guerre of Philippe de Hauteclocque) had joined de Gaulle in Britain after France fell in 1940, organized resistance in France's African colonies, and led a unit known as L Force, or the Leclerc Column, in North Africa and the Middle East. His armored division, an amalgam of longtime Free French campaigners and former Vichy Frenchmen, had arrived in Normandy on July 29. By the evening of August 24, the first elements of the division were rumbling through Paris streets and, on August 25, Leclerc had the signal honor of accepting the surrender of the German garrison. Joy reigned supreme throughout the city as the German garrison commander, General Dietrich von Choltitz, signed the instrument of surrender. This did not end all local fighting; some Germans, and Frenchmen who had collaborated with them, continued to snipe. Yet that hardly mattered to most Parisians. A French armored division was with them; the Americans were on the way. After four dark years of occupation, Paris could reclaim the title "City of Light."

Rue Lagrange ("Avenue Lagrange"), some of the Free French troops who liberated Paris. Photograph by P. Dubure, reproduced in *Paris de 19. au 26 Août 1944*, 1945.

SEPTEMBER 22

1943 Two British midget submarines penetrate Altenfjord in Norway and cripple the German battleship *Tirpitz*.

"**I** had thought that for me there could never again be any elation in war. But I had reckoned without the liberation of Paris," U.S. war correspondent Ernie Pyle wrote in August 1944. "The streets were lined as by Fourth of July parade crowds at home, only this crowd was almost hysterical. . . . As our jeep eased through the crowds, thousands of people crowded up, leaving only a narrow corridor, and frantic men, women and children grabbed us and kissed us and shook our hands and beat on our shoulders and slapped our backs and shouted their joy as we passed. Once when the jeep was simply swamped in human traffic and had to stop, we were swarmed over and hugged and kissed and torn at. Everybody, even beautiful girls, insisted on kissing you on both cheeks. . . . Of all the days of national joy I've ever witnessed this is the biggest." Celebrations continued even as some Germans and scattered bands of Vichy militia continued to resist. On August 26, these Axis loyalists opened fire on the crowds in the streets and on Charles de Gaulle, after the Free French leader entered the cathedral of Notre Dame to participate in a liberation ceremony. Resisting attempts to take him to safety, the general continued to walk, ramrod straight, down the cathedral aisle to two waiting priests—providing, in the words of BBC reporter Robert Reid, "the most extraordinary example of courage I have ever seen."

Crowds line the Champs-Élysées as Allied tanks and half-tracks pass through the Arc de Triomphe after the liberation of Paris. Photograph by Jack Downey, August 1944.

SEPTEMBER 23

1939 Germany declares that "the Polish Army of a million men has been defeated, captured, or routed."

1943 Mussolini announces the creation of the Salo Republic, comprising the portions of Italy where Germans are still in control.

While fighting continued in France, the Allies also moved into the Low Countries and closed in on Germany—so much faster than originally planned that, in August and September, supply lines were stretched almost beyond tolerable limits. The advance continued despite bitter reverses. On September 14, to support a drive on Aachen, the western-most city in Germany (taken October 21), the U.S. Ninth Infantry Division moved into the southern reaches of the Huertgen Forest, an area later described in the official U.S. Army history of the Second World War as "a seemingly impenetrable mass, a vast undulating blackish-green ocean." For the next three months, division after American division was torn apart in the effort to clear this impossible terrain—which the Germans were determined to hold. A portion of Germany's formidable Siegfried Line—two ranges of thoroughly camouflaged, interconnected pillboxes with overlapping fields of fire—lurked half-submerged in the forest. Mines and booby traps were hidden everywhere, and every artillery burst in the seventy-five-to-one-hundred-foot trees sent a lethal rain of metal and splintered wood showering down on the men below. The Americans gained little from what General James Gavin later called "the battle that should never have been fought," but they lost much: Of the 120,000 U.S. soldiers who took part, 33,000 were killed, wounded, or became victims of combat fatigue. An estimated 28,000 of the 80,000 Germans who faced them also became casualties.

ABOVE: S. Sgt. Elwin Miller, U.S. Army. Lithograph of a drawing by Howard Brodie (b. 1915).

RIGHT: U.S. Army infantrymen push through the Huertgen Forest near Vossenack, Germany. U.S. Army photograph, 1944.

SEPTEMBER 24

1944   San Marino declares war on Germany.

As the Ninth Infantry Division moved into the Huertgen Forest (see September 24), B-24 "Liberator" bombers of the U.S. Thirteenth Army Air Force made a round trip of 2,400 miles from Noemfoor Island off the New Guinea coast to bomb Japanese oil refineries on Balikpapan, Borneo. Known as the "Jungle Air Force," the Thirteenth supported General Douglas MacArthur's campaign to return to the Philippines—and included among its headquarters staff Technical Sergeant Samuel L. Boylston. Recipient of a special commendation for assisting airmen wounded during a Japanese air raid, Boylston was a man with special artistic talent that might have been lucrative, if he had charged for his services. "Both officers and enlisted men keep me drawing cartoon envelopes," he wrote to his parents on September 3. "Their friends always write back and remark about them. I would like to see all the envelopes I've fixed up. Would certainly be a site [sic]." From Noemfoor, Boylston moved to Morotai Island, about three hundred miles northwest of Sansapor, New Guinea, where U.S. troops landed on September 15 (without opposition from the thousand-man Japanese garrison, although the island was not completely secured until January). That same day, MacArthur visited Morotai. Looking toward the Philippines, a few hundred miles away, the general reportedly said: "They are waiting for me there, it has been a long time."

ABOVE: Technical Sgt. Samuel Lionel Boylston (b. 1923), 1944.

RIGHT: *Guard the Egg!*. Envelope decorated with a watercolor drawing by Sgt. Samuel Lionel Boylston, Thirteenth U.S. Army Air Force, September 30, 1944.

SEPTEMBER 25

1940 For the first time U.S. intelligence decodes a complete Japanese message transmitted in Tokyo's supersecret Purple diplomatic code.

1944 The *Volkssturm* (people's militia) is formed in Germany; men up to age sixty-five are pressed into the last-ditch defense effort.

Just over a month after he visited Morotai Island (see September 25), General Douglas MacArthur was able to begin his long-awaited campaign to return to the Philippines, from which he had been forced to retreat in 1942 (see May 7, June 11). The major objectives lay on the largest island, Luzon. First, however, it was necessary to secure the islands of Leyte and Mindero, to the south. Landings on Leyte, which was initially defended by a twenty-thousand-man Japanese garrison, began October 20, when U.S. troops secured their beachheads, started off-loading supplies, and began heading inland. Progress was such that MacArthur—along with Sergio Osmeña, successor to the late President Quezon—waded to shore through knee-deep water to announce triumphantly, "People of the Philippines, I have returned." Over the next several weeks, however, Japanese resistance on the island stiffened as the area commander sent reinforcements from Luzon. Implementing a new defense plan, Operation Sho-Go, the Japanese also precipitated the greatest naval battle in history. In the Battle of Leyte Gulf (October 23–26), fought over an area of more than one hundred thousand square miles, the Japanese sought to disrupt the U.S. landings on Leyte, defend the Philippines at all costs, and preserve Japan's supply lines. Instead, their devastating defeat marked the end of Japanese naval power. But the battle did introduce a new Japanese weapon: kamikaze ("divine wind") suicide pilots.

Two Coast Guard–manned Landing Ship Tanks (LSTs) deposit their cargoes on Leyte Island, the Philippines, as soldiers build sandbag piers out to the LST ramps to speed operations U.S. Coast Guard photograph, 1944.

SEPTEMBER 26

1940 President Roosevelt bars the export of scrap iron and steel to Japan.

Slogging along muddy rain-forest trails, into swamps, and through mountainous terrain stoutly defended by Japanese units, MacArthur's troops defeated the last organized resistance on Leyte by December 31. They then faced the next major Philippine operation: Luzon (see November 3). Throughout the long and bitter Philippine campaign, the Allies took some twelve thousand Japanese prisoners. Some were influenced to cease resistance by leaflets prepared and distributed by Allied psychological warfare experts. Others were convinced by skillful arguments made in their native language by members of the Military Intelligence Service (MIS, see July 6). MIS members also interrogated prisoners and, like Technical Sergeant Warren Tsuneishi, translated captured documents. Born in California on the Fourth of July, Tsuneishi (whose family was in a U.S. internment camp) volunteered with a buddy, Lloyd Shinsato, to join a reinforced battalion sent to a group of small islands not far from Leyte to rescue Filipino civilians who were being murdered by the Japanese. "Lloyd joined company leaders at the front lines while I remained at battalion headquarters," Tsuneishi remembered after the war. "Lloyd reported seeing bodies stacked up like cordwood in homes. I translated a document identifying the occupying force—a naval engineers unit of perhaps four hundred men. They were wiped out when they attacked our lines in a banzai attack."

LEFT: The cover of a leaflet produced by the U.S. Army, Psychological Warfare Branch, c. 1943–45.

RIGHT: Technical Sgt. Warren Tsuneishi, U.S. Army (left), with an unidentified buddy, on Leyte, in the Philippine Islands, where they were both translators for U.S. military intelligence. Photograph late 1944.

SEPTEMBER 27

1939 Warsaw surrenders to the Germans.

1940 In Berlin, Germany, Italy, and Japan sign the Tripartite Pact, a ten-year military and economic agreement. From London, the U.S. ambassador to Britain, Joseph Kennedy, cables Washington: "Britain is doomed."

ATTENTION AMERICAN SOLDIERS!

I CEASE RESISTANCE

THIS LEAFLET GUARANTEES HUMANE TREATMENT TO ANY JAPANESE DESIRING TO CEASE RESISTANCE. TAKE HIM IMMEDIATELY TO YOUR NEAREST COMMISSIONED OFFICER.

By Direction of the Commander in Chief.

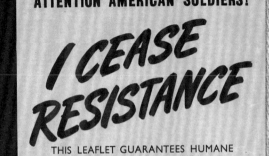

（左隅目の為の護保族家。本日し）

上の英文の内容は「この人は最早敵でな
く國際條約により生命・衣食住は勿論
醫療等が完全に保證さるべき者なり」と
云ふ小意味が書かれて居る
左圖は既に當方に来て居られる諸君の
戰友の一部

17-J-1

To secure MacArthur's right flank as his forces began the invasion of the Philippines (see September 26, 27), on September 15, U.S. Marines landed on Peleliu, in the Palau Islands, seven square miles of coral-encrusted real estate that became the site of one of the bloodiest battles of the war. On Peleliu the marines faced new Japanese tactics involving complex inland defenses calculated to make Americans pay the highest price possible for every square inch. It was, as marine Eugene Sledge later remembered, an "assault into hell." In his vivid postwar memoir, *With the Old Breed At Peleliu and Okinawa*, Sledge described being pinned down under Japanese fire: "The shells fell faster, until I couldn't make out individual explosions, just continuous, crashing rumbles with an occasional ripping sound of shrapnel tearing low through the air overhead amid the roar. The air was murky with smoke and dust. Every muscle in my body was as tight as a piano wire. I shuddered and shook as though I were having a mild convulsion. Sweat flowed profusely. I prayed, clenched my teeth, squeezed my carbine stock, and cursed the Japanese." After the marines were relieved by the army in mid-October, Sledge asked a buddy what he thought of Peleliu, expecting the usual sort of "hell, that wasn't nothin'" comment from the older combat veteran. What he got was: "Boy, that was terrible! I ain't never seen nothin' like it. . . . I've had enough after that." Peleliu was not declared secure until November 27.

U.S. Marines, reinforced by tanks, assault Japanese positions on Peleliu. U.S. Marine Corps photograph, October 7, 1944.

SEPTEMBER 28

1937 Before an estimated three million people at Berlin's Olympic City, Hitler and Mussolini affirm the "fraternity" of their two Fascist regimes.

1941 German troops begin massacring nearly thirty-four thousand Jews from the Kiev area at Babi Yar ravine.

While marines and infantrymen were enduring the horrors of Peleliu in support of MacArthur's Philippine Islands campaign (see September 28), civilians on the U.S. home front divided their attention between war news and the presidential election campaign. After briefly flirting with the idea of naming MacArthur as their candidate, members of the Republican Party chose New York governor Thomas E. Dewey to face Franklin Roosevelt in his fourth election bid, undertaken despite worries about the president's health. Few seriously doubted the outcome. On November 10, Eleanor Roosevelt (who had maintained her usual nonstop activities throughout the year) reported to readers of her "My Day" newspaper column: "It seems to be settled beyond any question that the President is going back to Washington to assume during four more years the very heavy responsibilities which those years must bring. One can only hope that the people and all their elected representatives will join with him in helping to meet these years with courage and efficiency." Just over a month later, all Americans faced the need for renewed courage when news reached them of a stunning new German offensive. On December 22, Mrs. Roosevelt's column began: "The news from Europe has been so bad that I cannot help thinking of the weariness and disappointment of the [Allied] men who have taken these miles of enemy territory and are now being driven back." (See September 30)

LEFT: First Lady Eleanor Roosevelt (seated, just right of center) enjoys a performance by folk singer Pete Seeger at the opening of the United Federal Labor Canteen for servicemen in Washington, D.C., which was sponsored by the Federal Workers of America, Congress of Industrial Organizations. Photograph by Joseph A. Horne, February 1944.

RIGHT: *I want you F.D.R.–Stay and finish the job!* Color lithograph poster by James Montgomery Flagg (1877–1960), 1944.

SEPTEMBER 29

1939 Germany and the Soviet Union sign a boundary and friendship treaty that formally divides Poland between them.

At 5:30 A.M. on December 16, a quarter million German troops smashed through the Ardennes Forest in Belgium, launching Operation Autumn Mist, Hitler's massive counteroffensive aimed toward the port city of Antwerp. Eighty thousand American troops, spread too thin in many spots to effectively resist, were stunned by the onslaught, which created a dangerous bulge in Allied lines. Some GIs broke and retreated; many others were captured—nearly nine thousand surrounded infantrymen surrendered at the tree-covered ridge of Schnee Eifel alone. Yet most of the Americans managed to hold on as U.S. commanders began rushing in reinforcements. On December 22, General Eisenhower's Order of the Day to his besieged troops was "to destroy the enemy on the ground, in the air, everywhere to destroy him." That same day, Major General Anthony McAuliffe, whose men were surrounded in the town of Bastogne, answered a German demand for surrender with one syllable: "Nuts!"—which puzzled the Germans until someone explained that the general meant "Go to hell." (McAuliffe's 101st Airborne Division did not surrender, and on December 26, the Fourth Armored Division of Patton's Third Army arrived and broke the siege of Bastogne.) By late January 1945, a total of six hundred thousand Americans had turned the tide of battle and pushed the Germans back to their starting point. The "Battle of the Bulge," Winston Churchill said, should "be regarded as an ever famous American victory."

Battered by a German offensive, American infantrymen of the 347th Infatry line up for chow from a field mess in frigid weather during the Battle of the Bulge, December 1944.

SEPTEMBER 30

1939 A Polish provisional government is established in Paris under Gen. Wladyslaw Sikorski.

1943 Near Naples, Italy, British troops surround Mt. Vesuvius.

Interlude: The Most Terrible Conflict

"I've become a beast of a man," Russian sniper Anatoly Chekhov told war correspondent Vasily Grossman in 1942, during the savage fighting for Stalingrad. "When I first got the rifle, I couldn't bring myself to kill a living being. Then I remembered our people and started killing [Germans] without mercy. . . . Sometimes I come out of the basement in the evening," the nineteen-year-old continued. "I look around . . . and think: the Volga is flowing so quietly, how come such terrible things are happening here?"

Chekhov looked out on a city smashed to rubble by weapons vastly more powerful than those used during World War I. The Luftwaffe had made the first devastating assault on Stalingrad—reflecting the dominant role that air power was assuming in World War II. Fighter aircraft, rockets, radio-controlled drones, and bombers carrying ever-larger loads of increasingly potent bombs hurtled through the heavens—ungoverned by any rules specifically covering aerial warfare. Though some rules had been drafted during the interwar years, they had never been formally adopted by any nation. As the war intensified, air power rained increasing destruction not only on battlefields and military forces, but also on countless cities and their civilian inhabitants, from Shanghai and Warsaw in 1937 and 1939 to Hiroshima and Nagasaki—which were nearly obliterated in 1945 by the most terrible weapon to emerge from the war, the atom bomb.

Rules did exist for sea and ground warfare. But such

OCTOBER 1

1939 The Polish navy surrenders; some ships, however, have escaped to Britain and will continue fighting as part of the Royal Navy.

1942 The first U.S. jet plane, a Bell XP-59, is flown over California.

carefully wrought legal constructs as the Hague Conventions of 1907 and the Geneva Conventions of 1929 were often overwhelmed by the scope, complexity, and chaos of World War II—and by the brutish philosophies of the Axis nations. While the Western democracies adhered to these legal precepts, Germany (which had ratified the Geneva Conventions) and Japan (which had not) repeatedly perpetrated atrocities of such enormity that they have been categorized as crimes against humanity. Yet even the Japanese military's often vicious mistreatment of prisoners of war, its savagery against civilians in occupied countries, paled beside the Third Reich's most heinous crime: the systematic killing of more than six million Jewish men, women, and children, and other people the Nazis deemed "subhuman"—an obscene industry of mass murder now known as the Holocaust.

The battle lines of World War II ranged from the covert struggles of anti-Axis resistance forces in occupied countries to military clashes on battlefields from Tarawa to Normandy. They wound through the combat-torn streets of cities and villages from Nanking to St. Lô; across embattled sea lanes, the graveyards of innumerable lost ships and sailors; through

hospitals where soldiers, sailors, and civilians struggled to cope with overwhelming physical and psychological injuries; and into the relative safety of combatant countries beyond the reach of enemy guns. In the United States, the "arsenal of democracy," gold stars in living room windows bore silent tribute to the more than four hundred thousand Americans who did not return from the war. Around the world, more than sixty million people perished. "So many bright futures consigned to the ashes of the past," as U.S. Marine Eugene Sledge wrote. "So many dreams lost in the madness that had engulfed us."

Calaveras [skeleton] in Battle. Illustration by Leopoldo Méndez for the poem "Corrido de Stalingrado" ("Battle of Stalingrad"). Relief cut on natural ground wood paper, c. 1943.

In his 1940 book, *I Saw France Fall: Will She Rise Again?* French diplomat René de Chambrun described a mobilization scene in the province of Lorraine, France: "When I reached the village, groups of men of all ages from twenty-one to forty were arriving in civilian clothes: some on bicycles, others on foot from neighboring villages. Some were accompanied by their wives, parents, children or sweethearts, who kissed them good-bye." Variations of this painful rending of families were taking place throughout vast areas of the world as countries crossed the line from peace into war. "Every man had his little package containing an extra shirt, a bottle of wine, and a loaf of bread," Chambrun continued. "After dressing and being equipped each man made up a bundle of his civilian clothes and his papers, and wrote out a tag, while hoping a little desperately that some day he would return from the war and find his belongings in a moldy cellar of the village." The people these new soldiers were leaving behind well remembered that millions of men had not returned from World War I, which had ended barely twenty years before. Now, in Europe, sons and husbands were departing again in response to Hitler's aggression—while in Asia, Chinese forces were reeling from the assaults of Hitler's Japanese allies. Worried civilians "talk sometimes, they even laugh, because they have to go on living," New York *Herald Tribune* correspondent Sonia Tomara reported from Bordeaux, France, in June 1940. "But the specter of the future is present in all minds."

Belgian women wave farewell to husbands and sons leaving for military service as the Germans launch their invasion of the Low Countries and France, May 1940.

OCTOBER 2

1941   Gestapo troops begin destroying the synagogues of Paris.

1944   After two months of fierce fighting, German forces crush the Warsaw uprising staged by the underground Polish Home Army. An estimated 250,000 Poles have been killed.

"**W**ith broken heart and head bowed in sadness but not in shame," General Jonathan Wainwright cabled President Roosevelt on May 6, 1942, "I report to your excellency that today I must arrange terms for the surrender of the fortified islands of Manila Bay." (See May 7, June 11.) Japan's occupation of the Philippine Islands placed tens of thousands of Filipino and American soldiers in Japanese hands as prisoners of war (POWs). In earlier conflicts, such as the Russo-Japanese War of 1904–05, the Japanese had won plaudits for their humane treatment of prisoners. But Japanese military doctrine and attitudes toward surrender had harshened considerably since then. In the Philippines, Allied POWs endured the horrors of the Bataan Death March, a tortuous sixty-five-mile move to a prison camp that killed an estimated twenty thousand prisoners from exhaustion, dehydration, exposure, and brutal treatment by their guards. All across Asia, conditions in Japanese-run prison camps—and aboard so-called Hell Ships that were used to transport thousands of POWs (see October 7)—generally ranged from bad to appalling, and worsened as the war turned against Japan. Chinese prisoners often suffered most cruelly. Some were subjected to horrific medical tortures at the hands of Japan's infamous Unit 731, which engaged in chemical and biological warfare and medical experimentation.

American and Filipino soldiers and sailors surrender to the Japanese on the fortress island of Corregidor in the Philippines. Captured Japanese photograph, May 1942.

OCTOBER 3

1943 Japanese troops open up offensive operations on a broad front in central China.

During the Battle of Britain (see March 22), when, as U.S. correspondent Ernie Pyle wrote, "London was ringed and stabbed with fire," Britain's *Daily Telegraph* celebrated the courage of London's civil defense workers. "The tales of brave acts performed by the man-in-the-street in a steel helmet are legion. . . . In indescribably exacting conditions, rendered perilous by a hail of bombs, they helped to fight . . . conflagrations which at one time threatened to match the classic fires of history . . . [and] cheered, comforted and marshalled women and children into the shelters." Such scenes were repeated in other British cities, across battered Europe, and throughout Asia—as each year brought greater levels of destruction. In June 1940, just before the fall of France, an exchange of gunfire between French and German tanks in Rouen ignited fires that soon raged out of control and consumed more than four hundred medieval houses. On the night of March 9–10, 1945, 334 U.S. B-29s, flying low over poorly defended Tokyo, dropped 1,665 tons of incendiary bombs. "As they fell, cylinders scattered a kind of flaming dew that skittered along the roofs, setting fire to everything it splashed," French eyewitness Robert Guillain later reported. "Under the wind and the gigantic breath of the fire, immense, incandescent vortices rose in a number of places, . . . sucking whole blocks of houses into their maelstrom of fire." The Tokyo firestorm incinerated much of the city and claimed more than one hundred thousand lives.

LEFT: An exhausted British air raid warden. Reproduction of a drawing by Feliks Topolski, published in *Britain in Peace and War*, 1941.

RIGHT: German tanks (right) moves through fiery ruins in Rouen, France. Color drawing by German artist Hans Liska in a reproduction of Liska's sketchbook published in Berlin, 1944.

OCTOBER 4

1943 French partisans, Moroccan Goums, and American Office of Strategic Service (OSS) agents complete the occupation of Corsica.

1944 British troops begin landing in Greece.

"There's a kite on fire dead ahead." December 1943: American war correspondent Edward R. Murrow was on board a British Lancaster bomber, part of a large wave of aircraft mounting a nighttime raid on Berlin (see July 9). Soon, the "kite" [aircraft] that the Lancaster's gunner had reported seeing on fire had become "a great golden, slow-moving meteor slanting toward the earth." Now approaching its target, Murrow's plane was hard-pressed to avoid a similar fate: "The sky ahead was lit up by bright yellow flares. Off to starboard, another kite went down in flames. The flares were sprouting all over the sky . . . and we were flying straight for the center of the fireworks." The sky was another battlefield, and aircrews of all the major combatants suffered heavy casualties from antiaircraft and machine-gun fire, midair collisions, and crash landings. Many airmen suffered terrible burns when their damaged aircraft burst into flames. "The plane was like an inferno," former RAF crewman Bill Foxley told a *Guardian* reporter in 2006. "I had 29 operations over three and a half years, rebuilding my face and repairing what was left of my hands." Fortunate enough to be cared for by the British plastic surgeon Archibald McIndoe at his hospital in East Grinstead, Foxley joined more than six hundred other McIndoe patients in forming the Guinea Pig Club, named for the innovative techniques McIndoe used to repair, as much as possible, the terrible damage air warfare had done to them.

ABOVE: Archibald McIndoe
(1900–1960), c. 1950

RIGHT: *Heinkel HE 177 – German Going Down Under Attack from Allied Planes*. Reproduction of a painting by Charles H. Hubbell published by Thompson Products, Inc., 1946.

OCTOBER 5

1940   Prime Minister Konoye states that a war between Japan and the United States is inevitable if the United States sees the Axis alliance as "hostile."

"When you get out on the sea with its vast distances, its storms and mists, and with night coming on and all the uncertainties which exist," Winston Churchill said to the House of Commons in 1940, "you cannot possibly expect that the kind of conditions which would be appropriate to the movements of armies have any application to the haphazard conditions of war at sea." On the moonless night of November 12, 1942, in the waters near Guadalcanal, a U.S. Navy task force sent to reinforce and resupply the American ground forces struggling to secure the island (see June 24, August 4) nearly collided with a Japanese naval force on a similar mission. Both sides loosed furious barrages at nearly point-blank range; both took heavy losses. The wounded USS *Juneau* limped on—until a torpedo from a Japanese submarine struck close to its ammunition stores. "The whole ship disappeared in a large cloud of black, yellow black, and brown smoke," one witness remembered. "It is certain," another reported, "that all on board perished." In fact, most of its crewmen were killed—including four of the five Sullivan brothers from Waterloo, Iowa, who had insisted on serving together on the same ship. The eldest brother, George, was among the few dozen men who made it into life rafts, but he was not among the ten who survived more than a week of drifting in dangerous seas. The tragic loss of five of Thomas and Alleta Sullivan's six children in this single engagement focused renewed home-front attention on the battles raging across the world's oceans.

LEFT: *They did their part—The five Sullivan brothers 'missing in action' off the Solomons.* Color poster with photographs of George, Francis, Joseph, Madison, and Albert Sullivan. U.S. Office of War Information, 1943.

RIGHT: *Scratch another meat ball—Saipan operations.* U.S. Navy photograph taken from the USS *Kitkum Bay*, 1944.

OCTOBER 6

1942 The United States signs a second protocol with the Soviet Union, promising to provide the Russians with 3.3 million tons of supplies between the signature date and July 1, 1943.

the five Sullivan brothers
"missing in action" off the Solomons

THEY DID THEIR PART

Since 1939, German U-boats in the Atlantic had operated in groups called "wolf packs," ravaging ship convoys, injuring thousands of navy crewmen and merchant mariners and sending thousands more to their deaths—yet never severing the Allied supply lines. As the Battle of the Atlantic turned decisively against the Germans in mid-1943 (see August 16), the Japanese began more regular use of a convoy system (previously considered "too defensive") to try to stem their own heavy merchant shipping losses. In response, American submariners began operating in wolf packs. In September 1944, one U.S. wolf pack, including the submarines *Pampanito*, *Sealion*, and *Growler*, attacked a convoy bound for Japan from Singapore. No special markings were on the vessels *Rakuyo Maru* and *Kachidoki Maru* to indicate that, in addition to oil and rubber, the ships also carried more than two thousand British and Australian prisoners of war. Not until four days after sinking both ships, when they came upon some of the POWs floating on a raft, did the Americans realize what had happened. "We . . . passed them below as quickly as possible," the *Pampanito*'s captain reported. "All of them were exhausted after four days on the raft and three years imprisonment. . . . All were very thin and showed the results of undernourishment. Some were in very bad shape. . . . A pitiful sight none of us will ever forget." The submariners rescued a total of 159 POWs before a typhoon ended their search. (The Japanese picked up 792.)

LEFT: Oil-soaked Australian and British prisoners of war, survivors of the Japanese transport *Rakuyo Maru*, are picked up by the USS *Sealion* in the China Sea, 1944.

RIGHT: *You bet I'm going back to sea!* Color poster sponsored by the War Shipping Administration, 1942.

OCTOBER 7

1940 Japan protests the U.S. embargo on aviation fuel and machine tools, and the ban on exporting iron and steel scraps, as an "unfriendly act."

"YOU BET I'M GOING
BACK TO SEA!"

Register at your nearest U.S. Employment Service Office

U.S. MERCHANT MARINE

War Shipping Administration

MAN THE VICTORY FLEET

"Victories are won in the forward areas," said American general Lesley J. McNair, "by men with brains and fighting hearts, not by machines." Pummeled by bombs, raked by artillery, machine-gun, and small arms fire, soldiers in forward areas from Kiev to Okinawa struggled against fear, battlefield chaos, and enemy troops—often in scenes that could have been taken from Dante's *Inferno*. In August 1944, Allied troops in France had a chance to capture or destroy the bulk of the Wehrmacht remaining in France in an area between Falaise and Argentan that became known as the Falaise Pocket. After a week of horrific combat, some 115,000 Germans managed to escape. They left behind ten thousand dead and fifty thousand prisoners—and took with them memories of a hell on earth. *Oberfeldwebel* (Master Sergeant) Hans Erich Braun later wrote of "the never-ending detonations . . . burning vehicles from which piercing screams could be heard . . . soldiers lying in their own blood—arms and legs torn off—others, driven crazy, crying, shouting, swearing, laughing hysterically. Close by a crossroads, caught by gunfire, lay a group of [French] men, women, and children." Supreme Allied Commander Dwight D. Eisenhower called Falaise "unquestionably one of the greatest 'killing grounds' of any of the war areas. Forty-eight hours after [the end of the battle] I was conducted through it on foot. . . . It was literally possible to walk for hundreds of yards, stepping on nothing but dead and decaying flesh."

Combat scene showing a flamethrower in action. Color drawing by German artist Hans Liska in a reproduction of Liska's sketchbook published in Berlin, 1944.

OCTOBER 8

1940 The U.S. government advises U.S. citizens to leave the Far East, "in view of abnormal conditions in those areas."

"**A**t this time, in addition to my usual duties, I was kept busy writing letters of condolence and answering the requests for more information concerning the death of a loved one. The few words of a War Department telegram left many questions unanswered and some people refused to believe the news until they heard from the Chaplain. . . .

"'I know that you and no one else can comfort me now that this tragedy has happened. You are the only one who can speak to the boys who saw my boy go down. The more you can tell me, the better I shall feel. Please, and as soon as possible, write to me about my boy.'

"'Father, you are the only one I believe and trust. Now that you have told me, I believe the War Department Telegram. Now I want one more favor, please Father. Enclosed is ten dollars. Please buy a flower and put it on my boy's grave. Also please take a snapshot of his grave and send it to me.'"

—Reminiscences of Chaplain Thomas J. Donnelly, 305th Regimental
Combat Team, Seventy-seventh Infantry Division, 1942–45

Chaplain R. T. DuBrau conducts a rainy GI funeral. Color slide by William R. Wilson (b. 1914), between 1941 and 1945.

OCTOBER 9

1942 The United States becomes the first nation to abandon the principle of special rights for foreigners living in China.

"I entered St. Malo while the city was half in American and half in German hands. . . . Sgt. Joe Thomas . . . and I entered the smoking town while white infantrymen were mopping up the last Nazi defenders. With snipers taking final pot-shots at us, we reached colored artillery positions on a hill as thirty-five Germans were being herded out of a building less than a hundred yards away. . . . Close to the German dugouts American machine guns were chattering and spitting lead at a small pocket of Germans still holding out, and the Germans returned the compliment from a smoking building. . . . This was one time that colored troops helped make possible the capture of an important city and actually entered with the first arrivals. From the hilltop I could see dirty white flags still dangling from a strongpoint [sic] just captured as we sat beside guns which had pummeled Hitler's crack soldiers. The prisoners were dazed and shaken from the incessant pounding from our artillery and dive-bombers. Dugouts were littered with grenades, ammunition, shattered guns and stale bread too hard to chew, but the concrete walls were too thick for anything to penetrate but big guns or flame throwers. French civilians, half naked, were begging for food and clothing every time we stopped. Our men were sleepy from night fighting. Said one, 'I could lie down on a live German and sleep.'"

—Report by Ollie Stewart, war correspondent for the Afro-American Newspapers, 1944

LEFT: Stretcher bearers, St. Malo, France. Photograph by Walter Rosenblum (b. 1919), 1944.

RIGHT: Drawing of an unknown GI by Donald Lester Dickson, U. S. Marine Corps, 1943.

OCTOBER 10

1942 U.S. Attorney General Francis Biddle announces that six hundred thousand Italian citizens living in the United States would no longer be regarded as enemy aliens, due to their "splendid showing . . . in meeting the test [of loyalty]."

"The Japanese emptied out the hospitals," U.S. Army veteran Anton Bilek told reporter Studs Terkel in 1984, looking back to 1942. "Anybody that could walk, they forced 'em into line. . . . If you fell out to the side, you were either shot by the guards or you were bayoneted and left there. We lost somewhere between six hundred and seven hundred Americans in the four days of the [Bataan Death] march. The Filipinos lost close to ten thousand." For nearly four years, the Philippine Islands were a battleground— guerrilla warfare replacing full-scale combat between the surrender of Allied forces there in May 1942 and the October 1944 Allied landings that began the long and bloody campaign to retake the islands. Tens of thousands were killed in battle or died from infected wounds, many more thousands were maimed or suffered from diseases and malnutrition. The Japanese occupation was brutal; when the Allies returned to the islands, the several thousand Japanese who surrendered to them were treated humanely. But most Japanese fought on. "The dilly-dallying over the surrender continues," combat surgeon Logan W. Hovis of the U.S. 503rd Parachute Infantry Regiment wrote home on August 21, 1945. "Occasionally, single [Japanese] soldiers or small groups turn themselves over to our custody. We know that there [are] several thousands in the mountains. We have no desire now to go in after them. The war is over and we have already lost too many good men." (See May 7, June 11, September 26, October 3)

LEFT: A Filipino corporal lies in an open-air Bataan hospital bed, his right arm suffering from a gangrenous infection, April 1942.

RIGHT: American film star and wartime medical corpsman Lew Ayres, a conscientious objector, treats wounded Japanese in a tent hospital on Leyte Island in the Philippines, December 1944.

OCTOBER 11

1942 The midnight Battle of Cape Esperance in the Solomon Islands ends in a victory for U.S. naval forces against the Japanese.

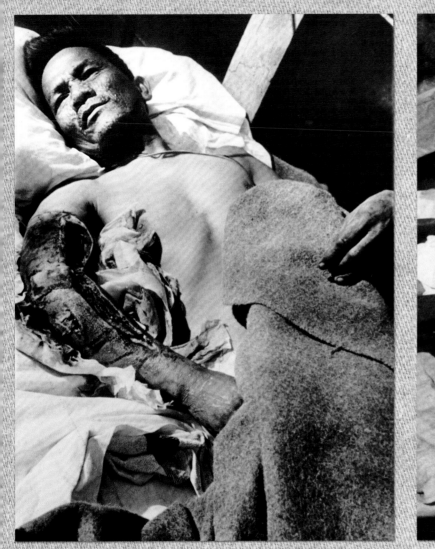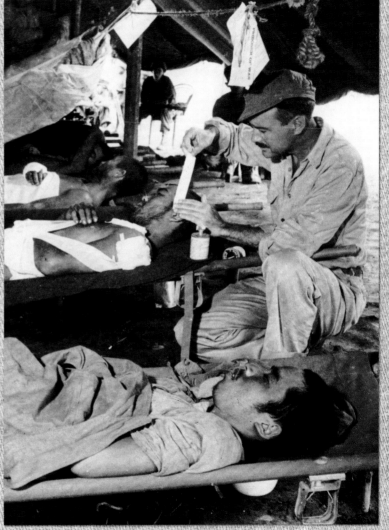

In 1945, U.S. Navy administrators received a letter from a civilian woman, whose name they did not reveal: "Please, for God's sake, stop sending our finest youth to be murdered on places like Iwo Jima. It is too much for boys to stand, too much for mothers and homes to take. . . .Why can't objectives be accomplished some other way? It is most inhuman and awful—stop! Stop!" Secretary of the Navy James V. Forrestal, who had witnessed part of the bitter fight for "Iwo" (see November 10, 11), responded personally. There was, he wrote, "no final means of winning battles except through the valor of the Marine or Army soldier, who . . . storms enemy positions, takes them and holds them." Yet, even in the midst of carnage, lives could be saved. Throughout the war, many thousands of people around the world—from researchers in civilian hospitals and universities, through military doctors who performed delicate surgery and treated both physical diseases and mental distress, to battlefield medics—worked to improve care for the wounded. In 1944 alone Harvard University chemists announced the development of synthetic quinine (used in treating malaria); the Eyebank for Sight Restoration (the world's first transplant agency) was established in New York City; and a new type of U.S. military aircraft, the helicopter, flew its first rescue mission when Coast Guard Commander Frank A. Erickson delivered forty units of blood plasma to aid survivors of an explosion on the USS *Turner*.

LEFT: *End of a Busy Day.* Reproduction of a painting by Franklin Boggs, one of a series of paintings sponsored by Abbott Laboratories depicting activities of the U.S. Army Medical Department during World War II, 1945.

RIGHT: *If he should fall is your blood there to save him?* . . . Color lithograph poster by Abram Games (b. 1914), published by His Majesty's Stationery Office between 1940 and 1945.

OCTOBER 12

1944 Germany launches V-weapons against Antwerp as punishment for Belgium's decision to open the city's port to the Allies. V–1s and V–2s will rain down on the city until March, killing about three thousand people and wounding fifteen thousand.

IF HE SHOULD FALL   IS YOUR BLOOD THERE TO SAVE HIM?

THE EMERGENCY BLOOD TRANSFUSION SERVICE NEEDS

BLOOD DONORS

In Yugoslavia, occupied since mid-1940, Josip Tito's Partisans were initially forced to leave their wounded behind after clashes with Axis forces. German troops almost invariably killed those abandoned men, in one instance laying the wounded Partisans out in a field and driving tanks over them. The Partisans soon established hidden hospitals. But no system was ever developed to peacefully heal the political schisms that divided Yugoslavia. As in other occupied countries, from neighboring Greece to distant Burma, political factions fought each other while at the same time fighting against (or for) the Axis. Agents of the British Special Operations Executive (SOE) and the American Office of Strategic Services (OSS) who operated in Yugoslavia from 1943 found themselves in the middle of a vicious civil war between two main adversaries, Tito's Communist-oriented Partisans and the Serbian Chetniks. "I couldn't tell who was . . . Communist or Reactionary," OSS major Linn Farish reported in the aftermath of one Partisan-Chetnik battle in which Americans had been caught. "What a very peculiar set of circumstances. . . . American airmen in American aircraft [were firing] at people who have rescued other American airmen and who were doing everything to make them comfortable. . . . If I am confused, what must be the state of mind of the people of Jugoslavia [sic]. Is it any wonder that hundreds of them have taken us aside and asked us to tell them . . . which way to turn." (See April 13, August 8)

Yugoslavs sabotaging Rail centre Subotitsa-Belgrade-Nish line. One of twenty-four plates from The United Nations at War, *produced by Charles A. Long, Jr., Inc., for the Dixie Cup Company. Gift to the Library of Congress and the people of the United States from Charles A. Long, Jr., Inc., 1944.*

OCTOBER 13

1942 The Americal Division becomes the first U.S. Army unit to reach Guadalcanal, two months after the initial American force of nineteen thousand Marines invaded.

1943 Italy declares war on Germany.

TED NATIONS AT WAR··· YUGOSLAVS sabotaging Rail centre Subotitsa-Belgrade-Nish line

Yugoslavs were among the five to seven million foreigners, both civilians and prisoners of war, whom the Nazis used as slave laborers in factories, mines, and farms within Germany. Most were taken from the Soviet Union and Poland. Hundreds of thousands came from Belgium, Italy, Holland, Bohemia-Moravia, and France. In February 1943, the Vichy French government, under heavy pressure from Germany's Commissar-General for Labor, Fritz Sauckel, introduced Compulsory Labor Service (STO), which required that men born between 1920 and 1922, except for those in a few excluded categories, go to work in Germany. Generally, the three hundred thousand Frenchmen who went to Germany under this order, like other Western Europeans, worked under better conditions than slaves from the East, whom the Germans regarded as subhuman. Still, the Westerners' circumstances were far from ideal. Dr. Wilhelm Jaeger, in charge of slaves laboring in the Krupp industrial works, reported that some French laborers "were kept for nearly half a year in dog kennels, urinals and in old baking houses." Some 350 U.S. soldiers captured during the Battle of the Bulge were also forced to be slave laborers: On the assumption that the men were Jewish, the Nazis separated them from other POWs and sent them to Berga, part of the Buchenwald concentration camp complex. By the time Allied troops reached them in April 1945, more than 20 percent of their number had perished and the rest were emaciated and scarred by their brutal treatment.

ABOVE: A gaunt Frenchman sits in rubble at the German slave labor camp at Nordhausen, Germany, waiting for an ambulance to take him to a hospital. U.S. Signal Corps photograph, April 1945.

LEFT: *We French Workers Warn You—Defeat Means Slavery, Starvation, Death.* Color poster by Ben Shahn (1898–1969), published by the U.S. War Production Board, 1942.

OCTOBER 14

1944 German field marshal Erwin Rommel is forced to commit suicide because of suspicions that he was involved in the July 20 attempt to kill Hitler. The Germans announce that he died from the effects of war wounds.

We French workers warn you... defeat means slavery, starvation, death

While foreign slaves labored to ease the burden of war on the German people (see October 14), the Nazi political machine continued indoctrinating German youth (see January 18). After her escape to America, German Jewish mother Marta Appel told of a visit to her children's school by an officer of the *Rasseamt*, the office of race. "He said that there are two groups of races, a high group and a low one. The high and upper race that was destined to rule the world was the Teutonic, the German race, while one of the lowest races was the Jewish race." To the officer's embarrassment, the tall blue-eyed blond girl he pointed to as a perfect example of Teutonic superiority proved to be Jewish—one of many such blunders that resulted in jokes generally told well out of earshot of Nazi Party members. "What does the ideal Aryan look like?" one went. "As tall as Goebbels [who was short], as slim as Göring [who was fat], as blond as Hitler [who was not]." But jokes could not mitigate the spreading poison of Nazi racial policies. As the Wehrmacht swept into country after country, it brought in its wake looting, slavery, starvation, punitive executions of hostages—and the systematic murder of millions of supposedly "racially inferior" people. One young Jewish girl, hiding in a cramped Dutch attic with her family and destined to become a victim of the Holocaust, refused to believe the world would tolerate such darkness forever. "Despite all that has happened," Anne Frank wrote in her diary, "I still believe that people are really good at heart."

Color illustration showing Jewish students and teachers being expelled from school from the virulently anti-Semitic children's book, *Trau keinem Fuchs auf gruner Heid und keinem Jud bei seinem Eid: Ein Bilderbuch für Gross und Klein* ("Don't Trust a Fox in a Green Meadow or the Word of a Jew: a Picture Book for Large and Small") by Elvira Bauer, published in Nuremberg, Germany, 1936.

OCTOBER 15

1942 About four thousand Japanese reinforcements land on Guadalcanal.

Children that Japanese soldiers left behind in their homeland are the focus of one of these American propaganda leaflets; the other demonstrates Allied power to choke off Japanese supply lines. The U.S. Army's Psychological Warfare Branch (PWB) distributed tens of millions of such leaflets throughout the Pacific Theater—increasingly emphasizing how badly the war was going for Japan. Carefully refraining from criticizing the revered Japanese emperor—and shunning the racial prejudices that flowed both ways in the brutal Pacific campaign—American psychological warriors in the Pacific adhered to a policy of telling the truth as they sought to establish a credibility that, they hoped, would encourage the emperor's troops to go against their military indoctrination and surrender. ("Reinforcements haven't come. There are no provisions," one captured Japanese diary noted. "Things are happening just as the enemy says.") At the same time, PWB found it necessary to urge Allied officers to remind their men, who had grown wary of Japanese deceptions during epically vicious combat, of the intelligence value of prisoners and the need to honor the guarantees given in PWB surrender leaflets. The leaflet campaign reached peak effectiveness in the Philippines, where the Allies took some twelve thousand Japanese prisoners, an unusually high number. Like Japanese prisoners taken elsewhere in the Pacific Theater, many were surprised at their humane treatment and proved to be very cooperative.

Two of the many propaganda leaflets distributed by the U.S. Army Psychological Warfare Branch in the Pacific Theater of Operations. In Japan, the kites shaped like carp symbolize pride in having a son in the family. The other leaflet depicts Adm. Chester Nimitz and Gen. Douglas MacArthur choking off Japan's lines of supply to its troops in the field, c. 1944.

OCTOBER 16

1940 A total of 16.4 million American men are registered for the draft.

1941 Nine Soviet armies are destroyed as Germans achieve victory in the battles of Bryansk and Vyazma.

端午の節句

日本の國民が昔から子供に對し非常に大きな愛情を持つてゐる事は全世界の人々に良く知られてゐます

徳川時代の初期の頃より毎年五月五日に家族の内の男の子の節義を象徴する爲に鯉のほりを立てる習慣が始まった

皆さんも御存知の様に之は武士が當時の戦に用ゐるのほり、槍、其他の武器を飾り其の偉勢を示してゐたのに對抗して一般庶民は空高く鯉のほりを吹き流し愛する子供の前途を祝したもので此の紙の鯉のほりは武士の如何なる紋章やのほりよりもはるかに壓倒してゐた

さて現在の烈しい戦の混亂の中にあつても此の美はしい物語りは皆さんの故國に於ける幾多の記憶を呼び起すのに充分でしょう、我々は皆さんの子供に對する限り無き愛情に對し深い理解と同情とを持つものであります

"Japanese planes! It was the most horrible and hated noise in China. Every child knew it, even the Miao and Lolo people in far West China recognized it and knew it to hate it. When I heard it, my blood would boil and bubble, and even my fingernails and my pores knew how to hate and wanted to fight. . . . I hated . . . Japan the ambitious, Japan the cruel, Japan the beastly, Japan the invader of my country! If these Japans I mention could be got rid of, I should not hate Japan. But even if they died out, the memories would live yet for a long time."

—Adet Lin, seventeen-year-old daughter of Chinese writer Lin Yutang, 1941

"The worst part of war, in my opinion, is what happens to the survivors—the widows without home or family, the ragged kids left to wander as orphans. I saw many of these in wartime Europe: a young British boy sitting by the rubble of the home where his parents lay buried shortly after a V-2 [German rocket-bomb] had hit; youngsters with shaven heads in a children's prison; human mascots, adopted by army units that had then moved on, leaving the children to fend for themselves. The aftereffects of war are never pretty to see. Neither should they be forgotten."

—Toni Frissell, American photographer who covered the war in Europe

LEFT: *China carries on*. Color lithograph poster sponsored by the U.S. National War Fund, between 1940 and 1945.

RIGHT: Abandoned child, Battersea, England. Photograph by Toni Frissell (1907–1988), January 1945.

OCTOBER 17

1941 The German submarine U-568 torpedoes and damages the U.S. destroyer *Kearney* while it is on convoy duty southwest of Iceland. Eleven crewmen are killed. General Hideki Tojo is named prime minister of Japan.

So rigid was government control in both Japan and Germany that there was little effective opposition at home to the Nazis' and Japanese militarists'conduct of the war. Yet some did resist. In Japan, where membership in neighborhood associations called *tonarigumis* was compulsory, and "irregular behavior" could be reported to the Thought Police, conservative legislator Seigo Nakano and his liberal counterpart Yukio Ozaki both criticized the government's war policies. In Germany, some civilians and members of the professional military, growing restive under Nazi repression and Hitler's increasingly irrational behavior, sought to assassinate the führer—their final attempt, in July 1944, unleashing a bloodbath of retaliation. Two years earlier, some exceptionally courageous university students, led by Sophie Scholl and her brother Hans and including their friend Christoph Probst, had formed the White Rose resistance organization, whose members painted anti-Nazi slogans on buildings and printed and distributed leaflets urging Germans to rise up against Hitler. Caught distributing leaflets on February 18, 1943, Sophie, Hans, and Cristoph were charged with sedition and "tried," on February 22, by the notorious Nazi judge Roland Freisler. Calm and challenging throughout, Sophie refused all opportunities to renounce her actions and possibly save her life. "Somebody, after all, had to make a start," she said. All three were executed by guillotine that same day.

Hans Scholl (1919–1943, left), Sophie Scholl (1921–1943), and Christoph Probst (1920–1943, right). Photograph by George J. Wittenstein, c. 1942.

OCTOBER 18

1942   In the wake of the Allied raid on Dieppe (see August 19), Hitler issues the "Commando Order." Calling commandos "bandits," the order calls for them to be shot on sight.

One particularly effective instrument of repression that functioned within Germany and throughout German-occupied countries was the much-feared *Geheime Staatspolizei* (State Secret Police), more commonly known as the Gestapo, part of SS chief Heinrich Himmler's ever-expanding complex of security organizations. Its agents had an entirely justified reputation for brutality. Staff Sergeant Doane Hage Jr. of the U.S. Army Air Forces had a brief taste of Gestapo interrogation methods after he was shot down over France in 1942 and captured trying to make his way into neutral Spain. He described the harrowing experience in a postwar memoir, written in the third person: "He was called a dirty American gangster and liar who came to spy on [Germany] and they would take no more lies. He was slapped some more times in the face and as he raised his handcuffed hands to protect his face the other man punched him in the stomach. . . ." [Taken into small, dark room, with cold water on the floor, he was stripped and, as his clothing was thoroughly searched, he was again accused of sabotage and beaten.] "He remembered the man he'd seen in one of the rooms upstairs that had been hanging upside down and with a bleeding back and he felt sure he would be in for similar treatment." Hage survived this encounter and was sent to prisoner-of-war camp Stalag 17B, where he honed his drawing skills depicting his own experiences and scenes described by his fellow prisoners.

ABOVE: *View from a Prison Cell.* Drawing by S. Sgt. Doane Hage Jr., USAAF, c. 1943.

RIGHT: *Interrogation at Gestapo Headquarters, Paris.* Drawing by S. Sgt. Doane Hage Jr., USAAF, c. 1943.

OCTOBER 19

1941   Complying with British and Russian demands, Afghanistan expels citizens of the Axis nations.

1942   Washington agrees to train and equip thirty Chinese divisions.

Not all Allied soldiers captured by the Germans made it to prisoner-of-war camps—or even as far as interrogation. On June 10, 1940, more than four hundred black African troops serving in the French army were forced to surrender near Lyon, France, after they ran out of ammunition. The German commander on the scene ordered the men, including the wounded, executed; those who attempted to escape were picked off by marksmen. In this case, the men's skin color seems to have been the primary reason for their murders. In other cases—such as the execution of nearly two hundred British POWs in France in May 1940—captured soldiers were slaughtered when keeping them in custody presented too great an inconvenience. The British were killed by members of Waffen SS divisions, the military arm of Himmler's SS. Four years later, during the last-ditch German offensive now known as the Battle of the Bulge (see September 30), Waffen SS troops commanded by *Standart-enführer* (colonel) Joachim Peiper disarmed captured American soldiers and marched them to a field near the town of Malmédy, Belgium. Suddenly, they began shooting the prisoners. Some, who feigned death after the first salvo, managed to survive. Others ran, but the Germans tracked them to nearby buildings, which they set on fire, killing the GIs who ran out to escape the flames. In all, the SS troops murdered some eighty Americans at Malmédy. Their bodies lay on the frozen ground until U.S. troops recaptured the area on January 13, 1945.

Massacre at Malmédy. Lithograph of a drawing, c. 1945, by Howard Brodie (b. 1915), based on a survivor's account.

OCTOBER 20

1941 With German forces sixty miles from the city, a state of siege is declared in Moscow.

1942 German forces are repulsed in a massive attack on Stalingrad.

"In the *izba*, surrounded by his staff, stands Khasin, with his bulging dark eyes . . . and cheeks blue from recent shaving," Soviet correspondent Vasily Grossman wrote of a Red Army officer in 1942. "He is explaining to me about the recent raid carried out by the tank brigade. . . . I was told back at the front headquarters that Khasin's family had all been killed in Kerch by Germans carrying out a mass execution of civilians. Purely by chance, Khasin saw photographs of the dead people in a ditch and recognized his wife and children. I was thinking, what does he feel when he leads his tanks into the fighting?" From Ethiopia to China, Greece to France, Axis forces—regular troops as well as specialized killing squads—systematically, and as a part of their assigned duties, murdered unarmed civilians. In German-occupied Europe, such mass murders often targeted certain ethnic or political groups. In both Asia and Europe, Axis troops sometimes massacred civilians in so-called retaliation for acts of resistance (see June 22, October 22), whether or not the victims were among those who had actually resisted. In March 1944, SS soldiers under *Obersturmbannführer* (lieutenant colonel) Herbert Kappler, assisted by Italian Fascist Pietro Caruso, took 335 Italian civilians—ten for each German that Italian partisans had recently killed with a bomb—to the Ardeatine Caves outside Rome and shot them, then sealed the cave with explosives to hide the evidence.

LEFT: Parents find their murdered son among the victims of a German massacre at Kerch, in the Soviet Union, 1942.

RIGHT: *They can take only our bodies*. Color lithograph poster by Ronay (first name unknown), sponsored by the U.S. National War Fund, between 1942 and 1945.

OCTOBER 21

1941 Germans murder about six thousand Serbians, including several hundred children, in reprisal for partisan attacks.

"THEY CAN TAKE
ONLY OUR BODIES..."

HELP HOLLAND TO RISE AGAIN!
The QUEEN WILHELMINA FUND, Inc.

Member Agency, National War Fund

The ruthless destruction of the Czechoslovakian town of Lidice by the Germans in 1942 as part of their retaliation for the assassination of Nazi official Reinhard Heydrich (see June 22) appalled the world. But the destruction of Lidice was not unique. As the Nazis erased it from the map of Europe, Japanese forces were beginning a murderous rampage in China, wreaking savage vengeance for the assistance a few Chinese had provided to American aircrews that had conducted the first American bombing raid on Japan (see June 16). Such acts of terror were a hallmark of Axis campaigns from the Rape of Nanking in 1937; through the destruction by Wehrmacht troops in 1943 of twenty-five Greek villages, and the murder of hundreds of civilians, in retaliation for partisan action that killed seventy-eight Germans; to the obliteration of the French town of Oradour-sur-Glane and the massacre of 642 townspeople in 1944 during an SS campaign to suppress the French Resistance. "The Nazis might have learned from the last war the impossibility of breaking men's spirits by terrorism," President Roosevelt declared on October 25, 1941. "Instead they develop their 'lebensraum' and 'new order' by depths of frightfulness which even they have never approached before." The president warned the invaders in both Europe and Asia "that the time will come when they shall have to stand in courts of law in the very countries which they are now oppressing and answer for their acts." (See December 17, 18)

Souvenir of Lidice. Lithograph by Benton Spruance (1904–1967), 1943.

OCTOBER 22

1944   Yugoslav partisans enter Belgrade.

In Axis-occupied Europe—beneath the storms of battle, behind the convulsions of "retaliatory" murder—the Nazis loosed a separate river of blood and kept it flowing relentlessly until the bitter end of the war. Born of Hitler's twisted hatred of "this Jewish bacillus infecting the life of peoples," what is now known as the Holocaust, a methodical attempt to exterminate all the Jewish people of Europe, was sustained by mindless prejudice and blind obedience to the führer's will—and administered with soulless efficiency by such Nazi officials as Heinrich Himmler, Hans Frank, and Adolf Eichmann, with the willing assistance of thousands of other Axis loyalists. By late 1942, reports of this murderous campaign had reached Allied authorities, who responded with a public declaration on December 17. "The German authorities, not content with denying to persons of the Jewish race . . . the most elementary human rights, are now carrying into effect Hitler's oft-repeated intention to exterminate the Jewish people in Europe. From all the occupied countries, Jews are being transported in conditions of appalling horror and brutality to eastern Europe. . . . None of those taken are ever heard of again. . . . The number of victims . . . is reckoned in many hundreds of thousands of entirely innocent men, women, and children. . . . [The signatories of this declaration] condemn in the strongest possible terms the bestial policy of cold-blooded extermination." By 1945, the Holocaust had claimed the lives of more than six million Jewish people.

River of Blood. Two-plate aquatint by Beatrice S. Levy (1892–1974), 1943.

OCTOBER 23

1942 The second Battle of El Alamein begins.

1943 In Singapore, the provisional government of India just proclaimed by pro-Axis Indian dissident Subhas Chandra Bose declares war on Britain and the United States.

In July 1944 and January 1945, units of the Soviet army became the first Allied force to liberate Nazi concentration and extermination camps when they opened the gates at Majdanek outside Lublin, Poland, and the largest of the death factories, Auschwitz, near Oswiecim, Poland. Moving toward Germany from the west, American troops did not discover the horrors of these camps until spring. When, on April 29, 1945, GIs arrived at Dachau, outside Munich, Germany, they made the first of many ghastly discoveries in the railway yards: More than fifty cattle cars filled with what, at first, they thought were rags and discarded clothing, were actually packed with corpses. "The dead were Hungarian and Polish Jews, children among them," Nerin E. Gun, a Dachau survivor, reported in his postwar book *The Day of the Americans*. "They had died of hunger, of thirst, of suffocation, of being crushed, or of being beaten by the guards." A week later, twenty-two-year-old Private First Class Harold Porter of the 116th Evacuation Hospital wrote his parents from Dachau of visiting the camp's crematory: "Dead SS troops [most of them killed by furious Americans] were scattered around the grounds, but when we reached the furnace house we came upon a huge stack of corpses piled up like kindling, all nude so that their clothes wouldn't be wasted by the burning. There were furnaces for burning six bodies at once, and on each side of these was a room twenty-feet square crammed to the ceiling with more bodies—one big stinking rotten mess."

ABOVE: A drawing made by Red Army artist Zinovii Tolkatchev during the liberation of Auschwitz, reproduced in *Osventsim*, 1965.

RIGHT: Starved bodies of prisoners who were transported to Dachau from another concentration camp by train, lie grotesquely as they died en route. U.S. Army photograph by Sidney Blau, April 30, 1945.

OCTOBER 24

1942 Vice Adm. William F. "Bull" Halsey assumes command of U.S. naval forces in the South Pacific.

When, in December 1942, the United Nations condemned Germany's "bestial policy" of exterminating European Jewry (see October 23), Nazi concentration and extermination camps lay beyond the range of Allied military action. As Allied forces advanced, Roosevelt and Churchill believed that the best way to rescue the surviving Jews was to concentrate on defeating Germany as quickly as possible. Day after day, Allied bombers targeted Axis industries and raided German cities. On the night of February 13–14, 1945, 244 British bombers loaded with incendiary bombs appeared in the skies over the ancient and heretofore largely untouched city of Dresden, Germany. The raid had originally been intended to target suburban industries and railroad marshaling yards through which more than twenty German troop trains had passed nearly every day early that month. Bombs fell, instead, on the old part of the city. Fires started by the first wave of bombers were augmented by incendiaries dropped by the second, and the flames quickly combined to form a raging firestorm that consumed more than eight square miles of the city and killed between twenty-five and thirty thousand people. The ghastly red glow from this incendiary horror was visible for miles. For Jewish slave laborer Ben Helfgott and his fellow slaves in a camp not far from Dresden, that terrible light was a beacon of hope: "To all of us, it was absolute salvation," he later recalled. "That was how we knew that the end was near."

LEFT: *The "V" for Victory.* Ink and opaque white drawing by Willard W. Combes (b. 1901), 1945.

RIGHT: Decomposing corpse in Dresden, Germany, 1945.

OCTOBER 25

1944   Britain, Russia, and the United States reestablish formal relations with Italy.

COLOGNE

Less than three months after the February 1945 firestorm in Dresden (see October 25), Germany capitulated. In the Pacific Theater, celebrations of the European peace were muted: Allied commanders were planning for what intelligence reports and hard combat experience told them would be an appallingly costly invasion of Japan. As preparation for that huge undertaking, the U.S. Army Air Forces continued its strategic bombing campaign, targeting Japanese cities—while in July, two top secret weapons arrived on the island of Tinian. The first atomic bomb opened a new age in human conflict when it devastated Hiroshima on August 6 (see November 25). When a B-29 nicknamed *Bockscar* released the second A-bomb over Nagasaki, correspondent William Laurence was in an accompanying plane. A "giant ball of fire" turned into a "pillar of purple fire, 10,000 feet high," he later reported. And out of that pillar erupted "a giant mushroom that . . . was . . . seething and boiling in a white fury of creamy foam. . . . . We last gazed at it from a distance of about two hundred miles. The boiling pillar of many colors could also be seen at that distance, a giant mountain of jumbled rainbows. . . . Much living substance had gone into those rainbows." The single atom bomb released over Nagasaki killed more than seventy thousand people outright, wounded thousands more, and permeated both the land and the stunned survivors with toxic radiation. Five days after it exploded, Japan surrendered.

Battered religious figures survive in the ruins of Nagasaki, Japan. U.S. Marine Corps photograph by Corp. Lynn P. Walker Jr., September 24, 1945.

OCTOBER 26

1939 Hans Frank becomes governor-general of Poland and immediately declares: "The Poles shall be the slaves of the German Reich."

1942 In the Battle of the Santa Cruz Islands, the U.S. Navy loses the carrier *Hornet* but buys time for Americans to reinforce the units battling to secure Guadalcanal.

The liberation of Paris in August 1944 ended a dark chapter in the history of the City of Light (see September 21–23). For more than four years the French capital had seethed with clandestine struggles that pitted resistance groups against Hitler's minions and their French collaborators—a shadow war of midnight arrests, beatings, torture, and summary executions. As Nazi authorities and their French helpmates deported Jewish Parisians to death camps, non-Jews and non-collaborators suffered through bitter-cold winters with little fuel for heat and stood in interminable lines to secure rationed food. In fertile French Indochina, meanwhile, Frenchmen began hoarding rice as the Japanese confiscated more and more of that vital crop. The Vietnamese peasants who raised the food were left with little to eat—especially after the Japanese ordered them to replace some of their rice crops with oil seeds, cotton, peanuts, and jute. Violent storms and Allied bombing exacerbated the food shortages and, by late 1944, full-scale famine was sweeping the country. "We saw hundreds of [starving] children," American Ray Grelecki of the OSS later remembered. "So, [on] our own authority [we] . . . brought in plane load after plane load of not only [food] but medical people." The Americans saved some lives—but the famine's effects were overwhelming. By the time conditions improved at the end of 1945, between one million and two million Vietnamese people had starved to death.

LEFT: *Ceux que Tombent* ("Those Who Fell"). A woman attends to the body of a Parisian killed during the liberation of the city. Photograph by R. Zuber, reproduced in *Paris de 19. au 26 Aout 1944*, 1945.

RIGHT: A Vietnamese woman and her child, two of the victims of the 1944–45 famine in Japanese-occupied French Indochina. Photograph given to U.S. Office of Strategic Services agent Archimedes L. Patti by his Vietnamese ally, Ho Chi Minh, 1945.

OCTOBER 27

1941 From Moscow, Russian forces launch a counterattack against German troops threatening the city.

1944 Allied forces contain a German counterattack in the Netherlands. Senator Harry S. Truman, Roosevelt's vice presidential running mate, makes a campaign stop in Peoria, Illinois.

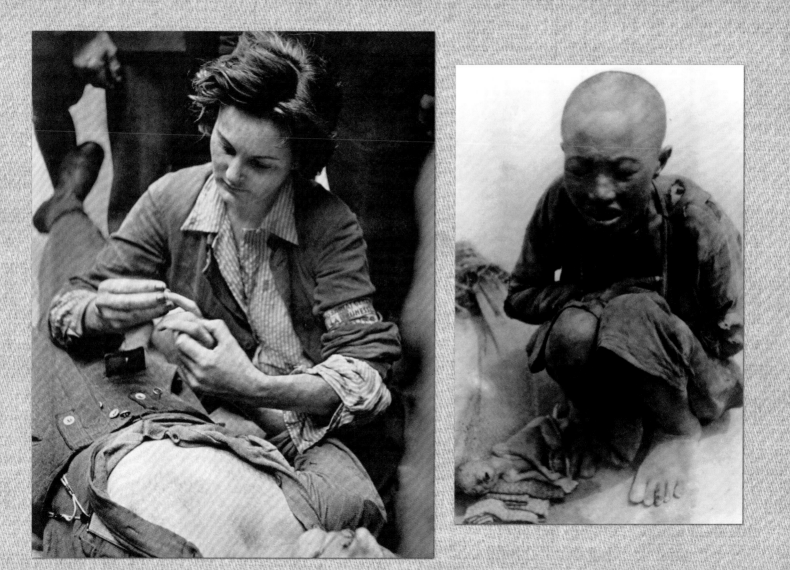

As famine enveloped French Indochina (see October 27), American troops were engaging in the bloody three-week battle for Saipan (June 15–July 9, 1944, see September 16). After ten days of fighting, Major General Keiji Igeta radioed his commander on Guam: "The enemy holds control of sea and air [and] . . . attacks with fierce concentration of bombs and artillery. . . . Wherever we go we are quickly surrounded by fire." The outcome of the battle was clear, but Japanese officers gave no thought to surrender. On the night of July 6–7, three thousand Japanese troops—the able-bodied in the front ranks, the wounded in the rear—hurled themselves against American lines in a final banzai charge that left most of them dead and the GIs shaken. Two days later, Rear Admiral Richmond Kelly Turner declared Saipan officially secured. But the Japanese wrote a horrific epilogue to this costly American victory. Soldiers whose code forbade surrender and civilians terrified of falling into the hands of American "beasts" slaughtered themselves with guns, bayonets, grenades, or by hurling themselves off island bluffs into the rocks and water below. Eighteen-year-old volunteer nurse Shizuko Miura failed in her attempt at suicide and was rescued by an American translator who shocked her by speaking Japanese. On the way to a field hospital, they looked down on water thick with corpses, including a woman who had tied her two children to her. The American began to weep. "Why," he said softly. "Why do Japanese kill themselves like this?"

Dead Japanese soldiers in a bomb crater on Saipan. Photograph by PFC Thomas H. Baird, U.S. Army, 1944.

OCTOBER 28

1940   Italy invades Greece.

1944   The first Japanese kamikaze to hit an American ship damages the U.S. cruiser *Denver* off Leyte, Philippines.

"From the icy rocks of the Aleutians, across the vast expanse of the Pacific . . . down the littoral of the Asiatic continent, through the fabled lands of the Indies to the very gates of the Antipodes, and then around into the Indian Ocean, the undisputed power of Japan has been established," the English-language *Japan Times* crowed on December 8, 1942. "The sting of Japan's lash has been felt . . . over tens of thousands of miles." Within the Japanese armies that wielded that lash were elite units of military police (MP), the *Kempeitai*. Powerful and much-feared by both soldiers and civilians, Kempeitai had duties that extended well beyond those normally associated with MPs, from mounting propaganda campaigns and securing human guinea pigs for medical experimentation to subversion and espionage. To help "pacify" civilians in occupied countries, the Kempeitai formed networks of spies and collaborators, whose information sometimes led to the brute treatment or mass annihilation of men, women, and children in reprisal for suspected rebellious acts or simply to terrorize survivors: Shanyway, Tharrawaddy, and Kalagon in Burma; Pontianak, Borneo; and Tigbuan and Santa Catalina in the Philippine Islands are only a few of the many occupied towns listed in the International Military Tribunal Far East's summary of Japanese war crimes as sites of mass murders. Little wonder that liberated populations sometimes dealt swiftly and harshly with people who had collaborated with the Japanese.

LEFT: A Chinese executioner holds the head of a Japanese spy. Photograph provided by T/Sgt. Robert John Kraft, U.S. Office of Strategic Services, 1945.

RIGHT: A Burmese man identifies one of the Japanese Kempeitai who massacred more than six hundred people in his village of Kalagon in July 1945, May 1946.

OCTOBER 29

1943 U.S. submarines begin mining the waters off French Indochina.

"The Army Air Force should carry out attacks . . . in order to terrorize the enemy forces and civilians," the chief of staff of Japan's Central China Expeditionary Force wrote War Minister Seishirō on July 24, 1939—confirming a policy of indiscriminate bombing that was already Japanese practice. That practice continued, even as Japanese authorities amended their laws to allow execution of Allied fliers for, among other things, attacking "private property of a non-military nature" after American B-17s conducted the first air raid on Japan in April 1942 (see June 15, 16). That October, the Japanese outraged Americans by executing three airmen who had participated in that raid: Dean E. Hallmark, William G. Farrow, and Harold A. Spatz. Thenceforward, they murdered many other Allied fliers—some after quick show trials, many summarily. The Japanese also eschewed legal niceties when they procured the "comfort women" who were forced to work in their military brothels. Most women were physically forced or threatened into this sexual slavery; some were tricked into service. A Japanese officer told sixteen-year-old Korean factory worker Yun Turi that he could find her a better job—then plunged her into a living nightmare from which she could not escape. "We had to serve soldiers all day long," she later reported. "When I had to serve many men, I would go out of my mind." Most comfort women who survived the war were physically and emotionally scarred for the rest of their lives.

LEFT: A defendant at the Far East war crimes trials demonstrates how, in May 1945, the Japanese beheaded captured B-29 crewman Lt. Darwin T. Emry, April 1946.

RIGHT: A young woman at a Japanese military garden party in Manchukuo (Manchuria), date unknown.

OCTOBER 30

1941   The nine-month siege of Sevastopol begins.

1944   The last murders by poisoned gas take place at the Nazis' largest death camp, Auschwitz.

"**M**r. President and Members of the Tribunal: . . . It is impossible in summation to do more than outline with bold strokes the vitals of this Trial's mad and melancholy record, which will live as the historical text of the twentieth century's shame and depravity. It is common to think of our own time as standing at the apex of civilization, from which the deficiencies of preceding ages may patronizingly be viewed in the light of what is assumed to be 'progress.' The reality is that in the long perspective of history the present century will not hold an admirable position, unless its second half is to redeem its first. These two-score years in the twentieth century will be recorded in the book of years as [among] the most bloody in all annals. . . . No half-century ever witnessed slaughter on such a scale, such cruelties and inhumanities, such wholesale deportations of peoples into slavery, such annihilations of minorities. . . . . These deeds are the overshadowing historical facts by which generations to come will remember this decade. If we cannot eliminate the causes and prevent the repetition of these barbaric events, it is not an irresponsible prophecy to say that this twentieth century may yet succeed in bringing the doom of civilization."

—Robert H. Jackson, Chief Prosecutor, the United States of America
Summation at the International War Crimes Trials
Nuremburg, Germany, July 26, 1946

Fascism. Silk-screen print by Harry Sternberg (1904–2001), 1947.

OCTOBER 31

1941 The U.S. loses its first combat vessel in the war when the destroyer *Reuben James* is torpedoed and sunk off the west coast of Iceland while escorting a British convoy; 115 men are killed.

Unconditional Surrenders: 1945

The year 1945 opened with the major Axis powers falling back on all fronts. Soviet troops pressed German forces hard in the East. In Belgium and Luxembourg, Americans gradually straightened the Bulge that December's German assault had made in their lines (see September 30), while Allied forces continued their contest with Germans still lodged in the Italian boot. As the Wehrmacht retreated, the Nazis sought to eradicate evidence of their appalling atrocities–while continuing to commit them. Concentration camps in the Allied lines of advance were emptied, surviving inmates forced onto the roads, and thousands massacred en route or as they reached their destinations. German V-weapons plunged out of the skies, killing thousands in Britain and

Belgium; the Luftwaffe deployed the last of its one hundred Messerschmitt 262 jet fighter aircraft. But these measures came far too late. Allied planes owned the air, and vast flights of bombers rained destruction on German and Japanese cities. In the Pacific Theater, Japanese troops continued to exhibit a singular contempt for surrender, fighting with fanatical intensity, inflicting thousands of casualties on Allied soldiers forced to dig, blow, or burn them out of every single jungle hideout and cave.

In February, President Roosevelt traveled to Yalta in the Crimea for a conference with Stalin and Churchill (see May 29). Upon his return, he delivered his report to Congress while seated rather than standing behind a podium

NOVEMBER 1

1940 By decree, Germany formally annexes western Poland.

1943 U.S. Marines invade Bougainville in the Solomon Islands.

as usual, one of many indications that his health was failing. His death in April badly shook the country that he had served as president for twelve crisis-filled years—but the American war effort did not flag under new commander in chief Harry S. Truman.

Victory in Europe, achieved in May, sparked wild celebrations. It also marked the beginning of a major redeployment of U.S. troops from the European Theater to the Pacific as Americans prepared for the invasion of Japan slated to begin in November—and projected to cost as many as one million Allied lives. As plans for amphibious landings took shape, a special group gathered at the Pentagon on May 31 to discuss whether the atomic bomb should be used on Japan—but no one in the room was certain what kind of damage the still-untested weapon might do. Six weeks later, a huge predawn explosion in the New Mexico desert shattered windows nearly two hundred miles away and inspired reports that the sun had come up and then gone down again. "We have discovered the most terrible bomb in the history of the world," Truman confided to his diary on July 25. Three days later, the Japanese rejected a final demand for unconditional surrender—despite a warning that the only alternative would be "prompt and utter destruction." Within two weeks, two

Japanese cities were in ruins, survivors of the atomic blasts terribly burned and poisoned by radiation. The most terrible bomb in history brought the Second World War to an end—even as a new kind of war was aborning, most ominously reflected in the widening rift between the United States and Britain on one side, and the Soviet Union on the other.

The Block Buster. Drawing by Edwin Marcus (1885–1961), December 1944.

On February 11, 1945, on his way back from the Allied conference at Yalta (see May 29), President Roosevelt stopped briefly in Egypt for separate meetings with monarchs Farouk of Egypt, Haile Selassie of Ethiopia, and Ibn Saud of Saudi Arabia. A presidential query to Ibn Saud about the possibility of letting more Jewish refugees into Palestine received a sharply negative answer: Arabs, the Saudi declared, would take up arms to prevent it. The president was also concerned about oil, aware, as interior secretary Harold Ickes had stated in a radio address nearly a year earlier, that the United States was "using up our oil reserves faster than we have been discovering new ones. . . .We don't have enough oil right now . . . [to] supply the military and essential industry with all that they require, and still have enough left for normal civilian consumption." Because the Saudis preferred ties to businesses from the United States, which had no apparent Mideast colonial ambitions, over companies based in Great Britain, American oilmen had been allowed in Saudi Arabia since the 1930s. After this meeting, from which the two national leaders emerged favorably impressed with each other, ties between the United States and Saudi Arabia were to grow stronger. Returning to Washington, Roosevelt reported to Congress that, at Yalta, the Allies had "made a good start on the road to a world of peace."

President Roosevelt meets with King Ibn Saud of Saudi Arabia aboard the USS *Quincy* north of the Suez Canal on February 14, 1945.

NOVEMBER 2

1941 Rival anti-Nazi Yugoslav guerrilla forces—the Chetniks and Tito's Partisans—begin fighting each other in Serbia.

As Roosevelt traveled home after meeting with King Ibn Saud in Egypt (see November 2), the Allies continued their campaign to liberate the Philippines. On January 9, Americans landed on the main island of Luzon, where the Japanese commander, General Tomoyuki Yamashita, had divided his forces into three main groups to conduct a war of attrition. One of Douglas MacArthur's main objectives on Luzon was the Philippine capital: "Go to Manila," he ordered his officers. "Go around the Nips [Japanese], bounce off the Nips, but go to Manila." Three separate American columns converging on the city slammed into hard resistance as they reached its outskirts. Rear Admiral Sanji Iwabuchi, commanding its twenty-one-thousand-man Japanese garrison, had ordered his men to fight to the death. Most of the garrison died in the ensuing monthlong battle—but not before engaging in an orgy of looting, rape, and murder against helpless civilians. By March 4, when the Americans secured the city at a cost of more than one thousand dead and nearly six thousand wounded, artillery barrages, explosions, and fires had destroyed much of the capital—and an estimated one hundred thousand Filipino civilians had been killed. By that time, Americans had also retaken the peninsula of Bataan and the island of Corregidor. But Yamashita and a force of 152,000 still remained in the north of Luzon; to the south, eighty thousand troops under General Shizuo Yokoyama were dug in. Months of hard and costly fighting lay ahead.

U.S. soldiers dig in, preparing to take the Philippine Islands capital, Manila, back from the Japanese. Photograph by S. Sgt. Charles Rosario Restifo, U.S. Army Signal Corps, 1945.

NOVEMBER 3

1939 Russia incorporates eastern Poland into the Soviet Union.

1941 Adm. Isoroku Yamamoto's plan to attack Pearl Harbor is approved by the Japanese command.

In late summer of 1944, U.S. Army Air Forces general Curtis E. LeMay, an experienced commander in the strategic bombing campaign against Germany, received orders to transfer to the Pacific Theater. After a brief visit to the United States, where he familiarized himself with America's new long-range heavy bomber, the B-29 (which was plagued, he noted unhappily, with "as many bugs as the entomological department of the Smithsonian Institution"), he took command of the Twentieth Bomber Command, set to fly missions against Japan from China. Logistics did not favor that enterprise, and by January 1945, LeMay was in command of the Twenty-first Bomber Command (part of the Twentieth Air Force) based on Guam, one of three islands in the Marianas chain that were designated B-29 bases. This move solved many of the logistical problems, but did nothing to debug the bombers, which continued to suffer from multiple mechanical problems. Inadequate aerial maps, extended periods of low visibility, and "that ferocious jet stream of the Pacific, high winds, sometimes at two hundred mph" were other problems LeMay's airmen faced as they launched their attacks on Japan. But "our major problem was the lack of practical experience in the new crews that were coming in all the time," LeMay wrote. "So I started some training procedures to try to whip the crews into shape. . . . In the end, the Twentieth Air Force probably flew more training missions than it did combat missions."

ABOVE: Maj. Gen. Curtis E. LeMay (1906–1990), USAAF, July 1945.

RIGHT: Airman asleep at a USAAF base on Guam. Photograph by Jack Delano, 1945.

NOVEMBER 4

1939 Congress approves the U.S. Neutrality Act of 1939 to permit arms sales to belligerent nations on a "cash-and-carry" basis.

1944 The first U.S. sighting of a Japanese balloon bomb occurs at San Pedro, California.

Confronted with long stretches of poor weather, problems related to flying bombing missions at high altitudes—and concomitant poor results from his command's air raids over Japanese territories—in February 1945 General Curtis LeMay switched tactics. His bombers would now fly nighttime low-level attacks against Japanese urban industrial areas and drop incendiaries rather than high explosives. The first incendiary raid, the night of March 9–10, targeted Tokyo and sparked a horrific firestorm that took more lives, LeMay later reported, than had been "caused by the big Allied raids on Hamburg and Dresden, or the nuclear strike to come in August on Hiroshima," (See October 4, November 25, 26.) More raids quickly followed: on Nagoya, "the heart of the Japanese aircraft industry"; on Osaka, Japan's second-largest city, where incendiary-sparked fires caused an arsenal to explode; on Kobe, where bombers used 4.7 million pounds of incendiaries. "We had dropped some warning leaflets over Japan," LeMay wrote, "which essentially told the civilian population that we weren't trying to kill them, but rather that we were trying to destroy their capability to make war. We were going to bomb their cities and burn them down. We suggested they leave for their own safety." Eventually, the USAAF alternated nighttime low-altitude incendiary raids with higher-altitude daytime raids. The strategic bombing campaign continued to the end of the war and ravaged more than sixty-five Japanese cities.

ABOVE: *Warning*. Propaganda leaflet dropped in Japan urging civilians to evacuate to avoid being bombed by the U.S. Army Air Forces. Psychological Warfare Branch, U.S. Army, 1944.

RIGHT: The view from the nose of an India-based U.S. B-29 bomber during a bombing run over Japanese railway yards at Kuala Lumpur, Malaya. U.S. Army Air Forces photograph, February 1945.

NOVEMBER 5

1940 Franklin Delano Roosevelt is elected president of the United States for an unprecedented third term.

1941 The U.S. Congress votes to stay in session indefinitely because of deteriorating relations with Japan.

As American bomber crews were preparing for their first nighttime incendiary raids on Japan (see November 5), Allied troops in western Europe reached the Rhine River, the last great natural barrier standing in the way of a drive into the heart of Germany. The Rhine had not been crossed by an enemy force since the time of Napoléon, and as the Germans retreated east across the rain-swollen river, they tried to maintain that record by detonating all the bridges. The Allies would have to stage amphibious assaults to reach the far bank while combat engineers built bridges for the main columns—except in one lucky instance. On March 7, 1945, the U.S. Ninth Armored Division found the Ludendorff railroad bridge in Remagen, Germany, intact—although it had been prepared for destruction. After engineers cut the wires on every German charge they could see, an American platoon began crossing the bridge—when charges at the far end went off. The bridge held, however, and U.S. troops and tanks that streamed across it established a firm bridgehead on the far bank. Meanwhile, engineers constructed additional pontoon bridges. These were in place when the Ludendorff span collapsed on March 17—killing twenty-eight of the engineers that were working on it. A few nights later, Third Army commander General George Patton sent his Fifth Infantry Division across the Rhine at Oppenheim, near Mainz. Other Allied units followed. To Hitler's fury, his enemies were now firmly established east of the Rhine.

Troops of the U.S. First Army stream across the Ludendorff bridge at Remagen, Germany, 1945.

NOVEMBER 6

1941 A committee of the U.S. National Academy of Sciences recommends immediate construction of an atomic bomb.

1943 Russian forces recapture Kiev, occupied by the Germans since September 19, 1941.

In late September 1944, with Allied forces pressing into Germany from both west and east, home-front morale plummeting, and fear of revolts by slave laborers and prisoners spreading, Third Reich authorities established the *Deutscher Volkssturm*, which Hitler placed under Nazi Party control. A last-ditch defense force comprising men and boys between the ages of sixteen and sixty (including some near-fanatical formations of Hitler Youth) as well as some women volunteers, the Volkssturm initially engaged primarily in support activities, such as laying mines and picking up downed Allied fliers. By early 1945, however, Volkssturm troops were increasingly being integrated into front-line units, with extremely uneven results. Where party-army cooperation was good and army officers were able (or inclined) to better arm, train, and support the militia units, Volkssturm battalions often held their own when facing the enemy. This was especially true when they had the added incentive of desperation, as on the eastern front, where the estimated 650,000 Volkssturm troops faced Soviets bent on vengeance. In the West, however (where only an estimated 150,000 of the more than one million Volkssturm troops taken prisoner experienced extended combat), their performance was generally poor. They had little fear of falling into the gentler hands of American and British troops—whose well-fed, well-clothed condition and apparently limitless resources also made it clear that Germany could not win the war.

LEFT: *The Last Drops* (of *Nazi Manpower*). Drawing by Edwin Marcus (1885–1961), c. 1945.

RIGHT: *Um freiheit und leben—volkssturm* ("For freedom and life—the people's militia"). Color poster reproducing a drawing by Mjölnir, published in Germany, c. 1944.

NOVEMBER 7

1941 Despite the existing state of siege, by German forces, Russian troops march through Moscow's Red Square in the traditional parade commemorating the Bolshevik Revolution. Tanks in the parade drive straight back to the front lines.

1944 Franklin Delano Roosevelt is elected president of the United States for a fourth term.

As Germany's situation grew ever more desperate, the Nazis took younger and younger boys into the *Volkssturm* (see November 7). After the war, the Allies found an eight-year-old in one of their POW camps—and learned that he had destroyed an American tank with a *panzerfaust* (the equivalent of an American bazooka). It was much more common, however, for Allied soldiers to encounter young children as hungry refugees. "The doggies [GIs] become accustomed to the abject poverty and hunger of the Italian refugees who stream out of towns which are being fought over, and who hang around bivouac areas," GI cartoonist Bill Mauldin wrote in his 1944 book *Up Front.* "It would take a pretty tough guy not to feel his heart go out to the shivering, little six-year-old squeaker who stands barefoot in the mud, holding a big tin bucket so the dogface can empty his mess kit into it. Many soldiers, veterans of the Italy campaign and thousands of similar buckets, still go back and sweat out the mess line for an extra chop and hunk of bread for those little kids. But there is a big difference between the ragged, miserable infantryman who waits with his mess kit, and the ragged, miserable civilian who waits with his bucket," Mauldin continued. "The doggie knows where his next meal is coming from. That makes him a very rich man in this land where hunger is so fierce it makes animals out of respectable old ladies who should be wearing cameos and having tea parties instead of fighting one another savagely for a soldier's scraps."

LEFT: *Up Front. The Prince and the Pauper.* Ink, white out, and pencil drawing by U.S. Army artist Bill Mauldin, c. 1944.

RIGHT: GI cartoonist Bill Mauldin (1921–2003) at work in the Il Messaggero building in Rome, c. 1945.

NOVEMBER 8

1939 Hitler escapes an assassination attempt; a bomb explodes, killing nine people, twenty minutes after he leaves a Munich beer hall celebration of the Nazis' abortive 1923 putsch.

1942 Anglo-American forces launch Operation Torch with landings on the Algerian and Moroccan coasts.

While Bill Mauldin's "doggies" slugged their way up the Italian boot (occasionally pausing to aid refugees, see November 8), pilots of the 332nd Fighter Group were on duty in the skies above them (see September 6). Like other American troops operating over or near enemy lines, the 332nd's pilots were issued "escape and evasion" kits in case something went wrong (each kit included such articles as a fishhook and line, bandages, gold coins, water purification tablets, and a compass). Still, evading capture by the enemy was often impossible and, once GIs were caught and imprisoned, escapes were relatively rare. Of the 95,532 Americans held by the Axis in Europe throughout the war, only 737 got away and returned to duty. In many cases, these more fortunate men made their way back to Allied lines with the help of underground organizations. Actual and potential escapees also had help from MIS-X, the U.S. Military Intelligence Service—Escape and Evasion Section, which was modeled on Britain's MI-9. MIS-X operatives masquerading as wives or sweethearts sent POWs care packages that concealed such useful items as saws, maps, foreign currency, and radios (cleverly hidden in cigarette packs or baseballs and useful for maintaining contact with MIS-X). Although conditions were even less favorable for POW escapes in Asia, where Westerners could not easily blend into the local population, both MIS-X and MI-9 did what they could in the China-Burma-India Theater to assist POWs and downed fliers.

LEFT: Playing cards provided to Allied prisoners of war sometimes concealed escape maps, divided into sections. Prisoners soaked the cards to dissolve the glue, peeled apart the layers, and assembled the maps. Facsimile escape map, c. 1990.

RIGHT: U.S. airmen of the 332nd Fighter Group receive precautionary escape kits at their air base at Ramitelli, Italy, prior to a mission. From left: Theodore G. Lumpkin Jr. (seated), Joseph L "Joe" Chineworth, Robert C. Robinson, Driskell B. Ponder, and Robert W. Williams. Photograph by Toni Frissell, March 1945.

NOVEMBER 9

1943 The United Nations Relief and Rehabilitation Administration (UNRRA) is established at Washington to aid countries subjugated by the Axis.

Downed fliers (see November 9) faced some unique problems in the Pacific Theater, where Allied forces were "hopping" from island to island. There, U.S. submariners added rescue services to their combat duties, forming a "Lifeguard League" that eventually saved more than five hundred airmen. On the ground, bitter combat continued. On February 19, 1945, fighting began on ten-mile-square Iwo Jima, just 660 miles south of Tokyo. A potential U.S. air base and the site of a radar facility that the Americans wished to destroy, "Iwo" was composed largely of volcanic pumice, making it decidedly unfriendly terrain. The Japanese had worked very hard to make it unfriendlier, digging thirteen thousand yards of tunnels, creating well-protected gun emplacements, and scattering defenders in some five thousand caves and camouflaged pillboxes. Pre-assault bombardments hardly touched these formidable defenses. Yet when the first wave of some ten thousand men of the Third, Fourth, and Fifth Marine Divisions landed and started struggling across terraces of volcanic ash, breathing air heavy with sulfur, they moved without opposition—for fifteen deceptive minutes. Then, as more marines followed, all hell broke loose. Day after day, shells smashed into the marines on the beachhead, incoming landing craft, and boats that attempted to transport the wounded to hospital ships. Taking heavy casualties (560 killed by the end of the first day), the marines battled on. (See November 11)

Marines dug in at the southeast edge of Motoyama Airfield #1 on Iwo Jima, covering the beach area from Mt. Suribachi to the east boat basin. U.S. Marine Corps photograph by Sgt. Scheer, 1945.

NOVEMBER 10

1941 Twenty-two thousand British troops sail from Halifax for the Far East aboard American ships protected by the U.S. Navy.

1942 U.S. troops enter Oran, Algeria.

The battle for Iwo Jima lasted from February 19 to March 16, eventually claiming nearly seven thousand American lives. Inching forward through artillery, sniper, and machine gun fire, U.S. Marines had to pry the Japanese out of their fortified positions with rifles, grenades, and flamethrowers. During this vicious fighting, twenty-two marines and five sailors acted with such stunning heroism that they were later awarded America's highest combat decoration, the Medal of Honor, thirteen of them posthumously. Among Americans on Iwo, as Admiral Chester Nimitz later said, "uncommon valor was a common virtue." On February 23, only four days into the battle, U.S. troops gained the top of Mt. Suribachi. When five marines of the Twenty-eighth Regiment, Fifth Division, and one navy corpsman raised a large U.S. flag on the summit, visible to all the GIs still struggling below, photographer Joe Rosenthal snapped their picture—creating an image that came to represent the courage and sacrifice of all U.S. servicemen during the war. Three of the men who raised that flag—Franklin Sousley, Harlon Block, and Michael Strank—were later killed on Iwo. Ira H. Hayes, John H. Bradley (USN), and Rene Gagnon survived. Soon after the picture appeared in American publications, they were plucked from their fighting units and sent on a tour of the United States to promote the sale of war bonds, during which they participated in jarringly festive reenactments of the flag raising that had occurred in the midst of such horrific tragedy and loss.

RIGHT: *7th war loan: now—all together*. Color poster by Cecil Calvert Beall based on Joe Rosenthal's photograph of Americans raising the flag on Mt. Suribachi, Iwo Jima. Published by the U.S. Government Printing Office, 1945.

LEFT: Surviving members of the group that raised the flag on Mt. Suribachi at the unveiling of a statue in New York City. From left: Rene Gagnon, John H. Bradley, and Ira H. Hayes. May 11, 1945.

NOVEMBER 11

1942 Immediately after the Allied invasion of North Africa, Hitler sends German troops into all the unoccupied areas of France except the Mediterranean coast, in violation of Germany's armistice agreement with the Vichy government.

7th WAR LOAN
NOW··ALL TOGETHER

While the marines were fighting for every inch on Iwo Jima (see November 10, 11), the naval armada supporting them was contending with a new Japanese suicide weapon. Named for the "Divine Wind," a huge storm that saved Japan from invasion in 1281 when it annihilated a Mongol fleet, kamikazes were meant to buy time for Japan to train new pilots and produce more war matériel. In the aerial equivalent of banzai charges, kamikaze aircraft, usually manned by young and inexperienced pilots, hurtled toward targeted Allied ships with the sole intent of crashing into them. The idea had been proposed by Vice Admiral Takajiro Onishi, who told his suicide pilots: "Nothing but the sacrifice of our young men's lives to stab at the enemy carriers can annihilate the enemy fleet and put us back on the road to victory." First used at the beginning of MacArthur's campaign to retake the Philippine Islands in October 1944, kamikazes were attacking en masse by 1945—though not all kamikaze pilots were of the same fanatical mind. "I must plunge into an enemy vessel," twenty-three-year old Ichizō Hayashi wrote in his diary on March 21, 1945. "As the preparation for the takeoff [for his final flight] nears, I feel a heavy pressure on me. I don't think I can stare at death. . . . I tried my best to escape in vain. So, now that I don't have a choice, I must go valiantly. . . . Despair, despair is a sin." He was killed on April 12, attacking Allied ships off Okinawa.

The flight deck of the aircraft carrier *Bunker Hill* after being hit by two kamikaze aircraft while on station off Okinawa. U.S. Navy photograph, May 11, 1945.

NOVEMBER 12

1942 A major three-day naval engagement begins off Guadalcanal. Both Japanese and U.S. fleets will suffer severe losses; Japanese losses will effectively isolate their Guadalcanal garrison.

On April 1, 1945, a vast armada of more than a thousand American and British ships, carrying an assault force of more than one hundred thousand men, arrived in the waters off the island of Okinawa. The largest of the Ryukyu Islands and a Japanese prefecture since 1879, Okinawa, only 350 miles southwest of Japan, had long been targeted by the Allies as a staging area from which to attack the Japanese home islands. To take this objective, American ground forces under General Simon B. Buckner would have to defeat nearly eighty thousand Japanese troops and the twenty-thousand-man Okinawan militia, all firmly entrenched in caves, tunnels, and other fortifications (as, offshore, the navy faced wave after wave of concerted kamikaze attacks). Within three weeks, the Americans secured the north of the island. But the Japanese commanding general, Mitsuru Ushijima, had concentrated his forces in the south, and there, progress was agonizingly slow. Tropical downpours that created a deep, glutinous mud caused "other problems besides chilly misery," Okinawa veteran Eugene Sledge later remembered. "Our tanks couldn't move up to support us. Amtracs had to bring a lot of supplies, because the jeeps and trailers bogged down." Then men had to haul those supplies by hand—through the mud and under fire—from where the amtracs dropped them. The Americans kept advancing, their heavy losses replaced by reinforcements as they moved through lethal torrents of enemy fire. (See November 14, 15)

LEFT: Maj. Gen. Simon Bolivar Buckner (1886–1945), U.S. Army, c. 1944.

RIGHT: *Map of Okinawa and the journey of the 383d Infantry.* Illustration included in *The Broken Urn*, a memoir by World War II veteran Carl Albin Hall (U.S. Army infantry, 1942–46), 2004.

NOVEMBER 13

1941 At the start of what will be the coldest Russian winter in 140 years, German eastern-front staff officers decide to renew the offensive against Moscow.

OKINAWA SHIMA
CT-383
MAJOR ENGAGEMENTS

CT-383 LANDED ON
BROWN BEACHES 1
APRIL '45
TIME: 0830

CORPS
RESERVE
4-22 APRIL '45

REST AREA
30 APRIL-
10 MAY

KAKAZU RIDGE
8-14 APRIL '45

THE GATE TO MAEDA
22-30 APRIL '45

YONABARU
FIELD

CONICAL HILL
10-30 MAY '45

MACHINATO
AIRFIELD

NAHA
AIRFIELD

NAHA

SHURI

KOCHI

YONABARU BAY

Sunaba

Kuo

Chatan

Sukuran

Atema

Nodako

Kochi

Kaniku

Tanabaru

Yonabaru

Kamizato

Iwa

Yunagusuku

Itoman

Ozato

Yuza

YUZA-DAKE
ESCARPMENT

As the fight for Okinawa continued (see November 13), Americans beat back a Japan-ese counterattack in early May, then continued pushing Ushijima's forces toward the southern tip of the island. But the retreating Japanese maintained their fierce resistance. Near the Okinawa capital, Naha, May 13–17, U.S. Marines of the Sixth Division suffered two thousand casualties in often hand-to-hand fighting before finally securing Sugar Loaf Hill. Everywhere, GIs had to engage in "cave flushing" to remove Japanese troops from well-hidden fortifications. After one cave was cleared, an American correspondent inspected it: "There in a room about fifteen feet square was a Japanese antitank gun mounted on pneumatic-tired wheels," he reported. "Piled high around three walls were cases of ammunition. . . . From the slit through which we entered the gun crew commanded the field of fire covering the broad, level plain across which American tanks had to advance to reach Kakazu Ridge." Overcoming such defenses was very slow, difficult, and costly. (One U.S. Tenth Army ordnance officer estimated that, in the first month of fighting, American forces expended an average if 1.65 *tons* of ground ammunition to kill each defending Japan-ese soldier.) Eventually, Americans on Okinawa developed successful anticave tactics: After artillery fire against the entrances forced the Japanese back into their tunnels, infantry and tanks closed in, sealing the caves with flamethrowers or explosives.

U.S. Marines engage in the harrowing process of flushing Japanese soldiers from caves that form part of their formidable defenses on Okinawa. U.S. Marine Corps photograph, 1945.

NOVEMBER 14

1940 More than four hundred German planes bomb the ancient English cathedral city of Coventry. The cathedral is destroyed, and sixty thousand other buildings, are destroyed or damaged. Hundreds of people are killed.

"I don't think Iwo Jima should have been taken, because of the cost to take it," retired U.S. Navy admiral Charles S. Adair—a captain and Pacific Theater amphibious operations planner in 1945—stated in 1976. "I don't think the value was there." (More than twenty-four thousand B-29 crewmen whose damaged planes landed on Iwo would probably have disagreed.) Nearly seven thousand Americans died on Iwo, some twenty thousand were wounded. The cost for Okinawa was even greater: more than 49,000 U.S. battle casualties, including 12,520 men killed. Among the dead: ground force commander Simon B. Buckner, killed just days before the fighting ended, and veteran war correspondent Ernie Pyle, hit by Japanese fire on April 18. On April 12, Pyle had described the passage of night on the island. "Flares in the sky ahead, the crack of big guns behind us, then of passing shells, a few dark figures coming and going in the night, muted voices at the telephones, the rifle shots . . . the feel of the damp night air under the wide sky . . . the old familiar pattern, unchanged by distance or time from war on the other side of the world. A pattern so imbedded in my soul that . . . it seemed to me as I lay there that I'd never known anything else in my life. And there are millions of us." On that same day, the commander in chief of all U.S. forces died of a cerebral hemorrhage—while two of his sons served on ships supporting the infantry, marines, and war correspondents on Okinawa.

ABOVE: American war correspondent Ernie Pyle (1900–1945). Photograph by Milton J. Pike, c. 1944.

RIGHT: The U.S. Fifth Marine Division cemetery on Iwo Jima, the flag at half-staff for the marines who died on the island and for their commander in chief, who died on April 12. Photograph by Murray Befeler, April 15, 1945.

NOVEMBER 15

1942   Five Sullivan brothers die when the ship on which they are all serving, USS *Juneau*, is sunk off Guadalcanal.

"In the capital's hush every sound was audible—the twitter of birds in new-leafed shade trees; the soft rhythmic scuffing of massed, marching men in the street; the clattering exhaust of armored scout cars moving past, their machine guns cocked skyward. And the beat of muffled drums. As Franklin Roosevelt's flag-draped coffin passed slowly by on its black caisson, the hoofbeats of the white horses, the grind of iron-rimmed wheels on pavement overrode all other sounds.

"Men stood bareheaded. Few people wept, so that the occasional sounds of sobbing seemed shockingly loud. As the coffin went past, part of the crowd began jostling quietly to move along, to keep it in sight. On Pennsylvania Avenue an elderly weeping Negro woman sat on the curb, rocking and crying, 'Oh, he's gone. He's gone forever. I loved him so. He's never coming back. . . .'

"To the White House. The caisson and its bright-colored burden rolled slowly along, small in the broad street from which Franklin Roosevelt had so often waved to cheering thousands. The sun seemed to grow hotter, the drums throbbed and muttered on & on. At last, the caisson ground up the graveled White House drive. The coffin was carried out of sight and into the executive mansion."

—*Time* Magazine, Monday, April 23, 1945

LEFT: Color reproduction of the unfinished portrait by Elizabeth Shoumatoff for which Franklin Delano Roosevelt was sitting just before he died, published by Gimbel Brothers, c. 1945.

RIGHT: Mourners line the streets of Washington, D.C., during President Roosevelt's funeral procession. Photograph by George Tames, April 14, 1945.

NOVEMBER 16

1944 Supporting ground operations, 2,807 U.S. and British planes drop more than ten thousand tons of bombs on German defensive positions near Aachen.

In February 1945, while U.S. Marines were struggling through the volcanic ash on Iwo Jima (see November 10 and 11), GIs in Europe were enduring the end of a frigid winter. "There's a lot of snow on the Western Front these days and the country looks like a Christmas card," Warrant Officer Frank J. Conwell wrote to his family on February 6. "But the Flexible Flyers have turned into tanks. The snow men are Schutstaffel [SS]. The snowballs are grenades. The wet stuff trickling down the back of necks is often blood. And when you're wet and numb with cold there's no place to go to." Bone tired and determined to achieve victory and go home, GIs in Europe, with their European Allies, had confronted some of the best troops Germany had to offer—and were pushing them back. The enemy was not all they had to deal with. They also suffered through miscalculations by the high command (as during the debacle of the Huertgen Forest, see September 24), tragic episodes of misplaced friendly fire, bad weather, supply shortages, and the peculiar bureaucratic quirks of the American military: *Snafu* ("situation normal, all f__ked up") was a common conversational term. In April, they learned of the death of their longtime commander in chief and Harry Truman's succession to the presidency—and confronted firsthand the Nazis' monstrous industry of death. (See October 23, 24, November 18)

LEFT: U.S. soldiers resting on the Siegfried Line. Photograph by Toni Frissell, February 1945.

RIGHT: Infantrymen of the 255th Regiment, Second Battalion, VI Corps, move down a street in Waldenburg, Poland. U.S. Army photograph, April 16, 1945.

NOVEMBER 17

1941 Congress amends the U.S. Neutrality Act, making it possible for U.S. merchant ships to be armed.

In April and May 1945, American troops opened the gates of Nazi slave labor and extermination camps and discovered earthly suburbs of hell. At Ebensee, in picturesque Austria, living skeletons populated a slave labor camp, part of the large Mauthausen complex. Here, under sadistic commandants Georg Bachmayer and Otto Reimer, prisoners labored from 4:30 A.M. until 6 P.M. building massive tunnels to house underground factories, then returned to their crowded and fetid barracks to face starvation and torture. So many people were tormented to death at the camp that it belatedly acquired its own crematorium—which could not keep pace with the number of bodies. Americans found stacks of corpses when they liberated Ebensee on May 9. Nearly two weeks earlier, Major Richard Winters of the 101st Airborne Division, who had led his men through tough clashes from D-Day to the Battle of the Bulge, arrived at a similar slave-labor prison at Landsberg, Germany, part of the Dachau complex (see October 24). Winters later wrote: "The memory of starved, dazed men who dropped their eyes and heads when we looked at them through the chain-link fence, in the same manner that a beaten, mistreated dog would cringe, leaves feelings that cannot be described and will never be forgotten. The impact of seeing those people behind that fence left me saying, only to myself, 'Now I know why I am here.'"

ABOVE: One of the sketches made by Soviet artist Zinovii Tolkatchev (1903–1977) when the Red Army liberated Auschwitz in January 1945. Published in *Osventsim,* 1965.

RIGHT: A scene at Ebensee concentration camp during its liberation by American forces. Photograph by S. Sgt. Charles M. Amsler (1913–2006), Medical Corps, U.S. Third Army, May 9, 1945.

NOVEMBER 18

1943 Cordell Hull becomes the first U.S. secretary of state to address a joint session of Congress when he reports to senators and representatives on the conference of Allied foreign ministers, held in Moscow, October 18–30.

1941 The Japanese Diet approves a "resolution of hostility" directed against the United States.

On April 12, 1945, as the United States was plunged into mourning by the death of President Roosevelt, the supreme Allied commander in Europe, General Dwight D. Eisenhower, first "came face to face with indisputable evidence of Nazi brutality and ruthless disregard of every shred of decency," as he later wrote in *Crusade in Europe*. With generals George Patton and Omar Bradley, he entered the Ohrdruf concentration camp near Gotha, Germany. "I visited every nook and cranny of the camp," Eisenhower reported, "because I felt it my duty to be in a position . . . to testify at first hand about these things in case there ever grew up at home the belief or assumption that 'the stories of Nazi brutality were just propaganda.'" Eisenhower ordered every citizen of Gotha to tour the camp. Elsewhere, American officers followed his example. "German civilians are being used to help clean up this . . . mountain of rotting corpses," Private First Class Harold Porter wrote his family from Dachau (see October 24). "They . . . exhibit every sign of genuine surprise, shock, and guilt. . . . I've talked with a French prisoner who was permitted to travel from camp to camp with an SS guard. He told of how the civilians on the trains recognized his striped uniform, exhibited genuine pity for him and even offered him cigarettes. He is sure that not one in a hundred of the German civilians has the faintest idea of what actually goes on in a concentration camp. Yet I wonder."

Citizens of Ludwigslust, Germany, inspect a nearby concentration camp under orders of the 82nd Airborne Division. U.S. Army photograph by T/4 Jack Clemmer, May 6, 1945.

NOVEMBER 19

1940 Although surrounded by Axis countries that have disregarded the neutrality of other nations, Switzerland nevertheless bans the Swiss Nazi Party.

While Allied troops were liberating survivors of the Holocaust (see October 24, November 18), the increasingly delusional Adolf Hitler huddled in his underground bunker in Berlin, intermittently convinced that he could still achieve victory. Haranguing generals who knew that much of what he said was nonsense, he hurled blame for the looming German defeat at world Jewry, the German high command—almost everyone except himself—as Russian artillery gutted the buildings above him and the Red Army moved into the city. On April 15, Eva Braun, his mistress for more than twelve years, arrived at the bunker. Hours after their marriage on April 30, Mr. and Mrs. Adolf Hitler committed suicide and, per Hitler's instructions, subordinates took their bodies outside and burned them. The day before, in Milan, Italy, partisans had displayed the bodies of former Fascist dictator Benito Mussolini and his mistress Clara Petacci in Piazzale Loreto—where people embittered by the ravages of the war into which Il Duce had led them battered and abused the corpses. Ineffectual head of a puppet government in German-controlled northern Italy since the Wehrmacht had rescued him from an Italian prison in September 1943, Mussolini had been attempting to escape to Switzerland when he and Petacci were captured on April 27. His execution rendered ironic a threat he had made against the Italian leaders who had deposed him: "Only blood," he said, "can cancel so humiliating a page from our country's history."

ABOVE: Eva Braun (1912–1945).

LEFT: The bodies of former Fascist dictator Benito Mussolini and his mistress Clara Petacci on display in Milan, Italy, 1945.

RIGHT: *The strange death of Adolf Hitler.* Color movie poster published by the Universal Film Corp, c. 1943.

NOVEMBER 20

1940
Chinese Communist forces continue their "100-Regiment Offensive"—guerrilla operations against Japanese military units and communications lines.

1943
As U.S. Marines fight on Tarawa, nearby Makin, an islander breathlessly greets the U.S. Navy beachmaster, Lieutenant Clarence B. Selden: "I-am-so-glad-you-have-come-we-have-waited-many-months-we-are-happy-you-have-come-may-I-get-your-men-coconuts?"

IS HE DEAD?

THE STRANGE DEATH OF ADOLF HITLER

with

LUDWIG DONATH
GALE SONDERGAARD
GEORGE DOLENZ
FRITZ KORTNER
LUDWIG STOSSEL
WILLIAM TRENK

Screen Play by Fritz Kortner   Original Story by Fritz Kortner and Joe May   Directed by JAMES HOGAN   Associate Producer, BEN PIVAR   A UNIVERSAL PICTURE

Less than a week after American generals Eisenhower, Patton, and Bradley toured the Ohrdruf concentration camp (see November 19), the Allied Twenty-first and Twelfth Army Groups successfully completed the largest double envelopment in history to date when they took into custody on April 18 the last of some 325,000 German troops that they had trapped in the Ruhr, Germany's prime industrial region. Not only had the Allies destroyed twenty-one Wehrmacht divisions, they had permanently deprived the Third Reich's remaining factories and fighting forces of resources vital to the war effort. With the Ruhr secured, Western Allied forces in central Germany moved northward toward the Elbe River, approximately seventy miles southwest of Berlin—as Soviet troops were approaching it from the east. "On 25 April patrols of the 273d Regiment, 69th Division, under V Corps, which had probed eastward from the Mulde [River], met elements of the Russian 58th Guards Division in the Torgau area, on the Elbe," Eisenhower later reported to the Combined Chiefs of Staff. "The junction of the Eastern and Western Fronts had been effected, and Germany was cut in two." When contact between the two converging Allied forces was imminent, Eisenhower and the Soviets agreed that, in central Germany, the Elbe and Mulde rivers would form the line of demarcation between the operations of their two forces. Eisenhower's decision to hold Western troops at the Elbe remains a subject of analysis and debate.

U.S. Ninth Army soldiers Capt. E. P. Grange (red cross on helmet), Bartow B. Falzinger (left of embracing Russian soldier), and John W. Standish (right of Russian soldier) greet Soviet troops of Marshal Ivan Koniev's army after the two forces link up at Apollensdorf, Germany, to the west of the first U.S./USSR meeting near Torgau. U.S. Signal Corps photograph, May 1945.

NOVEMBER 21

1942   American B-24s operating out of Libya bomb Tripoli harbor.

After Eisenhower decided that Western Allied forces would hold at the Elbe River (see November 21), Berlin became a purely Soviet military objective. Earlier Stalin had seemed to agree with Eisenhower's determination that "the Russian advance and the Allied bombing had largely destroyed [Berlin's] usefulness" as a major military objective. Therefore, Stalin assured Ike, "The Soviet Command . . . plans to allot secondary forces" to taking the German capital. In fact, the Soviet dictator had set April 16 as the starting date for an all-out effort by some 2.5 million Soviet troops to capture the city that—as capital of the German state of Prussia and of both Imperial and Nazi Germany—had for generations been a potent symbol of German militarism. At 5 A.M. that morning, Soviet forces launched their campaign from positions some thirty-five miles east of Berlin with one of the most powerful artillery barrages in history. By April 25, they had encircled the city. Soon, they were fighting in its streets against a cobbled-together defense force (including boys and older men of the *Volkssturm*, see November 7) that Hitler had ordered to resist "to the last man and the last shot." The führer committed suicide April 30; Berlin surrendered two days later. For some time thereafter, until belatedly restrained by their commanders, vengeful Soviet troops further despoiled the bomb- and artillery-ravaged city and attacked its people, committing countless atrocities—including looting, murder, and rape.

LEFT: Soviet soldiers in front of the Brandenburg Gate, Berlin, Germany. Photograph by Evgenii Khaldei, 1945.

RIGHT: *Tak budet s fashistskim sverem!* ("So it will be with the fascist beast!"). Color poster by Aleksei Kokorkin (1906–1959), 1945.

NOVEMBER 22

1942 Soviet forces surround the German Sixth Army near Stalingrad.

1943 U.S. Marines secure Makin, in the Gilbert Islands; marines also capture the western portion of Tarawa.

On May 5, 1945, three days after the Red Army took Berlin (see November 22), General Admiral Hans von Friedeburg, an emissary from the new German head of state, and Admiral Karl Dönitz, arrived at Eisenhower's headquarters in Reims, France, to open surrender negotiations on behalf of the German government. He commenced "playing for time," Eisenhower later wrote, "so that [the Wehrmacht] could transfer behind our lines [and away from the Soviets] the largest possible number of German soldiers still in the field." Friedeburg's efforts stopped when Eisenhower's representative, General Walter Bedell Smith, made it crystal clear that the Allies would only accept unconditional surrender on all fronts. This was accomplished at 2:41 A.M. on May 7, when German representatives signed the document of capitulation stipulating that all hostilities were to cease at midnight the next day. On May 8—Victory in Europe (V-E) Day for the Western Allies—Eisenhower issued a proclamation saluting "every man, every woman, of every nation" among the five million troops in his unified command. "Our common problems of the immediate and distant future can be best solved in the same conceptions of cooperation and devotion to the cause of human freedom as have made this Expeditionary Force such a mighty engine of righteous destruction. . . . This we shall remember—and in doing so we shall be revering each honored grave, and be sending comfort to the loved ones of comrades who could not live to see this day."

Col. Gen. Alfred Jodl, German chief of staff, signs the document of unconditional surrender in the war room of Supreme Headquarters, Allied Expeditionary Forces, Reims, France. Gen. Adm. Friedeburg sits on Jodl's left, German major Wilhelm Oxenius on his right. U.S. Army Signal Corps photograph, May 1945.

NOVEMBER 23

1939 Star of David badges become compulsory for all Jews in occupied Poland.

1942 The U.S. Women's Coast Guard Reserve (SPARS) is established.

UNCONDITIONAL SURRENDERS: 1945

Cooperation between the Soviet Union and its Western Allies had begun to deteriorate well before victory in Europe. Yet all remained cordial when on May 9 Allied representatives assembled in Berlin to witness German ratification of the surrender at Reims by signing a separate document—an event that resulted in the USSR adopting May 9 as their own V-E Day. "The second ceremony was, as we understood it . . . to give notice . . . that the surrender was made to all, not merely to the Western Allies," Eisenhower reported. Just over two months later, Stalin joined Churchill and Truman in Potsdam, Germany, for the final Allied strategy conference. From July 17 to August 2 the Big Three held often-contentious discussions of postwar arrangements in Europe and the continuing war in Asia. July 26 proved to be a signally important day: As Britain held an election that would result in defeat for Churchill's Conservative Party and his abrupt replacement as prime minister, the Big Three issued the Potsdam Declaration, which concluded with a demand that "the government of Japan . . . proclaim now the unconditional surrender of all Japanese armed forces. The alternative . . . is prompt and utter destruction." Ten days earlier, Americans had successfully tested the atom bomb. After so long a war, so much terror and destruction, when the Japanese failed to comply with this ultimatum, few Allied leaders expressed reservations about using the terrible new bomb against the only remaining Axis power.

Members of the Allied "Big Three" attending the Potsdam Conference include Winston Churchill (upper left, with cigar), Joseph Stalin (right, holding cigarette), and President Harry S. Truman (bottom, with back to camera, looking to the right). U.S. Army Signal Corps photograph, 1945.

NOVEMBER 24

1941 U.S. Navy commanders in the Pacific are warned that Japanese forces are preparing for military action, possibly against the Philippines or Guam.

UNCONDITIONAL SURRENDERS: 1945

On the morning of August 6, 1945, a B-29 Superfortress from the U.S. 509th Composite Group, Twentieth Air Force, took off from an airfield on Tinian, in the Mariana Islands. Named *Enola Gay* after the mother of its pilot, Colonel Paul Tibbets, the bomber was carrying "Little Boy," an eight-thousand-pound uranium-based atom bomb containing explosive power equivalent to 12,500 tons of TNT. Joined by two observation planes over Iwo Jima, the B-29 headed for Hiroshima, a city of some 245,000 people on Honshu, the largest of the Japanese home islands. Tibbets cautioned his crew to remember that, once the plane reached Japan, their communications would be recorded: "This is for history, so watch your language. We're carrying the first atomic bomb." At 8:09 A.M. Tibbets again went on the intercom: "We are about to start the bomb run. Put on your goggles and place them up on your forehead. When the countdown starts, pull the goggles over your eyes and leave them there until after the flash." The crew had no idea what the flash would be like; most of them had never heard of an "atomic bomb." At 8:15 A.M., Little Boy dropped from *Enola Gay*'s bomb bay. It exploded 660 yards above the city with a stunning flash that congealed into a massive ball of fire. From the midst of the maelstrom, a giant purple mushroom boiled upward, tail gunner George Caron later wrote, "like something terribly alive." Copilot Robert Lewis looked down, toward the fiery, roiling earth. "My God," he said. "What have we done?"

The crew of the *Enola Gay*, the B-29 that dropped the atom bomb on Hiroshima, Japan: front row, left to right: radar operator Jacob Beser, bomb operator Morris R. Jeppson, navigator Theodore Van Kirk, bombardier Thomas Ferebee, Navy technical adviser William Parsons, aircraft commander Paul W. Tibbets Jr., and copilot Robert Lewis. second row: assistant gunner and assistant flight engineer Robert Shumard, radio operator Richard Nelson, radar operator Joe Stiborik, flight engineer Wyatt E. Duzenbury, and gunner George Caron, 1945.

NOVEMBER 25

1943   In the battle of Cape St. George, New Ireland, five U.S. destroyers intercept five Japanese destroyers and sink three.

"**T**he force from which the sun draws its power has been loosed against those who brought war to the Far East," the Truman administration announced after Hiroshima exploded. "If [Japan's leaders] do not now accept our terms, they may expect a rain of ruin from the air, the like of which has never been seen." As maimed survivors of the Hiroshima blast and overwhelmed doctors began coping with ghastly injuries and the frightening effects of radiation, five hundred miles away in Tokyo Japan's leaders still debated whether to sue for peace or remain at war. Foreign Minister Shigenori Togo argued that the atom bomb "drastically alters the whole military situation and offers the military ample grounds for ending the war." War Minister Korechika Anami emphatically disagreed. "Such a move is uncalled for. Furthermore, we do not yet know that the bomb was atomic." Some in the military held out against capitulation even after a second atom bomb exploded over Nagasaki (see October 26). In the meantime, the chief of military intelligence, Lieutenant General Seizo Arisue, flew from Tokyo to Hiroshima to assess the damage. "The general had seen many cities laid waste by fire bombings," historian John Toland wrote in *The Rising Sun* (1970). "Usually there was smoldering debris, smoke from emergency kitchens and some signs of human activity—but below him stretched a lifeless desert. No smoke, no fires, nothing. . . . The pilot turned and shouted, 'Sir, this is supposed to be Hiroshima. What should we do?'"

Hiroshima, Japan, after the detonation of the atom bomb. Photograph by S. Sgt. Charles Restifo, U.S. Army Signal Corps, August 1945.

NOVEMBER 26

1940 The Belgian Congo declares war on Italy.

1943 In the Mediterranean, a remote-controlled glider bomb dropped by a Luftwaffe bomber strikes the British ship *Rohna*, which explodes and sinks in less than an hour. More than a thousand U.S. servicemen, and 134 Indian crewmen and British officers are lost.

Under constant air assault, and with few options remaining to them, the Japanese approached the Soviets (with whom they were still at peace, see April 11), hoping to enlist the USSR as an intermediary to negotiate with the Western Allies on terms short of unconditional surrender. The Soviets had other plans. At the Allied conference at Yalta (see May 29), Stalin had agreed that the USSR would enter the war against Japan "two or three months after Germany has surrendered." On August 8, Soviet foreign minister Vyacheslav Molotov read to Naotake Sato, the Japanese ambassador in Moscow, the Soviet Union's declaration of war. The next day, as Red Army troops poured into Manchuria and Korea, the second atom bomb demolished most of Nagasaki. Most Japanese leaders now realized that capitulation was the only remaining option—but some in the military still could not countenance the idea of surrender. Late on August 14, a thousand soldiers attacked the Imperial Palace, attempting a coup d'etat. After loyal troops quelled the revolt, the Japanese people heard their emperor's voice for the first time on the radio, informing them —in a carefully honed address that did not include the word surrender—that Japan had accepted the provisions of the Potsdam Declaration. The Allies proclaimed August 15 Victory in Japan (V-J) Day, but victory would not be official until September 2, when Allied and Japanese leaders assembled on the deck of the battleship USS *Missouri* to sign the instrument of surrender.

LEFT: Maj. Gen. Yatsuji Nagai, Japanese Imperial Army, boards the USS *Missouri* in Tokyo Bay. U.S. Army Signal Corps photo, September 2, 1945.

RIGHT: Spectators and photographers pick vantage spots on the deck of the USS *Missouri* in Tokyo Bay, to witness the formal Japanese surrender. U.S. Army Signal Corps photo, September 2, 1945.

NOVEMBER 27

1941 The Italians surrender Gondar, Ethiopia, to the Allies, bringing to an end the war for control over the Gulf of Aden and the Red Sea.

"**A**s we, eleven in all, climbed onto the veranda deck [of the USS *Missouri*] . . . we gathered into three short rows facing the representatives of the Allied powers across a table covered with green cloth, on which were placed the white documents of surrender. . . . There were also row upon row of American admirals and generals in somber khaki . . . war correspondents who, monkey-like, hung on to every cliff-like point of vantage . . . [and] a gallery of spectators who seemed numberless. . . . Never have I realized that the glance of glaring eyes could hurt so much."

—Japanese diplomat Toshikazu Kase

"**W**e are gathered here, representatives of the major warring powers, to conclude a solemn agreement whereby peace may be restored. . . . It is my earnest hope—indeed the hope of all mankind—that from this solemn occasion a better world shall emerge out of the blood and carnage of the past, a world founded upon faith and understanding, a world dedicated to the dignity of man and the fulfillment of his most cherished wish for freedom, tolerance, and justice."

—General Douglas MacArthur, September 2, 1945

ABOVE: U.S. Navy lieutenant Robert L. Balfour received this certificate after attending the Japanese surrender ceremonies.

RIGHT: Gen. Douglas MacArthur signing the official document of Japanese surrender aboard the USS *Missouri*. Standing behind him are American general Jonathan Wainright and British general Arthur E. Percival, both recently released from Japanese captivity. U.S. Navy photograph by Lt. C. F. Wheeler, September 2, 1945.

NOVEMBER 28

1943 After the most bitter and intense fighting of the Pacific war to date, Tarawa is completely secured. Allied leaders begin a three-day conference in Teheran, Iran.

V-E Day, May 8, sparked celebrations over the length and breadth of the Continent. Across the English Channel, huge, jubilant crowds occupied Trafalgar Square and the Mall and cheered King George VI, Queen Elizabeth, and Winston Churchill when they stepped out on a balcony at Buckingham Palace. In the United States, President Truman issued a proclamation of thanksgiving—but he reminded Americans that "our victory is but half won." V-J Day released another torrent of celebrations around the globe—particularly among Allied troops who were preparing for the invasion of Japan. One of them, U.S. Navy photographer's mate Robert Peters Eustace, nineteen, was aboard a vessel anchored in Buckner Bay, Okinawa, when "some kind of armistice" was announced. "The island lit up," he later reported. "Every gun in that island [shot] in the sky. Killed about seven or eight people that night from falling shrapnel." Combat had ceased on Okinawa less than two months before, and there were those on the island who could not celebrate, remembering the cost and the carnage—among them, U.S. Marine Eugene Sledge and the men of his unit. "We received the news with quiet disbelief," Sledge wrote after the war. "Sitting in stunned silence, we remembered our dead. So many dead. So many maimed. . . . Except for a few widely scattered shouts of joy, the survivors of the abyss sat hollow-eyed and silent, trying to comprehend a world without war."

ABOVE: A GI helmet and rifle mark the grave of a casualty of Sgt Lionel J. Paquette, killed in Burma, 1944.

RIGHT: Celebrating the outbreak of peace, civilians form a conga line in Lafayette Square, across from the White House, V-J Day, August 15, 1945.

NOVEMBER 29

1939 Spain ratifies a pact of friendship with Germany in which it promises the Germans "more than favorable" Spanish neutrality.

UNCONDITIONAL SURRENDERS: 1945

"Today is VE Day in the ETO [European Theater of Operation]—the greatest day of the war so far," U.S. Army nurse Mary Catherine McGarr wrote home from Germany on May 8, 1945. "I guess maybe we are selfish celebrating it because there are a lot of boys in the Pacific who will die tomorrow, and the next day, and the day after that." Less than four months later, all the firing had stopped. Yet for millions of people the war was not truly over. Great swaths of the world were in tatters, and for years medics and nurses of all the combatants continued to help heal and rehabilitate millions of physically and psychologically wounded military veterans and civilians. Not all wounds were apparent: "For the first twenty-odd years after my return, nightmares occurred frequently, waking me either crying or yelling, always sweating, and with a pounding heart," former U.S. Marine Eugene Sledge wrote in his posthumously published book *China Marine* (2002) . As he reentered civilian life in the prosperous and mercifully unscarred United States, he was also shocked by the incomprehension he encountered. "I was totally unprepared for how rapidly most Americans who did not experience combat would forget about the war, the evils we faced, and how incredibly tough it had been for us to defeat the Japanese and the Nazis," he wrote after describing an encounter with a particularly obtuse college registrar. "I felt like some sort of alien, and I realized that this sort of thing would confront me the rest of my days."

ABOVE: Eugene B. Sledge (1923-2001), c. 1945

LEFT: U.S. Army nurses Margaret Mary Eggleson, Karen Rasmussen, Mary Catherine McGarr, and Carolyn C. Cage on duty in the European Theater two months after V-E Day, July 1945.

RIGHT: Uniformed nurses were among the Japanese soldiers on Cebu, in the Philippine Islands, who surrendered to the Americans, in early August 1945.

NOVEMBER 30

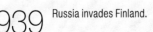

1939 Russia invades Finland.

1941 In Leningrad, USSR, eleven thousand Russians have starved to death this month.

UNCONDITIONAL SURRENDERS: 1945

Aftermath

Peace came gradually, and imperfectly, to the battered world. The ceremonies aboard the USS *Missouri* on September 2 (see November 27, 28) were followed by similar events throughout the Far East. In China, the Japanese surrender on September 9 ended one brutal chapter in the nation's long history—and opened another. The bitter rivalry between Chiang Kai-shek's Nationalists and Mao Tse-tung's Communist forces erupted into intermittent fighting that, despite American attempts to negotiate a settlement, soon exploded into full-scale civil war.

China was not the only site of postwar conflict. The final defeat of the Axis added fire to independence movements in European colonies from Africa and the Middle East to Indonesia and Vietnam. At the same time, a new worldwide ideological conflict was growing. Manifest in the Soviet blockade that led the United States to stage the Berlin Airlift, this "Cold War," as it came to be called, cast a deepening shadow over postwar international diplomacy—even as Allied authorities were examining the dark legacy of Axis aggression. In courtrooms in Europe and the Far East, Allied prosecutors confronted former Axis leaders with overwhelming evidence of atrocities "so calculated, so malignant, and so devastating that civilization cannot tolerate their being ignored," U.S. prosecutor in Europe Robert H. Jackson said, "because it cannot survive their being repeated."

From Norway to North Africa, Coventry to Canton, the

DECEMBER 1

1942   Ethiopia declares war on Germany, Italy, and Japan.

people of war-ravaged nations attempted to recover from the unprecedented devastation the Axis had unleashed on the world. Although the Allies had begun planning for postwar occupation and reconstruction well before victory was assured, by the end of 1946 it was apparent to the Western powers that more creative initiatives were needed to deal with the scope of the destruction, the vast numbers of displaced persons, and the changing world political climate. Thus, in June 1947, the new American secretary of state, George C. Marshall, proposed a cooperative economic program for rebuilding Europe that would prove to be one of the hallmarks of American diplomacy. That same year, Japan's postwar government adopted a new and more democratic constitution, developed under the auspices of General Douglas MacArthur, Supreme Commander of the Allied Powers in Japan.

Through all these events, men and women from all the combatant countries were returning home from military service abroad. Some were confined to hospitals, where they began long periods of physical and mental rehabilitation. Others were cheered and showered with ticker tape as they paraded through city streets before rejoining civilian life. In

the United States in 1947, more somber homecomings began. That October, the transport vessel *Honda Knot* arrived in San Francisco, while the Liberty ship *Joseph V. Connolly* docked in New York. Within the holds of those two vessels were 9,260 coffins containing the remains of Americans killed in the war—the first of 233,181 bodies that would eventually be brought home for burial. In New York, which had been the scene of wild ticker-tape celebrations two years before, more than four hundred thousand silent people, many of them weeping, lined the streets as one representative coffin was conveyed to Central Park for solemn ceremonies dedicated to all Americans who had made the ultimate sacrifice in the most terrible war the world has yet known.

The Repair Man? Drawing by Edwin Marcus (1885–1961), 1945 or 1946.

"**G**eneral Wainwright is a right guy and we are willing to go on for him," Brooklyn-born soldier Irving Strobing signaled before Corregidor fell in 1942 (see May 7, June 11, October 1). "But shells were dropping all night, faster than hell. Damage terrific. Too much for guys to take." Plunged with his troops into a brutal captivity after he was forced to surrender, Wainwright thinned to the point of emaciation during more than three years as a prisoner of war, as he and his fellow captives suffered from starvation rations, beatings, and myriad humiliations—while being almost completely cut off from news of home and the war. Liberated from a camp in Mukden, China, by U.S. Office of Strategic Services agents and Soviet troops, Wainwright reentered a changed world—and discovered that his gallantry in defeat and his conduct in captivity had made him a hero to his countrymen. After witnessing the formal Japanese capitulation in Tokyo and the surrender of Japan's Philippine garrison in Manila, the ill but unbowed officer returned to the United States and was greeted by huge crowds in San Francisco and Washington, D.C. (where Truman awarded him the Medal of Honor). In New York City, more than four million people lined the twenty-two-mile course of a massive ticker-tape parade. "Along the entire parade route, eyes glistened and throats were stilled at the sight of the gaunt, wrinkled soldier," one *Newsweek* reporter wrote. "Plainly, New Yorkers felt the impact of one American's sacrifice."

Left: General Jonathan Wainwright (1883–1953) arrives in the United States after more than three years as a prisoner of the Japanese, September 1945.

Right: In New York City, a ticker-tape parade welcomes Gen. Jonathan Wainwright home, September 1945.

DECEMBER 2

1941 The code message to proceed with the attack on Pearl Harbor, "Climb Mount Niitaka," is flashed to the Japanese task force.

1942 Scientists achieve the first nuclear chain reaction on the campus of the University of Chicago.

General Jonathan Wainwright (see December 2) returned to a vigorous United States, now the leading Allied nation. Its prosperity stood in stark contrast with the conditions in much of Europe and Asia, where ruin was rife, tens of millions were homeless, and millions were starving (see October 27). Coming to grips with such massive problems required stability—but the politics of peace were becoming ever more complicated. At the Potsdam Conference (see November 24), the United States, Britain, and the Soviet Union had established a Council of Foreign Ministers, which was to draw up treaties of peace with Italy, Romania, Bulgaria, Hungary, and Finland. (Treaties with Germany and Japan would have to wait until those shattered nations had acceptable governments in place.) By the summer of 1946, draft treaties were ready for review by delegates from twenty-one nations, who deliberated in Paris from July 29 to October 18—without settling on final terms. "Much has been said about acrimonious debates and the divisions in the Paris Conference," U.S. secretary of state James F. Byrnes stated in his post conference report. "Back of those debates and divisions were real and deep differences in interests, in ideas, in experience, and even in prejudices." Further discussions did yield treaties that were signed the following February. But one major problem evident at Paris continued to fester—"the continuing, if not increasing tension" as Byrnes reported, "between us and the Soviet Union."

Georges Bidault (right, back to camera), president and foreign minister of France, welcomes delegates to the peace conference in the Luxembourg Palace, Paris, July 29, 1946.

DECEMBER 3

1941 Yugoslav Partisans initiate organized attacks on German units. In minus 38-degree temperatures, German units begin pulling back from Moscow.

While the Soviet Union began to draw what Winston Churchill dubbed, in a March 1946 speech, an "iron curtain" between territories under its control and the Western democracies, the USSR was also facing what it regarded as an interior problem: Ukrainian, Estonian, Latvian, and Lithuanian guerrillas persisted in fighting against Soviet dominion over their homelands. On the other side of the "curtain," too, nationalist and anticolonial movements gained force all over the world—putting to the test one of the principles of the Allies' 1941 Atlantic Charter (see May 1, 2): "the right of all peoples to choose the form of government under which they will live." As soon as the larger war ended, the French battled nationalists in their overseas holdings, including Algeria and Vietnam, while the British faced strengthened independence movements throughout its empire. In the Dutch East Indies (now Indonesia), the Japanese occupation had cost many Indonesians their lives, yet it also encouraged the independence movement that the Dutch had long been attempting to disrupt. The movement's most prominent leader, Sukarno, thus cooperated with the Japanese—especially after Japan's assurance, in September 1944, that his country would become independent. Two days after Japan's surrender, Sukarno proclaimed the independent nation of Indonesia—sparking a five-year struggle during which nationalist forces battled both British and Dutch troops. The Republic of Indonesia finally became a reality in May 1950.

LEFT: Sukarno (1901–1970), 1945.

RIGHT: American political cartoonist Bill Mauldin (1921–2003) created this visual representation of the cycle of colonialism in Indonesia (the Allies rescuing the country from the Axis, the Netherlands trying to reassert control) in December 1948.

DECEMBER 4

1942   U.S. B-24s attack Naples harbor, the first U.S. air attack on Italy.

1943   The Yugoslav Partisans announce a provisional Yugoslavian government under Tito.

AFTERMATH

The first contingents of Allied troops did not reach Indonesia until late September 1945 (see December 4). Although they immediately found themselves grappling with nationalist groups, their principal objectives were to disarm the Japanese garrison there—and to liberate interned European civilians. All over the globe, as Allied forces liberated surviving prisoners of the Axis, they also took into custody vast numbers of surrendered Axis troops—temporarily increasing by millions the number of prisoners of war for which they were responsible. Axis soldiers taken into custody by the Red Army (including an estimated 600,000 to 850,000 Japanese) were confined in the system of Soviet camps until the mid-1950s. Many perished; others were put to work rebuilding the devastated USSR. In war-torn western Europe, the Allies had to cope with more than seven million surrendered soldiers, as well as millions upon millions of homeless and hungry civilians— a much greater problem than the Western Allies had anticipated. Providing adequate food and housing became agonizing logistical problems, especially in the first months, when much of the existing transport (in countries where transportation systems had been prime bombing targets) was occupied redeploying U.S. troops to the Pacific. "As I see it, conditions are going to be extremely difficult in Germany this winter," Eisenhower's deputy, General Lucius D. Clay, wrote in June 1945. "There will be much cold and hunger."

Some of the more than three hundred thousand Wehrmacht prisoners taken after the collapse of German resistance in the Saar and Palatinate areas of Germany. The largest mass surrender of German troops during the war, it constituted only a small portion of the Axis POWs with which the Allies had to cope. U.S. Army Signal Corps photograph, 1945.

DECEMBER 5

1941 U.S. naval facilities in Tokyo, Bangkok, Peking, Tientsin, Shanghai, Guam, and Wake Island are ordered to destroy all but absolutely essential communication codes and secret documents.

1943 Japanese planes attack Calcutta, India.

In country after war-ravaged country, peace brought an end to combat—and a new struggle to survive and restore smashed cities and towns, wrecked transportation systems, and ruined industries and farms. In Europe, where coal production had plummeted, people were desperate for warmth as the bitterly cold winter of 1945–46 descended. "We used to go through the ruins of the buildings to look for wood and anything we could burn," Inge John, a nineteen-year-old Berliner in 1945 remembered after the war. "People went to the parks and took the wood from the trees. After a while, there were no trees left." Anticipating the type of postwar problems many countries would face, in November 1943 forty-four Allied nations created the United Nations Relief and Rehabilitation Administration (UNRRA) "to plan, coordinate, administer or arrange for the administration of measures for the relief of victims of war." Two years later, a report by U.S. presidential adviser Samuel I. Rosenman gave UNRRA and the U.S. government an idea of the unprecedented scope of the postwar problems they were facing. Dispatched to Britain and liberated Europe by Roosevelt in January 1945, Rosenman submitted his report to Truman late that April. His detailed assessment of needs contained a cautionary political note: "The needs of the liberated countries . . . are grave not only from a humanitarian point of view, but also because . . . to a great extent the future permanent peace of Europe depends upon the restoration of the economy of these liberated countries."

LEFT: Two Germans search for food and fuel in the rubble of Berlin. Photograph by Emil Reynolds, 1945.

RIGHT: *Liberated but not free from want*. Color lithograph poster sponsored by the U.S. National War Fund, 1945.

For most people involved in the day-to-day struggles of postwar reconstruction, humanitarian considerations trumped political concerns as they tried to meet the nearly overwhelming needs of the war-weary peoples of Europe and Asia. Until V-J Day, the UNRRA (see December 6) lacked adequate personnel and shipping to organize many relief services; but by the end of 1945, it was sending supplies to both Europe and the Far East. "The face of UNRRA in the displaced persons camps of Upper Bavaria was a smiling 36-year-old Bronx Negro, Ernest C. Grigg, veteran of city and federal social-service agencies," *Time* magazine reported on December 31, 1945. "He had won the confidence of these strange latter-day slaves. . . . Grigg and his aides were slowly preparing them for a return to the world." Farther south, as the *Time* story noted, "Two Americans, Buell Maben and Spurgeon M. Keeny, represented UNRRA to the Greeks and the Italians." As tractors, mules, plows, and grain were being unloaded in Mediterranean ports, a special American ambassador visited Italian hospitals and orphanages. In November 1946, author and activist Helen Keller—whose personal story of triumph over disabilities had long been an inspiration to people around the world—visited children at an institution in Rome where they were recovering from grievous war wounds.

Escorted by a nun, American Helen Keller (1880–1968), herself blind and deaf from the age of nineteen months, visits a home for children maimed by the war, Rome, Italy, November 18, 1946.

DECEMBER 7

1941 Japanese forces attack Pearl Harbor and other U.S. and British territories in the Pacific, launching the war in the Pacific. Costa Rica declares war on Japan.

As United Nations relief efforts gathered force after V-J Day (see December 6, 7), Allied governments expended every effort to bring home, as quickly as possible, their troops who had been Axis prisoners of war. In the Far East, nearly 27 percent of all British, Commonwealth, and American POWs held by the Japanese had died while in captivity. Many who survived were in very bad shape. In late September 1945, the aircraft carrier USS *Enterprise*—only recently repaired after suffering a severe battering at the hands of kamikazes off Okinawa—was dispatched to Hawaii to pick up 1,149 sick and injured Americans who had just been released from POW camps in Japan. Photographs of these men in their impromptu hospital ward on the carrier's large hanger deck were widely circulated in the press to assure the American public that their long-imprisoned "boys" were on the way home. "Home" was a magical word to all released prisoners. A few months earlier, in Europe, GIs had liberated a POW camp crowded with twenty thousand troops from many Allied nations, torn down the German flag, and raised the Stars and Stripes. "Man, you never heard such a roar in all your life," liberated U.S. Army Air Forces colonel Clyde W. Bradley later remembered. "People who [weren't] Americans, they cheered and laughed and clapping [*sic*] and dancing and jumping up and down. . . . It was a tremendous feeling. You knew you were free. And you knew you were going to go home. The best thing, you knew you were going to go home."

Liberated American prisoners of war fill the hanger deck of the aircraft carrier USS *Enterprise*, which is carrying them back to the United States. Photograph by Photographer's Mate First Class William Thomas Barr, September 24, 1945.

DECEMBER 8

1941 The United States, Britain, and eleven other nations declare war on Japan. Japanese forces land in Malaya and Thailand. The Germans murder eighteen thousand Jews in Riga, Latvia.

For troops with horrific injuries, the eagerness to return home was often tinged with apprehension. How would people greet them? How would they get on with their lives? In 1944, twenty-two-year-old Mimi Korach Lesser accepted an invitation to become a sketch artist with the United Service Organizations (USO), beginning a tour of duty during which she visited hospitals and drew portraits of wounded GIs in the United States and Europe. "These men had been returned from the front with very serious injuries," she wrote in a postwar memoir. "Many would never leave the wards. Many were double amputees. But the support they gave each other was remarkable and the atmosphere was upbeat." The atmosphere was less upbeat at one hospital she visited that specialized in plastic surgery rehabilitation of facial and body wounds. "I was very nervous as I entered my first ward. The veterans were disbelieving that an artist would want to draw them. So it took great daring for a G.I., with half his face disfigured, to approach me with bravado and ask what I was going to do about him. Posing him with his good side facing me I was able to sketch what his face would look like after rehabilitation was complete. Talk about success—this opened up a stream of eager, brave, sad men. . . . Now they could have pictures sent to their loved ones that were positive." The time she spent in that hospital, she added, "was probably the best work I ever did."

ABOVE: Mimi Korach Lesser (b. 1922).

LEFT: This casualty was brought to a U.S. Army general hospital, where doctors were able to repair the wound, leaving minimal scars. Illustrations from *Medical Department, United States Army: Surgery in World War II*, 1964.

RIGHT: Sketch of PFC Oakley Gifford by USO artist Mimi Korach (Lesser), May 15, 1945.

DECEMBER 9

1940   The British launch their first offensive in North Africa, surprising and cutting off a much larger Italian force.

1944   Serbia and Macedonia are cleared of all German troops.

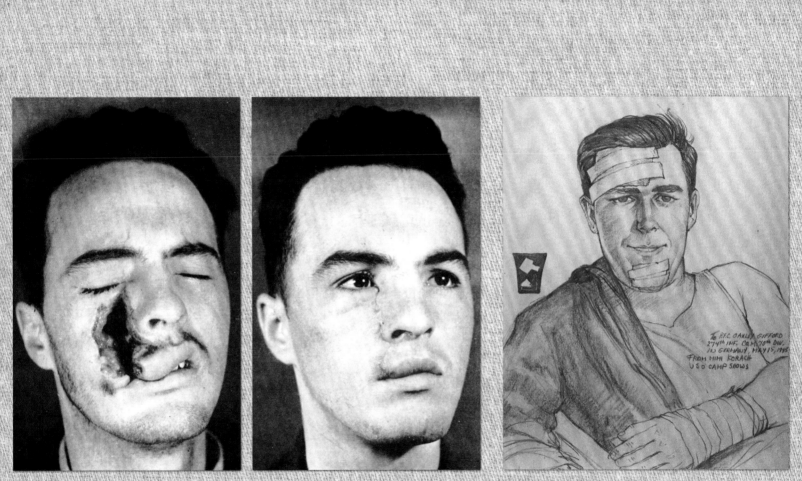

To P.F.C. OAKLEY GIFFORD
274th INF. CO. 70th DIV.
IN GERMANY, MAY 15, 1945
FROM MIMI KORACH
U S O CAMP SHOWS

Save for the Purple Heart, there were no U.S. medals to honor those struggling—sometimes for the rest of their lives—to cope with the effects of grievous physical or psychological war wounds (see December 9). Among all World War II combatants, many medals did exist to honor other forms of heroism, including several—such as the Medal of the French Resistance and Britain's George Cross (awarded to the entire Axis-besieged island of Malta)—that were created during the war. More than four hundred U.S. servicemen received the highest American military decoration, the Medal of Honor, for actions that were above and beyond the call of duty. In the Pacific Theater, Staff Sergeant Ysmael R. Villegas charged a succession of enemy positions during the 1944–45 Philippine Islands campaign. "Through his heroism and indomitable fighting spirit," his citation reads, "S/Sgt Villegas, at the cost of his life, inspired his men to a determined attack in which they swept the enemy from the field." In Europe, twenty-year-old Second Lieutenant Audie Murphy, when faced with advancing German tanks and artillery, sent his men to a safer location before calling Allied artillery fire on his own position. Standing his ground, he continued firing on the enemy until the barrage turned them back. The most decorated American soldier of the war, Murphy received his Medal of Honor six months after that act of exceptional bravery. Some valiant soldiers were not recognized with medals until decades after the war (see December 11, 13).

LEFT: The Medal of Honor (shown here with a neck band) was established as the highest U.S. military honor in 1863, during the American Civil War. Photograph by the Office of War Information, c. 1942.

RIGHT: France's Gen. Jean-Marie de Lattre de Tassigny congratulates U.S. Army Lt. Audie Murphy (1924–71), the most decorated soldier in the U.S. Army, after Murphy is awarded two French medals, July 16, 1948.

DECEMBER 10

1941 Japanese aircraft based in Saigon sink the British battleship *Prince of Wales* and the battle cruiser *Repulse* off Malaya. Guam surrenders to the Japanese.

On April 5, 1945, Private First Class Sadao Munemori of the all-Japanese-American 442nd Regimental Combat Team (see July 5) braved murderous fire to knock out two German machine guns in the mountains near Seravezza, Italy. As he turned to take shelter in a bomb crater, a grenade fell near two of his comrades. Munemori threw himself on the grenade and smothered its blast with his body. He was posthumously awarded the Medal of Honor. For more than fifty years, he was the only Japanese-American World War II serviceman to be accorded that honor. Like many other Japanese Americans in the armed forces during the war, Munemori served his country while his family was confined to an internment camp (see June 12). Nine of the ten camps established in 1942 were still open when a delegation from the 442nd visited the White House on September 11, 1945, to present President Truman with a contribution of $4,300 toward a memorial to Franklin D. Roosevelt. The last camp finally closed in March 1946—but the bitter effects of internment lingered. "Scars, even wounds from exclusion and detention still remain," the Commission on War-time Relocation and Internment of Civilians noted in 1983. Its two-volume report on the aftermath of internment led to passage of the Civil Liberties Act of 1988, in which Congress apologized on behalf of the nation. Twelve years later, President Bill Clinton awarded the Medal of Honor to twenty additional Japanese-American World War II veterans.

Tech. Sgt. Yeiichi Kelly Kuwayama and other members of the 442nd Regimental Combat Team, U.S. Army, present President Truman with a check for the team's contribution toward a Roosevelt memorial. From left: Earl Finch of the War Relocation Authority (WRA), Pvt. George M. Tsujimoto, Pvt. Terumi Kato, President Truman, Sgt. Kuwayama, Secretary of the Interior Harold L. Ickes, Pvt. Jesse Hirata, and Dillon Myer of the WRA. September 11, 1945.

DECEMBER 11

1941 U.S. Marines push back a Japanese force attempting to take Wake Island. Germany and Italy declare war on the United States.

1942 U.S. forces begin arriving in Iran and Iraq.

As internment camps for Japanese Americans were closing in late fall of 1945 (see June 12, December 11), many American soldiers on overseas duty were pressing to be released from military service and brought home. In September 1944, the War Department had announced a point system to facilitate an orderly demobilization. Servicemen received points for factors such as years in service, overseas duty, wounds, and citations; when they reached a specified total, they were eligible for release. Muddled by political complications, troop requirements for postwar occupation, logistical problems, and bureaucratic snafus, the system did not work smoothly (or, in the estimation of many GIs, equitably). Though some troops were brought home quickly, many others were not. Delays fed resentment, and resentment boiled over into the army "mutiny" of 1946. In Manila, Philippine Islands, on January 6, some twenty thousand soldiers marched on their command headquarters, confronted General William D. Styer—then interrupted his explanation of demobilization delays with catcalls and boos. Reports of this mass act of insubordination went out on the news wires, and soon GIs were demonstrating from Guam to Frankfort-am-Main. Soldiers also placed impassioned ads in newspapers and wrote to their congressmen. One sergeant stationed in Japan cabled Harry Truman (a denizen of Independence, Missouri, temporarily residing in the White House): "Give us our independence or go back to yours."

Twenty thousand homesick GIs gather in the square opposite city hall in Manila, Philippine Islands, to protest the U.S. Army's demobilization system. Photograph by Dave Davis, January 1946.

DECEMBER 12

1943 Erwin Rommel is appointed commander of German forces deployed along the coast of France for defense against an anticipated Allied invasion.

1944 A V-2 rocket hits a movie theater in Antwerp, killing 492 people and wounding about 500.

Some American troops with enough points for demobilization (see December 12) endured special hardships. In December 1945, naval authorities in Le Havre, France, barred 123 African American soldiers from boarding USS *Croatan* "because there was no means of segregating them" on that vessel. When those 123 men and other black veterans did succeed in demobilizing, they were plunged back into the continuing home-front battle for equality. The struggle was particularly vicious in the South, where the Ku Klux Klan was enjoying a postwar resurgence and violence against black Southerners was on the rise: In Georgia, black veteran Maci Snipes was dragged from his home and murdered after he dared to exercise his right to vote in a primary election. The struggle even cast its shadow over the Servicemen's Readjustment Act ("GI Bill," 1944). The bill included educational benefits that made college possible for millions of veterans who would otherwise have had little chance to acquire a higher education—thus sparking a revolution in American education. Both white and black veterans did participate in this revolution. But many blacks who applied for GI education benefits in the South confronted discriminatory implementation procedures established by their state governments. They were also restricted to historically black colleges that were unprepared to cope with the huge upsurge in applicants. In 1946–47, these schools were forced to turn away an estimated twenty thousand African American veterans.

LEFT: *The Return of the Soldier.* Pen and ink drawing by Charles White (1918–79), 1946.

RIGHT: Cover of *Shall I Go Back to School,* a U.S. War Department booklet, 1945.

DECEMBER 13

1939 A three-day running battle begins between three British cruisers and the German warship/raider *Graf Spee*. Trapped off the coast of Uruguay, the German vessel is scuttled by its captain— who later commits suicide.

AFTERMATH

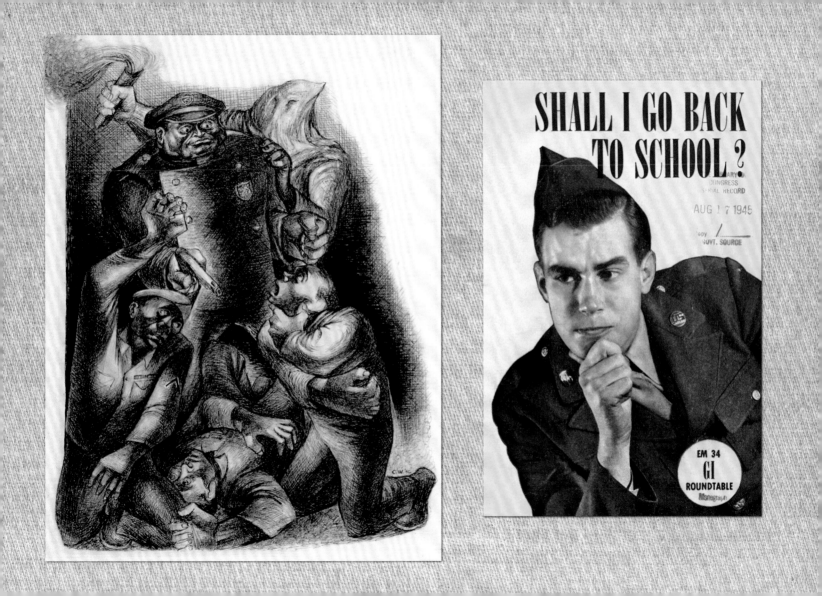

SHALL I GO BACK
TO SCHOOL?

AUG 17 1945

EM 34
GI
ROUNDTABLE

"**D**ear Folks: We will start [back to the States] sometime this month or next, if all goes as is scheduled," Sergeant Donald L. Spencer of the U.S. Army Air Forces, then stationed in France, wrote to his family in October 1945. "Boy, I can hardly wait to get back to the good old U.S.A." He arrived at New York Harbor aboard a crowded vessel on November 11. "As we passed the Statue of Liberty the decks were loaded with troops standing shoulder to shoulder cheering," Spencer later remembered. And, because it was Armistice (now Veterans) Day, New York gave them a very special greeting. "[T]wo motorized flat decked barges pulled alongside our ship. The port side barge had a 'Big Band' and singers on it. The starboard side barge had the New York City Rockette dancers on it doing their famous line kicks." Despite delays and snafus that sparked storms of protest from GIs and their families (see December 12), America was releasing its troops from service— at a rate that was causing considerable worry to the nation's top military commanders. Having emerged from the war the strongest Allied power, the United States faced heavy responsibilities for maintaining order in war-devastated lands and securing a lasting peace. But threats to that peace were growing, and top U.S. commanders feared that the rapid reduction in American military might would leave the nation without the forces required to meet those looming challenges.

Troops of the U.S. Twentieth Armored Division and units of the Ninth Army arrive in New York harbor aboard the SS *John Ericsson*, 1945.

DECEMBER 14

1939 The League of Nations expels Russia for violation of the League Covenant and various treaties in pursuing its war with Finland.

1944 Polish and British forces launch a new offensive in Italy.

"Smoke was still curling from the blasted ruins of Germany when the first teams began probing the desolation in search of [a] new kind of debris of modern war, the displaced ones," Kathryn Hulme wrote in 1953. Dispatched to Europe by UNRAA (see December 6, 7), Hulme lived and worked with Displaced Persons (DPs) for nearly five years. There were millions upon millions of these unwilling nomads and camp dwellers across the Continent: people whose homes had been destroyed during years of bombing, Eastern Europeans who had fled from Soviet domination, Germans evicted from lands on which Hitler had settled them after Nazi conquests, prisoners released from POW and concentration camps. Food, jobs, and privacy were scarce in DP camps. Despair was plentiful—especially for one group that had suffered losses unlike any other. Some three million European Jews had survived the Holocaust, emerging from the war bereft of families, homes, and all their possessions. Many placed their hopes for the future on the movement to establish a Jewish homeland in Palestine, where Jews and Arabs had been contentiously coexisting under British rule for years (see January 28). A well-organized underground movement helped thousands reach Palestine illegally; many others were caught and turned back. The new state of Israel was established on May 14, 1948. The next day, the first of many Arab-Israeli conflicts began.

ABOVE: *Zionist Organization jubilee; the Jews who will it, will have their state*. Color lithograph poster published in Tel Aviv, 1947.

RIGHT: Jewish refugees arrive at Poppendorf Camp near Luebeck, Germany, on September 8, 1947. They had just been removed from one of three British transports that returned 4,554 refugees who had reached Palestine aboard the *Exodus 1947*—only to be immediately forced to leave.

DECEMBER 15

1944 Under attack from kamikazes, U.S. Army troops land at Mindoro in the Philippines.
Russian troops cross into Czechoslovakia.

On the same day that General Eisenhower came face-to-face with the Holocaust at the Ohrdruf concentration camp near Gotha, Germany (see November 19), he also toured a salt mine, where GIs had made an astounding discovery. "In one of the tunnels was an enormous number of paintings and other pieces of art," Eisenhower wrote in his postwar book, *Crusade in Europe*. "In another tunnel we saw a hoard of gold, tentatively estimated by our experts to be worth about $250,000,000, most of it in gold bars. . . . Crammed into suitcases and trunks and other containers was a great amount of gold and silver plate and ornament obviously looted from private dwellings throughout Europe." The Americans had found evidence of systematic German looting that remains unique in the annals of warfare. German Jews were the first victims of this methodical thievery, but after the war began, Nazi avarice extended throughout all the occupied territories. In addition to taking every possession of value from Jewish people they deported to slave labor and extermination camps (including gold dental fillings), the Nazis stole precious items from churches, libraries, universities, museums, galleries, and private homes. Paintings, sculptures, objets d'art, jewels, books, tapestries, and more were instantly transformed into German assets. This unprecedented program of plunder constituted one of the lesser offenses for which Nazi leaders were called to answer during the war crimes trials at Nuremberg (see December 17).

An American soldier examines some of the treasures recovered from a cave in which passionate art "collector" Hermann Göring had stashed looted treasures, May 29, 1945.

DECEMBER 16

1944   The Battle of the Bulge begins as German forces launch a massive attack on the U.S. First and Ninth Armies along a forty-mile front in the Ardennes Forest in Belgium.

In London, on August 8, 1945, representatives of the governments of the United States, Britain, the French Republic, and the Soviet Union signed an agreement establishing "an International Military Tribunal for the trial of war criminals whose offenses have no particular geographical location." That November, twenty-two major Nazi figures—including Hermann Göring, Joachim von Ribbentrop, Alfred Jodl, Fritz Sauckel, Erich Raeder, and Karl Dönitz—faced judges and prosecutors from the four Allied powers in a courtroom in Nuremberg, Germany. The defendants all had legal representation. "That four great nations, flushed with victory and stung with injury, stay the hand of vengeance and voluntarily submit their captive enemies to the judgment of the law, is one of the most significant tributes that Power ever has paid to Reason," chief U.S. prosecutor Robert H. Jackson said in his opening statement. "[T]he forces which these defendants represent . . . are the darkest and most sinister forces in society—dictatorship and oppression, malevolence and passion, militarism and lawlessness. By their fruits we best know them. Their acts have bathed the world in blood." Eleven months later, eighteen of the twenty-two were convicted of one or more of four charges: conspiracy to wage aggressive war, crimes against peace, war crimes, and crimes against humanity. Of the eleven who were sentenced to death, only Göring evaded execution. He committed suicide two hours before he was to be taken to the gallows.

ABOVE: Justice Robert H. Jackson (1892–1954).

RIGHT: The International Military Tribunal convenes in a courtroom in Nuremberg, Germany. The defendants sit at the left, guarded by military police, 1946.

DECEMBER 17

1941 Adm. Chester W. Nimitz is named commander of the U.S. Pacific Fleet.

1944 On the second day of the Battle of the Bulge, German Waffen SS troops murder eighty unarmed American soldiers that they have taken prisoner in what will become known as the "Malmédy Massacre."

As the trial of twenty-two Nazis entered its sixth month in Nuremberg (see December 17), the Allied International Military Tribunal for the Far East commenced its first major trial in Tokyo on May 3, 1946. Like those at Nuremberg, the Far East proceedings focused on selected Japanese leaders. (Emperor Hirohito and other notable officials on whom Allied authorities were relying to ensure the smooth occupation of Japan were not charged.) Twenty-eight men listed as "Class A" defendants were indicted on fifty-five counts of "crimes against peace, conventional war crimes, and crimes against humanity." Each represented by counsel, they appeared before an eleven-member court headed by an Australian, Sir William Webb. American Joseph B. Keenan was the chief prosecutor. The trial concluded on April 16, 1948, and in the verdicts given that November, all the defendants were found guilty. Seven, including former prime minister and minister of war Hideki Tojo, were sentenced to death and executed by hanging on December 23. All but two of the remaining eighteen defendants were sentenced to life imprisonment. (Those still alive in 1958 were released.) The two-year trial that led to these convictions was the most prominent of more than two thousand similar proceedings held in the Far East under the auspices of American, Australian, British, Canadian, Chinese, Dutch, French, and Filipino military courts. In total, some three thousand people were convicted of war crimes; 920 were executed.

In Tokyo, eight of twenty-eight accused Japanese war criminals facing the International Military Tribunal in the Far East make an appearance in court, under guard. Front row (left to right): Hideki Tojo, Takasumi Oka, Yoshijiro Umezu, Sadao Araki, and Akira Muto. Second row: Baron Kiichiro Hiranuma, Shigenori Togo, and Mamoru Shigemitsu, May 1946.

DECEMBER 18

1944   Planes of the U.S. Fourteenth Air Force—including B-29 Superfortresses—attack Hangkow, China, a major Japanese supply base.

In Europe, as in the Far East, there were many war crimes trials. From Belgium to Yugoslavia, tens of thousands of people accused of collaborating with the Nazis were hunted down and brought before the bar. The French tried Vichy leaders Marshal Pétain and Pierre Laval. The Norwegians speedily convicted and executed Vidkun Quisling. In Italy, U.S. authorities arrested the seminal poet Ezra Pound, who had lived in the country for years. A devotee of Mussolini and Fascism, Pound broadcast virulently anti-Semitic, anti-Roosevelt screeds on Radio Rome from January 1941 through July 1943. Transported to the United States on November 18, 1945, he was examined by lawyers and psychiatrists, judged to be insane, and committed to St. Elizabeth's Hospital in Washington, D.C.—beginning a controversial thirteen-year confinement. Controversy also surrounded the 1949 trial and conviction for treason of Japanese-American Iva Toguri (d'Aquino). Stranded in Japan when the war started, she was one of several women who broadcast as "Tokyo Rose" on the *Zero Hour* radio program. They aired blatant propaganda—but it was propaganda that most GIs did not mind. "We looked forward to hearing from [Tokyo Rose] because she had up-to-date music," former U.S. Marine John Flack remembered in 2002. "People say [Toguri] should be executed because it endangered our morale. It never bothered us a bit." Released from prison in 1956 after serving six years of a ten-year sentence, Toguri was pardoned by President Gerald Ford in 1977.

LEFT: Ezra Pound (1885–1972), 1943.

RIGHT: Iva Toguri (1916–2006). Photograph by S. Sgt. Charles Rosario Restifo, U.S. Army Signal Corps, 1945.

DECEMBER 19

1941 Hitler assumes personal command of the German Eastern Front army.

1944 The fourth day of the Battle of the Bulge. As the U.S. 101st Airborne Division arrives at Bastogne, Luxembourg, the village is surrounded by German forces.

On March 12, 1947—with much of the war-torn world in continuing economic and political turmoil and Western relations with the Soviet Union on a sharpening decline—President Truman spoke before a joint session of Congress. After requesting emergency financial and technical aid for Greece, where Communist-backed and non-Communist factions were engaged in a bitter civil war, the president stated what came to be known as the Truman Doctrine: "I believe that it must be the policy of the United States to support free peoples who are resisting attempted subjugation by armed minorities or by outside pressures. . . . The seeds of totalitarian regimes . . . reach their full growth when the hope of a people for a better life has died. We must keep that hope alive." Three months later, Truman's new secretary of state, George C. Marshall, proposed a sweeping economic recovery program in which the United States would cooperate with all the willing countries of Europe. "Our policy is directed not against any country or doctrine," Marshall said, "but against hunger, poverty, desperation, and chaos." Nevertheless, only sixteen of twenty-two invited countries attended a July Conference on Economic Cooperation in Paris; the Soviet Union and countries under its sway declined. At home, support for Marshall's plan was by no means universal—but objections faded after the Soviets backed a successful Communist coup in Czechoslovakia in February 1948. Congress passed the Foreign Assistance Act on April 2 (see December 21).

LEFT: *Fred uden frygt* ("Peace without fear"). Color poster, published in Denmark, c. 1950.

RIGHT: Secretary of State George C. Marshall (1880–1959), U.S. State Department photograph, 1947.

DECEMBER 20

1941 Japanese troops land at Davao, Mindanao, in the Philippines. Claire Chennault's squadron of Flying Tigers enters combat for the first time, over Kunming, China.

FRED UDEN FRYGT

MARSHALLPLANEN
3År
HAR SKABT GRUNDLAGET FOR
SIKKERHED OG SAMARBEJDE

"**F**ew presidents have had the opportunity to sign legislation of such importance," Truman said April 3, 1948, as he signed the Foreign Assistance Act (see December 20). The legislation effectively launched the European Recovery Plan, popularly known as the Marshall Plan after its chief architect. "The American proposal for assistance to Europe is directed toward production, construction, and recovery," Marshall stated in November 1947. "It is a genuinely cooperative undertaking, which is being worked out in an atmosphere of mutual trust and with careful regard for the sovereignty of nations." From 1948 to 1952, the United States provided $13 billion for new housing projects, industrial revitalization, and massive amounts of machinery and supplies. The results were astonishing: By 1950, Europe was nearing or at its prewar levels in agricultural production and trade, and industrial output surpassed prewar levels. Substantial economic progress was crucial for European stability, but the tone of the program was almost as important—particularly to near-ruined Germany, divided into Communist and democratic blocks and warily regarded by its European neighbors. "I have always stressed the fact that it was not the 'money' but rather the spirit in which the aid was given that inspired Germans to make their effort," former German chancellor Ludwig Erhard said in 1972. "This spirit gave us hope that we would not be written off but treated as equal partners in the family of civilized nations."

LEFT: *Reconstruire l'europe* ("To rebuild Europe"). Color poster by Alban Wyss, c. 1948.

RIGHT: In the French sector of Berlin, German workers cover a Nazi anti aircraft bunker with earth, the first step toward turning this piece of land into a garden. Photograph by Dieter Giesecke , March 1951.

DECEMBER 21

1941 Japanese forces land 135 miles north of Manila.

1944 The U.S. Sixth Army secures the Ormoc Valley on Leyte, Philippines.

reconstruire l'europe

In 1948, as Americans launched the Marshall Plan in Europe (see December 20, 21), they were developing a separate economic stimulus program to help rebuild the shattered Japanese economy. Before the war, Japan had been the Far East's most highly industrialized nation; by September 1945 its manufacturing and transportation infrastructure was largely in ruins, millions of returning war veterans were jobless, food was scarce, and a quarter of the nation's housing had been destroyed. Such conditions favored instability (a fact that the Soviets tried to exploit when, in 1949, they repatriated thousands of Japanese POWs who had succumbed to years of indoctrination and adopted revolutionary ideology). Other factors strongly favored stability. Important among these was the mutual respect that developed between the Supreme Commander of the Allied Powers in Japan, General Douglas MacArthur, and Emperor Hirohito. On September 28, 1945, the emperor shocked his own people, and surprised the Americans, by breaking with strict imperial tradition and leaving the palace to call on the general. "I come to you," the emperor said, "to offer myself for the judgment of the powers you represent as the one to bear sole responsibility for every political and military decision made and action taken by my people in the conduct of [the] war." Deeply moved, MacArthur later wrote: "[Hirohito] was an Emperor by inherent birth, but in that instant I knew I faced the First Gentleman of Japan in his own right."

LEFT: A crowd gathers outside the Mitsukoshi department store in Tokyo to read a Communist Party election poster, April 16, 1946.

RIGHT: Emperor Hirohito of Japan with Gen. Douglas MacArthur at the general's home in the U.S. embassy in Tokyo. U.S. Army Signal Corps photograph, 1945.

DECEMBER 22

1944 At Bastogne, Brig. Gen. Anthony C. McAuliffe of the 101st Airborne is given a German ultimatum to surrender or face "annihilation." His refusal is eloquent, yet succinct: "Nuts."

Helping the Japanese restore their country's economy was one major priority for the Allies. Others were to eradicate Japanese militarism and promote democracy. Soon after his meeting with Emperor Hirohito (see December 22), MacArthur gave Prime Minister Kijuro Shidehara a list of reforms he wished to see made "as soon as they can be assimilated." Of fundamental importance was a radical revision of Japan's constitution. After a Japanese redraft proved unsatisfactory, MacArthur assigned the task to a group selected from occupation headquarters staff. The resulting constitution—promulgated by Hirohito in November 1946 and effective the following spring—included provisions that guaranteed popular liberties and established "essential equality" of the sexes. Article IX declared that "the Japanese people forever renounce war as a sovereign right of the nation. . . . Land, sea, and air forces, as well as other war potential will never be maintained." Many Americans soon questioned the wisdom of that provision. Communism was rapidly gaining ground in the Far East, and a democratic—and strong—Japan would be a welcome ally. Within six years, with Communist governments in power in North Korea and China (see December 24), Japan established Self-Defense Forces—with strict controls. Absorption of democratic tenets would take longer. "The spirit of a people cannot be changed overnight," Nobufumi Ito wrote in *New Japan* (1951). "Much will depend upon the encouragement given to us by the elder democracies."

LEFT: *The Yasukuni Jinja*, reproduction of a painting by Tadao Yoshimura, published in *Seisen Gafu* ("A Picture Album of the Holy War"), Tokyo, 1939. Built in 1869 to commemorate those who died in the service of the emperor, the Yasukuni shrine now houses the ashes of fourteen convicted war criminals, including Hideki Tojo. It became controversial after Japanese prime ministers revived the practice of making official state visits to venerate all who are honored there.

RIGHT: Cover of *New Japan: Six Years of Democratization* by Nobufumi Ito, edited by the Japan Peace Study Group, published in Tokyo in 1951.

DECEMBER 23

1941 Wake Island falls to the Japanese.

New Japan

Six Years of Democratization

edited by

The Japan Peace Study Group
Tokyo

In 1945, the Allies divided Korea (a Japanese possession since 1910) into two zones: Soviet troops occupied the north, Americans the south. By the time both nations withdrew their forces in 1949, tensions between the rival governments of North and South Korea were escalating toward a war that would soon involve the United States. That October in neighboring China, Communists under Mao Tse-tung declared victory over Chiang Kai-shek's Nationalists and established the People's Republic of China. Since 1946, Communist and Nationalist forces had been fighting each other in a brutal, roller-coaster war. The United States had long provided both financial and military aid to the Nationalists. In this conflict, however, the U.S. government left them increasingly to their own devices as the likelihood of Soviet military intervention in China receded—and the ineptitude of Nationalist battlefield leaders was compounded by the effects of massive corruption. ("They're all thieves," Truman growled at one point, "every damn one of them.") For three years, China devolved to a roiling chaos of corrosive inflation, riots, repression, battlefield carnage, and widespread starvation. By the end of 1948, waves of peasants and Nationalist military units were defecting to the Communists, whose disciplined forces were rapidly pushing forward. Chiang, meanwhile, had prepared a fall-back position on the island of Taiwan. By the time he retreated there at the end of 1949, the civil war had taken an estimated five million lives.

ABOVE: Hungry Chinese in Hunan Province beg for food. Photograph by Harlow Church, May 5, 1946.

RIGHT: *The glory of Mao's ideologies brightens up the new China.* Color poster by Zhou Zhenbiao, 1952.

DECEMBER 24

1941 On this grim Christmas Eve after Pearl Harbor, President Roosevelt and Prime Minister Churchill continue meeting with their top military leaders to plan Allied strategy.

As the triumph of Mao Tse-tung's Chinese forces on mainland China (see December 24) created lasting ripples in U.S. domestic politics—feeding subsequent anti-Communist excesses by Senator Joseph McCarthy and the House Un-American Activities Committee—the Truman administration faced growing Soviet intransigence in Europe. In response, George F. Kennan, a veteran diplomat who had extensive experience dealing with Stalin in Moscow, proposed a controversial, and variously interpreted, policy: "Soviet pressure against the free institutions of the Western world is something that can be contained," Kennan wrote in 1947, "by the adroit and vigilant application of a counterforce at a series of constantly shifting geographical and political points, corresponding to the shifts and maneuvers of Soviet policy." The following year, after the Communist coup in Czechoslovakia, indications were that the point of greatest danger was Germany, which was divided into sectors controlled by each of the four major Allied powers. On March 5, 1948, General Lucius D. Clay, military governor of the American sector, alerted Washington that he had noted "a subtle change in the Soviet attitude which gives me a feeling that [war] may come with a dramatic suddenness." Berlin was particularly vulnerable. Also partitioned among the four powers, Hitler's former capital housed more Soviet than Western-Allied troops, and was surrounded by Soviet-controlled territory (see December 26).

ABOVE: *Not the book of the month*. Soviet leaders watch approvingly as a bonfire consumes Wendell Willkie's book *One World*, which calls for international cooperation. Drawing by Edwin Marcus (1885–1961), September 1947.

RIGHT: British military police erect a sign to mark the division of British and Soviet sectors of Berlin. Photograph by Jack Chitham, 1948.

DECEMBER 25

1941   On a day when bread rations are increased after a supply shipment makes it into the city, 3,700 Russians die of starvation in Leningrad. Hong Kong's garrison surrenders to the Japanese.

1943   U.S. Marines land on New Britain.

In April 1948, soon after he warned Washington of the growing danger of military confrontation with the USSR in Germany (see December 25), General Clay learned that Soviet officials controlling the territory surrounding Berlin had turned back two trainloads of supplies bound for the city. He issued orders that the material be brought in by air—setting a precedent that would be followed and expanded when the USSR imposed a total blockade of the city two months later. Sparked by economic reforms made by the Western powers to strengthen the West German economy—which Stalin wished to keep weak—the blockade deprived two million people in West Berlin of essential services and vital supplies. American and British forces there were outnumbered and surrounded, but the British and Americans refused to abandon the city. ("We stay in Berlin—period," Truman said.) To avoid military confrontation, in late June they launched what became known as the Berlin Airlift. This massive undertaking involved some seventy-five thousand people, including twelve thousand members of the U. S. Air Force, eight thousand British Army and RAF personnel and forty-five thousand German cargo-handlers. At peak, planes carrying everything from coal to candy were landing at one of West Berlin's three airports every thirty seconds. The operation was not without human cost. Forty-eight Allied airmen had been killed in crashes by the time the outmaneuvered Soviets suspended the blockade in May 1949.

A U.S. Air Force plane, one of many participating in the Berlin Airlift, comes in for a landing in the beleaguered German city, 1948.

DECEMBER 26

1944   The siege of Bastogne is lifted when tanks of the U.S. Fourth Armored Division break the German encirclement.

To ensure adequate stockpiles of essential materials in West Berlin, British and American supply flights continued into September 1949 (see December 26). That same month, the U.S. government learned that the Soviet Union had opened a new and frightening chapter in its intensifying contest with the Western democracies. "We have evidence that within recent weeks an atomic explosion occurred in the USSR," Truman announced on September 23. Most people in the U.S. and British governments took the news calmly ("the eventual development of this new force by other nations was to be expected," the president said). Around the world, some even found artistic inspiration in the spread of nuclear weapons, concocting such bizarre creations as the "atomic hairdo." Generally, however, the fact that two powerful and increasingly antagonistic nations possessed these horrific weapons created waves of anxiety. By September 1951, *Time* magazine reported, U.S. civil defense chief Millard F. Caldwell was requesting $535 million because "cities and states were clamoring for civil-defense funds and guidance." Congress slashed the request by 88 percent, Mississippi Democrat Jamie L. Whitten saying, "If it were humanly possible and within financial reach to give complete protection . . . that would be the desire of all of us. But . . . you cannot build enough holes in the ground with all the money in the federal treasury . . . to be perfectly safe from the atomic bomb."

LEFT: Cover of *Atomic Bombing Care*, a child's picture box containing two strips of colored drawings depicting how children should behave in a shelter after an atom bomb attack, c. 1951.

RIGHT: Holding a photograph of an atomic explosion, Italian model Liliana Orsi, twenty-two, displays her new "atomic hairdo," painstakingly created over a period of twelve hours by Rome hairstylist Eusebio De Luca. Photograph by Albert Blasette, February 1951.

DECEMBER 27

1939 — Indian troops begin arriving in France to join the British Expeditionary Force.

1944 — U.S. B-29s launch their fifth attack on Tokyo.

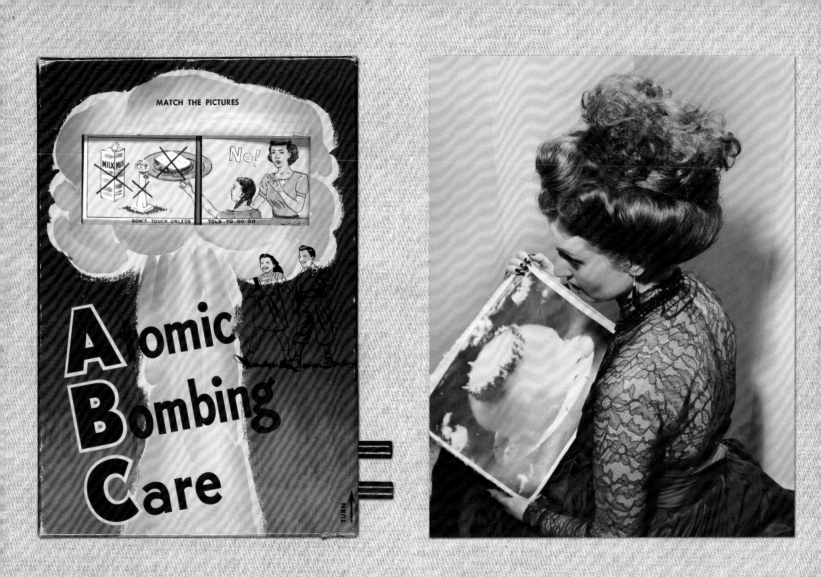

As the United States and the Soviet Union engaged in a nuclear arms race—eventually developing weapons more than a thousand times more powerful than the bombs dropped on Hiroshima and Nagasaki—those who had been grievously harmed in World War II continued to cope with their injuries. Airman Bert Shepard, whose right leg had been partially amputated after his plane was shot down over Germany in 1944, inspired America when he returned (after a prisoner exchange), joined the Washington Senators baseball team, and pitched in a major-league game in August 1945. Sent to the minors after the war, Shepard hoped to return to the majors—meanwhile striking out Stan Musial and Yogi Berra in exhibition games. "I don't want sympathy. All I want is a chance to play ball," he said in 1947. Eight years later, Sadako Sasaki, who had been two years old when the atom bomb fell on her city of Hiroshima, discovered she had developed leukemia, the blood cancer so prevalent among survivors it was called the "A-bomb disease." As she lay in the hospital, she began making origami (folded paper) cranes, having learned of the legend that a sick person who created a thousand paper cranes would soon get well. She died before she achieved that goal—but her story inspired other schoolchildren around the world. Young people continue to send origami cranes in her honor to the Children's Peace Monument in Hiroshima, which bears the legend: "This is our cry, This is our prayer, Peace in the world."

ABOVE: A Japanese survivor of the atomic bomb blast at Hiroshima, c. 1950.

RIGHT: After joining the Washington Senators as a coach, pitcher, and pinch-hitter, Lt. Bert R. Shepard (left), veteran P-38 pilot who lost part of his right leg in combat over Germany, adjusts his artificial limb under the watchful eye of the team's manager Ossie Bluege, March 30, 1945.

DECEMBER 28

1940 To stretch its petroleum supplies, Japan begins using charcoal and other substitute fuels to power automobiles.

"I hope I'll be here next year to send this message to future generations: Never forget the horror of war," American World War II veteran Jack Dickson told an Associated Press reporter on June 6, 2006. Dickson was in France, attending ceremonies marking the sixty-second anniversary of D-Day (see September 12, 13)—and his message continued: "Never forget that men died on these Normandy beaches to free the world." On June 8, 1944, two days after the D-Day landings, Normandy became the site of the first American military cemetery to be established in Europe during World War II. After the war, a permanent cemetery was established not far from the original site. Overlooking Omaha Beach, where Americans took heavy casualties before fighting their way inland, the 172-acre cemetery contains the graves of 9,387 members of the U.S. armed forces whose families chose to have them buried along with their comrades in the country where they had fallen. They are among the more than 93,000 World War II casualties buried overseas. At the ceremonies Dickson attended, French Veterans Minister Hamlaoui Mekachera praised the troops of eight Allied countries who had died defending the cause of freedom during the fierce combat at Normandy. Each veteran attending brought with him his own memories. "To see this beach where many friends lost their lives gives me chills," American Ken Ewing told the Associated Press, "and makes me think we should never forget; we must never forget."

Part of the United States cemetery above World War II's Omaha Beach, Normandy, France. Photograph by Susan Reyburn, May 29, 2007.

DECEMBER 29

1939 Finnish forces trounce invading Soviet units at Suomussalmi.

AFTERMATH

"**D**uring World War II my mother Bessie Reece Spencer . . . had four of her five sons in the military service," Donald L. Spencer wrote in the dedication to his memoir *World War II: Missions, Letters, Notes and Remembrances*. "To make her personal contribution to the war effort, at the age of 54, she went to school to become an aircraft parts inspector for the United States Army Air Corps. . . . My mother saved all of the letters, newspaper clippings and articles that are transcribed herein." Through decades of prosperity, recession, and political turmoil, Mrs. Spencer's careful preservation of World War II artifacts has helped keep alive the story of her sons' service in the world's greatest conflict—while her son Donald preserved an intriguing glimpse of Mrs. Spencer's role in that war in the dedication to his handcrafted book. In 1944, an artist drew an impromptu portrait of a soldier on his way to Guam, creating a graphic time portal through which the soldier's daughter, grandchildren, and great-grandchildren can see Private McCornick in the crowded belly of a ship, heading into his uncertain future. Once upon a time, sitting in an Illinois church, a woman heard the pastor, a World War II veteran who happened to be her father, tell of being a chaplain not only to the men of his U.S. Army regiment but also to German POWs—a story he had never told his children—and she saw her father, and the war he was in, in a clearer light. "There is a history," as Shakespeare wrote, "in all men's lives."

LEFT: Details from the cover of *World War II: Missions, Letters, Notes and Remembrances*, compiled by Donald L. Spencer, U.S. Army Air Forces, 1939–46, who served with the Ninth Air Force in the European Theater.

RIGHT: Portrait of PFC William S. McCornick, on board a U.S. Navy vessel bound for Guam. Charcoal drawing by Theodore D. Giavis, December 1, 1944.

DECEMBER 30

1943   The Allies gain control of western New Britain.

After World War II, thousands of memorials were created in all the former Allied countries—including the United States. But the country did not have a *national* commemorative site until the World War II Memorial, located on the National Mall in Washington, D.C., was dedicated over Memorial Day weekend in 2004. The dedication was the occasion for a World War II Reunion that brought thousands of veterans to the Mall. For three days, they met one another, described their experiences to eager audiences during thirty hours of programs held in large tents, and recorded their stories for the archives of the Library of Congress Veterans History Project (VHP). "Almost to a man they said they were only doing their jobs," VHP volunteer interviewer Susan Reyburn later said. "But what jobs for nineteen-year-olds—liberating concentration camps, fueling planes under fire, landing on Okinawa. When I thought about the summer jobs my friends and I had at that age, it was hard to believe what they were asked to do—and did do." Veteran Bob Dole had been severely wounded while attempting to save a comrade's life, but survived to serve with distinction in the U.S. Senate. "What we dedicate today is not a memorial to war," he told the huge crowd at the dedication ceremonies, "rather it is a tribute to the physical and moral courage . . . that inspires Americans in every generation to lay down their lives for people they will never meet, for ideals that make life itself worth living."

Veterans Richard Cozad of Miami, Florida, and Kenneth Johnson of Torrington, Wyoming, meet and exchange memories during the dedication ceremonies for the World War II Veterans Memorial on the National Mall, Washington, D.C. Photograph by Michaela McNichol, May 27, 2004.

DECEMBER 31

 1941 With Japanese forces thirty miles away, Manila is evacuated.

 1942 Free French troops from Chad advance into southern Libya.

Acknowledgments

Creating *World War II 365 Days* has been a moving and complex adventure. I am indebted to David M. Kennedy for the inspiration provided by his absorbing history of the World War II era, *Freedom from Fear*, and for his graceful and informative introduction to this book. Picture editor par excellence Athena Angelos was a tireless, thought-provoking, and endlessly inventive partner in creation. Both she and I benefitted from the guidance and expertise of many Library of Congress staff as we delved into the Library's massive World War II collections. I am particularly grateful to Helena Zinkham, Phil Michel, Jan Grenci, Barbara Natanson, and Lew Wyman in the Prints and Photographs Division; to Robert Patrick, Neil Huntley, and Rachel Mears in the Veterans History Project; to John Hébert and the staff of the Geography and Map Division; to Domenico Sergi of the LC Information Technology Service; and to Michaela McNichol in the Public Affairs Office. Athena and I also join in thanking Kevin Carroll.

At Harry N. Abrams, Inc., project manager Deborah Aaronson guided the development of the book with good humor and a firm hand. Sofia Gutierrez, our perpetually multitasking and miraculously patient editor, provided wise counsel as we confronted multiple challenges and our looming deadline. Designer Timothy Shaner expertly combined hundreds of disparate images and complex text. Any errors in that text are my responsibility alone.

Finally, I salute John Y. Cole, director of the Center for the Book in the Library of Congress, Director of Publishing Ralph Eubanks, and my dauntless colleagues in the Library's Publishing Office—with thanks to Evelyn Sinclair and Abby Colodner for their editorial assistance. I am especially grateful to Linda Osborne and Susan Reyburn, who worked with me on *The Library of Congress World War II Companion*. Their comments on draft text for this volume have made *World War II 365 Days* a richer and wiser book. — M. E. W.

Principal Sources and Further Reading

Adams, Stephen B. *Mr. Kaiser Goes to Washington: The Rise of a Government Entrepreneur* (Chapel Hill, NC: University of North Carolina Press, 1997)

Afro-American Company, The. *This Is Our War: Selected Stories of Six War Correspondents Who Were Sent Overseas by the AFRO-AMERICAN Newspapers* (The Afro-American Company, 1945)

Anderson, Mark M., ed. *Hitler's Exiles: Personal Stories of the Flight from Nazi Germany to America* (New York: The New Press, 1998)

Arnold, Henry Harley. *Global Mission* (New York: Harper & Brothers, 1949)

Bartholomew-Feis, Dixee R. *The OSS and Ho Chi Minh: Unexpected Allies in the War against Japan* (Lawrence, KS: University Press of Kansas, 2006)

Bartov, Omer. *Hitler's Army: Soldiers, Nazis, and War in the Third Reich* (New York, London: Oxford University Press, 1991)

Baynes, Norman H., ed. *The Speeches of Adolf Hitler*, 2 Vol. (London: Oxford University Press, 1942)

Beevor, Antony and Luba Vinogradova, ed. and trans. *A Writer at War: Vasily Grossman with the Red Army, 1941–1945* (New York: Pantheon Books, 2005)

Bernstein, Alison R. *American Indians and World War II* (Norman, OK: University of Oklahoma Press, 1991)

Bliss, Edward Jr., ed. *In Search of Light: The Broadcasts of Edward R. Murrow, 1938–1961* (New York: Knopf, 1967)

Bosworth, R. J. B. *Mussolini* (London: Arnold/Oxford University Press, 2002)

Brandon, Piers. *The Dark Valley: A Panorama of the 1930s* (New York: Knopf, 2000)

Bronson, Rachel. *Thicker than Oil: America's Uneasy Partnership with Saudi Arabia* (NY: Oxford University Press, 2006)

Bullitt, Orville H., ed. *For the President, Personal and Secret: Correspondence between Franklin D. Roosevelt and William C. Bullitt* (Boston: Houghton Mifflin, 1972)

Calvocoressi, Peter, Guy Wint, and John Pritchard. *The Penguin History of the Second World War* (London: Penguin Books, 1999)

Carroll, Andrew, ed., *War Letters: Extraordinary Correspondence from American Wars* (New York: Scribners, 2001)

Chadakoff, Rochelle, ed. *Eleanor Roosevelt's My Day: Her Acclaimed Columns, 1936–1945*, 3 vol. (New York: Pharos Books, 1989-91)

Churchill, Sir Winston. *The Second World War*, 6 vol. (Boston: Houghton Mifflin Co.

Collier, Richard. *Bridge Across the Sky, The Berlin Blockade and Airlift: 1948–1949* (New York: McGraw-Hill Book Company, 1978)

Colman, Penny. *A Woman Unafraid: The Achievements of Frances Perkins* (New York: Atheneum, 1993)

Craven,Wesley Frank and James Lea Cate, eds. *The Army Air Forces in World War II, Volume Six: Men and Planes* (Washington, DC: US Government Printing Office, 1983)

Daily Telegraph, London. David Marley, ed. *The Daily Telegraph Story of the War*, 5 vols (London: Hodder & Stoughton, 1942–46)

Deakin, F. W., *The Brutal Friendship: Mussolini, Hitler and the Fall of Italian Fascism* (New York: Harper & Row, 1962)

de Chambrun, René. *I Saw France Fall: Will She Rise Again?* (New York: William Morrow & Co, 1940)

Donnelly, Monsignor Thomas J. *"Hey Padre": The Saga of a Regimental Chaplain in World War II* (New York: 77th Division Association, Inc., 1986)

Editors of Time-Life Books. *World War II–The Aftermath: Asia* (Alexandria, VA: Time-Life Books, 1983)

Edwards, John Carver. *Berlin Calling: American Broadcasters in Service to the Third Reich* (Westport, CT: Praeger, 1991)

Eisenhower, Dwight D. *Crusade in Europe* (Garden City, NY: Doubleday & Company, Inc., 1948)

Erickson, John. *The Road to Berlin: Continuing the History of Stalin's War with Germany* (Boulder, CO: Westview Press, 1983)

Fenby, Jonathan. *Chiang Kai-shek: China's Generalissimo and the Nation He Lost* (New York: Carroll & Graff, 1004)

Ford, Kirk, Jr. *OSS and the Yugoslav Resistance, 1943–1945* (College Station, TX: Texas A&M University Press, 1992)

Frissell, Toni. *Toni Frissell, Photographs: 1933–1967* (New York: Doubleday, in association with the Library of Congress, 1994)

Fussell, Paul. *The Boys' Crusade: The American Infantry in Northwestern Europe, 1944–1945* (New York: The Modern Library, 2003)

Gibson, Hugh, ed. *The Ciano Diaries, 1939–1943* (New York: H. Fertig, 1973)

Gilbert, Sir Martin. *A History of the Twentieth Century, Volume 2: 1933–1951* (New York: William Morrow, 1998)

_____. *The Second World War: A Complete History* (New York: Henry Holt, 1989)

Gilmore, Allison B. *You Can't Fight Tanks with Bayonets: Psychological Warfare against the Japanese Army in the Southwest Pacific* (Lincoln, NE: University of Nebraska Press, 1998)

Goebbels, Joseph. *The Goebbels Diaries, 1942–43.* Louis P. Lochner, ed. and trans. (New York: Doubleday, 1948)

Goodwin, Doris Kearns. *No Ordinary Time: Franklin and Eleanor Roosevelt: The Home Front in World War II* (New York: Simon & Schuster, 1994)

Goralski, Robert. *World War II Almanac: 1931–1945* (New York: Bonanza Books, 1981)

Grew, Joseph C. *Ten Years in Japan: A Contemporary Record Drawn from the Diaries and Private and Official Papers of Joseph C. Grew* (NY: Simon & Schuster, 1941)

Griffin, Alexander R. *Out of Carnage* (New York: Howell, Soskin, Publishers, 1945)

Gutman, Yisrael, Ina Friedman, trans. *The Jews of Warsaw, 1939–1943: Ghetto, Underground, Revolt* (Bloomington, IN: Indiana University Press, 1982)

Harries, Meirion and Susie Harries. *Soldiers of the Sun: The Rise and Fall of the Imperial Japanese Army, 1868–1945* (London: Heinemann, 1991)

Harriman, W. Averell and Elie Abel. *Special Envoy to Churchill and Stalin* (New York: Random House 1975)

Harris, Sir Arthur. *Bomber Offensive* (Barnsley, South. Yorkshire, England: Pen & Sword Military Classics, 2005; originally published 1947)

Hitler, Adolf. *My New Order.* Raoul de Roussy de Sales, ed. (New York: Octagon Books, 1973)

Hurtsfield, Julian G. *America and the French Nation, 1939–1945* (Chapel Hill, NC: University of North Carolina Press, 1986)

James, Robert Rhodes ed. *Winston S. Churchill, His Complete Speeches, 1897–1963, Volume VII; 1943–1949* (New York: Chelsea House Publishers, 1974)

Kahn, E. J., Jr. *McNair, Educator of an Army* (Washington, DC: The Infantry Journal, 1945)

Kennedy, David. M. *Freedom from Fear: The American People in Depression and War* (New York: Oxford University Press), 1999

Kirkpatrick, Sir Ivone. *Mussolini: A Study in Power* (New York: Hawthorn Books, 1964)

Krug, Hans-Joachim, Yoichi Hirama, Berthod J. Sander-Nagashima, and Axel Niestle. *Reluctant Allies: German-Japanese Naval Relations in World War II* (Annapolis, MD: Naval Institute Press 2001)

Lamont-Brown, Raymond. *Kempeitai: Japan's Dreaded Military Police* (Phoenix Mill, Gloucestershire, England: Sutton, 1998)

Landau, Elaine. *The Warsaw Ghetto Uprising* (New York: New Discovery Books, 1992)

Lange, Dorothea and Paul Schuster Taylor. *An American Exodus: A Record of Human Erosion* (New York: Reynal & Hitchcock, 1939)

Larrabee, Eric. *Commander in Chief: Franklin Delano Roosevelt, His Lieutenants, and Their War* (New York: Harper & Row, 1987)

Laurence, William L. *Dawn over Zero: The Story of the Atomic Bomb* (New York: Alfred A. Knopf, 1946)

Lawson, Ted W., *Thirty Seconds over Tokyo* (New York: Random House, 1943)

LeMay, Curtis E., and Bill Yenne. *Superfortress: The Story of the B-29 and American Air Power* (New York: McGraw-Hill Book Company, 1988)

Lin, Adet, Anor and Meimei. *Dawn over Chungking* (New York: Da Capo, 1975, originally published 1941)

Lindsay, Franklin. *Beacons in the Night: With the OSS and Tito's Partisans in Wartime Yugoslavia* (Palo Alto, CA: Stanford University Press, 1993)

Loewenheim, Francis L., Harold D. Langley, and Manfred Jonas eds. *Roosevelt and Churchill: Their Secret Wartime Correspondence* (New York: Saturday Review Press/ E. P. Dutton & Co, Inc., 1975)

MacGregor, Morris J. *Integration of the Armed Forces, 1940–1965* (Washington, DC: Center of Military History, 1981)

MacLeish, Archibald. *A Time to Act: Selected Addresses* (Boston: Houghton Mifflin, 1943)

Manchester, William. *The Glory and the Dream: A Narrative History of America, 1932–1972* (New York: Bantam Books, 1990)

_____ *American Caesar, Douglas MacArthur, 1880–1964* (Boston: Little, Brown, 1978)

Masaoka, Mike with Bill Hosokawa. *They Call Me Moses Masaoka: An American Saga* (New York: William Morrow, 1987)

Mason, David. *Who's Who in World War II* (London: Weidenfeld and Nicolson, 1978)

Merridale, Catherine. *Ivan's War: Life and Death in the Red Army, 1939–1945* (New York: Metropolitan Books/Henry Holt, 2006)

Militärgeschichtliches Forschungsamt (Research Institute for Military History). *Germany and the Second World War*, 9 vol. (New York: Oxford University Press 1990-2008)

Murray, Williamson and Allan R. Millett. *A War to Be Won: Fighting the Second World War* (Cambridge, MA: Belknap Press of Harvard University Press, 2000)

Nicholas, Lynn H. *Cruel World: The Children of Europe in the Nazi Web* (New York: Alfred A. Knopf, 2005)

Nichols, David, ed. *Ernie's War: The Best of Ernie Pyle's World War II Dispatches* (New York: Random House, 1986)

Office of the Chief of Military History, Department of the Army. *The United States Army in World War II*, 78 vols.

Ohnuki-Tierney, Emiko. *Kamikaze Diaries: Reflections of Japanese Student Soldiers* (Chicago: University of Chicago Press, 2006)

Overy, Richard. *The Dictators: Hitler's Germany, Stalin's Russia* (New York: W.W. Norton, 2004)

Perrault, Gilles and Pierre Azema. *Paris under the Occupation* (London: The Vendome Press, 1989)

Read, Anthony. *The Devil's Disciples: Hitler's Inner Circle* (New York: W.W. Norton, 2003)

Salisbury, Harrison. *The Unknown War* (New York: Bantam Books, 1978)

Schultz, Duane P. *Hero of Bataan: The Story of General Jonathan M. Wainwright* (New York: St. Martin's Press, 1981)

Searle, Ronald. *To the Kwai and Back: War Drawings, 1939–1945* (Boston: Atlantic Monthly Press, 1986)

Sewell, Patricia W., ed. *Healers in World War II* (Jefferson, NC: McFarland & Company, Inc., 2001)

Shirer, William L. *The Rise and Fall of the Third Reich: A History of Nazi Germany* (New York: Simon & Schuster, 1981, most recent edition, 1990)

Sledge, E. B. *With the Old Breed at Peleliu and Okinawa* (Annapolis, MD: Naval Institute Press, 1981, most recent edition, 1996)

____ *China Marine* (Tuscaloosa, AL: The University of Alabama Press, 2002)

Stoler, Mark A. *Allies and Adversaries: The Joint Chiefs of Staff, the Grand Alliance, and U.S. Strategy in World War II* (Chapel Hill, NC: University of North Carolina Press, 2000)

Stone, Geoffrey. *Perilous Times: Free Speech in Wartime* (New York: W.W. Norton, 2004)

Sugarman, Tracy. *My War: A Love Story in Letters and Drawings* (New York: Random House, 2000)

Terkel, Studs. *"The Good War": An Oral History of World War Two.* (New York: Pantheon Books, 1984)

Toland, John. *The Rising Sun: The Decline and Fall of the Japanese Empire, 1936–1945* (New York: The Modern Library, 2003, originally published 1970)

Trevor-Roper, H. R., ed. *Hitler's War Directives, 1939–1945* (London: Pan, 1966)

Truman, Harry S. *Off the Record: The Private Papers of Harry S. Truman*, Robert H. Ferrell, ed. (New York: Harper & Row, 1980)

Tuchman, Barbara W. *Stilwell and the American Experience in China, 1911–45* (New York: Book of the Month Club, 1985)

Tucker, Spencer C., ed. *Encyclopedia of World War II: A Political, Social and Military History* (Santa Barbara, CA: ABC-CLIO, 2005)

Vance, Jonathan F. ed., *Encyclopedia of Prisoners of War and Internment* (Santa Barbara, CA: ABC-CLIO, 2000)

Wagner, Margaret E., Linda Barrett Osborne, Susan Reyburn, and Staff of the Library of Congress. *The Library of Congress World War II Companion* (New York: Simon & Schuster 2007)

Whiting, Charles and the editors of Time-Life Books. *The Home Front: Germany* (Alexandria, VA: Time-Life Books, 1982)

Young, Roland. *Congressional Politics in the Second World War* (New York: Columbia University Press, 1956)

Library of Congress Veterans History Project (VHP)

Among the thousands of discrete World War II collections held by the VHP, the papers of the following veterans provided information and images used in this book. (For further information on VHP and how to add material to its archives, visit the VHP website at www.loc.gov/vets/)

Charles M. Amsler
William Thomas Barr
Jesse A. Beazley
Sigmund S. Bialosky
Samuel Lionel Boylston
James George Brown
Ruth Deloris Buckley
Virginia C. Claudon (Allen)
René J. Défourneaux
Doane Hage, Jr.

Carl Albin Hall
Robert W. Johnsmiller
Yeiichi Kelly Kuwayama
Mimi Korach Lesser
Charles Rosario Restifo
Peter Sanfilippo
Donald L. Spencer
Tracy A. Sugarman
Warren Michio Tsuneishi

Information About Images

To order reproductions of Library of Congress images in this book, note the negative or digital ID number listed below. Most images can be viewed and some downloaded from the Library of Congress Prints & Photographs Online Catalog at www.loc.gov/rr/print/catalog.html Duplicates may also be ordered from the Library of Congress Photoduplication Service, Washington, D.C. 20540-4570; (202) 707-5640; fax (202) 707-1771; www.loc.gov/preserv/pds

KEY TO ABBREVIATIONS

GC: General Collections

G&M: Geography & Map Division

VHP: Veterans History Project

Other Sources

CMH: Center for Military History – Brochure Series: U.S. Army Campaigns of WWII

NARA: National Archives and Records Administration

USHMM: United States Holocaust Memorial Museum

Image positions: T = Thumbnail (small image accompanying text), L = left, R = right

JANUARY Jan01:LC-USZC4-11365; Jan02T: LC-USZC4-6635; Jan02L:LC-USZ62-29669; Jan02R:LC-USW33-038042; Jan03:LC-Dig-ppmsca-13321; Jan04:RBPE 13300900; Jan05L:LC-USZC4-3369; Jan05R:LC-Dig-yan-1a37717; Jan06:LC-Dig-ppmsca-08200; Jan07:LC-USZ62-94474; Jan08:G&M: G1046.F2M3 1924; Jan09T:LC-Dig-matpc-08277; Jan09:LC-Dig-ppmsca-15304-00014; Jan10L:LC-USZ62-47125; Jan10R:LC-USZC4-6419; Jan11:LC-USZC4-4675; Jan12L:LC-Dig-ppmsca-07437; Jan12R:GC: DS 777.53.S395; Jan13L:LC-Dig-npcc-11784; Jan13R:LC-USZ62-88492; Jan14L:LC-USZ62-43629; Jan14R:LC-USZ62-42896; Jan15:LC-Dig-ppmsca-05577; Jan16:LC-USA7-18242; Jan17:LC-USZ62-23569; Jan18L:LC-Dig-ppmsca-18359; Jan18R:RBSC DD253.S243; Jan19:LC-Dig-ppmsca-18370; Jan20L:LC-Dig-ppmsca-12896; Jan20R:LC-USZ62-93597; Jan21:LC-Dig-ppmsca-07216; Jan22:LC-Dig-ppmsca-18357; Jan23:LC-USZ62-62167; Jan24T:G&M: Neg #3962; Jan24: LC-USZ62-79595; Jan25L:LC-USZC4-4270; Jan25R: LC-USZ62-27663; Jan26:LC-USZ61-1362; Jan27T:LC-Dig-ppmsca-10853; Jan27:LC-USZC4-6441; Jan28:LC-Dig-ppmsca-18376; Jan29L:LC-USZ62-106389; Jan29R:LC-USZC4-1400; Jan30:LC-Dig-ppmsca-18373; Jan31:LC-Dig-ppmsca-18358

FEBRUARY Feb01:LC-USZC4-7350; Feb02L:LC-Dig-ppmsca-07453; Feb02R:GC: DP 269.N48; Feb03:GC: DS 777.53.S395; Feb04L:LC-USZ62-134169; Feb04R: LC-USZ62-49058; Feb05:GC: DS 777.53.S395; Feb06:GC: DS 777.53.S395; Feb07L:LC-USZ62-119395; Feb07R:LC-USZ62-10297; Feb08:LC-Dig-fsa-8b38632; Feb09:LC-Dig-ppmsca-18377; Feb10L:LC-USZC2-921; Feb10R:LC-USZ62-117148; Feb11L:LC-USZ62-132634; Feb11R :LC-USZC4-13000 © The Herb Block Foundation; Feb12:LC-Dig-ppmsca-05636; Feb13L:LC-Dig-ppmsca-18379; Feb13R: LC-USZ62-42714; Feb14:LC-USZ62-99270; Feb15:LC-USZ62-79578; Feb16L:LC-USZ62-132632; Feb16R:LC-Dig-ppmsca-18380; Feb17L:LC-Dig-ppmsca-18363; Feb17R:LC-Dig-ppmsca-18355; Feb18L:LC-USZ62-112306; Feb18R:LC-Dig-ppmsca-09441; Feb19T:LC-USZ62-116730; Feb19:LC-USZ62-90448; Feb20:LC-USZ62-104689; Feb21L:LC-Dig-acd-2a06640; Feb21R:LC-USZ62-105883; Feb22:GC: DS 777.53.S395; Feb23L:LC-USZ62-42443; Feb23R:LC-USZ62-42460; Feb24:LC-USZ62-91147; Feb25L:LC-Dig-ppmsca-18361; Feb25R:LC-Dig-ppmsca-18362; Feb26:LC-USZ62-104301; Feb27T:LC-USZ62-111579; Feb27:LC-Dig-ppmsca-18356; Feb28:LC-Dig-ppmsca-18369

MARCH Mar01:LC-USZ62-77424; Mar02L:USHMM #30690; Mar02R: Mar02R:LC-USZC4-2117; Mar03:LC-Dig-ppmsca-18368; Mar04:GC: DS 777.53.S395; Mar05:LC-USE6-D-008873; Mar06:LC-USZ62-87807; Mar07L:LC-USZ62-99475; Mar07R:LC-USZ62-104645; Mar08L:LC-Dig-ppmsca-18364; Mar08R: LC-Dig-acd-2a12308; Mar09L:LC-Dig-acd-2a07453; Mar09R:LC-USZ62-103540; Mar10:LC-USZ62-125828; Mar11T:LC-USZ62-13325; Mar11T:LC-Dig-ppmsca-13335; Mar12:LC-Dig-ppmsca-18374; Mar13:LC-Dig-ppmsca-18365; Mar14L:LC-USZC4-13394; Mar14R:LC-Dig-ppmsca-05361; Mar15:LC-Dig-ppmsca-18367; Mar16:LC-USZ62-50036; Mar17L:LC-USZ61-1558; Mar17R:LC-Dig-ppmsca-05363; Mar18T:LC-Dig-ppmsca-18527-0010; Mar18:LC-Dig-ppmsca-18381; Mar19:LC-Dig-ppmsca-18372; Mar20T:LC-USZC2-5571; Mar20:LC-Dig-ppmsca-18366; Mar21L:LC-USZC2-866; Mar21R:LC-Dig-ppmsca-04289; Mar22:NARA: 306-NT-2734V; Mar23L:LC-Dig-ppmsca-18384; Mar23R:LC-Dig-ppmsca-18383; Mar24:LC-USZ62-43398; Mar25L:LC-Dig-ppmsca-18527-0012; Mar25R:GC: D753.C52; Mar26:LC-Dig-ppmsca-05649; Mar27:LC-USZ62-12199; Mar28L:LC-USW33-000890-ZC; Mar28R:LC-Dig-ppmsca-18564; Mar29L:LC-Dig-fsac-1a33871; Mar29R:LC-Dig-ppmsca-18378; Mar30L:LC-Dig-acd-2a05739; Mar30R:LC-USZ62-48851; Mar31:GC:DS 777.53.S395

APRIL Apr01:LC-Dig-ppmsca-12900; Apr02:GC: DS 777.53.S395; Apr03:LC-USZ62-130661; Apr04:LC-Dig-ppmsca-13336; Apr05L:LC-Dig-ppmsca-18385; Apr05R:LC-USZC2-803; Apr06:LC-Dig-ppmsca-18527-0011; Apr07L:LC-USZ62-128765; Apr07R:LC-USZ62-90200; Apr08:LC-Dig-ppmsca-18371; Apr09:LC-USZ62-95099; Apr10L:LC-Dig-ppmsca-03394 © The Herb Block Foundation; Apr10R:GC: AP4. I3 Folio; Apr11:LC-USZ62-64857; Apr12L:LC-Dig-ppmsca-18541; Apr12R:LC-USZC4-8737; Apr13T:LC-USZ62-136498; Apr13:LC-Dig-ppmsca-13366; Apr14:GC: D772.B5B8; Apr15:LC-USZC4-3885; Apr16L:LC-Dig-acd-2a05841; Apr16R:G&M: G1038. U5 1942; Apr17:LC-USZC4-6819; Apr18:LC-Dig-ppmsca-18386; Apr19:LC-USZ62-52710; Apr20L:LC-Dig-ppmsca-18352; Apr20R:LC-USZ62-84955; Apr21T:NARA:111-SC-192258; Apr21:LC-USZ62-107499; Apr22:LC-USZ62-12198; Apr23:LC-Dig-ppmsca-18375; Apr24 :LC-Dig-ppmsca-19279; Apr25T:LC-USW33-029456-C; Apr25 :LC-USZ62-52708; Apr26L:LC-USZC4-4723; Apr26R:LC-USZ62-129810; Apr27T:LC-USZC4-2328; Apr27:LC-USW33-018432-C; Apr28:LC-USZ62-91315; Apr29:LC-Dig-ppmsca-13360; Apr30L:LC-Dig-yan-1a37602; Apr30R:LC-Dig-yan-1a37606

MAY May01:LC-USZC4-12529; May02:LC-USZC4-1472; May03L:LC-USZ62-86800; May03R:LC-USZC4-5877; May04:GC:D769A533 Vol 4, Pt 4; May05T:LC-Dig-ppmsca-18560; May05:LC-USZC4-7403; May06:LC-USZ62-128366; May07L:LC-USW33-019075-C; May07R:LC-Dig-acd-2a10758; May08L:LC-USZ61-1572; May08R:LC-Dig-ppmsca-18538; May09:LC-Dig-ppmsca-18528; May10:LC-USZ62-90452; May11:LC-USZ62-98901; May12L:LC-USZC4-4327; May12R:LC-USZC4-6151; May13:GC: D769A53, Vol 4, Pt 4; May14 L:LC-USZC4-702; May14 R:LC-Dig-ppmsca-19023; May15L:LC-US-Dig-ppmsc-03387 © The Herb Block Foundation; May15R:LC-USZ62-42438; May16:LC-USZC4-3626; May17T:LC-USZ62-5210; May17L:LC-USZ61-40; May17R:LC-USZ62-110949; May18:LC-USZ62-132630; May19:LC-USZ62-54521; May20L:LC-USZ62-77383; May20R:LC-Dig-acd-2a10490; May21:CMH: Algeria-French Morocco; May22L:LC-USZ62-105236; May22R:LC-USW33-055039-ZC; May23:LC-USZ62-98900; May24:LC-Dig-ppmsca-13345; May25:GC: DS 777.53. S395; May26:LC-Dig-ppmsca-19503; May27L:LC-USZ62-38316; May27C:LC-USZ62-120136; May27R:LC-USZ62-83950; May28:VHP:Rene Defourneaux (AFC/2001/001/03357); May29:LC-USZ62-7449; May30:LC-USZ62-104251; May31T:LC-USZ62-42456; May31:LC-USZ62-111632

JUNE Jun01:LC-USZC4-1663; Jun02:LC-Dig-ppmsca-18533; Jun03T:LC-USZC2-1170; Jun03:LC-USZ62-104034; Jun04T:LC-USZ62-86003; Jun04:LC-Dig-ppmsca-18553; Jun05T:LC-Dig-ppmsca-19010; Jun05 :LC-USZ62-120361; Jun06L:GC: UB 250 U33 No217b; Jun06R:GC: UB 250 U33 No217b; Jun07L:LC-Dig-ppmsca-18525; Jun07R:LC-USZC4-7408; Jun08L:fsa 8e06539; Jun08R:LC-Dig-ppmsca-18529; Jun09:LC-USZC4- 1773; Jun10:LC-USZ62-133829; Jun11T:LC-USZ62-21027; Jun11: LC-DIG-fsa-8b08336; Jun12T:LC-USZ62-95994; Jun12:LC-USZ62-61122; Jun13T:LC-USE613-D-000178; Jun13:LC-USZC4-7238; Jun14:LC-Dig-fsac-1a35297; Jun15T:LC-USZ62-49898; Jun15:GC: D 790 L3; Jun16L:LC-USZ62-70161; Jun16R:GC: DS 777.53.S395; Jun17:LC-USZC4-3603; Jun18L:GC:D 742J3 R7; Jun18R:LC-Dig-ppmsca-19502; Jun19:LC-Dig-ppmsca-18551;

Jun20T:GC: DS 777.53.S395; Jun20:LC-USZ62-80648; Jun21:LC-USZ62-93195; Jun22T:LC-Dig-ppmsca-18539; Jun22:LC-USZ62-41944; Jun23L:LC-USZ62-85201; Jun23R:LC-USW33-000646-ZC; Jun24:LC-Dig-ppmsca-18532; Jun25:LC-USZ62-132626; Jun26T:GC: D7435D3; Jun26:LC-USZ62-128337; Jun27:LC-Dig-ppmsca-18531; Jun28:LC-Dig-ppmsca-18556; Jun29:LC-Dig-ppmsca-18555; Jun30:LC-USZ62-133904

JULY Jul01:LC-USZC4-6033; Jul02:GC: 743.2.V46; Jul03:LC-USZ62-122720; Jul04:LC-USZ62-87996; Jul05:LC-USZ62-111188; Jul06L:LC-USZ62-132790; Jul06R:Deutsches Historisches Museum; Jul07L:LC-USW3-59181-C; Jul07R:LC-Dig-ppmsca-18561; Jul08L:LC-USZC2-1588; Jul08R:LC-USZ62-126662; Jul09L:LC-USZ62-119757; Jul09R:LC-USZ62-117758; Jul10:GC: D743.2.V46; Jul11:LC-Dig-fsac-1a34948; Jul12:LC-USZC4-4265; Jul13L:LC-USZC4-1653; Jul13R:LC-Dig-ppmsca-18524; Jul14L:LC-USZ6-1295; Jul14R:LC-USZ6-123275; Jul15:LC-Dig-ppmsca-13323; Jul16T:LC-USZ62-86688; Jul16:LC-USZ62-92190; Jul17L:LC-Dig-fsac-1a34614; Jul17R:LC-Dig-fsac-1a34676; Jul18L:GC: D743.2.L5; Jul18R:LC-USZ62-16191; Jul19L:LC-USZ62-107199; Jul19R:LC-USW33-000127-ZC; Jul20:VHP: Mimi Lesser (AFC/2001/001/11904); Jul21:LC-Dig-fsac 1a34584; Jul22:LC-USZ62-97776; Jul23:LC-Dig-ppmsca-18549; Jul24L:LC-USZC2-1109; Jul24R:LC-USZC4-4430; Jul25T:LC-Dig-ppmsca-18559; Jul25:LC-Dig-ppmsca-12899; Jul26L:LC-USZC4-2683; Jul26R:LC-USZC4-2290; Jul27T :GC: DS 777.53.S395; Jul27:LC-USZ62-121814; Jul28L:GC: DS821.H813; Jul28R:GC: D742.J3 N6; Jul29L:LC-USZ62-13334;

Jul29R:GC: DS 777.53.S395; Jul30L:LC-USZ62-61847; Jul30R:LC-USZ62-116523; Jul31:GC: D 743 .2 .L6

AUGUST Aug01:LC-USZC4-2289; Aug02:VHP: Peter Sanfilippo (AFC/2001/001/5844); Aug03T:FDR Presidential Library; Aug03:LC-USW33-027834-ZC; Aug04T:LC-Dig-ppmsca-18534; Aug04:LC-USW33-018822-C; Aug05L:LC-Dig-ppmsca-18548; Aug05R:LC-Dig-ppmsca-18530; Aug06L:LC-USZC4-2752; Aug06R:LC-USZ62-49735; Aug07L:LC-USZ62-121789; Aug07R:G&M: Neg #3594; Aug08T:LC-USZ62-73301; Aug08:LC-USE6-D-009168; Aug09:LC-USE6-D-009115; Aug10T:LC-USZC4-1676; Aug10:LC-USE623-D-010845; Aug11:LC-USZ62-74701; Aug12T:GC: TX 740.04; Aug12:GC: TX 357.B53; Aug13:NARA: 238-NT-288; Aug14T:LC-Dig-ppmsca-13330; Aug14:LC-Dig-ppmsca-18526; Aug15:VHP: Peter Sanfilippo (AFC/2001/001/5844); Aug16L:LC-USZ62-101969; Aug16R:LC-USZC4-10296; Aug17:LC-USZ62-113677; Aug18L:LC-USZ62-130597; Aug18R:LC-USZ62-75515; Aug19L:LC-Dig-ppmsca-18562; Aug19R:LC-USZ62-72926; Aug20:LC-Dig-ppmsca-18536; Aug21T:LC-Dig-ppmsca-19271; Aug21L:LC-Dig-ppmsca-18550; Aug21R:LC-Dig-ppmsca-18535; Aug22:NARA:111-SC-180476; Aug23L:LC-Dig-ppmsca-19026; Aug23R:LC-Dig-ppmsca-19027; Aug24L :LC-Dig-acd-2a07397; Aug24R:CMH: Naples-Foggia Aug25:LC-USZ62-23573; Aug26L:LC-USZC4-7598; Aug26R:TimeLife-Getty # 50659710; Aug27L:LC-Dig-ppmsca-18547; Aug27R:LC-Dig-ppmsca-18544; Aug28L:LC-USZ62-91780; Aug28R:LC-USZC2-798; Aug29T:LC-USZC4-9891; Aug29:VHP: James Brown (AFC/2001/001/32354); Aug30L:LC-USW33-040023-ZC;

Aug30R:LC-USZ62-98191; Aug31:LC-USZ62-105509

SEPTEMBER Sep01:LC-Dig-acd-2a10518; Sep02L:LC-Dig-ppmsca-04649; Sep02R:LC-USZ62-85024; Sep03L:VHP: Peter Sanfilippo (AFC/2001/001/5844); Sep03R:GC: D 769.A533 V 5, Pt 1; Sep04:LC-Dig-ppmsca-19007; Sep05:LC-USZ62-121825; Sep06L:MSS Noel Parrish Papers; Sep06R:NARA: 80-G-424329; Sep07:LC-USW33-040237; Sep08L:LC-USZ62-86118; Sep08R:LC-USZC4-6031; Sep09L:VHP: Virginia Allen(AFC/2001/001/33674); Sep09R:VHP: Sigmund Bialosky (AFC/2001/001/33662); Sep10:GC:DS 777.53.S395; Sep11L:LC-USZ62-83210; Sep11R:LC-USZ62-121096; Sep12L:LC-Dig-ppmsca-04246; Sep12R:LC-Dig-ppmsca-04237; Sep13:LC-Dig-ppmsca-13373; 71240; Sep14T:LC-USZC4-9618; Sep14:LC-Dig-ppmsca-19265; Sep15:G&M: France D-Day Normandy 743rd Tank Battalion; Sep16L:LC-USZ62-118813; Sep16R:LC-Dig-ppmsca-19012; Sep17T:LC-Dig-ppmsca-19275; Sep17L:GC: DS 777.53.S395; Sep17R:LC-Dig-ppmsca-19272; Sep18:LC-USZ6-1888; Sep19:LC-USZ62-104195; Sep20:LC-USZ62-13333; Sep21 & Sep22:GC: D762. P3P32; Sep23:LC-Dig-fsac 1a55001; Sep24T:LC-USZC4-9535; Sep24:LC-Dig-ppmsca-19022; Sep25 (both):VHP: Samuel Boylston (AFC/2001/001/01848); Sep26:NARA:026-G-3738; Sep27L:LC-Dig-ppmsca-19018; Sep27R:VHP: Warren Tsuneishi (AFC/2001/001/02153); Sep28:LC-USZ62-92428; Sep29L:LC-USW3-040956-D; Sep29R:LC-Dig-ppmsca-12898; Sep30:NARA: 111-SC-198849

OCTOBER Oct01:LC-Dig-ppmsca-19036; Oct02:LC-Dig-ppmsca-19028; Oct03:NARA: 111-SC-334296;

Oct04T:GC:1165.T6L3; Oct04:LC-Dig-ppmsca-19019; Oct05T:Queen Victoria Hospital NHS Foundation Trust, East Grinstead, UK; Oct05:LC-Dig-ppmsca-19009; Oct06L:LC-USZC4-4434; Oct06R:GC: D 743.2.U485; Oct07L:LC-Dig-ppmsca-19031; Oct07R:LC-USZC4-6779; Oct08:LC-Dig-ppmsca-19020; Oct09:LC-Dig-ppmsca-15789; Oct10L:LC-Dig-ppmsca-19035; Oct10R:LC-USW33-040056-ZC; Oct11L:LC-Dig-ppmsca-19030; Oct11R:LC-Dig-ppmsca-19021; Oct12L:LC-Dig-ppmsca-19013; Oct12R:LC-USZC4-5077; Oct13:GC: D743.2. L6; Oct14T:LC-USZ62-120280; Oct14:LC-USZC4-1664; Oct15:GC: DS145 .B35; Oct16L:LC-Dig-ppmsca-13370; Oct16R:LC-Dig-ppmsca-19017; Oct17L:LC-USZC4-13399; Oct17R:LC-Dig-ppmsca-19004; Oct18:USHMM: Courtesy of Dr. George J. Wittenstein; Oct19(both):VHP: Doane Hage(AFC/2001/001/01202); Oct20:LC-USZC4-9532; Oct21L:LC-USW33-000956-ZC; Oct21R:LC-USZC4-13397; Oct22:LC-USZC4-5538; Oct23:LC-Dig-ppmsca-19006; Oct24T:GC: NC 1165 .T56A55; Oct24:NARA: 111-SC-264811; Oct25L:LC-Dig-acd-2a07424; Oct25R:LC-USZ62-94462; Oct26:NARA: 127-N-136176; Oct27L:GC: D762 .P332; Oct27R:Special Collections and University Archives Department, University of Central Florida Libraries, Orlando, Florida; Oct28:VHP: Thomas Baird (AFC/2001/001/28182); Oct29L:VHP: Robert John Kraft (AFC/2001/001/01593); Oct29R:LC-Dig-ppmsca-19025; Oct30L:LC-Dig-ppmsca-19024; Oct30R:NARA: 306-NT-1318; Oct31:LC-Dig-ppmsca-19264

NOVEMBER Nov01:LC-USZ62-42461; Nov02:LC-USZ62-65203; Nov03:VHP:Charles Restifo

(AFC/2001/001/ 05849); Nov04T:LC-USZ62-90022; Nov04R:LC-Dig-ppmsca-13573 #53; Nov05L:LC-Dig-ppmsca-13367; Nov05R:LC-Dig-ppmsca-19011; Nov06:LC-USZ62-99268; Nov07L:LC-Dig-acd-2a10383; Nov07R:LC-Dig-ppmsca-18614; Nov08L:LC-Dig-ppmsca-17140; Nov08R:LC-Dig-ppmsca-03235; Nov09L:G&M: G6426.A9 1943.W6 1990; Nov09R:LC-Dig-ppmsca-09549; Nov10:LC-USZ62-113919; Nov11L:LC-USZC4-3352; Nov11R:LC-Dig-ppmsca-13342; Nov12:NARA: 80-G-323712; Nov13L:LC-USZ62-90331; Nov13R:VHP:Carl Albin Hall (AFC/2001/001/27180); Nov14:LC-USZ63-110863; Nov15T:LC-USZ62-61128; Nov15:LC-USZ62-132799; Nov16L:LC-USZC4-3166; Nov16R:LC-USZ62-90257; Nov17L:LC-USZC4- 4489; Nov17R:LC-USZ62-99266; Nov18T:GC: NC 1165. T56A55; Nov18:VHP: Charles Amsler (AFC/2001/001/320); Nov19:NARA: 111-SC-207193; Nov20T:LC-Dig-ppmsca-19270; Nov20L:LC-USZ62-76691; Nov20R:LC-USZC4-13333; Nov21:LC-Dig-ppmsca-09148; Nov22L:LC-USZ62-121815; 71240; Nov22R:LC-USZC4-3629; Nov23:LC-USZ62-105517; Nov24:LC-USZ62-122603; Nov25:LC-Dig-ppmsca-19032; Nov26:VHP:Charles Restifo (AFC/2001/001/ 05849); Nov27L:LC-Dig-ppmsca-19034; Nov27R:NARA: 111-SC-210644; Nov28T:VHP: Robert Balfour (AFC/2001/001/2531); Nov28:LC-Dig-ppmsca-19289; Nov29T:LC-Dig-ppmsca-19278; Nov29:LC-USW3-59181-C; Nov30T:GC:D 767.99.P4 S55 1996; Nov30L:Courtesy of Athena Angelos; Nov30R:LC-Dig-ppmsca-19033

DECEMBER Dec01:LC-Dig-acd-2a10505; Dec02L:LC-Dig-ppmsca-19277; Dec02R:LC-Dig-

ppmsca-19276; Dec03:LC-Dig-ppmsca-19285; Dec04L:LC-USZ62-105693; Dec04R:LC-Dig-ppmsca-19260 ; Dec05:LC-USZ62-99271; Dec06L:LC-Dig-ppmsca-13354; Dec06R:LC-USZC4-13393; Dec07:LC-Dig-ppmsca-19283; Dec08:VHP: William Barr (AFC/2001/001/10509); Dec09T & Dec09R:VHP: Mimi Lesser (AFC/2001/001/11904); Dec09L:GC: RD 209 .A5; Dec10L:LC-Dig-ppmsca-1a35466; Dec10R:LC-Dig-ppmsca-19269; Dec11:VHP: Yeiichi Kuwayama (AFC/2001/001/07423); Dec12:LC-Dig-ppmsca-19320; Dec13L:LC-USZC4-4886; Dec13R:GC: UB 357. A658; Dec14:LC-Dig-ppmsca-19287; Dec15T:LC-USZC4-6798; Dec15:LC-Dig-ppmsca-18558; Dec16:LC-Dig-ppmsca-19288; Dec17T:LC-USZ62-135297; Dec17:USHMM #93626; Dec18:LC-Dig-ppmsca-19319; Dec19L:LC-USZ62-116969; Dec19R:VHP:Charles Restifo (AFC/2001/001/ 05849); Dec20L:LC-USZ62-99150; Dec20R:LC-USZ62-41497; Dec21L:LC-Dig-ppmsca-19291; Dec21R:LC-Dig-ppmsca-19281; Dec22L:LC-USZ62-95422; Dec22R:LC-USZ62-111645; Dec23L:GC: DS 777.53.S395; Dec23R:GC: DS 889 .I8; Dec24T :LC-USZ62-134165; Dec24:LC-USZC4-3345; Dec25T:LC-USZ62-132578; Dec25L:LC-Dig-ppmsca-13353; Dec26:LC-Dig-ppmsca-19280; Dec27L:LC-Dig-ppmsca-19267 ; Dec27R:LC-Dig-ppmsca-19282; Dec28T :NARA: 111-SC-285580; Dec28:LC-Dig-ppmsca-19274; Dec29:Courtesy of Susan Reyburn ; Dec30L:VHP: Donald Spencer (AFC/2001/001/ 02975); Dec30R:Courtesy of Blaine Marshall; Dec31:Courtesy of Michaela McNichol

Index

Page numbers in *italics* refer to illustrations.

Project Manager: Deborah Aaronson
Editor: Sofia Gutierrez
Designer: Timothy Shaner
Production Manager: Alison Gervais
Photo Editor: Athena Angelos

Library of Congress Cataloging-in-Publication Data:
Wagner, Margaret E.
    World War II 365 days / by Margaret E. Wagner.
        p. cm.
    Materials drawn from the Library of Congress' collections.
    ISBN 978-0-8109-9637-3
1. World War, 1939–1945. 2. World War, 1939–1945—Sources. I. Library
of Congress. II. Title. III. Title: World War Two. IV. Title: World War 2.

D743.W25 2009
940.54—dc22   2008016922

Text and Illustrations/photographs © 2009 Library of Congress
Introduction © 2009 David M. Kennedy

US cover: General Dwight D. Eisenhower, Supreme Commander, Allied
Expeditionary Force, with members of the 101st Airborne Division, on the
eve of the invasion of Normandy, June 5, 1944.

UK cover: Aircraft spotter on the roof of a building in London with St.
Paul's Cathedral in the background, c. 1940.

Back cover: Workers at the Chattanooga Stamping and Enameling
Company form a V for Victory outside their "defense plant." Office of War
Information photograph between 1941 and 1946.

Printed and bound in China
10 9 8 7 6 5 4 3 2 1

Abrams books are available at special discounts when purchased in
quantity for premiums and promotions as well as fundraising or
educational use. Special editions can also be created to specification.
For details, contact specialmarkets@hnabooks.com or the address below.

HNA ▪▪▪▪
harry n. abrams, inc.
a subsidiary of La Martinière Groupe

115 West 18th Street
New York, NY 10011
www.hnabooks.com